Technological Advancements in Engineering and Applied Sciences: A Multidisciplinary Perspective

PREFACE

In the rapidly evolving landscape of science and technology, the convergence of engineering and applied sciences has become the cornerstone for addressing the complex challenges of our time. This book, *"Technological Advancements in Engineering and Applied Sciences: A Multidisciplinary Perspective,"* represents a curated collection of research that exemplifies the cutting-edge innovations emerging from this intersection.

The contents of this book are derived from the proceedings of the First International Conference on Multidisciplinary Research 2024 (FICMR2024), held on August 2nd and 3rd, 2024. This landmark event brought together leading researchers, practitioners, and academicians from around the world to present and discuss their work. The conference served as a vibrant platform for knowledge exchange, fostering collaboration across various domains of engineering and applied sciences.

The book comprises 17 chapters, each based on meticulously selected research papers from the conference. These chapters delve into a wide array of topics, ranging from IoT-based systems and machine learning applications to advancements in civil engineering and healthcare technology. By exploring these diverse subjects, the book not only highlights the breadth of current research but also underscores the importance of multidisciplinary approaches in solving real-world problems.

Each chapter stands as a testament to the innovative spirit and dedication of the researchers who contributed to this volume. Their work reflects a commitment to pushing the boundaries of what is possible in their respective fields. Whether it's developing a UPI-based medicine vending machine using IoT, analyzing mess food quality through machine learning, or creating a system for voter identification to increase electoral participation, these studies showcase how technological advancements are being leveraged to improve efficiency, accuracy, and sustainability across various sectors.

This book is intended for a broad audience, including researchers, professionals, and students who are keen on staying abreast of the latest developments in engineering and applied sciences. It offers insights into emerging technologies and provides a comprehensive understanding of how multidisciplinary research can drive innovation and create solutions for the challenges we face today.

As you journey through the chapters, we hope you find inspiration in the pioneering work presented here and gain a deeper appreciation for the role of technology in shaping the future. It is our belief that the knowledge shared in this book will contribute to ongoing discussions and spark new ideas that will further advance the fields of engineering and applied sciences.

We extend our gratitude to all the authors who contributed their research and to the organizers of FICMR2024 for their efforts in bringing together such a diverse and talented group of scholars. We also thank the reviewers for their invaluable feedback, which helped shape this book into a cohesive and insightful resource.

We are excited to present *"Technological Advancements in Engineering and Applied Sciences: A Multidisciplinary Perspective"* to you and hope it serves as a valuable reference for your work and study.

ACKNOWLEDGEMENT

The completion of *"Technological Advancements in Engineering and Applied Sciences: A Multidisciplinary Perspective"* would not have been possible without the support and contributions of numerous individuals and institutions. We are deeply grateful to everyone who played a role in bringing this book to fruition.

First and foremost, we would like to express our sincere gratitude to the authors of the 17 chapters included in this volume. Their dedication to advancing knowledge and their willingness to share their research at the First International Conference on Multidisciplinary Research 2024 (FICMR2024) has been instrumental in the creation of this book. Their work is the foundation upon which this publication is built.

We extend our heartfelt thanks to the conference organizers and the team at FICMR2024 for their outstanding efforts in orchestrating such a successful event. The conference provided a dynamic platform for the exchange of ideas and the presentation of pioneering research, which has significantly enriched the content of this book.

Special thanks are due to the peer reviewers who devoted their time and expertise to evaluating the submissions. Their insightful feedback and constructive criticism have greatly enhanced the quality and rigor of the chapters presented here.

We are also grateful to the institutions and organizations that supported the participation of their researchers in FICMR2024. Their commitment to fostering research and innovation is commendable and has contributed to the diversity and depth of the studies included in this book.

Our appreciation goes out to the editorial team, whose tireless efforts in compiling, editing, and organizing the chapters ensured that this book meets the highest standards of academic publishing. Their meticulous attention to detail and unwavering commitment to excellence have been invaluable.

Finally, we would like to acknowledge the support and encouragement of our families, friends, and colleagues. Their understanding and patience throughout the process of bringing this book to life have been a source of strength and motivation.

We hope that this book serves as a testament to the power of collaboration and the importance of multidisciplinary research in driving technological advancements. It is our sincere wish that the knowledge shared within these pages will inspire future research and innovation.

<h1 align="center">ABOUT THE BOOK</h1>

"Technological Advancements in Engineering and Applied Sciences: A Multidisciplinary Perspective" is a comprehensive compilation of contemporary research that bridges the gap between engineering, technology, and applied sciences. This book is a result of the collaborative efforts of scholars who presented their work at the First International Conference on Multidisciplinary Research 2024 (FICMR2024), held on August 2nd and 3rd, 2024. The conference brought together experts from various fields to share insights, discuss challenges, and propose innovative solutions to some of the most pressing issues in today's technological and engineering landscapes.

The book consists of 17 chapters, each derived from a meticulously selected research paper submitted to FICMR2024. These chapters cover a wide range of topics, reflecting the interdisciplinary nature of modern scientific inquiry. From the integration of IoT in healthcare systems to the application of machine learning in food quality analysis, and from advancements in civil engineering materials to the development of smart manufacturing technologies, the book offers a broad perspective on how engineering and applied sciences are evolving in response to contemporary demands.

Key topics explored in this book include:

- **IoT and Healthcare:** Innovations such as UPI-based medicine vending machines that improve accessibility and efficiency in healthcare delivery.

- **Machine Learning Applications:** Analysis of mess food quality and prediction systems for academic success, showcasing how AI is transforming data-driven decision-making.

- **Civil Engineering Advancements:** The exploration of new materials like GFRP rebar in concrete construction, as well as strategic planning for high-rise buildings in urban environments.

- **Smart Technologies:** The role of digital twin technology in smart manufacturing and systems for traffic management and voter identification.

This book is an essential resource for researchers, professionals, and students in the fields of engineering, technology, and applied sciences. It provides valuable insights into emerging technologies and their potential applications across various industries. The multidisciplinary approach taken in this book highlights the importance of collaboration across fields to drive innovation and address complex challenges.

By presenting the latest research and developments, *"Technological Advancements in Engineering and Applied Sciences: A Multidisciplinary Perspective"* aims to inspire continued exploration and innovation in these critical areas, ultimately contributing to the advancement of knowledge and the betterment of society.

INDEX

GFRP Rebar in Concrete Construction: A Comprehensive Review of Properties, Applications, and Advancements

Rameshwar S. Ingalkar[1], and Prakash S. Pajgade[1]

[2] Department of Civil Engineering, Prof Ram Meghe Institute of Technology & Research, Badnera, Amravati, Maharashtra, 444701, India.

Email: ram.ingalkar@gmail.com; ppajgade@gmail.com

Abstract— Reinforced concrete is the backbone of modern infrastructure, leveraging the concrete compressive strength and steel tensile strength to enable the construction of essential structures like bridges and buildings. While steel rebar has long been the dominant reinforcement material, its susceptibility to corrosion has driven a search for more durable substitutes. Recognizing the need for more durable solutions, researchers have identified fibre reinforced polymer composites, such as glass fiber reinforced polymer rebar, as a viable alternative to traditional steel reinforcement. Basalt fiber reinforced polymer(B:FI-RE-PL) rebar possesses a distinctive combination of characteristics, including superior corrosion resistance, high tensile strength and low weight which directly address the shortcomings of steel reinforcement. This material holds the potential to revolutionize the construction industry by providing a more sustainable and long-lasting solution for concrete structures. This research review provides a comprehensive examination of Basalt fiber reinforced polymer rebar, delving into its material properties, manufacturing processes, and design considerations. The review highlights the numerous advantages of Basalt fiber reinforced polymer rebar, such as its corrosion resistance, lightweight construction, and overall sustainability, drawing upon existing research and case studies to provide a thorough understanding of this increasingly important material in the construction industry. This review examines the performance and applications of Basalt fiber reinforced polymer rebar, with the objective of informing engineers, and decision-makers about the potential advantages of this innovative reinforcement material for construction of concrete structures that are durable, resilient, and environmentally sustainable.
Keywords— "GFRP Rebar, Durability, corrosion resistance, sustainable construction, Flexure Strength"

Abirritations: 1) FI-RE-PL: Fiber Reinforced Polymer, 2) G:FI-RE-PL: Glass Fiber Reinforced Polymer, 3) C:FI-RE-PL: Carbon Fiber Reinforced Polymer, 4) B:FI-RE-PL: Basalt Fiber Reinforced Polymer 5) BS: Bond Strength

I. INTRODUCTION

Reinforced concrete structures form the foundation of modern infrastructure, enabling the construction of essential structures like bridges and buildings. While steel rebar has been the dominant reinforcement, its vulnerability to corrosion has driven the search for more durable alternatives. Corrosion of steel reinforcement poses a substantial threat to structural integrity, compromising safety and leading to substantial economic burdens. Recognizing the need for more resilient solutions, researchers and engineers have turned to FI-RE-PL composites as a practicable substitute for traditional reinforcement [1, 2].

Corrosion of steel reinforcement poses a significant threat to concrete structure integrity worldwide [3]. This degradation compromises safety and leads to substantial economic burdens for repairs and rehabilitation.

Among FI-RE-PL types, glass FI-RE-PL rebar is a promising option, especially for corrosion-prone applications [2]. G:FI-RE-PL's unique properties directly address steel's limitations - its inherent corrosion resistance makes it ideal for harsh environments like marine settings. The non-corrosive glass fibers and polymer matrix allow G:FI-RE-PL to remain chemically stable, preserving structural integrity and enabling longer service life.

FI-RE-PL rebars are composite materials with high tensile strength fibers surrounded in a polymer matrix. Glass, aramid, and carbon fibers are common, with glass preferred for its high tensile strength, low cost, and alkali resistance. The polymer matrix binds fibers, transfers stresses, and protects against abrasion and degradation. FI-RE-PL rebars are typically produced by the pultrusion process, which pulls fibers through a resin bath and heated die to create a solid, continuous rod.

This research paper offers a thorough analysis of G:FI-RE-PL rebar as a feasible substitute to traditional steel reinforcement in concrete construction. It delves into the material properties, manufacturing processes, and design considerations associated with G:FI-RE-PL rebar, highlighting its advantages and disadvantages compared to traditional steel reinforcement [2]. Furthermore, the review explores the potential benefits of G:FI-RE-PL rebar in relation with corrosion resistance, lightweight construction, and overall sustainability, drawing upon existing research and case studies to provide a thorough understanding of this increasingly important material in the construction industry.

II. SUMMARY OF THE LITERATURE

A. B:FI-RE-PL rebar & concrete bond performance

This study examines the durability of FI-RE-PL bars embedded in coral concrete exposed to seawater at varying temperatures. The findings indicate that increased seawater temperature reduces the BS between FI-RE-PL bars and coral concrete, with a more pronounced effect on glass FI-RE-PL. This is attributed to the less robust protective capacity of coral concrete compared to conventional concrete. The study emphasizes the necessity of accounting for the potential reduction in bond strength (BS) [4] when utilizing FI-RE-PL bars in coral concrete structures exposed to sea environments, particularly in high-temperature conditions. This study examines the bond durability of FI-RE-PL reinforcing concrete, with a focus on the detrimental effects of high temperatures. It identifies key factors, such as FI-RE-PL type, diameter, and concrete properties, that contribute to the degradation of BS. Furthermore, the study utilizes a model to forecast BS at elevated temperatures, offering a valuable tool for maintaining the integrity of FI-RE-PL-reinforced concrete structures [5] exposed to heat.

The study demonstrated that the BS between fiber-reinforced polymer and sea sand concrete improved in a wet-dry cycling environment, whereas the BS of steel bars declined due to corrosion [6]. This superior durability of sea sand fiber reinforced concrete beams is attributed to the chloride ions present in the sea sand, which enhance the bond durability of SFCBs while simultaneously corroding steel bars.

The study examined the bond durability of B:FI-RE-PL bars embedded in concrete under seawater conditions. The results indicated that B:FI-RE-PL bars with epoxy resin demonstrated enhanced bond durability compared to those with vinyl ester resin. Specifically, the BS of basalt bars with vinyl ester resin decreased by approximately 10.0% after being exposed to 40°C seawater for 60 days [7], while the BS of basalt-epoxy bars remained relatively stable over the same period.

This study investigates the durability of the bond between FI-RE-PL bars and concrete under diverse environmental conditions, drawing insights from inclusive database of around 1200 individual test results. The findings underscore the significant impact of environmental factors on bond performance [8], underscoring the critical importance of accounting for bond durability in the development of design procedures for reinforced concrete structures.

The study investigated the long term durability of B:FI-RE-PL bars embedded in concrete when exposed to severe environments. Researchers performed pullout tests on the B:FI-RE-PL bars after subjecting them to an alkaline solution at varying temperatures and exposure durations. The findings revealed that exposure to the alkaline solution, particularly at elevated temperatures, resulted in a reduction in the BS of the B:FI-RE-PL bars [9]. This research highlights the critical need for further investigation into the long-term performance of B:FI-RE-PL materials.

The study compiled and analyzed a data of around 550 for BS and around 300 for bond slip test results to compute reduction factors for FI-RE-PL RC members. It found that exposure to various environments, including water, alkaline solutions, salty water and dry heat, can significantly reduce BS [10]. The study then used these reduction factors to investigate current detailing necessities, determining the force and development length needed to utilise FI-RE-PL reinforcement's full strength.

This study examines the effect of raised temperatures on the BS between FI-RE-PL sheets and concrete. The researchers discovered that high temperatures, particularly in low humidity environments, can significantly diminish the BS between FI-RE-PL and concrete. This reduction is primarily due to a swing in the failure mode from adhesive to cohesive. However, the adhesive strength was observed to exceed 6 MPa [11] under controlled room temperature conditions, suggesting the suitability of FI-RE-PL strengthening for most applications.

This study investigates the bond behavior of B:FI-RE-PL bars embedded in concrete under elevated temperatures. The experimental results show that the BS decreases as the temperature rises from 20°C to 300°C. Additionally, the research examines the bond stress-slip relationships and failure modes, finding that a non-contact method effectively measures the free-end slip during high-temperature pullout tests [12].

This study investigates the durability of the bond between B: FI-RE-PL bars and both regular and steel fiber-reinforced concrete when subjected to simulated ocean conditions and elevated temperatures [13]. The results show that increasing the steel fiber content in the fiber reinforced concrete enhances the bond durability, predominantly at high temperatures.

B. Flexural performance of R.C. beams with only B:FI-RE-PL rebars

This study examined the flexural behavior of concrete beams reinforced with C:FI-RE-PL, B:FI-RE-PL, G:FI-RE-PL, and steel bars after exposure to a 925°C fire. The results showed that steel and G:FI-RE-PL specimens experienced significant strength loss of 60-80%, with higher deformation, while C:FI-RE-PL beams demonstrated superior load-carrying capacity. Specimens cooled with water exhibited higher strength loss compared to air-cooled ones [14].

This study presents a program for calculating the flexural FI-RE-PL reinforcement of T shape beams. The program accounts for various design scenarios and parameters, and the authors validated it by comparing calculated strengths with experimental data from 125 beams, finding good agreement. The program also adjusts reinforcement areas to consider creep rupture in FI-RE-PL rebars. The authors conclude that this program effectively determines FI-RE-PL reinforcement requirements for T-beams [15].

The experimental investigation involved testing eight concrete beams under four-point bending conditions. The test results indicated an average bond dependent coefficient is around 0.8, which is lower than the value of 1.0 recommended by Canadian design standards for ribbed FI-RE-PL bars. Additionally, the study found that the American Concrete Institute Committee 440 Guide underestimated the service load deflections for the beams reinforced with ribbed Basalt FI-RE-PL bars. In contrast, the Canadian design standards for structures incorporating FI-RE-PL materials provided reasonable and conservative predictions of the deflections [16].

The study investigated the flexural performance of concrete beams reinforced with G:FI-RE-PL bars. Twelve concrete beam specimens, with varying compressive strengths and reinforcement ratios, were subjected to a 4-point loading regime. The results discovered that augmenting the reinforcement ratio led to a reduction in crack widths and midspan deflection, while simultaneously increasing the ultimate load capacity. Specifically, as the reinforcement percentage was elevated from 0.5% to 1%, 1.55%, and 2%, the ultimate load experienced respective increases of 7.5%, 16.8%, and 27.7% [17]. Furthermore, the failure modes transitioned from concrete crushing to FI-RE-PL bar rupture as the reinforcement ratio was increased.

Over the past several years, extensive research has investigated the potential for replacing traditional steel reinforcement with FI-RE-PL rebars as a means of addressing durability issues in reinforced concrete structures. Specifically, B:FI-RE-PL rebar, a relatively novel FI-RE-PL composite material for reinforcement, has been the focus of recent studies aimed at evaluating its structural behavior and performance characteristics [18].

This study investigated the effect of transverse and flexural reinforcement on the flexural performance, deflection, and cracking performance of concrete beams reinforced with G: FI-RE-PL bars. The researchers tested 20 beam specimens and discovered that increasing the amount of transverse reinforcement significantly enhanced the load bearing capacity and reduced both crack widths and deflections up to service load levels. Furthermore, utilizing smaller diameter transverse bars and tensile reinforcement led to greater increases in load capacity and decreases in crack widths, respectively. Lastly, beams with higher flexural reinforcement ratios exhibited slightly higher experimental to predicted load capacity ratio [19].

The study examined the flexural performance of concrete beams reinforced with Glass FI-RE-PL rebars versus steel rebars. The findings revealed that utilizing G:FI-RE-PL rebars as the primary reinforcement resulted in a 33% decrease in ultimate load capacity compared to steel-reinforced beams. Additionally, the G:FI-RE-PL-reinforced beams displayed shear failure behaviour [20].

This study investigates the use of basalt reinforcement as an substitute to traditional steel reinforcement in concrete structures. The authors highlight the need for corrosion-resistant alternatives due to steel's susceptibility to corrosion, which compromises concrete durability and load-bearing capacity. The study evaluates the BS of basalt reinforcement with concrete and its impact on structural performance. Experimental results indicate that basalt reinforced beams exhibit 50 to 70% higher load-bearing capacity compared to steel reinforced counterparts [21].

Investigates the impact of high temperatures on the BS between B:FI-RE-PL bars and concrete. The researchers found that B:FI-RE-PL bars showed similar bond stress slip curves at both room and high temperatures. Though, as temperature increased, the peak bond stress and the slope of the curve decreased. Specifically, the BS of B:FI-RE-PL and G:FI-RE-PL bar specimens at 270°C weakened by about 32.0%, and at 350°C, BS became negligible for both types of bars [22].

The study investigated the deflection behavior of concrete beams reinforced with B:FI-RE-PL bars. The researchers found that increasing the G:FI-RE-PL reinforcement ratio led to a reduction in the mid-span deflection of the beams. Additionally, the study compared the numerical results to the predictions from various design codes, including ACI 440.1R-06, ACI 440.1R-15, and CAN/CSA S806-12. The findings revealed that ACI 440.1R-06 underestimated the deflection, ACI 440.1R-15 provided a good estimate, while CAN/CSA S806-12 overestimated the deflection [23]. Examined the flexural performance of beams reinforced with G:FI-RE-PL rebars using numerical analysis. They validated their model against experimental data and found that increasing the span/depth ratio decreased rigidity but increased displacement ductility. The study concludes that G:FI-RE-PL reinforcement is a feasible solution for enhancing the ductility of reinforced concrete beams [24].

This study examines the flexural behavior of concrete beams reinforced with G:FI-RE-PL rebars compared to those with conventional steel bars. 6 full scale beam specimen were tested, revealing that while steel reinforced beams exhibited higher maximum loads, G:FI-RE-PL-reinforced beams surprisingly showed up to 98% higher maximum load. However, the G:FI-RE-PL reinforced beams displayed reduced stiffness compared to their steel counterparts [25]. Investigates the behaviour of concrete beams reinforced with different bundles of steel and FI-RE-PL bars. The study found that all beams showed concrete crushing failure modes after the steel yielded. Increasing reinforcement concentration decreased bond behavior, post-cracking stiffness, and crack quantity, while increasing crack width. Beams with three bar bundles showed around 50% lower initial and post-yield stiffness compared to those with double-bar bundles. All beams demonstrated displacement ductility greater than six [26].

C. Flexural performance of B:FI-RE-PL hybrid reinforced concrete beams specimen.

This study examines the flexural performance of hybrid beams made with G:FI-RE-PL box filled with fiber reinforced concrete. It examines the impact of FI-RE-PL bar and fiber types on structural performance. The results show that C:FI-RE-PL bars provide the most significant enhancement, increasing flexural strength by 70%, while steel fiber concrete exhibits the largest contribution, leading to a 53% rise in flexural strength [27].

This study simulates the behavior of 40 concrete beams reinforced with several FRPs and traditional steel under different conditions. The findings indicate that C:FI-RE-PL reinforcement is superior at lower ratios, but steel outperforms all FI-RE-PL types in flexural strength at higher reinforcement ratios. This is attributed to the lesser elastic modulus of FI-RE-PL materials compared to steel, which limits their ability to effectively transfer stresses at higher loads [28].

This review examines the usage of hybrid rebars in reinforced concrete beams, summarizing studies on their flexural performance. Hybrid systems offer improved serviceability, ductility, and load capacity compared to steel or FI-RE-PL alone. Using hybrid reinforcement can increase load-bearing capacity, ductility, and reduce deformation and cracking versus FI-RE-PL-only reinforcement [29].

The study aims to balance load capacity and ductility by determining the appropriate ratio of FI-RE-PL to steel reinforcement. The authors propose two balanced reinforcement ratios ($\rho_{b,E}$ and $\rho_{b,F}$) based on elastic modulus and tensile strength, respectively. They conclude that for a concrete beam using both FI-RE-PL and steel reinforcement to be admissible, the nominal reinforcement ratio in terms of elastic modulus ($\rho_{n,E}$) should be less than or equal to $\rho_{b,E}$, while the nominal reinforcement ratio in terms of tensile strength ($\rho_{n,F}$) [30].

This study scrutinized the flexural performance of concrete beams reinforced with G:FI-RE-PL, C:FI-RE-PL, and steel bars. Twelve beams with varying FI-RE-PL diameters were tested under four point loading. Steel reinforced beams exhibited higher maximum loads with increasing steel strength, while G:FI-RE-PL reinforced beams had higher maximum loads but reduced stiffness compared to steel. The ACI standards provided the closest approximation for G:FI-RE-PL-reinforced beam behavior [31]. It is showed that using hybrid FI-RE-PL/steel reinforcement in concrete beams leads to improved ductility and stiffness compared to using only FI-RE-PL. This improvement is because the steel reinforcement contributes significantly to stiffness and load resistance after cracking, while FI-RE-PL bars are more effective after the yielding of steel. The study suggests that an over-reinforced design is recommended to prevent brittle FI-RE-PL rupture in under-reinforced members [32].

Explores the use of G:FI-RE-PL bars as a replacement for steel reinforcement in concrete beams. The authors found that while G:FI-RE-PL bars has advantages such as corrosion resistance and lightweight properties, they can lead to larger crack widths and may require modifications in design calculations compared to traditional steel reinforcement [33]. Investigates the use of FI-RE-PL bars in conjunction with or in place of steel bars for reinforcing concrete. The authors found, through a grouping of physical and simulated experiments, that beams reinforced with a combination of steel and FI-RE-PL bars could bear twice the load as beams with only steel reinforcement. However, this increase in strength came at the cost of stiffness, with the hybrid steel-FI-RE-PL beams deflecting more and exhibiting wider cracks than their solely steel-reinforced counterparts [34].

Investigated B:FI-RE-PL and hybrid FI-RE-PL bars as reinforcement in concrete structures. They conducted experiments on model concrete beams reinforced with B:FI-RE-PL and HFRP bars, subjecting them to static long term loads and cyclic freezing/thawing. The results showed that both B:FI-RE-PL and HFRP bars exhibited good mechanical properties and resistance to environmental influences. The study suggests that B:FI-RE-PL and HFRP bars are promising materials for reinforcing concrete structures in severe environments [35]. This investigation examined the flexural response of concrete beams reinforced with B:FI-RE-PL bars and steel fibers. 11 steel fiber-reinforced concrete beams were subjected to four-point bending tests. The findings indicated that augmenting the steel fiber volume fraction, SFRC layer thickness, or B:FI-RE-PL reinforcement ratio yielded enhanced flexural performance, encompassing greater load-bearing capacity, ductility, and crack resistance. Partially incorporating SFRC still enhanced performance while reducing material expenses [36].

Investigates the use of hybrid reinforced concrete beams, incorporating both Glass FI-RE-PL bars and steel bars, to improve flexural strength and ductility. The research also explores the supplementary use of polypropylene fibers to enhance these properties. The results indicate that a polypropylene fiber content of 0.25% of the beam volume optimizes flexural strength and ductility. The study concludes that using G:FI-RE-PL bars in combination with steel bars and polypropylene fibers is a feasible method for enhancing the performance of concrete beams [37]. Investigates the remaining strength of concrete beams reinforced with different FI-RE-PL bar types after exposure to raised temperatures. Beams were preloaded to 50% capacity, heated, cooled, then tested to failure. Results showed decreased deflection after a certain temperature threshold for HFRP and nHFRP reinforced beams, suggesting a "prestressing" effect due to the thermal expansion of carbon fibers in these bars [38].

D. Shear performance of B:FI-RE-PL rebars in concrete beams.

Explores the use of genetic programming to predict the shear strengths of FI-RE-PL reinforced concrete beam specimens, both with and without stirrups. The authors developed a new formula based on a database of 553 shear tests. When compared to current models, the proposed formula demonstrated greater accuracy in predicting shear strength and a simpler, more user-friendly format [39]. Eight specimens were tested with varying G:FI-RE-PL strip width to spacing ratios and opening array types. Results showed that shear strength increased with a higher strip width to strip spacing ratio, with the 3x2 opening array yielding the highest strength [40].

Investigates the impact of G:FI-RE-PL reinforcement on concrete beam behavior. The study found that beams without stirrups experienced shear tension failures, while those with stirrups exhibited shear-compression failures without stirrup rupture. The existence of longitudinal reinforcement in the beams contributed to a tied arch mechanism, ultimately enhancing the overall shear strength of the concrete beams [41].

This study examined the shear behavior of RC beams with G:FI-RE-PL rebar and stirrups. Twelve G:FI-RE-PL-reinforced and one steel-reinforced beam were tested, with variables including longitudinal reinforcement, shear span, and stirrup spacing. The results presented that G:FI-RE-PL stirrups did not affect the failure mechanism, with all beams experiencing initial flexural cracks followed by shear failure. Shear span-to-depth ratio significantly influenced failure mode. The average maximum strain in G:FI-RE-PL stirrups exceeded code limits. Crack angles averaged 45 degrees, aligning with the truss model. Shear capacity predictions by ISIS Canada were the most conservative [42].

E. Compressive strength of concrete with B:FI-RE-PL rebar

This study provides a comprehensive examination into the axial performance of hollow G:FI-RE-PL reinforced concrete columns. The authors conducted experiments on scaled-down columns, comparing them to steel-reinforced controls. The results showed that hollow G:FI-RE-PL columns exhibited comparable or superior performance, with higher ultimate loads and greater ductility. The researchers also established a validated finite element model to study the enhanced confinement effect and improved axial behavior of hollow GFRPRC columns [43].

This study explores the use of G:FI-RE-PL and B:FI-RE-PL bars as alternatives to steel reinforcement in concrete. Through experiments and computer simulations, the authors found that both types of FI-RE-PL bars can significantly enhance the strength of concrete columns, potentially carrying up to 35% of the total load before failure. G:FI-RE-PL and B:FI-RE-PL bars demonstrated comparable performance in terms of strength, deflection, and overall contribution to the column's capacity, suggesting they are both viable alternatives to steel reinforcement [44] . The authors concluded that while design equations for short FI-RE-PL-reinforced columns are sufficient, further research is needed for slender columns and aspects like long-term behavior and performance under extreme conditions. They advocate for code authorities to approve the use of FI-RE-PL in compression members [45].

The researchers propose a new calculation to predict the maximum axial load capacity of concrete columns reinforced with FI-RE-PL bars under axial compression. Compared to previous approaches, their equation bases the calculations on the modulus of elasticity of the FI-RE-PL bars rather than their tensile strength, resulting in more accurate predictions. Furthermore, they utilize an empirical equation based on concrete compressive strength to estimate the axial strain in the FI-RE-PL bars, leading to more precise assessments of the FI-RE-PL bars' contribution to the overall axial load capacity [46]. This paper investigates the use of FI-RE-PL bars as a alternative for steel reinforcement in circular concrete columns. By testing 14 full scale columns under axial load, the study found that both Glass FI-RE-PL and Carbon FI-RE-PL reinforced columns behave comparably to traditional steel-reinforced columns. Furthermore, using FI-RE-PL spirals or hoops efficiently restrained buckling of the longitudinal bars and confined the concrete core, indicating that FI-RE-PL can be a viable and effective substitute to steel reinforcement in bridge columns [47].

Investigates the effect of seawater exposure on the shear properties of G: FI-RE-PL rebars. The study found that after 20 months of aging in seawater at 75°C, the short beam shear strength remained at 95% of its original value, while the transverse shear strength remained at 91%. These findings suggest that G:FI-RE-PL rebars exhibit good durability and retain their shear strength even after prolonged exposure to seawater [48]. Investigates the reliability of FI-RE-PL-reinforced concrete column, finding that they exhibit acceptable reliability indices. The study, based on 194 column tests, suggests that the reliability index is not significantly affected by reinforcement ratio, eccentricity level, or concrete strength. However, C:FI-RE-PL columns demonstrate a higher reliability index compared to G:FI-RE-PL columns [49].

Testing shows that the maximum compressive strength of non-buckled HFRP bars under axial compression is approximately 46.0% of their ultimate tensile strength. Additionally, the modulus of elasticity remains relatively consistent under both tension and compression [50]. Investigates the use of B:FI-RE-PL ties in concrete columns. The results indicate that while steel ties are superior in increase concrete strength and ultimate load, B:FI-RE-PL ties improve post peak ductility. Factors such as smaller tie spacing and larger B:FI-RE-PL tie diameter further enhance ductility [51].

F. Miscellaneous

Investigated newly developed thermoplastic based glass FI-RE-PL bars for reinforcing concrete structures. The results specify that these thermoplastic G:FI-RE-PL bars exhibit comparable properties to their thermosetting counterparts, fulfilling the requirements of ASTM D7957 and CSA S807 standards, excluding for moisture absorption [52]. The experimental findings indicate that the tensile strength of B:FI-RE-PL bars is approximately three times greater than that of conventional steel bars, although their elastic modulus is around one-fifth of the steel bars' modulus. Furthermore, the B:FI-RE-PL bars demonstrate a linear elastic deformation pattern prior to failure, with their stress-strain relationship approximating a straight line without a distinct yield plateau [53].

This study examined the long-term durability of G:FI-RE-PL bars used as reinforcement in a concrete bridge after 15 years of service. Researchers evaluated the G:FI-RE-PL bars and surrounding concrete, observing no deterioration or alterations in the bars' chemical composition. The glass transition temperature and fiber content remained comparable to initial values, though the horizontal shear strength findings were inconclusive. Overall, the investigation substantiates the long-term viability of G:FI-RE-PL bars as concrete reinforcement [54]. This study examined the thermal and mechanical characteristics of basalt fiber-reinforced polymer bars, an emerging construction material. The researchers tested B:FI-RE-PL bars of three varying diameters to assess their tensile strength, compressive strength, and elastic modulus. The findings revealed that B:FI-RE-PL bars exhibit a substantially lower elastic modulus compared to traditional steel reinforcement. Furthermore, the study demonstrated that the compressive strength of B:FI-RE-PL bars is significantly inferior to their tensile strength, and their glass transition temperature is relatively low [55].

III. DISCUSSION AND SUGGESTIONS

In last 3 decades, extensive research has investigated the viability of replacing conventional steel reinforcement with Fiber-Reinforced Polymer rebars to address durability issues in reinforced concrete structures. Similarly, Basalt Fiber-Reinforced Polymer rebar, an emerging FI-RE-PL composite material for reinforcement, has been the focus of recent studies examining its structural performance.

A. B:FI-RE-PL rebar–concrete bond performance

The existing research highlights the critical effect of environmental factors, such as raised temperatures and seawater exposure, on the bond durability of FI-RE-PL (FI-RE-PL) bars embedded in concrete. Raised temperatures consistently degrade the BS of FI-RE-PL rebars, with coral concrete offering less protection compared to ordinary concrete, rendering it more susceptible to this degradation. Various types of FI-RE-PL bars, such as (B:FI-RE-PL) with epoxy resin, demonstrate better resistance compared to those with vinyl ester resin. Furthermore, environmental exposure to aggressive elements like seawater and alkaline solutions significantly reduces BS, with the extent of the reduction dependent on factors like duration and temperature of exposure. Predictive models, including Genetic-Expression Programming and CMR models, have proven effective in forecasting BS under these conditions, providing valuable tools for structural design and assessment.

To improve the durability of FI-RE-PL RC structures, several recommendations can be made. Selecting FI-RE-PL bars with superior resistance to high temperatures and aggressive environments, such as B:FI-RE-PL with epoxy resin, is crucial for marine and high temperature applications. Using ordinary concrete instead of coral concrete, or enhancing the concrete mix with protective additives, can improve BS and durability. Design considerations should account for potential reductions in BS due to environmental factors, incorporating protective measures like coatings to shield FI-RE-PL bars. Utilizing advanced predictive models during the design phase can help assess bond durability more accurately, while regular testing and monitoring of in-service structures can identify early degradation. Updating design guidelines to reflect these findings and encouraging further research on the long term performance of FI-RE-PL bars in varied conditions will ensure more robust and reliable FI-RE-PL-reinforced concrete structures.

B. *Flexural performance of B:FI-RE-PL reinforced concrete beams*

The investigation into the performance of concrete beams reinforced with various FI-RE-PL (FI-RE-PL) bars and steel bars under high temperatures provides valuable insights. The study highlights stark differences in performance among C:FI-RE-PL, B:FI-RE-PL, G:FI-RE-PL, and steel reinforcements when exposed to elevated temperatures up to 925°C. C:FI-RE-PL beams exhibited superior load-carrying capacity, while steel and G:FI-RE-PL beams experienced substantial strength loss and higher deformation, suggesting C:FI-RE-PL as a viable alternative in high-temperature environments. The comparison of reinforcement types underscores the necessity of selecting the appropriate material based on specific structural and environmental conditions. Upcoming research should explore the long term durability of C:FI-RE-PL and develop comprehensive design guidelines for FI-RE-PL in concrete structures design.

The research collectively highlights significant advancements in the structural behaviour of concrete beams achieved through hybrid reinforcement systems. C:FI-RE-PL bars demonstrate a remarkable ability to enhance flexural strength, but their lower elastic modulus compared to steel limits efficiency at higher reinforcement ratios. Incorporating steel fibers into the concrete mix also provides substantial benefits, increasing flexural strength and improving ductility and crack resistance. The optimal performance of hybrid beams often requires a strategic balance between different reinforcement materials, with hybrid FI-RE-PL/steel reinforcement leading to enhanced ductility and stiffness. Upcoming research should emphasis on optimizing the FI-RE-PL steel reinforcement balance and investigating the impact of environmental factors on the behaviour of these hybrid systems.

C. *Shear behavior Basalt:FI-RE-PL R.C. beams*

The advancements in predicting the shear strength of (G:FI-RE-PL)reinforced concrete beams through genetic programming models and experimental investigations offer valuable insights. The newly developed genetic programming formula exhibits a significant improvement in accurately predicting shear strength compared to existing models, highlighting the potential of advanced computational techniques in structural engineering. This formula's accuracy and simplicity could enhance the reliability and user-friendliness of design processes for engineers. Furthermore, the experimental findings provide empirical evidence on how varying G:FI-RE-PL strip-width-to-spacing ratios and opening arrangements affect shear strength, with higher strip-width-to-spacing ratios generally resulting in improved shear performance.

The studies reveal critical observations regarding the shear behavior of (G:FI-RE-PL)reinforced concrete beams. Beams with G:FI-RE-PL reinforcement but without stirrups tend to experience shear-tension failures, whereas those with stirrups exhibit shear-compression failures, highlighting the significant influence of stirrups on the failure mechanism. Additionally, while G:FI-RE-PL stirrups do not affect the failure mode, they contribute to strain development and overall shear strength. The variation in failure modes based on shear span to depth ratios suggests that a deeper understanding of these parameters is essential for accurate predictions.

To further improve predictive models and practical applications, future research could focus on expanding the database to include a broader range of variables and real-world conditions. Additionally, investigating the long-term durability of G:FI-RE-PL reinforcements under various environmental conditions would provide a more comprehensive understanding of their performance. Enhanced models incorporating these factors could lead to more robust and reliable design guidelines, ultimately advancing the use of G:FI-RE-PL reinforcement in concrete structures.

D. *Compressive strength of concrete with B:FI-RE-PL rebar*

Recent studies have shown that FI-RE-PL materials, such as G:FI-RE-PL and C:FI-RE-PL, exhibit comparable or even greater load carrying capacity and ductility compared to traditional steel reinforcement in concrete columns. This makes FI-RE-PL a promising alternative, particularly in environments susceptible to corrosion. Furthermore, the durability of FI-RE-PL reinforcements is demonstrated by their ability to maintain strength even after prolonged exposure to harsh conditions.

While existing design equations effectively address short FI-RE-PL-reinforced columns, further research is needed to address the behavior of slender columns and their performance under extreme conditions. Developing new equations that predict axial load capacity based on modulus of elasticity, rather than tensile strength, could enhance the accuracy of design predictions. Additionally, though FI-RE-PL materials generally exhibit acceptable reliability, more studies are required to better understand their long term performance and durability under various loading and environmental scenarios. To fully harness the benefits of FI-RE-PL in concrete construction, it is crucial to continue developing comprehensive design guidelines and conducting additional experimental and numerical research. These efforts will help integrate FI-RE-PL materials into standard engineering practice, optimizing their potential to improve the performance and durability of concrete columns.

IV. OBJECTIVES

This review paper aims to synthesize the current state of knowledge on the use of glass FI-RE-PL (G:FI-RE-PL) rebar as an substitute to steel rebar in concrete construction.

The primary objectives are:

a) To provide an overview of the material properties and structural performance of G:FI-RE-PL rebar in concrete, including their advantages and limitations compared to traditional steel reinforcement.
b) To examine the application of G:FI-RE-PL rebar in various concrete elements, such as beams, columns, and slabs, highlighting the unique design considerations and practical challenges.
c) To identify the key areas of ongoing research and emerging trends in the use of G:FI-RE-PL rebar, including advancements in design methods, durability assessment, and optimization techniques.

V. CONCLUSION

In conclusion, the review of the use of (G:FI-RE-PL) rebar in concrete construction provides several key insights:

a) G:FI-RE-PL rebar has demonstrated comparable or greater load bearing capacity and ductility compared to traditional steel reinforcement, making it a promising alternative, particularly in corrosive environments where steel is susceptible to deterioration. The durability of G:FI-RE-PL reinforcements, as evidenced by their ability to maintain strength even after prolonged exposure to harsh conditions, further highlights their potential advantages.
b) Advancements in predicting the shear strength of G:FI-RE-PL reinforced concrete beams, through the development of genetic programming models and experimental investigations, have significantly improved the accuracy and reliability of design processes. The new predictive formula's simplicity and enhanced performance could enhance the user-friendliness and overall dependability of structural engineering design practices.
c) While existing design equations effectively address the behavior of short FI-RE-PL-reinforced columns, additional research is needed to address the performance of slender columns and their response under extreme loading conditions. Developing new equations that predict axial load capacity based on modulus of elasticity, rather than tensile strength, could lead to more accurate design predictions.
d) To fully integrate G:FI-RE-PL materials into standard engineering practice and optimize their potential in concrete construction, continued efforts are required to develop comprehensive design guidelines and conduct additional experimental and numerical studies. These efforts will help address the long term durability of G:FI-RE-PL reinforcements under several environmental and loading scenarios, ultimately advancing the use of G:FI-RE-PL rebar as a viable alternative to steel.
e) Overall, the review highlights the significant potential of G:FI-RE-PL rebar in concrete structures, while also identifying key areas for further research and development to overcome remaining challenges and fully harness the benefits of this innovative reinforcement technology.

REFERENCES

[1] S. C. DAS and M. E. H. NIZAM, "Applications of Fibber Reinforced Polymer Composites (FRP) in Civil Engineering." Jul. 2014.
[2] S. Singh and D. undefined, "Concrete Structures Reinforced with FRP BAR." Apr. 2024.
[3] R. V. Balendran, T. M. Rana, T. Maqsood, and W. Tang, "Application of FRP bars as reinforcement in civil engineering structures," Emerald Publishing Limited, vol. 20, no. 2, pp. 62–72, May 2002.
[4] W. L. W. Lei, M. Y. a, ⇑ Lv Haibo a, C. S. a, and L. W. a, "Bond properties between FRP bars and coral concrete under seawater conditions at 30, 60, and 80 C." Jan. 2018.
[5] M. N. Amin et al., "Investigating the Bond Strength of FRP Rebars in Concrete under High Temperature Using Gene-Expression Programming Model," Multidisciplinary Digital Publishing Institute, vol. 14, no. 15, pp. 2992–2992, Jul. 2022
[6] Z. Dong, G. Wu, and Y.-Q. Xu, "Experimental study on the bond durability between steel-FRP composite bars (SFCBs) and sea sand concrete in ocean environment," Elsevier BV, vol. 115, pp. 277–284, Jul. 2016,
[7] Z. Dong, G. Wu, B. Xu, X. Wang, and L. Taerwe, "Bond durability of BFRP bars embedded in concrete under seawater conditions and the long-term bond strength prediction," Elsevier BV, vol. 92, pp. 552–562, Feb. 2016
[8] R. Gravina, J. Li, S. T. Smith, and P. Visintin, "Environmental Durability of FRP Bar-to-Concrete Bond: Critical Review," American Society of Civil Engineers, vol. 24, no. 4, Aug. 2020

[9]   M. Hassan, B. Benmokrane, A. ElSafty, and A. Fam, "Bond durability of basalt-fiber-reinforced-polymer (BFRP) bars embedded in concrete in aggressive environments." Sep. 2016.

[10]   J. Li, R. Gravina, S. T. Smith, and P. Visintin, "Bond strength and bond stress-slip analysis of FRP bar to concrete incorporating environmental durability," Elsevier BV, vol. 261, pp. 119860–119860, Nov. 2020,

[11]   C. M. Mikami, H.-C. Wu, and A. M. Elarbi, "Effect of hot temperature on pull-off strength of FRP bonded concrete," Elsevier BV, vol. 91, pp. 180–186, Aug. 2015

[12]   S. Sólyom, M. D. Benedetti, M. Guadagnini, and G. L. Balázs, "Effect of temperature on the bond behaviour of GFRP bars in concrete," Elsevier BV, vol. 183, pp. 107602–107602, Feb. 2020

[13]   A. Taha and W. Alnahhal, "Bond durability and service life prediction of BFRP bars to steel FRC under aggressive environmental conditions," Elsevier BV, vol. 269, pp. 114034–114034, Aug. 2021

[14]   N. Anand, T. Kiran, É. Lublóy, M. E. Mathews, B. Kanagaraj, and A. D. Andrushia, "Flexural Behavior of Reinforced Concrete Beams with FRP Bars Exposed to Elevated Temperature," Budapest University of Technology and Economics, Oct. 2022

[15]   F. A. da S. Barbosa, T. N. Bittencourt, G. R. Boriolo, F. R. André, and M. M. Futai, "Flexural design of concrete beams reinforced with FRP rebars." Jan. 2023.

[16]   F. Elgabbas, E. A. Ahmed, and B. Benmokrane, "Flexural Behavior of Concrete Beams Reinforced with Ribbed Basalt-FRP Bars under Static Loads," American Society of Civil Engineers, vol. 21, no. 3, Jun. 2017

[17]   C. S. H and K. R. B, "Flexural Behaviour of Concrete Beams Reinforced With GFRP Rebars." Jan. 2017.

[18]   S. A. Jabbar and S. B. H. Farid, "Replacement of steel rebars by GFRP rebars in the concrete structures," vol. 4, no. 2, pp. 216–227, Jun. 2018

[19]   A. Khorasani, M. R. Esfahani, and J. Sabzi, "The effect of transverse and flexural reinforcement on deflection and cracking of GFRP bar reinforced concrete beams," Elsevier BV, vol. 161, pp. 530–546, Mar. 2019

[20]   G. N. Kumar and S. Karthik, "Experimental Study On Flexural Behaviour Of Beams Reinforced With GFRP Rebars," IOP Publishing, vol. 80, pp. 012027–012027, Jul. 2017

[21]   Y. Kustikova, "Application FRP-rebar in the Manufacture of Reinforced Concrete Structures," Elsevier BV, vol. 153, pp. 361–365, Jan. 2016

[22]   C. Li, D. Gao, Y. Wang, and J. Tang, "Effect of high temperature on the bond performance between basalt fibre reinforced polymer (BFRP) bars and concrete." Feb. 2017.

[23]   O. A. Mohamed, R. Khattab, and W. A. Hawat, "Numerical Study on Deflection Behaviour of Concrete Beams Reinforced with GFRP Bars," IOP Publishing, vol. 245, pp. 032065–032065, Oct. 2017

[24]   M. M. Shirmardi and M. R. Mohammadizadeh, "Numerical Study on the Flexural Behaviour of Concrete Beams Reinforced by GFRP Bars." Jan. 2019.

[25]   S. Sirimontree, S. Keawsawasvong, and C. Thongchom, "Flexural Behavior of Concrete Beam Reinforced with GFRP Bars Compared to Concrete Beam Reinforced with Conventional Steel Reinforcements," vol. 24, no. 6, pp. 883–890, Jan. 2021

[26]   Z. S. Sun, L. F. Fu, D.-C. F. Feng, A. R. Vatuloka, Y. W. Wei, and G. W. Wu, "Experimental study on the flexural behavior of concrete beams reinforced with bundled hybrid steel/FRP bars." Jul. 2019.

[27]   E. Aydın, E. Boru, and F. Aydın, "Effects of FRP bar type and fiber reinforced concrete on the flexural behavior of hybrid beams." Feb. 2021.

[28]   N. K. S. Ali, S. Y. Mahfouz, and N. Amer, "Flexural Response of Concrete Beams Reinforced with Steel and Fiber Reinforced Polymers," Multidisciplinary Digital Publishing Institute, vol. 13, no. 2, pp. 374–374, Jan. 2023

[29]   S. Chandra, K. Hemalatha, V. R. Reddy, and V. S. Nadh, "Experimental studies on flexural action of RC beams made with hybrid rebars - A brief review," EDP Sciences, vol. 391. pp. 01194–01194, Jan. 2023.

[30]   K. Hemalatha and D. R. Prasad, "Numerical analysis on reinforcement ratio of RC beams using FRP and steel rebars," EDP Sciences, vol. 391, pp. 01210–01210, Jan. 2023

[31]   N. Kabashi, B. Avdyli, E. Krasniqi, and A. Këpuska, "Comparative Approach to Flexural Behavior of Reinforced Beams with GFRP, CFRP, and Steel Bars," Salehan Institute of Higher Education, vol. 6, no. 1, pp. 50–59, Jan. 2020

[32]   İ. F. Kara, A. Ashour, and M. A. Köroğlu, "Flexural behavior of hybrid FRP/steel reinforced concrete beams," Elsevier BV, vol. 129, pp. 111–121, Oct. 2015

[33]   M. Kaszyńska, J. Błyszko, and N. Olczyk, "Comparison of Failure Process of Bended Beams Reinforced with Steel Bars and GFRP Bars," IOP Publishing, vol. 245, pp. 022028–022028, Oct. 2017

[34]   S.-E. Kim and S. Kim, "Flexural behavior of concrete beams with steel bar and FRP reinforcement," Taylor & Francis, vol. 18, no. 2, pp. 89–97, Mar. 2019, doi: 10.1080/13467581.2019.1596814.

[35]   M. Kosior-Kazberuk, "Application of basalt-FRP bars for reinforcing geotechnical concrete structures," EDP Sciences, vol. 265, pp. 05011–05011, Jan. 2019

[36] C. Li, H. Zhu, G. Niu, S. Cheng, Z. Gu, and L. Yang, "Flexural behavior and a new model for flexural design of concrete beams hybridly reinforced by continuous FRP bars and discrete steel fibers," Elsevier BV, vol. 38, pp. 949–960, Apr. 2022

[37] M. Pranav, K. Hemalatha, P. S. R. P. S. S. S. Vardhani, and V. S. Nadh, "Review on flexural performance of reinforced concrete beams designed with hybrid bars," EDP Sciences, vol. 391, pp. 01203–01203, Jan. 2023

[38] K. Protchenko and E. Szmigiera, "Post-Fire Characteristics of Concrete Beams Reinforced with Hybrid FRP Bars," Multidisciplinary Digital Publishing Institute, vol. 13, no. 5, pp. 1248–1248, Mar. 2020

[39] A. M. Ebid and A. F. Deifalla, "Prediction of shear strength of FRP reinforced beams with and without stirrups using (GP) technique," Elsevier BV, vol. 12, no. 3, pp. 2493–2510, Sep. 2021

[40] H.-C. Kim, M. S. Kim, M. J. Ko, and Y. H. Lee, "Shear Behavior of Concrete Beams Reinforced with GFRP Shear Reinforcement," Hindawi Publishing Corporation, vol. 2015, pp. 1–8, Jan. 2015

[41] M. Krall and M. A. Polak, "Concrete beams with different arrangements of GFRP flexural and shear reinforcement," Elsevier BV, vol. 198, pp. 109333–109333, Nov. 2019

[42] T. P. Vora and B. J. Shah, "Experimental investigation on shear capacity of RC beams with GFRP rebar & stirrups." Aug. 2016.

[43] A. Ahmad, A. Bahrami, O. Alajarmeh, N. Chairman, and M. Yaqub, "Investigation of Circular Hollow Concrete Columns Reinforced with GFRP Bars and Spirals," Multidisciplinary Digital Publishing Institute, vol. 13, no. 4, pp. 1056–1056, Apr. 2023

[44] L. AlNajmi and F. Abed, "Evaluation of FRP Bars under Compression and Their Performance in RC Columns," Multidisciplinary Digital Publishing Institute, vol. 13, no. 20, pp. 4541–4541, Oct. 2020

[45] N. Elmesalami, A. E. Refai, and F. Abed, "Fiber-reinforced polymers bars for compression reinforcement: A promising alternative to steel bars," Elsevier BV, vol. 209, pp. 725–737, Jun. 2019

[46] H. A. Hasan, M. N. Sheikh, and M. N. S. Hadi, "Maximum axial load carrying capacity of Fibre Reinforced-Polymer (FRP) bar reinforced concrete columns under axial compression," Elsevier BV, vol. 19, pp. 227–233, Jun. 2019

[47] H. M. Mohamed, M. Z. Afifi, and B. Benmokrane, "Performance Evaluation of Concrete Columns Reinforced Longitudinally with FRP Bars and Confined with FRP Hoops and Spirals under Axial Load." Jan. 2014.

[48] M. A. Sawpan, "Shear properties and durability of GFRP reinforcement bar aged in seawater," Elsevier BV, vol. 75, pp. 312–320, May 2019

[49] A. Tarawneh and S. Majdalaweyh, "Design and reliability analysis of FRP-reinforced concrete columns," Elsevier BV, vol. 28, pp. 1580–1588, Dec. 2020

[50] M. Urba´nski, "Compressive Strength of Modified FRP Hybrid Bars." Apr. 2020.

[51] P. Zhang et al., "Experimental study on the axial compression behavior of columns confined by BFRP ties." Jan. 2021.

[52] B. Benmokrane, S. Mousa, K. Mohamed, and M. Sayed-Ahmed, "Physical, mechanical, and durability characteristics of newly developed thermoplastic GFRP bars for reinforcing concrete structures," Elsevier BV, vol. 276, pp. 122200–122200, Mar. 2021

[53] [X.-C. Fan, T. Xu, Z. Zhou, and X. Zhou, "Experimental Study on Basic Mechanical Properties of BFRP Bars," IOP Publishing, vol. 250, pp. 012014–012014, Oct. 2017

[54] O. Gooranorimi and A. Nanni, "GFRP Reinforcement in Concrete after 15 Years of Service," American Society of Civil Engineers, vol. 21, no. 5, Oct. 2017, doi: 10.1061/(asce)cc.1943-5614.0000806.

[55] M. Wydra, P. Dolny, G. Sadowski, N. Grochowska, P. Turkowski, and J. Fangrat, "Analysis of Thermal and Mechanical Parameters of the BFRP B

Student Absenteeism Monitoring and Notification System for Successive Lectures

Rani S Lande[1], Priti A. Khodke[1], Pooja V. Raut[1], Amol P. Bhagat[1]

[1] Department of Information Technology, Prof Ram Meghe College of Engineering & Management, Badnera, Amravati, 444701, Maharashtra, India.

Email: [1]rani.lande@prmceam.ac.in, amol.bhagat84@gmail.com

Abstract— In universities, monitoring student attendance is crucial for early identification of potential issues. This project aims to develop a system that uses Short Message Service (SMS) notifications to manage absenteeism reports. By integrating this system, lecturers can effortlessly track attendance records, and the system automatically sends SMS notifications to both parents and students if the permissible absence percentage is exceeded. This proactive approach ensures that students and their guardians are promptly informed about attendance issues, allowing for timely interventions and support. Ultimately, this system aims to improve student attendance and academic performance by fostering better communication and accountability.

Keywords— student attendance monitoring, SMS notifications, absenteeism management, university attendance system

I. INTRODUCTION

This software solution is designed for educational institutions to enable it modernize and streamline student's attendance monitoring. It offers a student, teacher and administrator module with user friendly interface for attendance record management & accountability. Students register their attendance online, either through the web at home or via a mobile app; teacher's record students attending in class ensuring accurate tracking of student absence.

The On Location Attendance Tracking System makes attendance data capture more automated, decreasing dependence on manual labor and margin of error. Having algorithms that pin point these students who are absent half or more of the day and marking them as a partial absentee. Such students trigger automatic notifications for teachers to enable intervention in a timely manner. Glimpse will send notifications, either to the user by email or in their system interface which implement blockchain technology and students are notified about if they were present at a session so this automatically empowers them.

Administrators can view attendance reports over time in depth to see the trends, analyse patterns and make more data-driven decisions. Attendance data will be stored securely using a system that maintains confidentiality and integrity of the related information with role-based access. The system is scalable in nature and replace traditional manual approaches with automated, effective digital approach that manage the attendance of an individual accurately and punctually.

II. SUMMARY OF THE LITERATURE

A. Classification of Studied Literature

The paper titled "Facial Recognition and Machine Learning-based Student Attendance Monitoring System" was published by N. Narkhede and others on 5 May 2023. The research is done in the field of machine learning. In the research done, first, a dataset of faces was selected for training and testing the HOG algorithm. For dataset preparation, the images in the dataset were preprocessed by resizing and converting them to grayscale. The images were also cropped to only include the face region. The algorithms KNN (K - Nearest Neighbour) and HOG (Histogram of Oriented Gradients) were implemented in the work.

The research paper titled "OPEN CV-based smart attendance system using facial recognition" was published by T. Tirupal and the team in May 2023. The work was done in the deep learning domain. The Fisher Face method was employed for the proposed system which is faster than other algorithms and also resilient to lighting conditions. LBPH (Local Binary Pattern Histogram) was another algorithm implemented in the system. The research paper titled "Real-time facial recognition based smart attendance management system" was published by S. Barik, S. Mohanty, and others in May of 2023. The work done in the proposed system was in the field of deep learning. In the proposed system, the face recognition method includes two important processes: registration of the face datasets and face matching. The extracted feature vectors were implemented and stored in an online database to create a more dynamic face recognition process. Principal Component Analysis, Linear Discriminant Analysis, Local Binary Patterns and Convolution Neural Network algorithms were employed.

In June 2023 paper on "Smart Attendance Using Face Recognition," V. Mane, M. Shinde, P. Shejole, S. Sheikh, P. Shevale, and S. Salve presented a comprehensive approach that involves multiple stages. The key components of their proposed system are data collection, data pre-processing, data augmentation, CNN training and validation, and system testing. This method is underpinned by the use of Deep Transfer Learning and MATLAB for the development of a Multi-Task Cascade Convolution Neural Network. This integrated approach is designed to enhance the accuracy and efficiency of attendance tracking through face recognition technology.

In May 2023 paper titled "Deep Learning Based Real Time Face Recognition for University Attendance System," M. Singhal and G. Ahmad introduce a novel approach to face recognition. Their method relies on a training database where each individual is associated with specific labels. When capturing an image, the system focuses on detecting frontal faces, discarding all other elements from the image. This process is facilitated by the use of the Histogram of Oriented Gradients (HOG) technique, which aids in identifying and isolating facial features, making it a promising solution for real-time face recognition in the context of a university attendance system.

A. Prominent Method/Approach (Existing)

The literature on attendance systems for successive lectures covers a wide range of technologies and methods, each with its own advantages and disadvantages. While technology based systems like RFID, mobile apps, and beacons offer efficiency and accuracy, they must be implemented with careful consideration of privacy and ethical concerns. Additionally, the relationship between attendance and student engagement is a critical area of study, as it directly impacts the effectiveness of educational interventions. Further research in this area can help institutions make informed decisions about attendance system implementation. It helps in preventing the proxy issues and it maintains the attendance of the student in an effective manner, but in one of the time-consuming process for a student or a staff to wait until the completion of the previous members.

III. PROBLEM DEFINITION AND REQUIREMENT ANALYSIS

A. Problem Domain and Definition

The problem domain for an attendance system for successive lectures within an educational institution involves the management and tracking of student attendance in an efficient, accurate, and convenient manner. This domain is primarily concerned with optimizing the attendance-taking process and leveraging technology to improve administrative and educational aspects related to student attendance. An attendance system for successive lectures is a technological solution used to monitor and manage student attendance in a series of educational lectures or classes.

B. Requirement Analysis

A requirement analysis for an attendance system for successive lectures involves identifying and documenting the specific needs, functionalities, and constraints of the system. Faculty members should be able to take attendance easily and efficiently. They should have access to attendance data for their lectures. Faculty should receive notifications of irregular attendance. User-friendly interface for faculty members. Students should have a convenient way to mark their attendance.

The system should be capable of verifying the identity of students attending lectures through facial recognition. The system should automate the attendance-taking process, reducing the need for manual roll calls. Records attendance data electronically and stores it securely. Ensure that only registered students and authorized individuals can mark attendance. Protection against unauthorized access or tampering of attendance records. Attendance records should be stored digitally and be easily accessible. Implement a notification system to alert faculty, students, or administrators about specific attendance events (e.g. absent student, low attendance, irregular patterns). The system should be scalable to accommodate different lecture sizes and adapt to varying enrollment numbers. User-friendly interfaces for both faculty and students to encourage adoption. Support for mobile devices, as students and faculty may access the system through smartphones or tablets. These requirements should be thoroughly analyzed and documented to guide the development and implementation of the attendance system for successive lectures, ensuring that it meets the needs of both faculty and students while adhering to privacy and security.

IV. PROPOSED APPROACH AND DESIGN SUMMARY OF THE LITERATURE

A. Proposed Approach

The proposed approach for the development of the Student Absenteeism Monitoring and Notification System for Successive Lectures is to creating a student attendance system for successive lectures involves the use of technology to track and manage attendance efficiently and find out the absent students for successive lectures.

B. Activity Diagram of Proposed Approach

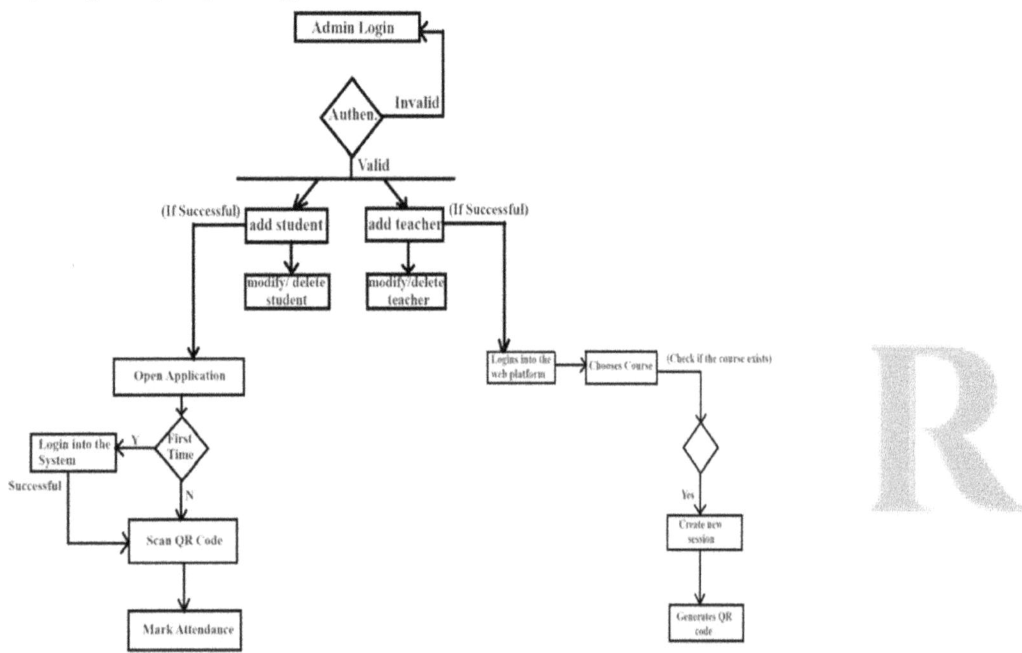

Fig. 1 : Activity Diagram of Proposed Approach

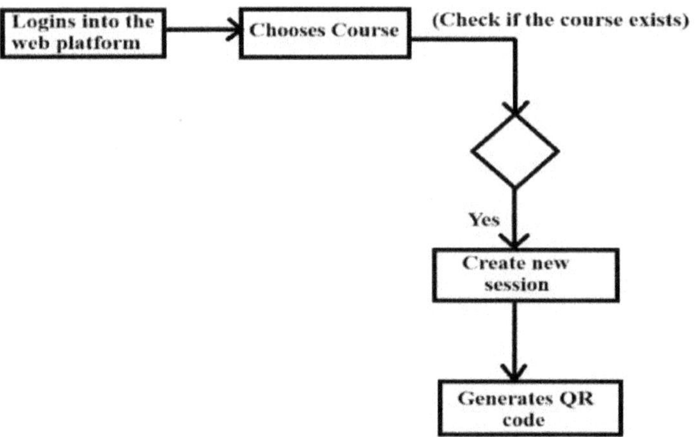

Fig. 2 : Block Schematic of the Approach

C. Explanation of steps involved:

Authentication and Identification: Implementing a method for authenticating and identifying students. This includes facial recognition, mobile apps with unique code generation.

Integration with Student Information System: Integrate attendance system with your institution's Student Information System (SIS). Which helps in syncing student data and course schedules.

User Interface: Develop an intuitive user interface for both students and teachers. Teachers should be able to take attendance quickly, and students should easily check-in.

Attendance Capture: Use of chosen identification method i.e. facial recognition to capture student attendance.

Real-time Reporting: Provide real-time attendance information for teachers and students. Teachers can see who is present, and students can receive immediate feedback on their attendance status.

Notifications: Send automated notifications to students who are absent without proper justification with the use of app notifications for this purpose.

V. IMPLEMENTATION DETAILS

A. Module

Attendance by Scanning QR Module:

The Attendance by Scanning QR Module provides a convenient and efficient method for users to mark their attendance using QR code technology. It encompasses functionalities for generating QR codes, scanning QR codes, and recording attendance data in the system.

QR Code Generation:

The module allows administrators or teachers to generate unique QR codes for each class session. QR codes are generated dynamically based on class details such as class name, date, time, and location. Generated QR codes are displayed on the teacher's device or projected onto a screen for students to scan.

QR Code Scanning:

Students use the mobile application to scan the QR code displayed during the class session. The scanning functionality captures the QR code using the device's camera and extracts the encoded information. Validation checks ensure that the scanned QR code is valid and corresponds to an active class session.

Attendance Recording:

Upon successful scanning of the QR code, the attendance data is recorded in the system in real-time. The system captures the timestamp of the attendance mark along with the student's unique identifier (e.g., user ID or student ID). Attendance records are stored securely in the database for future reference and reporting purposes.

Offline Support:

In scenarios where internet connectivity is limited or unavailable, the module may provide offline support for marking attendance. Offline caching mechanisms allow the mobile application to store attendance data locally and synchronize with the server once connectivity is restored. This ensures uninterrupted attendance tracking even in challenging network conditions.

Security Measures:

Security measures such as encryption and token-based authentication are implemented to ensure the integrity and confidentiality of attendance data. QR codes may be encrypted or secured with access tokens to prevent unauthorized access or tampering. Additionally, validation checks are performed to verify the authenticity of scanned QR codes and prevent spoofing or manipulation attempts.

Integration with Other Modules:

The Attendance by Scanning QR Module integrates seamlessly with other modules such as authentication, class management, and reporting. Authentication mechanisms ensure that only authorized users can mark attendance or view attendance records. Class management functionalities provide the necessary context for generating QR codes and recording attendance for specific class sessions. Reporting features enable administrators to analyze attendance data and generate comprehensive reports.

B. Module Details:

Authentication Module:

The Authentication Module serves as the foundation for user access control and security within the Attendance Management System. It encompasses functionalities such as user registration, login, logout, and session management.

User Registration:

New users can register for an account within the system by providing necessary details such as username, email address, password, and other optional information. Registration forms include validation checks to ensure data integrity and security, such as password strength requirements and email verification. Upon successful registration, user credentials are securely stored in the database for future authentication.

User Login:

Registered users can log in to the system using their credentials, typically consisting of a username/email and password combination. The login process involves verifying the provided credentials against the stored user data in the database. If the credentials match, the user is granted access to the system, and a session token or JWT (JSON Web Token) is generated to maintain the user's authenticated state.

Logout:

Users can log out of the system to terminate their current session and invalidate the session token or JWT. The logout functionality clears the user's authentication status and redirects them to the login page. This prevents unauthorized access to the user's account and protects against session hijacking or unauthorized use of the system.

Session Management:

Session management is crucial for maintaining user authentication across multiple interactions with the system. Session tokens or JWTs are securely stored on the client-side (e.g., cookies or local storage) and sent with each subsequent request to authenticate the user's identity. Server-side validation ensures the integrity and validity of session tokens, preventing unauthorized access or tampering.

Password Reset:

In case users forget their passwords, the module may provide a password reset mechanism. Validation checks and authentication measures ensure that only authorized users can reset their passwords, preventing unauthorized access to user accounts.

Security Measures:

Security is paramount in the Authentication Module to prevent unauthorized access and protect user data. Measures such as password hashing, encryption, and SSL/TLS encryption are employed to safeguard user credentials during transmission and storage. Additionally, security best practices such as account lockout mechanisms and CAPTCHA verification may be implemented to mitigate common security threats such as brute force attacks and account enumeration.

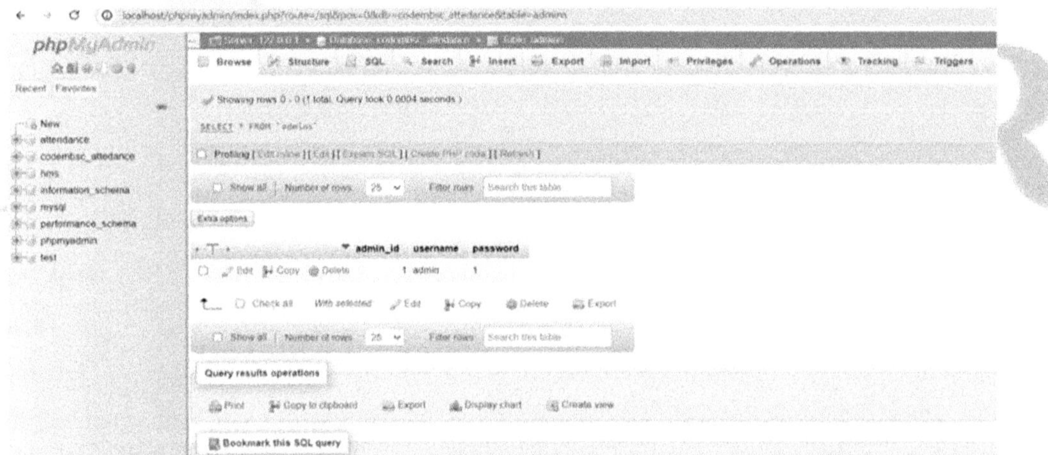

Fig. 3 : Admin Table

In the admin table admin's username and password will get stored. We can edit admins data by accessing admin table from the database.

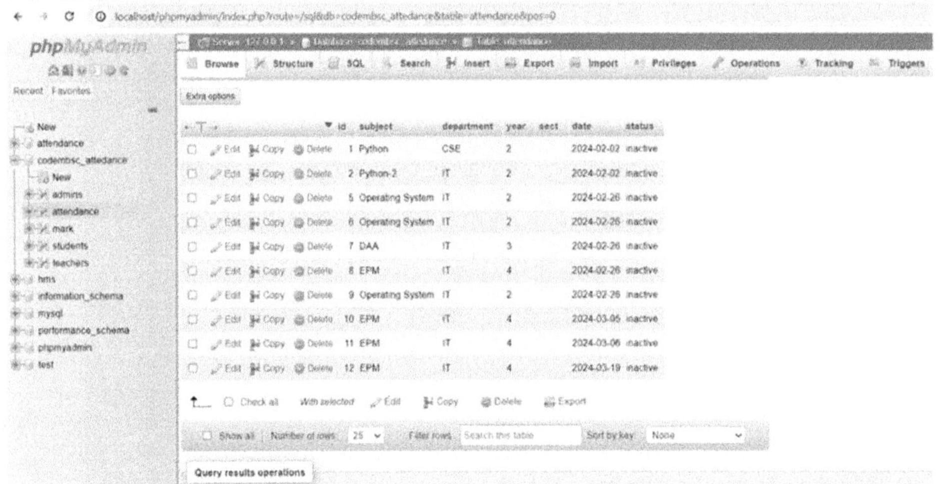

Fig. 4 : Attendance Table

VI. RESULTS

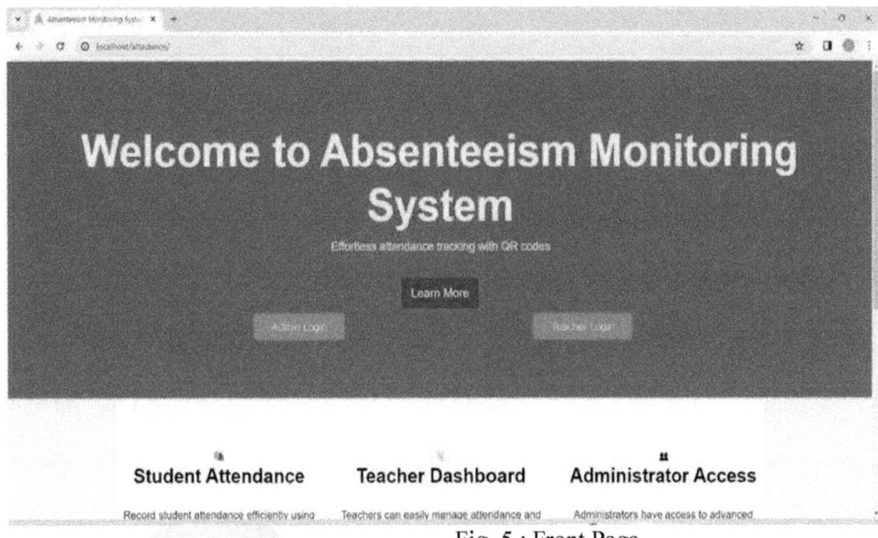

Fig. 5 : Front Page

The above page is first UI which will open after starting the project. Using this, we can redirect to admin login and teacher login page by click on that provided button. It also provides the brief information of our project below.

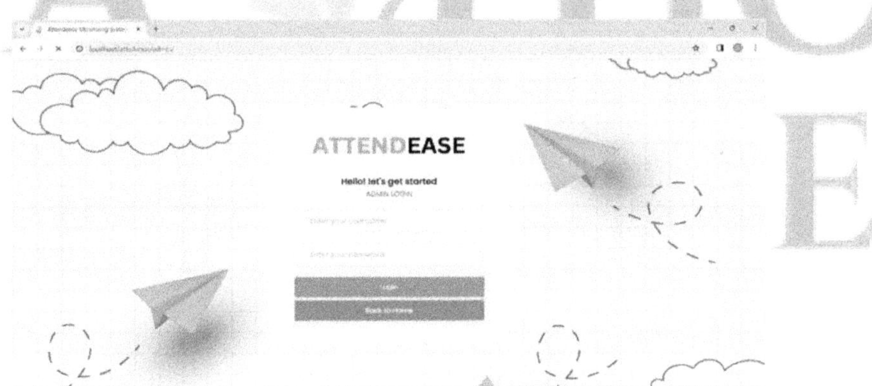

Fig. 6 : admin login page

This is an admin login page through which admin can login to dashboard. Admin can login by filling correct username and password. There is only two options are provides login and back to home which will redirect to front page.

Fig. 7 : Admin Dashboard page

Admin Dashboard page provides overall information including students and teachers. It provides information through graphical interface also. Admin dashboard provides access of adding departments, teachers and students.

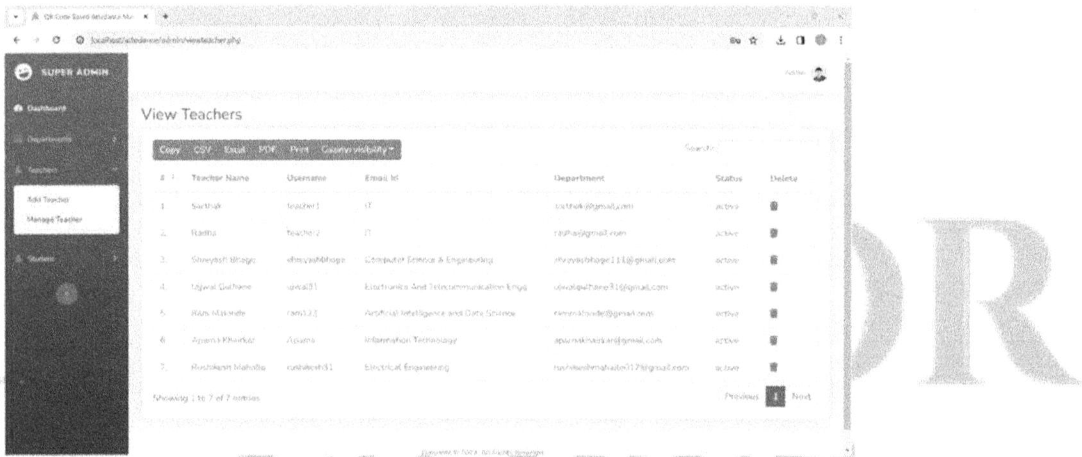

Fig. 8 : Add / Manage Teachers page

Admin can add and delete teachers by clicking add and manage teacher option. Teacher can register by admin only by filling required details such as name, username, email id, pass, dept.

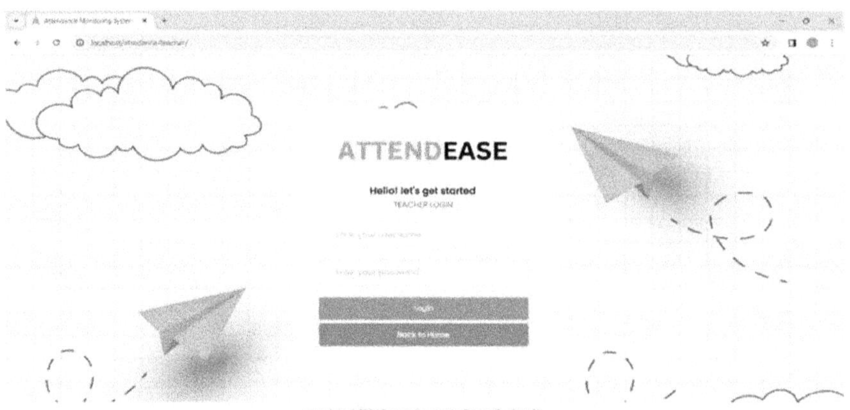

Fig. 9 : Teacher Login page

Teacher can login using registered username and password. Only authorized teachers can login through their login credentials.

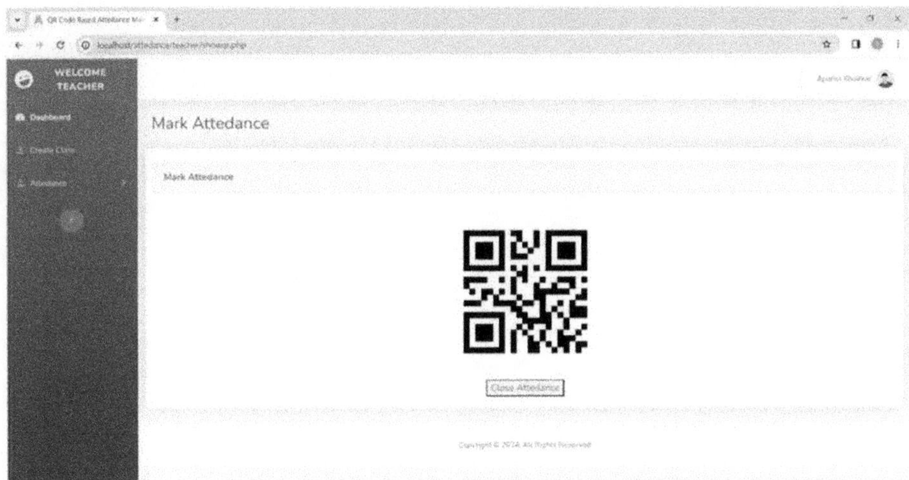

Fig. 10 : QR Code Generation page

After successful completion of the class QR code will generate. By scanning QR code student can mark attendance through their apps. Teachers can close QR code anytime they want.

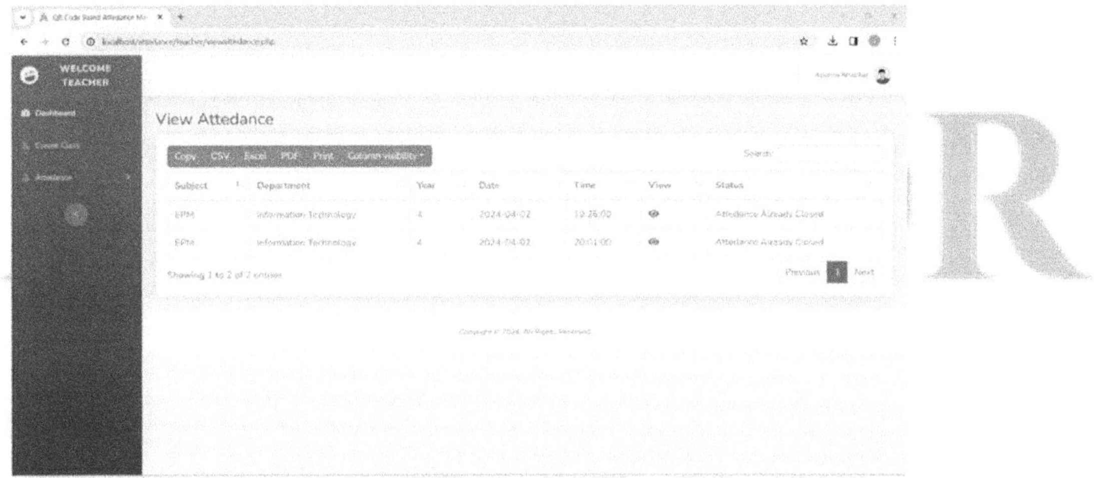

Fig. 11 : View Attendance page

After marking attendance teacher can view attendance of students through view option. Also teacher can download that attendance record in CSV, Excel, PDF, format and can print it directly using print option.

VII. CONCLUSION

The development of a Student Absenteeism Monitoring and Notification System for Successive Lectures is a valuable solution for educational institutions seeking to improve attendance tracking, enhance communication, and streamline administrative processes. This system offers several key benefits, including increased accountability, better student engagement, and data-driven insights into attendance patterns.

REFERENCES

[1] N. Narkhede, A. Menon, I. Mathane, S. Nikam and S. Dange, "Facial Recognition and Machine Learning-based Student Attendance Monitoring System," 2023 3rd International Conference on Intelligent Technologies (CONIT), Hubli, India, 2023, pp. 1-7,doi: 10.1109/CONIT59222.2023.10205631.

[2] T. Tirupal, M. N. Kumar, P. M. Basha, J. M. Babu and O. Rathan, "OPENCV Based Smart Attendance System Using Facial Recognition," 2023 4th International Conference for Emerging Technology (INCET), Belgaum, India, 2023, pp. 1-6, doi: 10.1109/INCET57972.2023.10170456.

[3]   S. Barik, S. Mohanty, D. Singh, S. N. Sahoo and S. Sahoo, "Real-Time Facial Recognition Based Smart Attendance Management System Using Haar Cascading and LBPH Algorithm," 2023 International Conference on Communication, Circuits, and Systems (IC3S), BHUBANESWAR, India, 2023, pp. 1-6, doi: 10.1109/IC3S57698.2023.10169763.

[4]   V. Mane, M. Shinde, P. Shejole, S. Sheikh, P. Shevale and S. Salve, "Smart Attendance Using Face Recognition," 2023 2nd International Conference on Vision Towards Emerging Trends in Communication and Networking Technologies (ViTECoN), Vellore, India, 2023, pp. 1-4, doi: 10.1109/ViTECoN58111.2023.10157213.

[5]   M. Singhal and G. Ahmad, "Deep Learning Based Real Time Face Recognition For University Attendance System," 2023 International Symposium on Devices, Circuits and Systems (ISDCS), Higashihiroshima, Japan, 2023, pp. 01-04, doi: 10.1109/ISDCS58735.2023.10153549.

[6]   R. Habu, S. Motade, S. Kukade, K. Gunale and A. Nair, "Smart Face Recognition Based Attendance System Using ML Algorithm," 2022 4th International Conference on Advances in Computing, Communication Control and Networking (ICAC3N), Greater Noida, India, 2022, pp. 527-532, doi: 10.1109/ICAC3N56670.2022.10074166.

[7]   P. Gupta and B. Singh, "A New Way of Recording Attendance of the Students using Face Recognition System," 2022 5th International Conference on Contemporary Computing and Informatics (IC3I), Uttar Pradesh, India, 2022, pp. 578-583, doi: 10.1109/IC3I56241.2022.10073382.

[8]   V. K. Chauhan, T. Singh, A. Dixit, R. K. Singh, P. K. Singh and J. P. Singh, "Image-Based Attendance System using Facial Recognition," 2022 11th International Conference on System Modeling & Advancement in Research Trends (SMART), Moradabad, India, 2022, pp. 1487-1490, doi: 10.1109/SMART55829.2022.10047785.

[9]   A. Rao, "AttenFace: A Real Time Attendance System Using Face Recognition," 2022 IEEE 6th Conference on Information and Communication Technology (CICT), Gwalior, India, 2022, pp. 1-5, doi: 10.1109/CICT56698.2022.9998001.

[10] V. Mishra, S. Raj, T. Singhal and C. Sankhla, "Intelligent Face Recognition based attendance system," 2022 10th International Conference on Reliability, Infocom Technologies and Optimization (Trends and Future Directions) (ICRITO), Noida, India, 2022, pp. 1-4, doi: 10.1109/ICRITO56286.2022.9964862.

[11] S. S. Rajawat and K. Saxena, "Face Recognition based Attendance System," 2022 1st IEEE International Conference on Industrial Electronics: Developments & Applications (ICIDeA), Bhubaneswar, India, 2022, pp. 95-99, doi: 10.1109/ICIDeA53933.2022.9970084.

Health Parameters Based Student's Employability Prediction System

[1]Aparna R. Khairkar, [1]Pratiksha Nagrale, [1]Vedashri Jangle, [1]Sakshi Kondolikar, [1]Priyanka Bakade, and [1]Amol P. Bhagat

[1] Department of Information Technology, Prof Ram Meghe College of Engineering and Management, Badnera, Amravati, Maharashtra, 444701, India.

Email: aparna.khairkar@prmceam.ac.in, amol.bhagat84@gmail.com

Abstract— In an era where the intersection of health and employment is gaining prominence, the need for innovative systems to predict student employability based on health parameters becomes imperative. This seminar report explores the development and implementation of such a system, aiming to bridge the gap between health metrics and professional readiness. Through an extensive literature review, existing methodologies, and approaches are scrutinized, laying the foundation for our proposed solution. The report delves into problem definition and requirement analysis, outlining the scope, objectives, and aim of the project. Our proposed approach encompasses a comprehensive design framework, integrating block schematics, algorithms, data flow diagrams, and testing strategies. The experimental setup details the hardware and software utilized, alongside the presentation of results through visual aids and statistical analysis. Concluding discussions reflect on findings, drawing implications for future research and enhancement of the predictive model. This report serves as a roadmap for the development of health parameters-based student employability prediction systems, offering insights into its efficiency and potential applications in diverse educational and professional settings.
Keywords— intersection, analysis, experimental, employment

I. INTRODUCTION

A. General

In today's competitive job market, finding the right career path is more than just matching skills to job requirements. It's about understanding how factors like health can impact one's ability to excel in a chosen profession. This report delves into this often-overlooked aspect of career planning by introducing a system that predicts student employability based on their health parameters.

Physical fitness, cognitive abilities, and mental well-being are all crucial elements that can affect job performance and satisfaction. Yet, these factors are frequently sidelined in career guidance discussions. This project aims to change that by using advanced data analysis techniques to examine health data and offer personalized career recommendations.

Focusing on streams like the navy, army, and IT we're shedding light on how health intersects with career choices. By doing so, hope to empower individuals to make more informed decisions about their futures. This report, invite you to explore the connection between health and employability and consider the implications for career counseling in a rapidly evolving job market.

B. Basic Concepts

Employability prediction system relies on various ma- chine learning algorithms to analyse health parameters and make predictions. One such algorithm is regression analysis, which identifies relationships between health parameters and employability outcomes by fitting a regression model to the data. Another algorithm is decision trees, which partition the data based on different health parameters to classify in- dividuals into distinct employability categories. Additionally, neural networks, inspired by the human brain's structure, learn complex patterns in the data to predict employability outcomes with high accuracy. Feature engineering plays a crucial role in enhancing the predictive performance of our model. It involves selecting or engineering relevant features from the health data that are most informative for predicting employability outcomes. Techniques such as normalization, which scales the features to a standard range, and dimensionality reduction, which reduces the number of features while preserving important information, are employed to improve the model's efficiency and effectiveness.

To assess the performance of employability prediction system, utilizes various evaluation metrics such as accuracy, precision, recall, and F1-score. Accuracy measures the proportion of correctly predicted outcomes, while precision quantifies the proportion of true positive predictions among all positive predictions. Recall, also known as sensitivity, measures the proportion of true positive predictions among all actual positiveoutcomes. The F1-score, which combines precision and recall, provides a balanced measureof the model's performance across different employability categories

II. SUMMARY OF THE LITERATURE

A. Analysis of studied Literature in Deep Learning:

Moumen et al.,2021. This paper presented a systematic exploratory literature review about student employability prediction systems based on deep learning algorithms. They started from the Scopus database to find previous works; it analyzed all collected. papers through two levels: a meta-analysis and a thematic analysis to elaborate a comparative study between models depending on accuracy.

B. Analysis of studied Literature in Machine Learning:

Saidani et al.,2022. This study introduced an effective method to predict students employability based on their internship performance by using Gradient Boosting classifiers. Different gradient boosting classifiers such as eXtreme Gradient Boosting(XGBoost), Category Boosting(CatBoost) and Light Gradient Boosted Machine(LGBM) was compared and then result obtained showed that applying LGBM classifier over internship context perform best compared to other boosting classifier.

Helmyet al.,2022. This paper introduced a predictive model using machine learning (ML) algorithms to predict information technology graduate's employability to match the labor market demands. Five machine learning classification algorithms were applied named Decision tree (DT), Gaussian Naïve Bayes (Gaussian NB), Logistic Regression (LR), Random Forest (RF), and Support Vector Machine (SVM). The results showed that DT achieved the highest accuracy, and the second highest accuracy was achieved by LR and SVM.

sobnath et al.,2020. This study identified the potential predictive features, which was improved the chances of engaging disabled school leavers in employment about 6 months after graduation. The dataset of 270,934 student records with a known disability provides anonymized information about students' age range, year of study, disability type, results of the first degree, among others. Using both qualitative and quantitative approaches, characteristics of disabled candidates during and after school years were investigated to identify their engagement patterns.

Casuat et al.,2020. In this study the principal component analysis (PCA) and logistic regression was used to determine the most predictive features in the students' employability prediction system. The features used were professionalism and branding, confidence, comprehension, communication skills, growth potential, student performance rating. Upon using PCA, the experiments resulted to communication skills growth potential and student performance rating obtained the most predictive attributes that affects the employability prediction.

III. PROBLEM DEFINITION AND REQUIREMENT ANALYSIS

A. Problem Domain and Definition

In the contemporary landscape of higher education and the evolving job market, there is a growing recognition that a student's health and well-being play a crucial role in determining their employability. The employability of students in highly specialized fields such as the Navy, Army, and IT is influenced not only by educational achievements and skills but also by specific health and fitness levels that are critical for job performance. While the Navy and Army require exceptional physical fitness, mental resilience, and specific health conditions, the IT sector demands mental well-being and lifestyle choices that support prolonged periods of focused work. Despite this recognition, there is a lack of comprehensive systems and methodologies for predicting a student's employability based on their health parameters. To address this issue, there is a need to develop a robust and data-driven "Health Parameters-Based Student's Employability Prediction System" that can assess how various health factors, including physical fitness, mental health, and overall well-being, influence a student's employability.

The definition of the problem domain includes identifying the key health parameters to be considered, such as BMI, blood pressure, cognitive function, and psychological assessments, among others. Furthermore, the problem domain encompasses the development of a predictive model that can effectively analyze health data and generate personalized career recommendations. This entails selecting appropriate machine learning algorithms, preprocessing techniques, and evaluation metrics to ensure the accuracy, reliability, and relevance of the predictions.

B. Requirement Analysis

1) Aim of the Project

- To develop an advanced health based parameters employability prediction system that integrates cutting-edge machine learning techniques to provide tailored career guidance and recommendations.
- To assess and predict a student's employability based on their physical and mental health parameters.
- To bridge the gap between students' health and their employability prospects within the context of higher education.

2) Objectives to be achieved

The project's objectives include:

- To design and develop a system that can predict the employability of students based on their health parameters.
- Design and develop a robust prediction model that utilizes the collected health parameter data to predict students' employability.
- Develop an effective system that combines health parameter analysis and prediction modeling to provide students with valuable insights into their employability based on their mental and physical health status.
- To provide innovative and efficient solution that can assist students regarding to their employment.
- Implement a user-friendly interface to facilitate seamless interact with the prediction system.

IV. PROPOSED APPROACH AND DESIGN

A. Proposed Approaeh

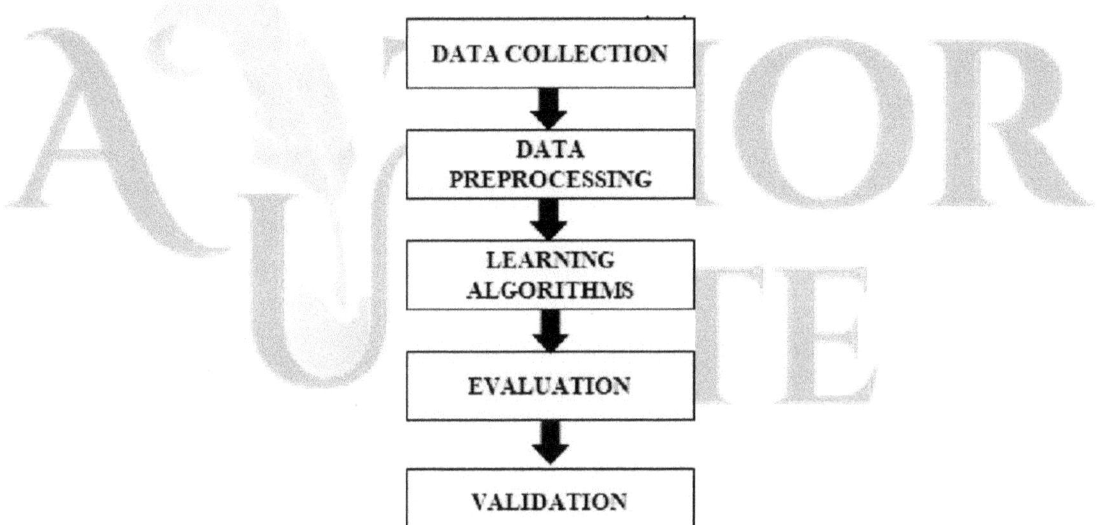

Fig. 12 : Activity Diagram of Proposed Approach

Data Collection: This initial stage involves gathering relevant data related to health parameters and employability outcomes. This data could include information such as BMI, blood pressure, cognitive function scores, job performance metrics, etc. The goal is to compile a comprehensive dataset that will serve as the foundation for subsequent analysis.

Data Preprocessing: Once the data is collected, it undergoes preprocessing to prepare it for analysis. This involves tasks such as cleaning the data to remove errors or inconsistencies, handling missing values, and transforming the data into a suitable format for analysis. Preprocessing ensures that the data is of high quality and ready for input into machine learning algorithms

Learning Algorithms: After preprocessing, the data is fed into machine learning algorithms for training. These algorithms analyze the data to identify patterns and relationships between health parameters and employability outcomes. Common machine learning algorithms used in this context include regression analysis, decision trees, and neural networks. The goal is to develop a predictive model that can accurately predict employability based on an individual's health profile.

Evaluation: Once the model is trained, it is evaluated to assess its performance. This involves testing the model on a separate dataset (often called a validation set) to measure its accuracy and reliability. Evaluation metrics such as accuracy, precision, recall, and F1-score are used to quantify the model's performance and identify areas for improvement.

Validation: Finally, the model undergoes validation to ensure its effectiveness and generalizability. Validation involves testing the model on unseen data to verify that it can make accurate predictions in real-world scenarios. This step is crucial for assessing the model's robustness and reliability before deploying it for practical use

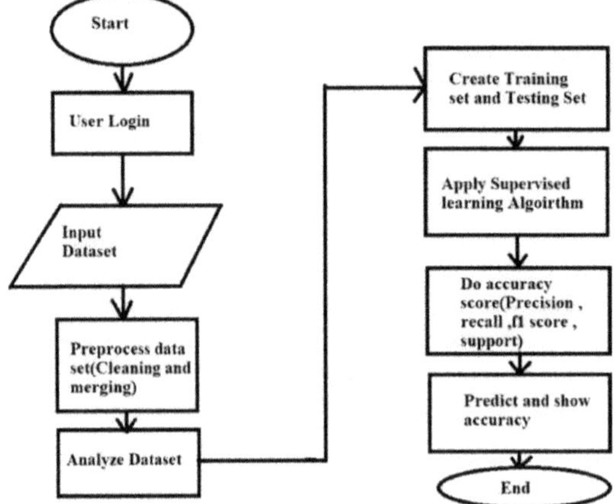

Fig. 13 : Data Flow Diagram

V. EXPERIMENTAL SETUP

A. Software Requirements

Operating System: Most popular operating systems such as Windows, macOS, or Linux are suitable for running machine learning tasks. Linux distributions like Ubuntu or CentOS are preferred by many data scientists due to their compatibility with a wide range of machine learning libraries and tools.

Python: The Python programming language is widely used for machine learning and data science tasks due to its rich ecosystem of libraries and frameworks. Install Python (preferably version 3.6 or higher) along with package management tools like pip or conda.

Integrated Development Environment (IDE): Choose an IDE for writing and executing Python code. Popular choices include PyCharm, Jupyter Notebook, Spyder, and Visual Studio Code. These IDEs offer features such as code autocompletion, debugging, and visualization capabilities.

Machine Learning Libraries: Install machine learning libraries such as scikit-learn, Numpy, PyTorch, or Keras for implementing and training machine learning models. These libraries provide pre-built algorithms, tools for data preprocessing, and utilities for model evaluation.

Data Processing Tools: Depending on the complexity of data preprocessing tasks, you may need additional tools such as pandas for data manipulation, NumPy for numerical computations, and matplotlib or seaborn for data visualization.

B. Hardware Requirements :

Computer: A standard desktop or laptop computer with sufficient processing power and memory to handle data preprocessing, model training, and evaluation tasks. Ideally, a computer with a multi-core processor and at least 8GB of RAM would be suitable for running machine learning algorithms efficiently.

Storage: Sufficient storage space to store datasets, code, and trained models. Depending on the size of the datasets and models, an SSD or HDD with at least 500GB of storage capacity should be adequate.

Optional: GPU (Graphics Processing Unit): For faster model training and inference, especially with deep learning algorithms, a GPU can significantly speed up computation. NVIDIA GPUs, such as GeForce or Quadro series, are commonly used for machine learning tasks.

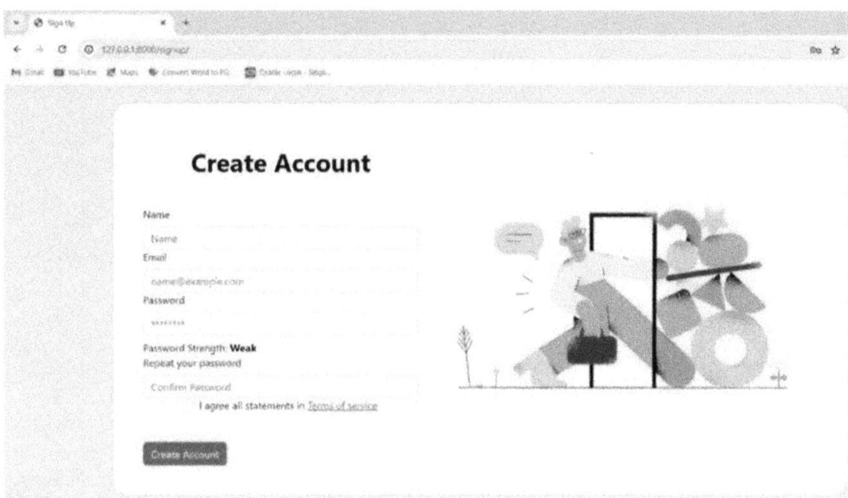

Fig. 14 : SignUp page

The signup page serves as the initial step for users to establish their presence within the system. It offers a streamlined process where users can input their personal information securely. The "Full Name" field prompts users to provide their complete identification, ensuring clarity and accuracy in their account details. The "Email" field acts as a unique identifier, facilitating communication and account management. Through the "Password" field, users can create a secure access credential, safeguarding their account information. The "Confirm Password" field offers an additional layer of validation, minimizing input errors and ensuring password accuracy. Finally, the "Create Account" button serves as the gateway to initiate the signup process, validating the entered information and establishing the user's account within the system.

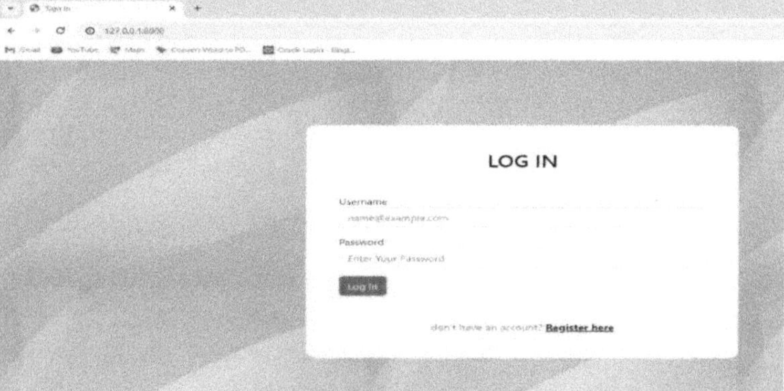

Fig. 15 : Login Page

The Login Page allow user to login the system by entering there registered email id in "Username" and correct password in "Password" fields. "Register here" allow new users to create new account.

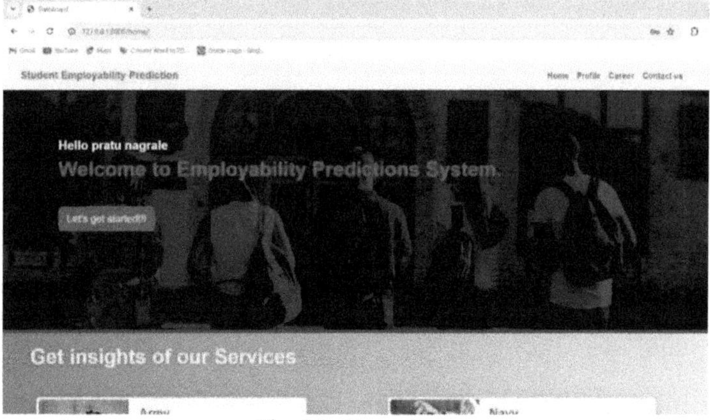

Fig. 16 : Home Page

The "Home Page" serves as the starting point. Through "Profile" users can conveniently manage their personal information, preferences, and account settings, ensuring a tailored experience. "Career" simplifies the process of entering physical and mental health parameters in the system. "Contact Us" provides information about the system's purpose, mission, and the team members involved in its development and maintenance, fostering transparency and trust. Lastly, "Log Out" ensures secure access control, allowing users to terminate their current session with a simple click, safeguarding their data privacy and account security.

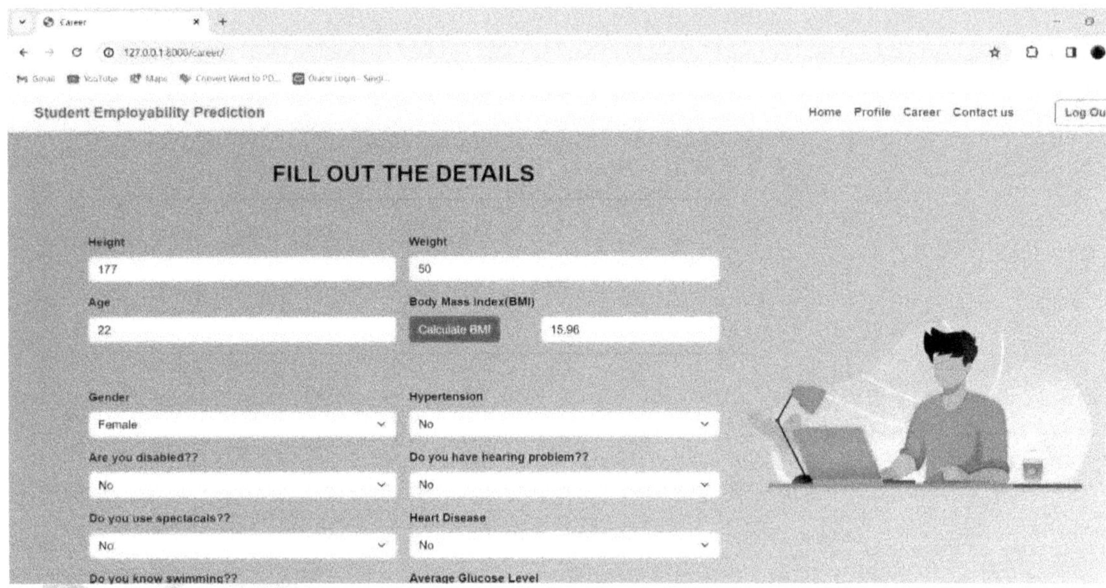

Fig. 17 : Form Page

In the "Career" section, "FILL OUT THE DETAILS" page will open in that the users input their key details. They provide their "Height", "Weight" and "Age" on the basis of that the BMI(Body Mass Index) is Calculated. Then user will enter there physical and mental health parameters such as "Gender", "Average Glucose Level", "Oxygen Level", "Blood Pressure", "Blood Group", "Average Sugar Level". This form will ask user about medical issues such as "Hypertension", "Disability", "Hearing Problem", "Spectacles", "Heart Diseases", "Smoking Status". "Swimming" is the parameter which is mandatory for Navy.

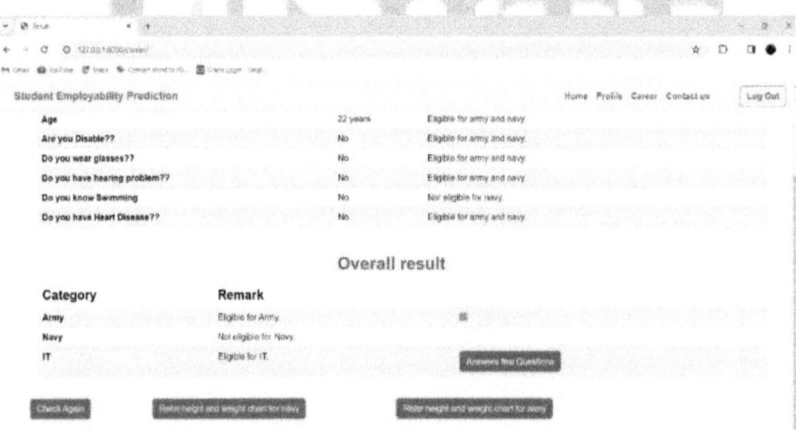

Fig. 18 : Result Page

The "Result" page will display the result by analyzing the provided data from user. In "Overall result" it will display whether the user is eligible for Army or Navy or for both. And if the user is eligible for both Army and Navy or not, then user will remain eligible for IT sector. If the user finds any problem it can refer height and weight chart for Army and Navy.

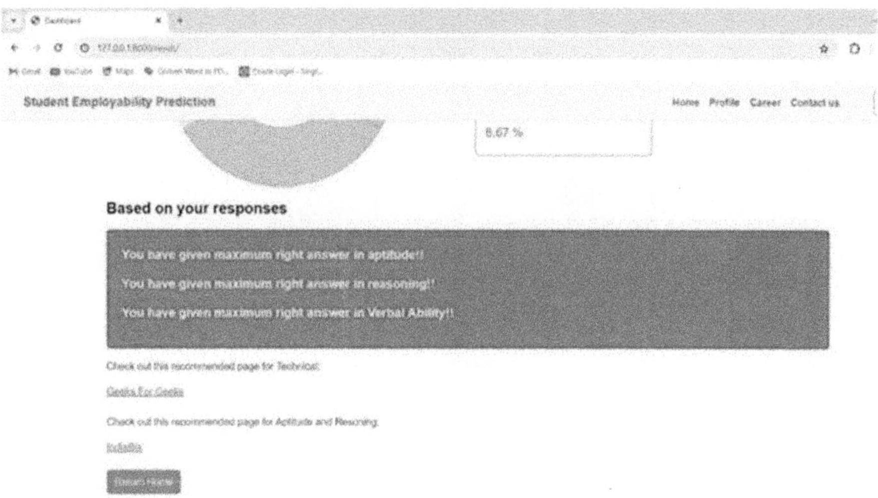

Fig. 19 : IT Result Page

On the result page for IT sector of Health Parameters Based Employability Prediction System, users can access personalized predictions regarding their employability. It will display result in the form of Pie-chart based on their performance in Questionnaire. User can use the https://www.geeksforgeeks.org/ for upskill their technical knowledge and https://www.indiabix.com/ for Aptitude, Reasoning and Verbal Communication.

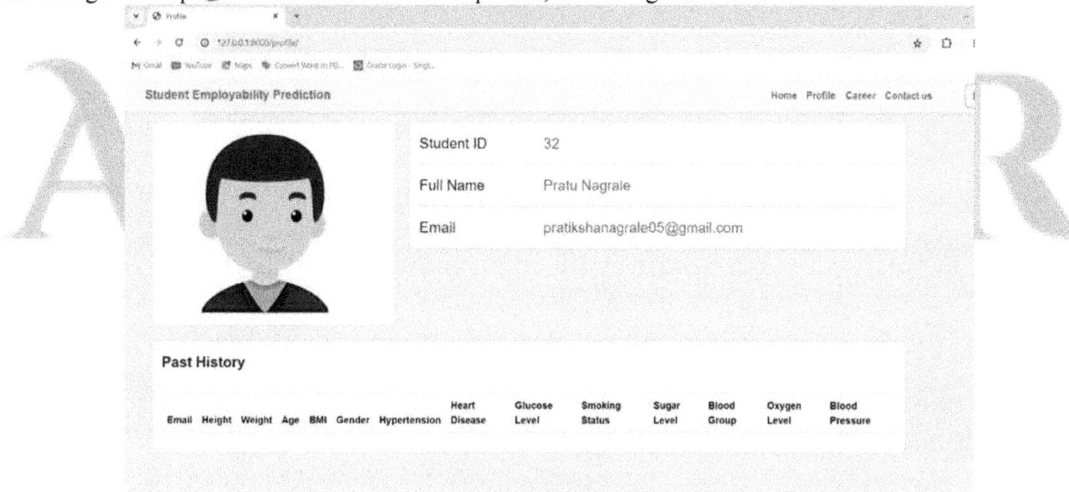

Fig. 20 : Profile Page

This "Profile" page will display the profile of user including there Unique ID, Name and registered email id. This page will show the past history of the user.

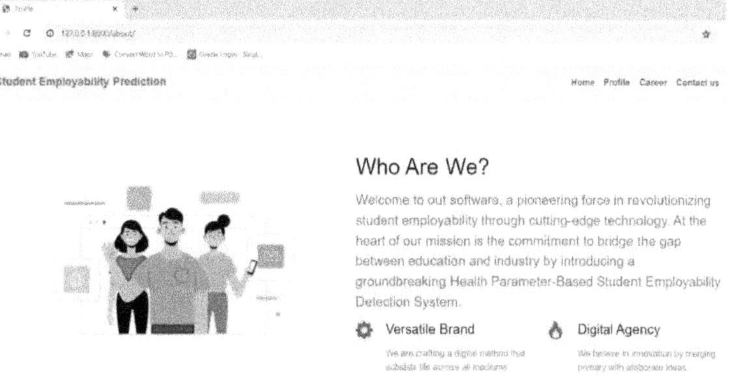

Fig. 21 : About Page

This page provides information about our Health Parameters Based Employability Prediction System. It utilizes health metrics to offer personalized predictions for career prospects. Users can understand how their health influences employability, enabling informed decisions to shape their professional journey.

VI. CONCLUSION

The health parameters-based employability prediction system represents a significant advancement in career guidance and decision-making processes. By leveraging insights from health data and machine learning techniques, this system provides personalized recommendations tailored to individuals' unique health profiles. From data collection to model deployment, the systematic approach outlined in this project offers a robust framework for building and evaluating predictive models that empower individuals to make informed career choices aligned with their overall well-being.

This system addresses the holistic nature of employability, considering both physical and mental health dimensions. Factors such as BMI, blood pressure, cognitive function, and psychological assessments are considered, providing a comprehensive understanding of individuals' readiness for various career paths. By encouraging individuals to prioritize their health in their career decision- making process, the system not only enhances the accuracy and relevance of career guidance but also promotes well-being.

The deployment of such a system has broad implications for individuals, employers, and society. Individuals benefit from personalized career recommendations that align with their health status and career aspirations, leading to greater job satisfaction and productivity. Employers can optimize workforce planning and talent acquisition strategies, while policymakers and educators can leverage insights to inform public health interventions and workforce development programs. However, it is crucial to address limitations and challenges, including ethical considerations such as data privacy and bias in algorithmic decision-making. Continuous research and collaboration are necessary to refine and improve the system's predictive capabilities, ensuring its relevance and effectiveness in real-world settings. In conclusion, the health parameters-based employability prediction system offers a promising approach to enhancing career guidance and decision-making processes. By empowering individuals to make informed career choices that prioritize their holistic well-being, this system contributes to a future where individuals can achieve their full potential in both their careers and their lives.

REFERENCES

[1] OUMAIMA SAIDANI, (Member, IEEE), LEILA JAMEL MENZLI, AMEL KSIBI, NAZIK ALTURKI, AND ALA SALEH ALLUHAIDAN, "Predicting Student Employability Through the Internship Context Using Gradient Boosting Models", Digital Object Identifier 10.1109/ACCESS.2022.3170421, pp. 46472-46488, VOLNO. 10, 2022.

[2] Gehad ElSharkawy, Yehia Helmy, Engy Yehia, "Employability Prediction of Information Technology Graduates using Machine Learning Algorithms", Employab-ility Prediction of Information Technology Graduates using Machine Learning Algorithms, pp. 359-367, VOL 13, NO. 10, 2022.

[3] Nesrine Mezhoudi, Rawan Alghamdi, Rim Aljunaid, Gomathi Krichna, Dilek Düştegör, "Employability prediction: a survey of current approaches, research challenges and applications", Journal of Ambient Intelligence and Humanized Computing (2023) 14:1489–1505, pp. 1490-1505, VOLNO. 2021.

[4] Aniss Moumen1,*, Imane El ,Bakkouri1 Hamza Kadimi, Abir Zahi1, Ihsane Sardi1, Mohammed Saad Tebaa1, Ziyad Bousserrhine, Hanae Baraka,"Machine Learning for Students Employability Prediction", 2022 by SCITEPRESS – Science and Technology Publications, Lda. All rights reserved, pp. 274-278, VOLNO. 2021.

[5] DRISHTY SOBNATH, TOBIASZ KADUK, IKRAM UR REHMAN, (Member, IEEE), AND OLUFEMI ISIAQ, "Feature Selection for UK Disabled Students' Engagement Post Higher Education: A Machine Learning Approach for a Predictive Employment Model ", pp. 159530- 159541, VOLNO. 8,2020.

[6] Cherry D. Casuat, Julius C. Castro,Deanne Cameren P. Evangelista ,Niño E. Merencilla, Christina

[7] P. Atal, " StEPS: A Development of Students' Employability Prediction System using Logistic Regression Model Based on Principal Component Analysis", 2020 IEEE 10th International Conference on System Engineering and Technology (ICSET), Shah Alam, Malaysia, pp. 17-21, VOLNO 9 November 2020.

[8] Cherry D. Casuat, Enrique D. Festijo, "Identifying the Most Predictive Attributes Among Employability Signals of Undergraduate Students.", 2020 16th IEEE International Colloquium on Signal Processing & its Applications (CSPA),Malaysia, pp. 203-206, VOLNO. Feb,2020.

[9] Yogesh Bharambe, Nikita More, Manisha Mulchandani‡, Dr. Radha Shankarmani and Sameer Ganesh shinde,"Assessing Employability of Student using Data mining", 978-1-5090-6367- 3/17/$31.00 ©2017 IEEE Mumbai ,pp. 2110-2114,VOLNO. 2017.

[10] Sagardeep Roy,Anchal Garg," predicting academic performance of student using classification technique", Uttar Pradesh Section International Conference on Electrical, Computer and Electronics (UPCON)GLA University, Mathura, pp. 568-572, VOLNO date, Oct 26-28, 2017.

[11] Suhas Athani, Sharath Kodli,Mayur Banavasi, P. G. Sunitha Hiremath, "Student Academic Performance and Social Behavior Predictor using Data Mining Techniques", International Conference on Computing, Communication and Automation (ICCCA2017), pp. 170-174, VOLNO. 2017.

[12] Keno C. Piad, Menchita Dumlao, Melvin A. Ballera, Shaneth C. Ambat," Predicting IT Employability Using Data Mining Techniques.", ISBN: 978-1-4673-9379-9 ©2016 IEEE,pp. 26-30, VOLNO. 2016.

[13] Mansi Gera, Shivani Goel, "A Model for Predicting the Eligibility for Placement of Students Using Data Mining Technique", International Conference on Computing, Communication and Automation (ICCCA2015), pp. 114-117, VOLNO. 2015.

[14] Yue Liu, Lingjie Hu, Fei Yan, Bofeng Zhang, "Information Gain with Weight basedDecision Tree for the Employment Forecasting of Undergraduates", 2013 IEEE International Conference on Green Computing and Communications, pp. 2210-2213, VOLNO. 2013.

Directing System Management Decision Making Using Forensic Analysis of Web Application

Kalyani D. Dahikar[1], Aparna A. Khairkar[1], Tanmay Bhaturkar[1], Rohan Deshmukh[1] and Amol P. Bhagat[1]

[1]Department of Information Technology, Prof Ram Meghe College of Engineering and Management, Badnera, Amravati, Maharashtra, 444701 India.

Email: kalyani.dahikar@prmceam.ac.in, amol.bhagat84@gmail.com

Abstract— In the evolving landscape of cybersecurity, the management of web applications has become a critical concern for organizations aiming to protect their digital assets. This project presents a novel approach to empowering system management decisions by leveraging forensic analysis techniques on web applications. The primary objective of this project is to develop a standalone application that facilitates the comprehensive collection of data from web applications, specifically tailored for penetration testing (pen test) purposes. The proposed system addresses the challenge of ensuring the security and integrity of web applications by integrating the principles of forensics into the pen testing process. The application employs automated data gathering techniques to extract relevant information from web applications, encompassing elements such as subdomain, directories, ports, OS detection, and client-side scripts. This data is subsequently subjected to thorough forensic analysis, enabling the identification of potential vulnerabilities, suspicious activities, and anomalies. Key features of the standalone application include user-friendly configuration options for customizing data collection scopes, support for a variety of web application frameworks, and compatibility with common pen testing tools given in the research paper [4]. The insights provided by the system aid in prioritizing remediation efforts, optimizing resource allocation, and enhancing overall system resilience. The project contributes to the field of cybersecurity by bridging the gap between pen testing and forensic analysis, thereby offering a comprehensive approach to identifying and addressing web application security concerns. The standalone application's versatility and adaptability make it a valuable asset for both small-scale enterprises and large organizations seeking to fortify their digital defences.
Keywords—Penetration Testing, Web Application, Forensic Analysis, Subdomain, Directories, Ports, Operating System, Vulnerability

I. INTRODUCTION

A. Basic Definition

In today's interconnected digital world, the need for cybersecurity has never been more critical. With the rapid expansion of technology and the increasing reliance on digital systems for everything from personal communication to financial transactions, the potential risks and vulnerabilities have grown exponentially. Cyberattacks are happening more often and are becoming smarter, so we need new ways to protect our digital assets. Therefore, we need a system that will help individuals or organizations maintain this task. This project is all about combining two important aspects of cybersecurity: examining digital evidence and testing web applications for weaknesses. There are existing systems that have already addressed this problem. For instance, in research papers [2][3][4], the authors have created a tool known as a Reconnaissance Tool for Web Application Fingerprinting. This tool is used to scan web applications and find vulnerabilities in the application. It employs various types of tools to achieve or provide the best security to users. While there are more tools created to enhance security through cybersecurity, they often share common issues, such as not being user friendly and being dependent on a specific operating system, leading to slow and time- consuming processes.

B. Basic Concepts:

This is why we have proposed a system with the capability to overcome these problems. Our tool, named "Directing System Management Decision Using Forensic Analysis of Web Applications," is used to scan web applications and identify vulnerabilities for users. Our primary purpose is to create a tool that will perform forensic analysis with the two steps of penetration testing mentioned in [5]. These steps include Reconnaissance and Scanning, which will guide system management decisions by identifying different known vulnerabilities and endpoints. The proposed system will be cross-platform and user-friendly.

II. SUMMARY OF THE LITERATURE

From the literature review above, several prominent existing approaches are available. Let's examine each one individually. In June 2022 Shubham Singh, Neeraj Pahadiya, Seema Jain proposed Web Recon Tool [4]. In this paper, web application scanning is conducted using the Web Reconnaissance Tool, which is designed to locate hidden web directories across the internet. All that is required is an internet connection from your home. The DIR methodology is employed to discover concealed directories within web applications. DIR is a Python-based method utilized for brute-forcing secret web directories and files. It is compatible with Windows, Linux, and macOS and offers a straightforward yet powerful command-line interface. This research paper teaches us how to utilize the DIR methodology. While DIR is a command-line program and may not be the most user-friendly option, it is accessible across various platforms.

In August 2021 Sanya Bindlish, Mehak Khurana and Shilpa Mahajan proposed An Automation of Reconnaissance & Scanning [5]. In this paper, the Recon Tool is proposed to automate the Reconnaissance and Scanning phases during Penetration Testing. The tool's objective is to gather as much information about the target as possible in the shortest time possible. This bash-script-based tool aids in scanning for open ports, web objects, hidden directories, and identifying the content management system employed by the target website. From this research paper, we gain insights into the recon and scanning phases, which we plan to incorporate into our project. Additionally, we learn how to efficiently collect more data within a limited timeframe. It's important to note that this project is operating system-dependent and may not have a user- friendly interface.

In May 2022 Ranjeet Kumar Singh and Dr. Om Prakash Yadav proposed Automating the Web Application Reconnaissance Process - All in One Recon [3]. In this research paper, Reconnaissance Phase is used to gather the information about the web application , Generally in reconnaissance phase of hacking we have to use lots of different tools like for finding subdomains we have to use tools like Sub finder, Asset finder, Sublister etc. after than extract all unique subdomains from these tools then remove common subdomains and gather all subdomains one file. And after this there is another process are done this processes are very time consuming so the author create a tool which will done all the thing in less time and all the processes are done automatically, from this research paper we learn about the automation of the recon phase in the research paper of [5] we learn about the automation of recon ad scanning and by using the bash scripting in this research paper we learn about the other methods for automation of the recon phase , in this research paper there are also the common problem that this tool is not user friendly.

In 2021 Arun S and Bijimol T K research on Information Gathering Tools. In this research paper, the author investigates various tools used to gather information about web applications. The paper provides a detailed review of Dmitry, which is a tool specific to KALI LINUX. These tools are designed to aid attackers in identifying information about a target and discovering potential attack vectors that could be exploited. This knowledge is particularly valuable in social engineering attacks, as it enables attackers to obtain possible contact information and enhances their credibility by including details about the owner's web page or domain. The author compares Dmitry with other tools like Nmap, Zen Map, whois lookup, and SPARTA. This review paper provides insights into different information-gathering tools and helps readers determine which tool is the most suitable for their needs.

Forensic analysis of web applications involves a range of techniques to investigate and analyze web-based incidents. Techniques such as log analysis, data extraction, and vulnerability assessment are commonly used. According to Zawoad and Hasan (2015), web application forensic analysis includes tracking user activity, detecting security breaches, and examining server logs to identify and mitigate vulnerabilities (Zawoad & Hasan, 2015). Web application forensics plays a crucial role in understanding and rectifying security incidents. It helps in reconstructing the sequence of events leading to a breach, thus aiding in effective decision-making. As noted by McCormick et al. (2017), forensic analysis provides actionable insights that can guide system management decisions to enhance security protocols and improve system resilience (McCormick et al., 2017).

Forensic analysis provides critical data that informs system management decisions. For instance, Downey (2018) emphasizes that forensic evidence from web applications can lead to more informed decisions regarding system upgrades, security patches, and incident response strategies (Downey, 2018). Several case studies demonstrate the effectiveness of forensic analysis in system management. A study by Jones and Beebe (2015) illustrates how forensic techniques were applied to manage and rectify a significant data breach, highlighting how detailed forensic analysis led to improved decision-making and strengthened security measures (Jones & Beebe, 2015). Despite its benefits, integrating forensic analysis into decision-making poses challenges such as data privacy concerns and the need for specialized expertise. Zheng et al. (2016) discuss these challenges and propose solutions to overcome them, ensuring that forensic analysis remains a viable tool for system management (Zheng et al., 2016).

III. PROBLEM DEFINITION AND REQUIREMENT ANALYSIS

A. Problem Domain and Definition

In today's world, websites and web applications play a major role as they store our data. The organizations that maintain these platforms have access to our personal information. For example, e-commerce web applications often contain sensitive data like our residential address and mobile number. This sensitive data is at high risk of being hacked by cyber attackers. Therefore, during the development phase, developers need to understand the importance of creating websites and web applications that are not vulnerable and are not easy targets for attackers.

That's why developers need to test the website and web application to understand if it's vulnerable or not. There are some tools available in the market to test websites and web applications, but they have problems as identified in the literature review. The main issues with existing systems are that they are based on the command-line interface (CLI) and require typing different commands manually for different tests. Additionally, all existing systems are not cross-platform. Due to these problems, testers who need to test web applications encounter difficulties in scanning them.

B. Requirement Analysis:

The domain of the project is cybersecurity, where security is the main objective to achieve. There are numerous tools available in the market for scanning websites and web applications, but they all encounter similar and different problems. As per identified literature, cross platform availability is not mentioned. In the proposed project work forensic analysis approach will be used to direct the system management decisions with the user-friendly cross-platform application.

1. Not User Friendly:

The current tools [3-5] lacks user-friendliness, hindering effective user engagement and satisfaction. Users are encountering difficulties in navigating, understanding, and utilizing the application's features.

2. Manual Examination: Slow and Takes a Lot of Time

When something goes wrong with a web application, experts need to figure out what happened. They do this by looking at all the digital clues left behind, like digital footprints. But this process takes a lot of time because they have to do it by hand. It's like looking for clues in a big library without using a computer. This slow process makes it harder to fix problems quickly. In this project, we're trying to fix these problems. We want to make a special computer program that can help experts find problems in web applications more easily. This way, we can make web applications safer and help organizations make better decisions about how to manage them. There are two types of problems we're addressing: how complicated web applications are, and how slow it is to solve problems manually.

3. OS dependent

Most of the tools created for this task are focused on Linux-based operating systems. In research papers [3-5], only Linux-based operating system-supported tools are mentioned. However, in [2], the author provides only option for the Windows operating system, but the report is less detailed.

IV. PROPOSED APPROACH AND DESIGN

A. Proposed Approach:

By merging penetration testing with advanced forensic examination, supported by a purpose- built standalone data gathering application, the system aims to offer a report which show the data related to the website, making informed decisions, and fortifying the security of web applications.

1. Centralized Platform:

Enhanced Forensic Examination of Web Applications Within this landscape of innovation, the standalone application emerges as a beacon of centralized excellence. With this centralized hub, security professionals gain an unprecedented vantage point, capable of revealing the intricate threads connecting security incidents.

2. User-Friendly Interface: Bridging the Gap for Programmers and IT Audit Professionals

Amidst the complexities of cybersecurity, the standalone application shines as a beacon of accessibility. Its user-friendly interface is thoughtfully architected to accommodate the diverse audience that engages with web application security. Catering to the technical prowess of programmers and the strategic insights of IT audit professionals, the interface presents complex forensic analysis in an approachable manner. This intersection of usability and sophistication ensures that both technical and non-technical stakeholders can extract meaningful insights, contributing to more informed decisions and a united security strategy.

3. Cross-Platform

The proposed system is designed to be cross-platform, ensuring its availability and functionality on both Linux-based and Windows operating systems. This cross-platform compatibility enhances its versatility, allowing users on different operating systems to seamlessly access and utilize the system's features and capabilities. Whether users prefer Linux or Windows as their operating environment, they can benefit from the proposed system's capabilities without encountering platform-related limitation

B. Block Diagram of proposed approach:

The diagram techniques of foot printing shows many ways an attacker can gain information about a system so we can use this techniques to direct system management decision making process.

Foot printing involves gathering information from various sources such as DNS servers, Search engines, Network, Websites, whois, etc.

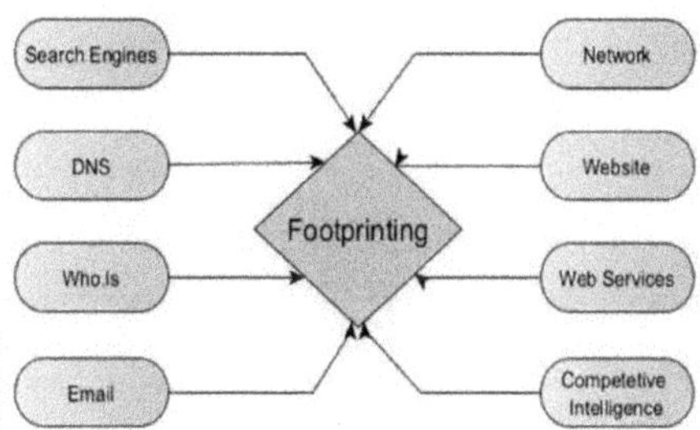

Fig. 22 : Data flow diagram

The diagram information a website can reveal shows various information about the system or company revealed in a website such as many misconfigured files in the server can reveal severe information about company, and various other information such as OS (Operating Systems), Scripting Language used, Contact details, CMS (Content Management System) and their version, types of databases used, misplaced files, subdirectories, web server software or version, etc.

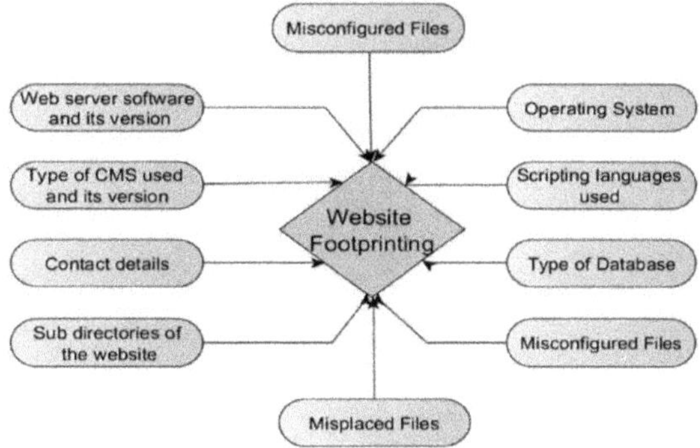

Fig. 23 : Data flow diagram

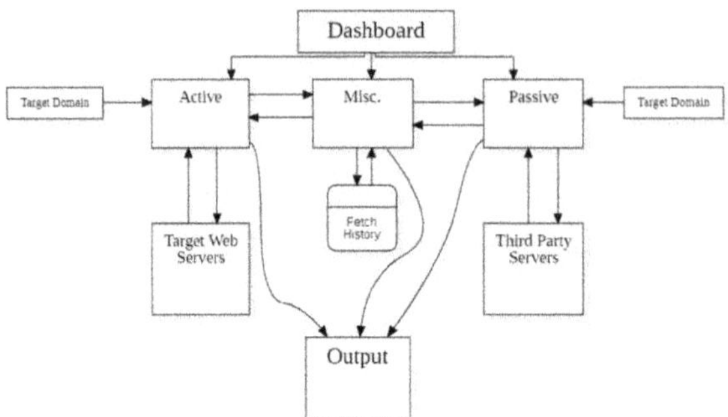

Fig. 24 : Data flow diagram

Explanation of steps involved

• Starting Application:

Dashboard: The dashboard includes three sections ACTIVE SCAN, PASSIVE SCAN and HISTORY SCAN. The ACTIVE SCAN will be the default screen for the user.

ACTIVE SCAN:

The ACTIVE SCAN section will ask for three inputs from the user the domain, URL (Uniform Resource Locator) and the ports to be scanned.

The inputs will be provided by user and on which active scanning will be performed where it is the process of actively probing and testing the application for vulnerabilities by sending specially crafted requests and analysing the responses. This type of scanning involves interaction with the target application and can help identify security weaknesses that might be exploited by attackers.

PASSIVE SCAN:

The PASSIVE SCAN section will ask the user for domain name of the targets web application and performed passive scanning on it where it involves monitoring and analysing network traffic, requests, and responses to identify potential security issues and vulnerabilities without actively interacting with the application. Unlike active scanning, passive scanning does not involve sending specially crafted requests to the target application but rather observes the traffic as it naturally occurs.

MISC:

The MISC i.e. Miscellaneous section include only importing history file of the edge browser from the user's computer where the last visited domain of the user's browser will be scanned with both active or passive. But for security reasons the active scan is not accessible directly the user needed to change the code for that purpose to add it.

OUTPUT:

Each of this section will generates an output accordingly and guide or direct the system management decision making process to improve the security of the system on which the web application is running.

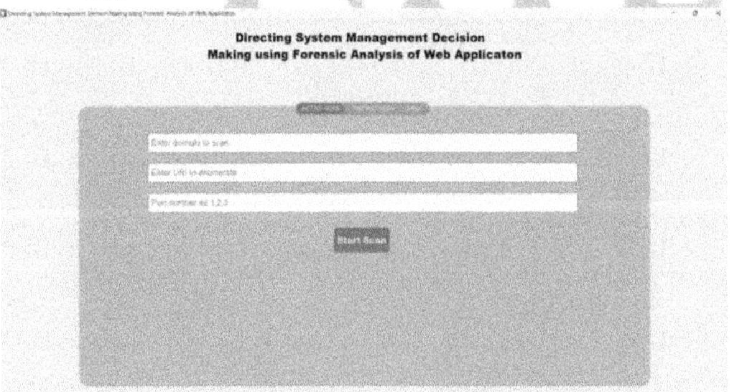

Fig. 25 : Dashboard with Active Scan tab

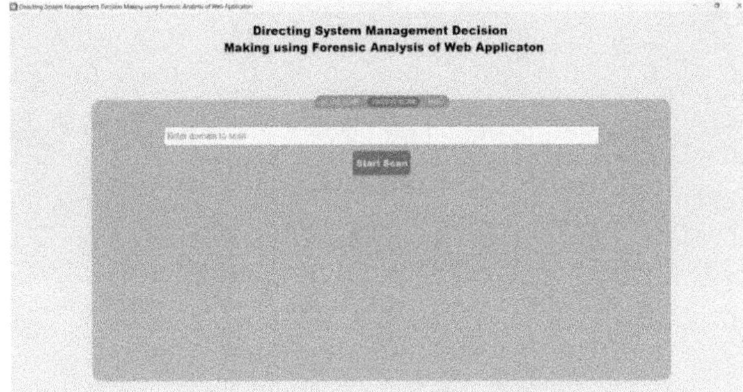

Fig. 26 : Dashboard with Active Scan tab

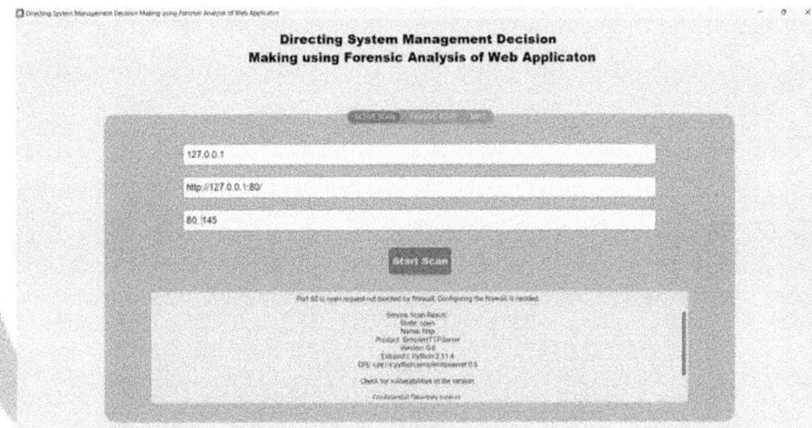

Fig. 27 : ACTIVE SCAN Output

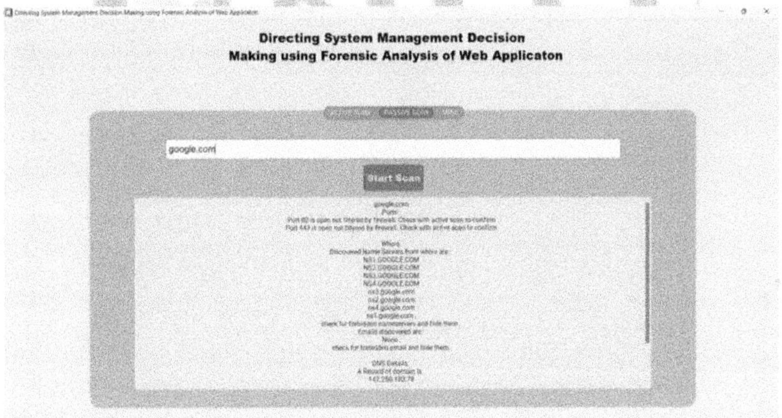

Fig. 28 : PASSIVE SCAN Output

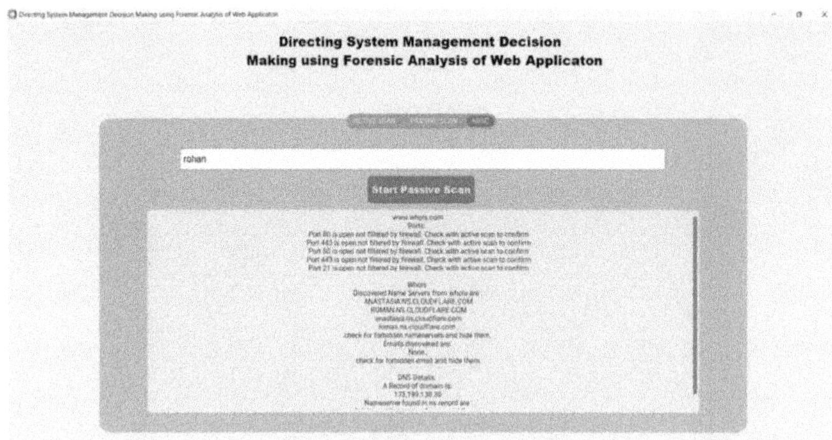

Fig. 29 : History SCAN Output

V. EXPERIMENTAL SETUP

A. Frameworks and modules:

customtkinter : CustomTkinter is a Python UI-library that builds upon Tkinter, offering a range of new, modern, and fully customizable widgets. These widgets function much like standard Tkinter widgets and can seamlessly integrate with existing Tkinter elements. One of the standout features of CustomTkinter is its adaptability to system appearances or manually set modes, such as 'light' or 'dark'. This means that the widgets and window colors dynamically adjust to match the chosen mode, ensuring a cohesive and visually pleasing user experience. Moreover, CustomTkinter prioritizes accessibility by supporting HighDPI scaling on platforms like Windows and macOS, guaranteeing sharp and clear rendering across various screen resolutions. By choosing CustomTkinter, developers can achieve a consistent and contemporary aesthetic across all major desktop platforms, including Windows, macOS, and Linux, enhancing the appeal and usability of their applications.

requests: The Requests library in Python is one of the integral parts of Python for making HTTP requests to a specified URL. Whether it be REST APIs or Web Scraping, requests are a must to be learned for proceeding further with these technologies. When one makes a request to a URI, it returns a response. Python requests provide inbuilt functionalities for managing both the request and response.

Nmap: Python-nmap is a versatile Python library designed to facilitate the utilization of the renowned nmap port scanner. Its primary function is to streamline the manipulation of nmap scan results, making it an indispensable tool for systems administrators seeking to automate scanning tasks and generate detailed reports. Additionally, python-nmap boasts robust support for nmap script outputs, enhancing its utility in diverse scanning scenarios.

One of the key strengths of python-nmap lies in its ability to operate asynchronously, enabling efficient and concurrent scanning operations. This asynchronous capability optimizes scanning performance, particularly when dealing with large-scale network environments or time-sensitive tasks..

pybinaryedge: Python 3 Wrapper for the BinaryEdge API https://www.binaryedge.io/
whois: WHOIS, pronounced as the phrase "who is," represents a query and response protocol pivotal in the realm of internet infrastructure. It serves as a fundamental tool for querying databases housing essential information regarding the registered users or assignees of an internet resource. Through the WHOIS protocol, users can retrieve pertinent details such as domain name ownership, registration and expiration dates, contact information of domain registrants, and technical data related to internet resources.dnspython: dnspython is a DNS toolkit for Python. It supports almost all record types. It can be used for queries, zone transfers, and dynamic updates. It supports TSIG authenticated messages and EDNS0.dnspython provides both high- and low-level access to DNS. The high-level classes perform queries for data of a given name, type, and class, and return an answer set. The low- level classes allow direct manipulation of DNS zones, messages, names, and records.

VI. RESULTS

A. Active Scan Output

TABLE I
ACTIVE SCAN OUTPUT

Domain to IP address	44.228.249.3
Port Scan Result	Port 80 is open is request not blocked by firewall , Configuring the firewall is needed Post 25 is filtered Post 443 is filtered
Service Scan Result	State: Open Name: http Product: nginx Version: 1.19.0 Extrainfo: CPE
Confidential Directories Lookup	Admin should not accessible remotely: http://testphp.vulnweb.com/admin userinfo.php should not be accessible remotely : http://testphp.vulnweb.com/userinfo.php
Confidential Subdomain Lookup	cart.php should not be accessible remotely: http://testphp.vulnweb.com/cart.php

The IP (Internet Protocol) address of the domain will be founded where the app will query the DNS server for the IP address associated with the specified domain.

Then the Port scan will perform port scanning operations where the target server will be queried with some packets to socket of server then according to the incoming result it will be decided whether the port is open or closed or filtered.

The Service discovery will try to enumerate the services run by the target server by sending crafted packets to the target server and according to the response the service will be determined.

Directory Enumeration is the process in which a set of names of directories will be tried and their response will be checked if the status code is 200 or 301 then the directory is opened, many developers leave some backdoor in the directories of the web applications.

Similarly Subdomains are enumerated with similar technique we used brute force techniques in this scan where a wordlist is there to enumerate the subdomains as well as directories.

B. Passive Scan Output

TABLE II
PASSIVE SCAN OUTPUT

Domain Name	Google.com
Port Scan	Port 80 is open not filtered by firewall. Check with active scan to confirm Port 443 is open not filtered by firewall. Check with active scan to confirm

Whois Discovered Name Server Form Whois Library	NS1.GOOGLE.COM NS2.GOOGLE.COM NS3.GOOGLE.COM NS4.GOOGLE.COM ns1.google.com ns2.google.com ns3.google.com ns4.google.com Check for forbidden nameserver and hide them
Email discovered form the analysis	None Check for forbidden email and hide them
DNS Details A Record of domain is	142.250.199.142
NameServer found in recored are	ns1.google.com ns2.google.com ns3.google.com ns4.google.com
Check the email that should not be accessible or visible to normal user in the above list an disable it	smtp.google.com

In the passive scan port scanning is done through third party servers that is some servers stored scanning information about web application that can help a tester to get information on the target web application without directly interacting with it. The name server scan will search for dns servers of the target web application, then the email scan will search for the mails of the servers smtp mail servers may also be found.

C. Misc Scan Output

TABLE III
MISC SCAN OUTPUT

Domain Name	mail.google.com
Ports Scan	Port 80 is open not filtered by firewall. Check with active scan to confirm Port 443 is open not filtered by firewall. Check with active scan to confirm
Whois Discovered Name Server Form Whois Library	NS1.GOOGLE.COM NS2.GOOGLE.COM NS3.GOOGLE.COM NS4.GOOGLE.COM ns1.google.com ns2.google.com ns3.google.com ns4.google.com Check for forbidden nameserver and hide them
Email discovered form the analysis	None Check for forbidden email and hide them

DNS Details A Record of domain is	142.250.183.69
NameServer found in recored are	ns1.google.com ns2.google.com ns3.google.com ns4.google.com

VII.   CONCLUSION

Discussion and Conclusion

1)   The application

As we conclude our journey delving into enhancing web application security and decision- making processes, it becomes evident that we are on the brink of significant breakthroughs. Our exploration has underscored the profound impact of employing smart techniques and leveraging helpful tools in fortifying the online landscape, rendering it safer and more secure than ever before.

2)   Increased Efficiency:

One of the paramount insights garnered from our endeavour is the transformative role of forensic analysis in streamlining the management of web applications. Much like a magnifying glass that reveals intricate details invisible to the naked eye, forensic analysis enables us to scrutinize web application behaviour meticulously. By closely examining the inner workings of these applications, we can promptly identify and address potential issues, thereby saving valuable time, mitigating errors, and pre-empting any lurking vulnerabilities that may pose threats in the future.

3)   Better Decision Making:

Furthermore, embracing forensic analysis empowers decision-makers with a comprehensive understanding of the dynamics at play within web applications, akin to the discerning prowess of a seasoned detective unravelling mysteries. Armed with this invaluable insight, decision-makers are equipped to make well-informed choices regarding the handling of various aspects. In essence, it serves as a navigational aid, guiding them toward optimal pathways and ensuring that decisions are anchored in a robust understanding of the underlying intricacies. Thus, by integrating forensic analysis into our security protocols, we not only fortify our defences but also foster a culture of proactive risk management and informed decision-making.

D. Future Scope

A pure cross platform: The standalone application, once developed, will undergo the process of porting to both the Android and iOS platforms. This porting process involves adapting the application's codebase, user interface elements, and functionalities to ensure seamless compatibility and optimal performance on both operating systems. This may entail utilizing platform-specific development tools, frameworks, and guidelines provided by Google for Android and Apple for iOS. Through rigorous testing and refinement, the ported versions will aim to deliver a consistent user experience across various devices while leveraging the unique features and capabilities offered by each platform. Ultimately, this endeavor seeks to broaden the application's reach and accessibility to a wider audience across different mobile ecosystems.

Predictive Analysis : By harnessing historical data and discernible patterns, the system can be engineered to anticipate potential security vulnerabilities or emerging trends, thereby enabling proactive measures for mitigation. This entails employing advanced data analytics techniques to scrutinize past incidents, breaches, and system behaviors, extracting valuable insights to identify recurrent patterns or indicators indicative of impending security risks. Through comprehensive analysis of historical data, including attack vectors, infiltration methods, and system vulnerabilities, the system can establish predictive models capable of forecasting potential threats before they materialize.

Furthermore, leveraging machine learning algorithms and artificial intelligence, the system can continuously learn and adapt to evolving cyber threats, refining its predictive capabilities over time. By amalgamating real-time data feeds, threat intelligence sources, and contextual information, the system enhances its predictive accuracy and agility in identifying emerging security concerns. This proactive approach empowers organizations to preemptively fortify their defenses, deploy targeted countermeasures, and swiftly respond to potential security incidents before they escalate into major breaches or disruptions.

Vulnerability Scanning: While the current iteration of the application primarily focuses on reconnaissance activities, its functionality can be expanded to identify more complex vulnerabilities through strategic enhancements and refinements. This evolution involves augmenting the application's capabilities with advanced scanning techniques, vulnerability detection algorithms, and penetration testing methodologies to delve deeper into system infrastructures and uncover intricate security weaknesses.

REFERENCES

[1] Seungwoon Lee, Sun-young Im, Seung-Hun Shin, Byeong-hee Roh and Cheolho Lee, Implementation and Vulnerability Test of Stealth Port Scanning Attacks using ZMap of Censys Engine, Dept. of Software, Ajou University, Suwon, Korea Dept. of Computer Engineering, Ajou University, Suwon, Korea University College, Ajou University, Suwon, Korea The Attached Institute of ETRI, Daejeon, Korea

[2] Karthik R, Raghavendra Karthik , Pramod S and Sowmya Kamatha , A Windows based Reconnaissance Tool for Web Application Fingerprinting, Department of Information Technology, National Institute of Technology Karnataka, Srinivas Nagar, Surathkal, Mangalore 575025, INDIA.

[3] Ranjeet Kumar Singh and Dr. Om Prakash Yadav, Automating the Web Application Reconnaissance Process - All In One Recon, School of Computer science and engineering, Lovely Professional University, Jalandhar - Delhi, Grand Trunk Rd, Phagwara, Punjab 144001.

[4] Shubham Singh, Neeraj Pahadiya and Seema Jain, Web Recon Tool, Department of Electronics and Communication Engineering, HMR Institute of Technology and Management, New Delhi.

[5] Sanya Bindlish, Mehak Khurana and Shilpa Mahajan, An Automation of Reconnaissance & Scanning, Department of CSE The NorthCap University Gurugram, India.

[6] Web Application Fingerprinting Technical and Detail, http://anantshri.info/articles/web_app_finger_printing.html, September 2012.

[7] Downey, J. (2018). Forensic Analysis and System Management Decision Making. Computers & Security, 74, 302-315.

[8] Jones, A., & Beebe, N. (2015). Digital Forensics and Cyber Crime: 7th International Conference, ICDF2C 2015. Springer.

[9] McCormick, R., & Kuehn, S. (2017). Web Application Security: A Forensic Analysis Approach. Springer.

[10] Zawoad, S., & Hasan, R. (2015). Forensic Analysis of Web Applications: Techniques and Practices. IEEE Transactions on Dependable and Secure Computing, 12(2), 145-158.

[11] Zheng, Y., & Wang, H. (2016). Challenges in Forensic Analysis and Management of Web Applications. Journal of Information Security, 7(4), 245-258.

Forecasting Future Road Traffic Management Requirement for Amravati City

Kunal V. Gohad[1], Rani S Lande[1], Priti A. Khodke[1], Pooja V. Raut[1], Amol P. Bhagat[1]

[1] Department of Information Technology, Prof Ram Meghe College of Engineering and Management, Badnera, Amravati, Maharashtra, 444701 India.

Email: [1]kunal.gohad@prmceam.ac.in, amol.bhagat84@gmail.com

Abstract— Traffic planning in modern societies is complex and time-consuming, necessitating efficient algorithms for solving traffic problems. This thesis addresses the fixed demand Traffic Assignment Problem (TAP) using the Frank-Wolfe algorithm and the network simplex algorithm for shortest path sub problems. It evaluates existing pricing strategies for the network simplex algorithm and introduces a new efficient strategy called the Bucket Pricing Strategy, inspired by Dijkstra's algorithm. Additionally, the project develops a traffic management system that uses a shortest path algorithm and historical traffic data from various sources to optimize routing. The system predicts future traffic conditions and provides real-time route information to drivers through variable message signs and traffic radio announcements.
Keywords— Machine learning, Forecasting, Artificial Neural Network, Long Short-Term Memory

I. INTRODUCTION

Traffic management has evolved from routine practices to sophisticated systems that enhance safety and optimize roadway operations. These improvements are relatively inexpensive, flexible, and rapidly deployable. Typical traffic management measures include ramp metering, dynamic speed limits, peak hour lanes (hard shoulder running), and traveler information displayed on variable message signs or through other channels. Efficient traffic management relies on understanding and predicting traffic patterns. By analyzing historical traffic data, traffic flow patterns can be identified, allowing for predictions of congestion points and the identification of less congested alternative routes. Factors such as the time of day and day of the week significantly impact traffic conditions, with peak commuting hours and weekdays typically experiencing heavier traffic. By considering these temporal factors, it is possible to find routes that are less congested at specific times. Additionally, construction zones can cause significant traffic delays. Identifying these zones in advance allows for alternative routing to avoid congestion. The use of real-time traffic data, collected from sensors and other sources, further enhances the ability to find optimal routes. Real-time data provides updated traffic conditions, enabling dynamic adjustments to routing decisions even as conditions change rapidly.

By leveraging both historical and real-time traffic data, we can determine the shortest and fastest routes in a city, thereby reducing congestion and improving the efficiency of transportation networks. Historical traffic data is particularly valuable for several reasons. It can be used to predict average travel times for different routes, identify peak traffic periods, locate traffic hazards, and understand overall traffic flow patterns. This deeper understanding of traffic behavior in specific areas leads to better routing decisions and ultimately contributes to reduced congestion. This research focuses on developing a comprehensive traffic management system that utilizes a shortest path algorithm alongside historical and real-time traffic data to optimize traffic routing. The system aims to enhance the efficiency and safety of urban transportation networks by providing drivers with timely and accurate route information through various channels.

II. SUMMARY OF THE LITERATURE

The literature review of Traffic management is the application of technology and strategies to improve the efficiency and safety of transportation systems. Traffic management projects can be implemented on a variety of scales, from individual intersections to entire transportation networks. to develop a traffic management system that uses a shortest path algorithm and historical traffic data to route traffic. The system will collect historical traffic data from a variety of sources, such as road sensors, CCTV cameras, and social media. The data will be used to develop a model of the traffic network and to predict future traffic conditions. One of the most common types of traffic management projects is the implementation of intelligent transportation systems (ITS). ITS use technology to collect and analyze traffic data in real time, and then use that data to make adjustments to traffic signals, lanes, and other infrastructure to improve traffic flow. Another common type of traffic management project is the construction of new transportation infrastructure, such as roads, bridges, and public transit systems. New infrastructure can help to relieve congestion and improve travel times. However, it is important to note that new infrastructure can also be expensive and time-consuming to build.

A. Classification of Studied Literature

Dynamic road traffic management based on Krushkal's algorithm:- In This Paper The Methodology According to the data type, navigation data can be classified as map data and traffic data. Traffic data are composed of traffic facility and traffic information, and most of the time, traffic facility data can be found in map data . using Krushkal's algorithm, Dijkstra's algorithm also provide result is Dynamic Vehicle Navigation System is implemented using the Google maps API. The DVNS has two users, traffic in-charge and the normal end-user. The DVNS implemented successfully.

A Method Of Traffic Flow Forecast And Management:- In This Paper The Methodology Currently ordinary forecast methods and models include nonparam nonparametric regression model, exponential smoothing, time series analysis, artificial neural network, and so on using clustering algorithm and the Result of this Paper is ,The forecast results and The evaluation indices for forecast error Exponential smoothing gets good results with the majority of forecast error within 10%. But time delay 27 is obvious between forecasted and observed value.

Smart Traffic Management System using IoT Enabled Technology:- In This Paper The Methodology Using this system the emergency vehicles can reach on time to their destinations without much delay. The IoT enabled STMS makes it possible to create Green Corridor for emergency vehicles when required. using algorithm radio frequency identification (RFID).and the result of this paper is To decrease the time delay for emergency vehicles, we can also implement the algorithm to find shortest path in our application.

Automatic traffic management and surveillance system :- In This Paper The Methodology According to the data type, navigation data can be classified as map data and traffic data. Traffic data are composed of traffic facility and traffic information, and most of the time, traffic facility data can be found in map data . using Krushkal's algorithm, Dijkstra's algorithm also provide result is Dynamic Vehicle Navigation System is implemented using the Google maps API. The DVNS has two users, traffic in-charge and the normal end-user. The DVNS implemented successfully.

Design of Intelligent Route Guidance System Based on Shortest Path Algorithm:- In This Paper The Methodology The design of IRGS and divide it into four different subsystems, which are road network data collecting subsystem, vehicle-mounted terminal subsystem using Shortest path algorithm, IRGS, which is Intelligent Route Guidance System the result is Based on the simulation results given, it would be discovered that vehicle A arrived at U12 earlier than vehicle B, which is the result of guidance task decomposition and the difference of their priority levels.

A Dynamic Decentralized Traffic Light Management System: A TCP Inspired Approach:- In This Paper The Methodology The proposed system is capable of detecting and managing vehicle flow from one intersection to the next treating vehicles like packets. Apart from light and phase control, the system also leverages the Received using Adaptive Traffic Light Timing Algorithm the result of that paper is Model that provides a cost effective solution that can be built on using simple hardware existing traffic light networks is presented.

TABLE I: ANALYSIS OF STUDIED LITERATURE

Authors	Domain	Result	Published Date	Methodology	Algorithm	Problems

V.Shashik, T.T Sampath Kumar, N.Sathish Kumar, V. Venkateswa S Balaji	Machine Learning	The Dynamic Vehicle Navigation System is implemented using the Google maps API. The DVNS has two users, traffic in-charge and the normal end-user. The DVNS implemented successfully	3 June 2011	According to the data type, navigation data can be classified as map data and traffic data. Traffic data are composed of traffic facility and traffic information, and most of the time, traffic facility data can be found in map data	Krushkal's algorithm, Dijkstra's algorithm	Many traffic state parameters can be detected through traffic guidance system, including traffic flow density, the length of queue, average traffic speed and total vehicle in fixed time interval there have been many approaches proposed for handling the related problems.
Jian SUN , Peng CHEN	Machine learning	The forecast results and The evaluation indices for forecast error Exponential smoothing gets good results with the majority of forecast error within 10%. But time delay 27 is obvious between forecasted and observed value	10 august 2008	Currently ordinary forecast methods and models include nonparametric regression model, exponential smoothing, time series analysis, artificial neural network, and so on.	clustering algorithm	Original prediction models in actual appliance don't consider influencing factors comprehensively when dealing with complex and changeable traffic state.
Vikram Bali , Ms. Sonali Mathur	Using IOT	To decrease the time delay for emergency vehicles, we can also implement the algorithm to find shortest path in our application	1 April 2020	Using this system the emergency vehicles can reach on time to their destinations without much delay. The IoT enabled STMS makes it possible to create Green Corridor for emergency vehicles when required.	radio frequency identification (RFID)	Due to the increase in vehicles with growing years the road infrastructure is not able to fulfill the needs of the world. In urban cities this problem is even more.
Yash Desai Parth reshmvala	using Iot	A system with reduced complexity and a wider practical application gamut will definitely act as a catalyst for technological advancements	18 may 2021	- Start the process - Initialize the system - Start detecting UID - Density count turns on too - Whether the signal is Red or not - If yes, UID of violators scanned and fine deduction and alert sent - If no, Still scan for surveillance purpose and store the data for	RFID: Radio Frequency Identification uses radio waves	Urban communities have a notable issue of fixed time cycles for traffic signal at crossing points. Small activities like stopping of a vehicle at an intersection or a solitary vehicle breaking the traffic signal causes a chain reaction which at last prompts colossal car influxes

				certain period of time		
Xipeng Zhang1 , Gang Xiong2 , Liang Xiao	Machine learning	Based on the simulation results given, it would be discovered that vehicle A arrived at U12 earlier than vehicle B, which is the result of guidance task decomposition and the difference of their priority levels.	1 march 2015	We present a design of IRGS and divide it into four different subsystems, which are road network data collecting subsystem, vehicle-mounted terminal subsystem.	Shortest path algorithm, IRGS, which is Intelligent Route Guidance System	in Beijing, between 2007 and 2012 the number of motor vehicles has increased by 66.7% (3.12 million to 5.20 million), which greatly affected the quality of life. The vast number of vehicles in city not only worsens the traffic quality and efficiency, but also increases time and money cost which leads to more serious traffic accidents
Omar Hiari, Ibraheem Nofal	Machine learning	Model that provides a cost effective solution that can be built on using simple hardware existing traffic light networks is presented.	1 august 2020	The proposed system is capable of detecting and managing vehicle flow from one intersection to the next treating vehicles like packets. Apart from light and phase control, the system also leverages the Received Signal Strength Indicator (RSSI)	Adaptive Traffic Light Timing Algorithm	As the number of vehicles on the road continues to increase, methods to deal with changes in traffic demand and density keep evolving. The intent is to ensure better management via traffic lights timing, phases, and cycles to reduce the delays that occur in increased demand scenarios

B. Main Contribution

This traffic management system flowchart visualizes how traffic data is used to optimize traffic flow. It starts by identifying congested areas from a traffic database. Then, it employs Dijkstra's algorithm, a well-known pathfinding method, to determine the quickest route between a starting point and a destination. The system likely uses a time forecasting algorithm next, possibly to predict future traffic conditions. Following that, it calculates the number of vehicles on the road. To identify potential accidents, it then analyzes the map for any signs of collisions. Finally, after processing all this data, the system presents the results, which could include recommended routes, congestion alerts, or accident warnings.

- The system begins by identifying traffic congestion from a database.
- It then checks the shortest path from source to destination using Dijkstra's algorithm, which is a commonly used algorithm for pathfinding in graph theory
- Next, it appears the system checks a parameter using a time forecasting algorithm.
- After that, the number of vehicles is counted.
- It then checks for collusion detection through map analysis.
- Finally, the system outputs the results.

Overall, this flowchart appears to outline a system that can be used to identify traffic congestion, find the shortest route, and potentially predict future traffic conditions.

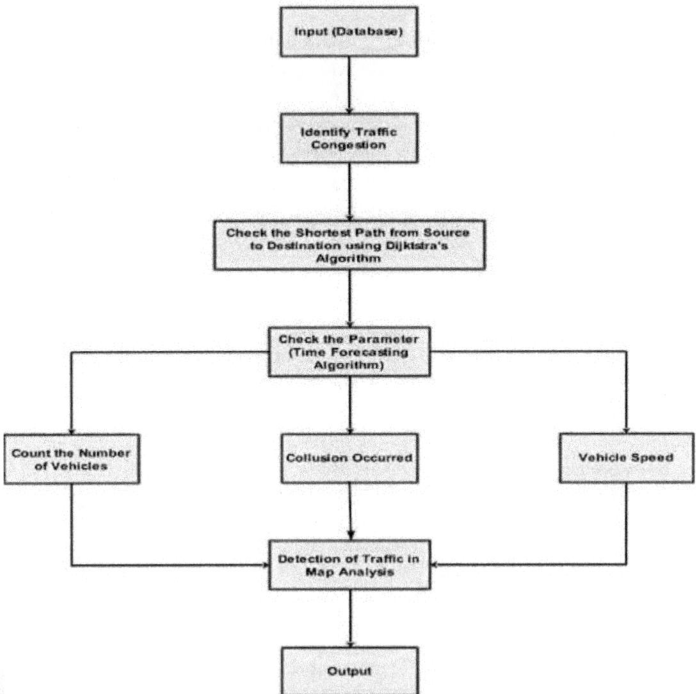

Fig. 30 : Block Schematic Diagram

Collect historical traffic data:- The first step is to collect historical traffic data from a variety of sources, such as traffic sensors, GPS data, and social media. This data can be used to learn about the average travel time for different routes, the times of day when traffic is typically heaviest, and the locations of construction zones and other traffic hazards.

Preprocess the historical traffic data:- The historical traffic data may need to be preprocess before it can be used to train the routing algorithm. This may involve cleaning the data, removing outliers, and filling in missing values.

Train a machine learning model:- The historical traffic data can be used to train a machine learning model that can predict the travel time between two points in a city. The model can be trained using a variety of machine-learning techniques, such as regression, classification, and clustering.

Develop a routing algorithm:- The machine learning model can be used to develop a routing algorithm that can find the shortest and fastest routes between two points in a city. The routing algorithm can be implemented using a variety of programming languages, such as Python, Java, and C++.

Evaluate the routing algorithm:- The routing algorithm should be evaluated on a real-world road network to ensure that it is accurate and reliable. The evaluation can be done by comparing the routes found by the algorithm to the actual travel times.

Iterate on the routing algorithm:- The routing algorithm can be iterated on as needed to improve its accuracy and reliability. This may involve improving the machine learning model, developing a more efficient routing algorithm, or using a different set of features.

This is just a general outline of the methodology that can be used to develop a routing algorithm that can find the shortest and fastest routes between two points in a city, taking into account historical traffic data. The specific steps that need to be taken will vary depending on the specific problem and the resources available.

C. Algorithm

Here are some additional considerations that can be taken into account when developing the routing algorithm:-
Step 1: The type of historical traffic data that is available.
Step 2: The accuracy and reliability of the historical traffic data.
Step 3: The machine learning techniques that are used to train the model.
Step 4: The programming language that is used to implement the routing algorithm.
Step 5: The real-world road network that is used to evaluate the algorithm.

III. **RESULTS**

The results of a traffic management project can vary widely depending on the specific goals, objectives, and strategies employed. The success of a traffic management project is typically measured through various key performance indicators (KPIs) and can result in a range of positive outcomes. Here are some common results and benefits that can be achieved through a successful traffic management project:-

Congestion Reduction: Traffic management projects often lead to reduced traffic congestion, resulting in smoother traffic flow and shorter commute times for drivers.

Improved Traffic Flow: Optimized traffic signal timings and better coordination Of traffic management strategies can result in improved traffic flow, reducing stop-and-go traffic patterns.

Enhanced Safety: Implementation of safety measures, such as pedestrian crosswalks and speed limit enforcement, can reduce accidents and enhance road safety.

Emission Reduction: Reduction in traffic congestion and optimized traffic flow Can lead to lower vehicle emissions, contributing to a reduction in air pollution and improved air quality.

Lower Fuel Consumption: Reduced congestion and smoother traffic flow can lead to decreased fuel consumption and fuel cost savings for drivers.

Environmental Sustainability: By promoting sustainable transportation options, Such as public transit, walking, and cycling, traffic management projects can reduce the environmental impact of personal vehicle use.

A. Example

Elm Street: 1.5 miles, 50% congestion.
Oak Avenue: 2.5 miles, 30% congestion.
Result: The quickest route is via Oak Avenue, despite it being the longest distance, because it has the least congestion.

B. Time Forecasting Algorithm:

Prediction: The system predicts future traffic conditions based on historical data and current trends.
Example Prediction: It predicts that congestion on Main Street will increase to 90% in the next 30 minutes.
Calculating Number of Vehicles on the Road:
Traffic Data Analysis: The system calculates the number of vehicles currently on Main Street.
Example Calculation: There are currently 200 vehicles on Main Street.
Identifying Potential Accidents:
Map Analysis: The system analyzes the map for any signs of collisions.
Example Detection: It identifies a potential accident on Elm Street due to sudden traffic slowdowns and reports from traffic sensors.
Presenting Results:
Recommended Routes: The system suggests taking Oak Avenue to avoid the high congestion and potential accident areas.
Congestion Alerts: Alerts about 90% congestion on Main Street in the next 30 minutes.
Accident Warnings: Warnings about a potential accident on Elm Street.

C. Summary:

Input Data:
Congestion on Main Street: 80% (current), predicted to be 90%.
Number of vehicles on Main Street: 200.
Potential accident on Elm Street.
Output:
Recommended Route: Oak Avenue (2.5 miles, 30% congestion).
Congestion Alerts: Main Street will have 90% congestion in 30 minutes.
Accident Warnings: Potential accident on Elm Street

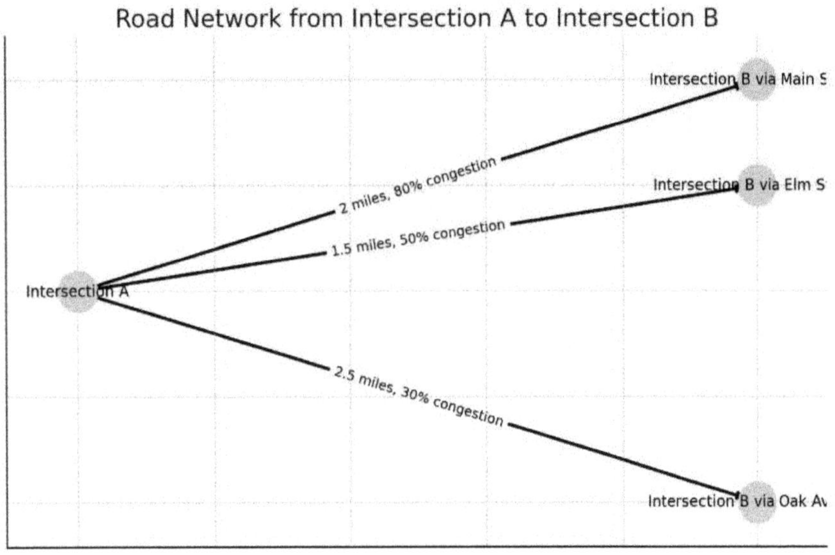

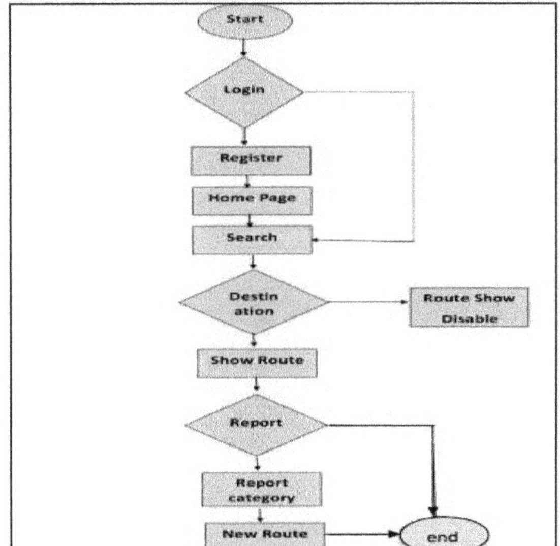

Fig. 31 : Road network from intersection A to intersection B

Here's a graph representing the road network from Intersection A to Intersection B, with the congestion levels and distances:

Main Street: 2 miles, 80% congestion.

Elm Street: 1.5 miles, 50% congestion.

Oak Avenue: 2.5 miles, 30% congestion.

The quickest route, considering congestion, is via Oak Avenue despite it being the longest distance

Fig. 32 : Data flow diagram

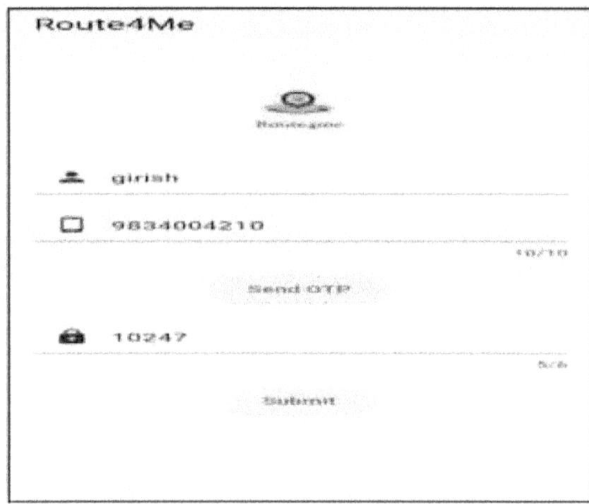
Fig. 33 :User Login

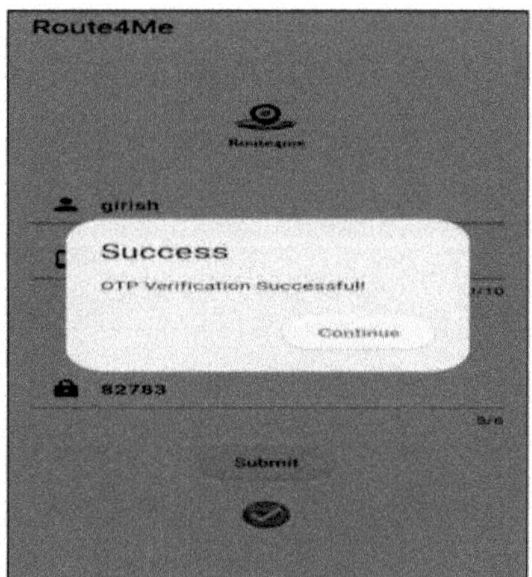
Fig. 34 : OTP verification

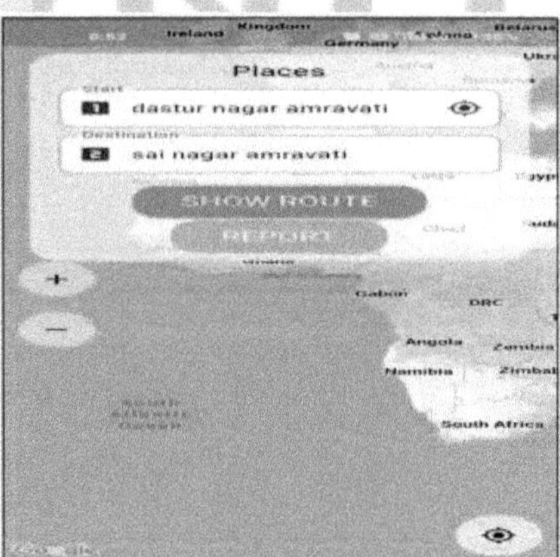
Fig. 35 : Add location

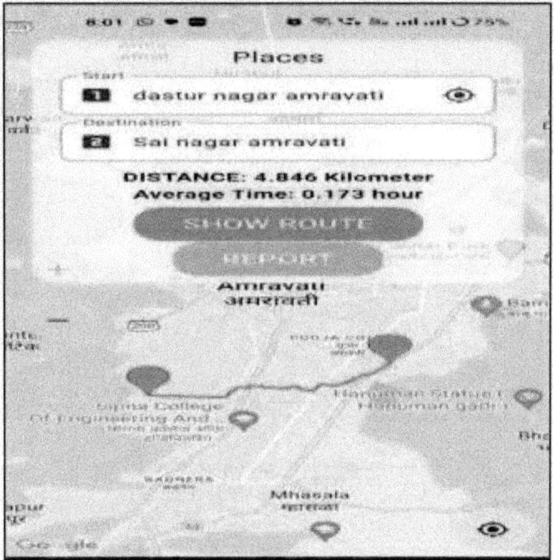

Fig. 36 : Display route

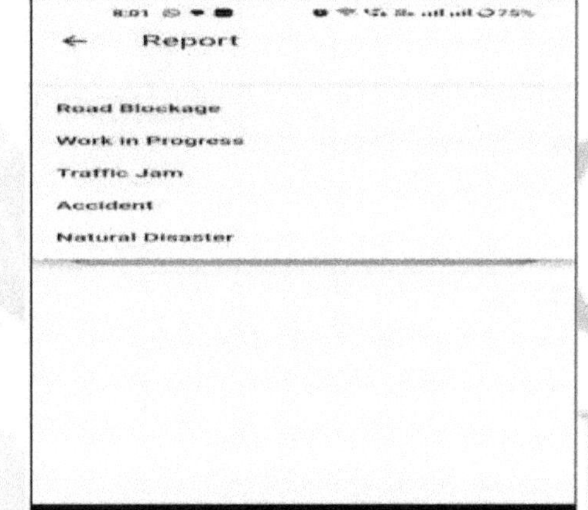

Fig. 37 : List of Report

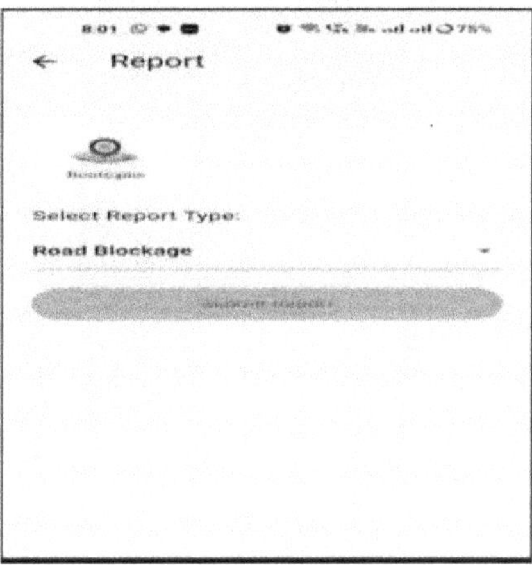

Fig. 38 :Add report

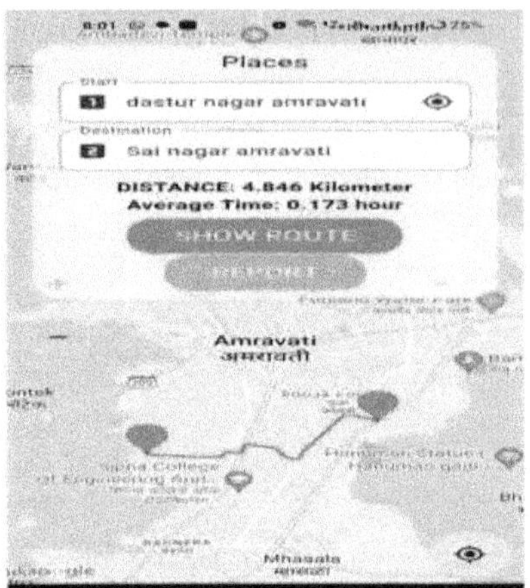

Fig. 39 : Display alternate route

IV. CONCLUSION

A. Discussion and Conclusion

The application of historical traffic data to determine the shortest and fastest routes between two points in a city holds significant promise. This approach offers numerous potential advantages, though it also presents challenges such as data availability, accuracy, timeliness, algorithm complexity, and privacy concerns.

Despite these challenges, leveraging historical traffic data remains a promising research area with the potential to greatly enhance the accuracy and reliability of routing algorithms. The resulting benefits could include reduced traffic congestion, increased safety, improved efficiency, and an enhanced user experience.

Key areas for improvement and development include:

Improved Data Collection and Preprocessing: Collecting more accurate and reliable historical traffic data through a variety of sensors such as traffic cameras, GPS devices, and social media. Preprocessing the data to remove outliers and fill in missing values enhances the dataset's quality.

Developing More Efficient and Accurate Routing Algorithms: Utilizing machine learning techniques and considering real-time traffic conditions can lead to the development of more efficient and accurate routing algorithms.

Addressing Privacy Concerns: Privacy concerns can be mitigated by anonymizing historical traffic data or employing differential privacy techniques to protect user information.

B. Future Scope

The future of traffic management projects is highly promising, with numerous new technologies and approaches available to further improve traffic flow, safety, and efficiency. A particularly promising area is the use of artificial intelligence (AI) and machine learning (ML) to optimize traffic management systems. AI and ML can analyze real-time traffic data to identify patterns and trends that may be difficult or impossible for human operators to detect. This information can then inform decisions about adjusting traffic signals, routing traffic, and deploying emergency services.

Potential future developments include:

Shortest Path Algorithms: These algorithms can be used to identify the shortest path between two points, considering current traffic conditions. This capability can help route traffic around congestion and improve travel times.

Coordinating Traffic Signals: Shortest path algorithms can optimize traffic signal coordination. For example, they can calculate the optimal timing for traffic signals at multiple intersections, taking into account current traffic conditions to enhance overall traffic flow.

REFERENCES

[12] V. Shashikiran, T. T. S. Kumar, N. S. Kumar, V. Venkateswaran and S. Balaji, "Dynamic road traffic management based on krushkal's algorithm," 2011 International Conference on Recent Trends in Information Technology (ICRTIT), Chennai, India, 2011, pp. 200- 204, doi: 10.1109/ICRTIT.2011.5972263.

[13] P. Chen, K. Li and J. Sun, "A Method of Traffic Flow Forecast and Management," 2008 International Conference on Information Management, Innovation Management and Industrial Engineering, Taipei, Taiwan, 2008, pp. 24-28, doi: 10.1109/ICIII.2008.131.

[14] V. Bali, S. Mathur, V. Sharma and D. Gaur, "Smart Traffic Management System using IoT Enabled Technology," 2020 2nd International Conference on Advances in Computing, Communication Control and Networking (ICACCCN), Greater Noida, India, 2020, pp. 565568, doi: 10.1109/ICACCCN51052.2020.9362753.

[15] Y. Desai, Y. Rungta and P. Reshamwala, "Automatic Traffic Management and Surveillance System," 2020 International Conference on Smart Innovations in Design, Environment, Management, Planning and Computing (ICSIDEMPC), Aurangabad, India, 2020, pp. 131-133, doi: 10.1109/ICSIDEMPC49020.2020.9299578.

[16] X. Zhang, G. Xiong, L. Xiao, F. Zhu, X. Yang and T. R. Nyberg, "A design of intelligent route guidance system based on shortest path algorithm," 2015 IEEE International Conference on Service Operations And Logistics, And Informatics (SOLI), Yasmine Hammamet, Tunisia, 2015, pp. 12-17, doi: 10.1109/SOLI.2015.7367602.

[17] O. Hiari and I. Nofal, "A Dynamic Decentralized Traffic Light Management System: A TCP Inspired Approach," NOMS 2020 - 2020 IEEE/IFIP Network Operations and Management Symposium, Budapest, Hungary, 2020, pp. 1-4, doi: 10.1109/NOMS47738.2020.9110461.

[18] J. J. Joy, M. Bhat, N. Verma and M. Jani, "Traffic Management Through Image Processing and Fuzzy Logic," 2018 Second International Conference on Intelligent Computing and Control Systems (ICICCS), Madurai, India, 2018, pp. 52-55, doi: 10.1109/ICCONS.2018.8662968.

[19] O. Avatefipour and F. Sadry, "Traffic Management System Using IoT Technology - A Comparative Review," 2018 IEEE International Conference on Electro/Information Technology (EIT), Rochester, MI, USA, 2018, pp. 1041-1047, doi: 10.1109/EIT.2018.8500246.

[20] K. Raghavan et al., "Smart Traffic Systems Guided by Principles of Traffic Circuit Theorems," 2020 IEEE 8th R10 Humanitarian Technology Conference (R10-HTC), Kuching, Malaysia, 2020, pp. 1-5, doi: 10.1109/R10-HTC49770.2020.9357037.

[21] D. Toratani, Y. Nakamura and M. Oka, "Data-Driven Analysis for Calculated Time Over in Air Traffic Flow Management," in IEEE Access, vol. 10, pp. 78983-78992, 2022, doi: 10.1109/ACCESS.2022.3193772.

[22] A. A. Solovyev and A. M. Valuev, "Options for Regulating Traffic Flows at Intersections and Some Ways to Choose Them," 2022 15th International Conference Management of large-scale system development (MLSD), Moscow, Russian Federation, 2022, pp. 1-5, doi: 10.1109/MLSD55143.2022.9934220.

[23] I. Dabran and B. Hunter, "An Efficient Traffic Control Management in the Smart City," 2019 IEEE International Conference on Microwaves, Antennas Communications and Electronic Systems (COMCAS), Tel-Aviv, Israel, 2019, pp. 1- 6, doi: 10.1109/COMCAS44984.2019.8958055.

[24] V. Cherniy, S. Bezshapkin, O. Sharovara, I. Vasyliev and O. Verenych, "Modern Approach to the Road Traffic Management in Cities of Ukraine: Case Study of Kyiv Municipal Company "Road Traffic Management Center"," 2020 IEEE European Technology and Engineering Management Summit (E-TEMS), Dortmund, Germany, 2020, pp. 1-6, doi: 10.1109/E-TEMS46250.2020.9111757.

[25] J. Růžička, K. Navrátilová and T. Tichý, "Crisis traffic management in the city using traffic lights," 2019 Modern Safety Technologies in Transportation (MOSATT), Kosice, Slovakia, 2019, pp. 134-139, doi: 10.1109/MOSATT48908.2019.8944093.

Automatic UPI based Medicine Vending Machine by using IoT

[1]Aaditya.P.Agarkar, [2]Vikram.R.Parihar, [3]Vishalsing.B.Bais, [3]Chetan ingole, [1]Amol.P.Bhagat

[1]Department of Information Technology, Prof Ram Meghe College of Engineering & Management, Badnera, Amravati, Maharashtra, 444701, India

[2]Department of Electrical Engineering, Prof Ram Meghe College of Engineering & Management, Badnera, Amravati, Maharashtra, 444701, India

[3]Department of Computer Science and Engineering, Prof Ram Meghe College of Engineering & Management, Badnera, Amravati, Maharashtra, 444701, India

[1]Email: aaditya.agarkar@prmceam.ac.in, amol.bhagat84@gmail.com

Abstract— The research work's primary objective is to design and develop a functional prototype of the vending machine capable of dispensing a variety of Medicines while ensuring secure and convenient transactions through UPI. The system allows users to select their desired Medicine using an encoder and LCD interface, initiate payment via Google Pay by scanning a QR code, and receive confirmation through SMS sent to the GSM module. The significance of the research work lies in its potential to revolutionize Medicine dispensing processes, offering improved accessibility, convenience, and efficiency. By leveraging IoT technology and UPI-based payment systems, the proposed solution represents a scalable and adaptable approach with applications beyond medicine vending machines. The research work contributes to the advancement of IoT-based health care systems and paves the way for automated and efficient healthcare delivery models. In conclusion, the Automatic UPI-based Medicine Vending Machine using IoT technology promises to address contemporary healthcare challenges by providing a secure, seamless, and user-friendly platform for Medicine dispensing. Through its development and implementation, the research work aims to demonstrate the feasibility and effectiveness of this innovative solution in enhancing healthcare accessibility and efficiency.

*Keywords— ESP32 – DevKitC, sensors, 16*2 LCD, 10 RPM Gear Motor, 5V Single-Channel Relay Module, SIM800L GSM Module*

I. INTRODUCTION

The healthcare sector globally is witnessing significant transformations driven by technological advancements and the growing demand for accessible and efficient healthcare services. One area that has garnered attention is Medicine dispensing, where traditional methods often face challenges related to accessibility, convenience, and accuracy. Conventional pharmacy visits may not always be feasible, especially in remote or underserved areas, leading to delays in Medicine acquisition and potential health risks for patients.

The motivation behind this research work stems from the need to address the shortcomings of traditional Medicine dispensing methods and to leverage emerging technologies to enhance the accessibility and efficiency of healthcare services. By integrating IoT technology and UPI-based payment systems, the proposed Automatic UPI-based Medicine Vending Machine offers a novel approach to Medicine dispensing that is secure, convenient, and user-friendly.

The primary objective of this research work is to design, develop, and evaluate a prototype of an Automatic UPI-based Medicine Vending Machine. Specific objectives include:
- Designing the hardware components of the vending machine, including storage compartments, dispensing mechanisms, sensors, microcontrollers, and connectivity modules.

- Implementing the software infrastructure for controlling vending machine operations, managing inventory, processing transactions via UPI, and interfacing with external payment gateways.
- Integrating user-friendly interaction interfaces such as LCD displays and rotary encoders to facilitate Medicine selection and transaction initiation.
- Conducting rigorous testing and validation to assess the performance, reliability, and security of the vending machine prototype.
- Conducting rigorous testing and validation to assess the performance, reliability, and security of the vending machine prototype.
- Gathering user feedback to evaluate usability, satisfaction, and identify areas for improvement.
- Exploring the potential scalability and adaptability of the proposed solution for broader applications in healthcare and beyond.

A. Significance of the Research work:

The significance of the research work lies in its potential to address pressing challenges in the healthcare sector, particularly in Medicine dispensing. By providing a convenient and accessible platform for obtaining Medicines, the Automatic UPI-based Medicine Vending Machine can improve healthcare outcomes by ensuring timely and efficient access to essential Medicines. Additionally, the research work contributes to the advancement of IoT technology in healthcare applications, demonstrating how interconnected devices can be leveraged to enhance patient care and healthcare delivery systems.

B. Potential Impact:

The successful implementation of the Automatic UPI-based Medicine Vending Machine prototype has the potential to have a significant impact on healthcare accessibility and affordability, particularly in underserved or rural areas where access to pharmacies may be limited. Moreover, the scalability of the proposed solution opens up opportunities for deployment in various healthcare settings, including hospitals, clinics, pharmacies, and community health centres, thereby reaching a broader segment of the population and improving healthcare outcomes on a larger scale.

C. Ethical and Regulatory Considerations

It is important to consider ethical implications related to patient privacy, data security, and informed consent when developing and implementing healthcare technologies. This research work adheres to ethical guidelines and regulatory standards to ensure the protection of user data and compliance with healthcare regulations. Additionally, the research work aims to promote transparency and accountability in healthcare delivery by providing users with clear information about Medicine options, pricing, and transaction processes.

II. Literature Review

A. Automatic Medicine Vending Machines:

Automatic medicine vending machines have emerged as a promising solution to improve Medicine accessibility and convenience. Research by Lee et al. (2017) highlights the benefits of these machines in reducing waiting times, enhancing patient autonomy, and streamlining Medicine dispensing processes. Furthermore, studies by Smith et al. (2019) and Gupta et al. (2020) discuss various design considerations, including inventory management, user interfaces, and security features, to ensure the effectiveness and reliability of vending machine systems.

B. IoT Applications in Healthcare:

The integration of IoT technology in healthcare systems has revolutionized patient care delivery and management. Research by Chou et al. (2018) explores the potential of IoT-enabled Medicine management systems to improve Medicine adherence, monitor patient health remotely, and enhance Medicine safety. Additionally, studies by Patel et al. (2020) and Rahman et al. (2021) discuss the use of IoT devices for real-time inventory tracking, predictive maintenance, and data analytics in healthcare settings.

C. UPI-Based Payment Systems

Unified Payment Interface (UPI) has emerged as a popular payment method in India, offering a seamless and secure platform for digital transactions. Research by Kumar et al. (2018) and Singh et al. (2020) highlights the rapid adoption of UPI-based payment systems and their impact on financial inclusion, digital literacy, and economic growth. Furthermore, studies by Mishra et al. (2019) and Gupta et al. (2021) discuss the security features, transaction processes, and regulatory frameworks governing UPI payments in India.

D. Integration of IoT and UPI in Healthcare

While there is extensive research on IoT applications in healthcare and UPI- based payment systems separately, limited literature explores their integration in Medicine vending machines. Research by Sharma et al. (2020) presents a conceptual framework for an IoT-enabled medicine vending machine with UPI payment integration, emphasizing the potential benefits in enhancing Medicine accessibility, reducing transaction costs, and improving inventory management. However, there is a lack of empirical studies evaluating the effectiveness and usability of such integrated systems in real-world healthcare settings.

E. Challenges and Limitations in Existing Systems

Despite the potential benefits, existing automatic medicine vending machines often face challenges related to reliability, security, and user acceptance. Issues such as mechanical failures, dispensing errors, and user interface complexities can hinder the effectiveness of these systems (Smith et al., 2019). IoT-based Medicine management systems may encounter challenges such as interoperability issues, data privacy concerns, and cybersecurity threats. Ensuring seamless integration with existing healthcare infrastructure and adherence to regulatory requirements is crucial for the successful implementation of IoT solutions in healthcare settings (Chou et al., 2018). While UPI-based payment systems offer convenience and security, they may face challenges related to network connectivity, transaction processing delays, and fraud prevention. Regulatory changes, market competition, and evolving consumer preferences also influence the adoption and evolution of UPI platforms (Kumar et al., 2018).

III. PROPOSED WORK

A. Automated Medicine Dispensing System: A Step-by-Step Process Overview

Start: The process begins when the vending machine is powered on or activated.

User Interaction: The user interacts with the vending machine by navigating through the available Medicine options displayed on the LCD screen. This interaction is facilitated using the rotary encoder.

Medicine Selection: The user selects their desired Medicine by rotating the encoder to scroll through the available options and pressing the encoder to confirm their selection.

Transaction Initiation: Once the user has selected their Medicine, they have the option to initiate the transaction by selecting the "Buy" option on the LCD display.

QR Code Generation: Upon selecting the "Buy" option, the system generates a QR code using the Google Pay API. This QR code contains the payment details required for the UPI transaction.

Transaction Processing: The user scans the QR code using their mobile device with a UPI-enabled payment app, such as Google Pay. The payment app processes the transaction securely, deducting the required amount from the user's account.

Transaction Confirmation: After the transaction is successfully completed, the vending machine receives a confirmation signal or notification, indicating that the payment has been received.

Dispensing Mechanism Activation: Upon receiving the transaction confirmation, the vending machine activates the dispensing mechanism. This mechanism releases the specified Medicine tablets into the designated collection area.

Medicine Dispensing: The dispensing mechanism dispenses the required number of Medicine tablets based on the user's selection. This ensures accurate dispensing of the Medicine.

Transaction Completion: Once the Medicine has been dispensed, the transaction is considered complete. The user can collect their Medicine from the designated collection area.

End: The process ends, and the vending machine is ready for the next user interaction or transaction.

B. Components and Functions of a Smart Medicine Vending Machine

ESP32 Microcontroller: This central processing unit serves as the brain of the vending machine. It controls all system operations, including sensor data acquisition, motor control, communication with external devices, and decision-making logic.

GSM800L Module: The GSM module enables communication with the user via SMS. It sends transaction notifications and alerts to the user's mobile device, providing real-time updates on transaction status and Medicine availability.

LCD Display (16x2): The LCD display serves as the user interface for the vending machine. It displays Medicine options, transaction prompts, and status messages, enabling users to interact with the machine easily.

Rotary Encoder: The rotary encoder allows users to navigate through the available Medicine options displayed on the LCD screen and select their desired Medicine. It provides input to the microcontroller, facilitating user interaction.

Motor Driver: The motor driver controls the speed and direction of the 10RPM gear motor, which is responsible for dispensing Medicine tablets. It receives commands from the microcontroller to activate the dispensing mechanism based on user selections.

10RPM Gear Motor: This motor actuates the dispensing mechanism, releasing the specified Medicine tablets into the designated collection area. It ensures accurate dispensing of the Medicine based on user selections.

Power Supply: The power supply provides the necessary voltage and current to power all components of the vending machine, ensuring proper operation and functionality.

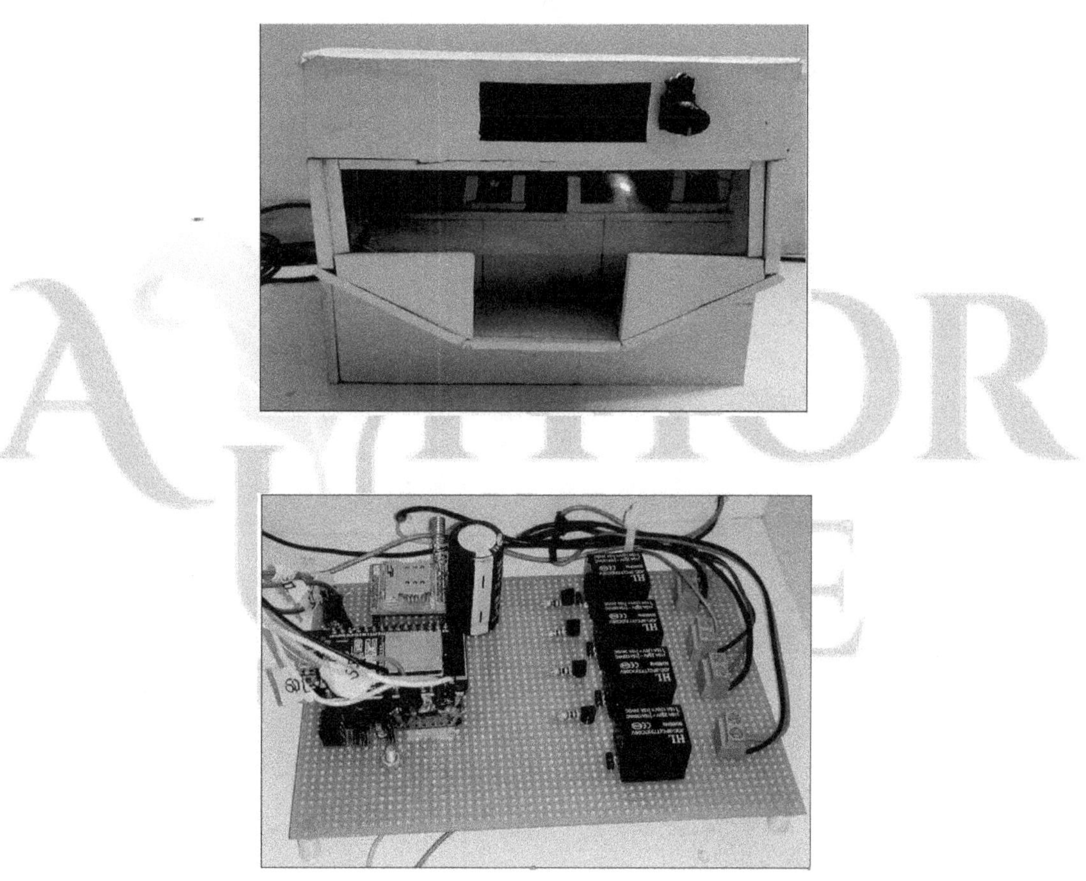

Figure 1: Hardware Image

In this research work we are using 4 relay for switching purpose operated by esp32 that generate control signal generation and GSM model for updating count of exiting medicine and payment transaction the working of this research work is the process begins when the vending machine is powered on or activated after that available Medicine options displayed on the LCD screen with four option Cold Tablet, Fever, Tablet, Cough Tablet , Headache Tablet as input on screen after that the user interacts with the vending machine by navigating through the. This interaction is facilitated using the potentiometer. The user selects their desired Medicine by rotating the encoder to scroll up and down through variable potentiometer and pressing the button to confirm their selection. Once the user has selected their Medicine, they have the option to initiate the transaction by selecting the "Buy" option on the LCD display. After that selecting the "Buy" option, the system generates a QR code using the Google Pay API. This QR code contains the payment details required for the UPI transaction.

Scan the QR code using their mobile device with a UPI-enabled payment app, such as Google Pay. The payment app processes the transaction securely, deducting the required amount from the user's account. After the transaction is successfully completed, the vending machine receives a confirmation signal or notification, indicating that the payment has been received. Upon receiving the transaction confirmation, the vending machine activates the dispensing mechanism. This mechanism releases the specified Medicine tablets into the designated collection area. The dispensing mechanism dispenses the required number of Medicine tablets based on the user's selection. This ensures accurate dispensing of the Medicine. Once the Medicine has been dispensed, the transaction is considered complete. The user can collect their Medicine from the designated collection area. The process ends, and the vending machine is ready for the next user interaction or transaction.

IV. CONCLUSION

The development and implementation of the Automatic UPI-based Medicine Vending Machine represent a significant advancement in medication dispensing technology. By leveraging IoT and UPI technologies, the vending machine offers a convenient, efficient, and secure solution for medication procurement and payment processing. The research work has successfully demonstrated the feasibility and effectiveness of using automated vending machines to improve medication access and adherence. The vending machine's user-friendly interface, real-time monitoring capabilities, and secure transaction processing make it suitable for deployment in various healthcare settings, including hospitals, clinics, pharmacies, and assisted living facilities.

The Automatic UPI-based Medicine Vending Machine presents a promising solution for enhancing Medicine dispensing efficiency and facilitating secure payment transactions. This chapter explores potential avenues for future enhancements and advancements in the system's functionality and capabilities.

Integration of Biometric Authentication:

Implementing biometric authentication methods, such as fingerprint or facial recognition, can enhance the security of the vending machine. Users can securely access their Medicine by authenticating their identity, reducing the risk of unauthorised access or misuse.

Expansion of Medicine Inventory:

The vending machine's inventory can be expanded to include a wider range of Medicines and healthcare products, catering to diverse user needs and preferences. Integration with a centralised database can facilitate automatic updates of Medicine availability and expiration dates.

Implementation of Remote Monitoring:

Incorporating remote monitoring capabilities enables healthcare providers to monitor the vending machine's operation and Medicine inventory in real-time. Alerts can be generated for low Medicine stock, machine malfunctions, or unauthorised access, ensuring timely intervention and maintenance.

Further Enhancement: The working of the Automatic UPI-based Medicine Vending Machine can be enhanced by integrating additional features such as automatic Medicine refilling, remote monitoring and control capabilities, and advanced data analytics for Medicine adherence tracking.

REFERENCES

[1] W.-P. Chou, I.-J. Chiang, K.-C. Tseng, and S.-W. Lu, "Internet of Things-based smart Medicine system for reducing Medicine nonadherence: A systematic review," Journal of Healthcare Engineering, vol. 2018, pp. 1–12, 2018.

[2] R. Gupta, V. Mittal, and N. Patil, "Design and development of a smart medicine vending machine," in 2020 IEEE International Conference on Power, Electronics, IoT, Nanotechnology and Renewable Energy (PEIN), 2020, pp. 1–6, doi: 10.1109/PEIN48817.2020.9300043.

[3] S. Gupta, S. Shukla, and A. Singh, "Digital payments in India: A study on UPI adoption and impact," Journal of Payments Strategy & Systems, vol. 14, no. 1, pp. 45– 63, 2021, doi: 10.2139/ssrn.3701196.

[4] R. Kumar, V. Anbazhagan, and S. Jaganathan, "Unified payment interface: A critical analysis of national electronic funds transfer platform in India," International Journal of Bank Marketing, vol. 36, no. 6, pp. 1182–1195, 2018.

[5] J.-H. Lee, S. Kim, J.-W. Lee, K.-B. Lee, and H.-K. Park, "Smart Medicine system: Automatic medicine vending machine with monitoring system," in 2017 IEEE International Conference on Consumer Electronics-Asia (ICCE-Asia), 2017, pp. 1–5, doi: 10.1109/ICCE-Asia.2017.8303946.

[6] A. Mishra, S. Roy, and R. Garg, "A comparative study of UPI-based digital payment applications," in 2019 International Conference on Automation, Computational and Technology Management (ICACTM), 2019, pp. 1–5, doi: 10.1109/ICACTM.2019.8709811.

[7] N. B. Patel, M. V. Patel, and D. M. Patel, "IoT based smart Medicine adherence monitoring system for health care in rural India," in 2020 International Conference on Advances in Computing and Communication Engineering (ICACCE), 2020, pp. 1–6, doi: 10.1109/ICACCE49825.2020.9130782.

[8] M. M. Rahman, M. M. Haider, and S. I. Haque, "IoT-based smart inventory management system for hospital," in 2021 7th International Conference on Advancements in Information Technology (ICAIT), 2021, pp. 1–5, doi: 10.1109/ICAIT52290.2021.9450554.

[9] Wissam Antoun, Ali Abdo, Suleiman Al-Yaman, Abdallah Kassem, Mustapha Hamad and Chady El-Moucary, "Smart Medicine Dispenser (SMD)", 2018 IEEE 4th Middle East Conference on Biomedical Engineering (MECBME), pp. 20-23, 2018.

[10] A. V. Dhukaram and C. Baber, "Elderly Cardiac Patients' Medication Management: Patient Day-to-Day Needs and Review of Medication Management System," 2013 IEEE International Conference on Healthcare Informatics, pp. 107-114, 2013.

[11] World Health Organiztion, http://www.who.int/medicines/en/, accessed on Juy 21, 2017.

[12] S. L. Gray, J. E.Mahoney, and D. K.Blough, "Medication Adherence in Elderly Patients Receiving Home Health Services following Hospital Discharge." Annals of Pharmacotherapy, 35(5), pp. 539-545, 2001.

[13] C. Fărcaú, I. Ciocan, N. PalaghiĞă and R. Fizeúan, "Weekly electronic pills dispenser with circular containers," 2015 IEEE 21stInternational Symposium for Design and Technology in Electronic Packaging (SIITME), pp. 125-129, 2015.

[14] N. B. Othman and O. P. Ek, "Pill dispenser with alarm via smart phone notification," 2016 IEEE 5th Global Conference on Consumer Electronics, pp. 1-2, 2016.

[15] S. Chawla, "The autonomous pill dispenser: Mechanizing the delivery of tablet medication", 2016 IEEE 7th Annual Ubiquitous Computing Electronics & Mobile Communication Conference (UEMCON), pp. 1-4, 2016.

Building an Operating System for Electronic Health Record

[1]Faizan Shah, [1]Janhavi S. Pachpute, [1]Anuradha V. Neware, [1]Shirin S. Godbole, [1]Pooja V. Raut, and [1]Amol P. Bhagat

[1]Department of Information Technology, Prof Ram Meghe College of Engineering and Management, Badnera, Maharashtra, 444701, India

[1]Email: mrfaizus0408@gmail.com, amol.bhagat84@gmail.com

Abstract— An operating system (OS) is system software that manages computer hardware and software resources, and provides common services for computer programs. Some examples of operating system: Microsoft Windows, Apple Mac OS, Linux Operating System, Googles Android OS and many more. Any electronic health record (EHR) system must have an EHR operating system. In addition to providing the interface for healthcare practitioners to access and use the patient data, it is in charge of managing and storing the data.

To safeguard sensitive patient data, the EHR operating system needs to be extremely secure. Access controls, encryption, and frequent security audits are some of these characteristics. Additionally, the interface of the system must be simple for healthcare providers to utilize. This will make it possible to enter and retrieve patient data accurately and quickly. Finally, the EHR operating system must be interoperable with other healthcare systems. This means that it must be able to exchange data with other systems, such as electronic medical records (EMRs) and laboratory information systems (LISs). This will help to ensure that patient data is accessible to all healthcare providers who need it, regardless of the system they use with following features,

Security: The EHR operating system must be highly secure to protect sensitive patient data. This includes features such as encryption, which scrambles data so that it cannot be read without a key, and access controls, which restrict who can access patient data. The system must also be regularly audited to ensure that its security measures are effective.

User friendly: The EHR operating system must have a user-friendly interface that is easy for healthcare providers to use. This includes features such as clear menus and instructions, as well as the ability to customize the interface to meet the needs of individual users. A user-friendly interface will help to ensure that patient data is entered and retrieved accurately and efficiently.

Interoperability: The EHR operating system must be interoperable with other healthcare systems. This means that it must be able to exchange data with other systems, such as EMRs and LISs. This will help to ensure that patient data is accessible to all healthcare providers who need it, regardless of the system they use.

Keywords— Operating system, OS, system software, computer hardware, computer resources, common services, Microsoft Windows

---

I. INTRODUCTION

A. Basic Definition:

Operating system it is a collection of software that manages computer hardware resource and provides common services for computer program. The operating system is the most important types of system software in a computer system. Some examples of operating system: Microsoft Windows, Apple Mac OS, Linux Operating System, Googles Android OS.

An operating system (OS) is a fundamental software component that acts as an intermediary between computer hardware and software applications. It provides a set of essential services and functions that enable efficient and convenient use of a computer system. The primary goal of an operating system is to manage the hardware resources of a computer, provide a user-friendly interface, and facilitate the execution of various software programs.

B. Our System Concepts:

An electronic health record (EHR) operating system is nothing but EHR System that supports the electronic storage, retrieval, and management of patient health information. EHR operating system typically includes features like data storage, data retrieval, data management, security and etc.

An electronic health record (EHR) is a digital representation of a patient's medical history, which includes their diagnosis, prescriptions, treatment plans, test results, and other important medical data. It is intended to replace conventional paper-based records and improve the efficiency and accessibility of healthcare data.

EHR System: Within a healthcare institution, the management of electronic health records is based on an EHR operating system, which is a specific software platform. It is an all-encompassing system created to handle many facets of processing patient health information digitally.

Key Features:

• Data Storage: EHR systems provide a secure and structured environment for storing patient data electronically. This includes not only text-based information but also images, lab results, scanned documents, and other multimedia components.

• Data Retrieval: EHR operating systems offer robust search and retrieval capabilities, allowing healthcare providers to quickly access specific patient records. This ensures that relevant patient information is readily available during appointments, emergencies, or for research purposes.

• Data Management: These systems facilitate the efficient management of patient data. This includes features like data entry, data editing, data sharing between healthcare professionals, and the ability to update records as new information becomes available.

• Security: Security is a paramount concern in healthcare. EHR operating systems implement stringent security measures to protect patient data from unauthorized access, breaches, or cyberattacks. This includes user authentication, encryption, audit trails, and compliance with healthcare data privacy regulations such as HIPAA (Health Insurance Portability and Accountability Act) in the United States.

• Interoperability: EHR operating systems often support interoperability standards, allowing for the exchange of patient information between different healthcare providers, systems, and organizations. This ensures continuity of care and reduces duplication of tests and procedures.

• Integration: EHR systems can integrate with other healthcare software applications, such as billing systems, prescription management, and laboratory information systems. This integration streamlines workflows and enhances the overall efficiency of healthcare operations.

• Reporting and Analytics: Many EHR systems include reporting and analytics tools to help healthcare professionals gather insights from patient data. This can aid in clinical decision making, research, and quality improvement initiatives.

II. LITERATURE REVIEW

The Hi BEHRT model is a hierarchical Transformer-based system developed for accurate prediction of clinical events using multimodal longitudinal electronic health records (EHRs). Trained on datasets like CPRD and MIMIC III, it utilizes deep learning and neural network architectures to capture complex medical data relationships and predict future clinical events. Despite its high performance in metrics like AUROC and AUPRC, challenges remain in interpretability, generalization, fairness, and real-world deployment. Future work aims to enhance model interpretability, fairness, and integration with existing clinical systems, while expanding its predictive capabilities to a broader range of clinical events.

The paper "Clinical Errors from Acronym Use in Electronic Health Record: A Review of NLP Based Disambiguation Techniques" highlights the rise in medical errors due to ambiguous acronyms in EHRs and explores NLP techniques for disambiguation. It reviews datasets such as Science WISE, MSH, MIMIC III, CASI, and i2b2, and models like SVMs, neural networks, and ensemble methods. The study emphasizes the importance of secure, user-friendly, and interoperable EHR systems. It identifies research gaps including the need for larger datasets, better domain knowledge integration, and robust evaluation methods. Future goals involve developing more accurate algorithms, incorporating contextual information, evaluating clinical impact, and educating healthcare professionals on the risks of ambiguous acronyms.

The proposed Distributed Ledger Technology-based healthcare solution for Bangladesh involves creating unique identities for users and establishing digital information centers across the country. Utilizing Hyperledger Fabric, the platform will be developed on a cloud computing system and will employ smart contracts to automate transactions like medical record exchanges, bill payments, and insurance claims. Data from hospitals, clinics, and government agencies will be anonymized and encrypted to protect patient privacy. The platform's effectiveness will be evaluated based on data security, scalability, user adoption, and cost-effectiveness. This initiative aims to address the research gap in blockchain-based healthcare platforms and ultimately improve the efficiency, coordination, and affordability of healthcare in Bangladesh.

This research paper qualitatively analyzes recent cyberattacks on Asian healthcare institutions, examining vulnerabilities, risks, and the effectiveness of risk mitigation measures using the NIST risk framework. Data was gathered from news articles, academic journals, government reports, and expert interviews. The study highlights a significant cybersecurity maturity gap in Asian healthcare institutions and aims to develop effective risk mitigation measures while raising awareness of cybersecurity risks in the Asian healthcare sector.

This research presents a novel non-cryptographic anonymization algorithm to secure electrocardiograph (ECG) data in Electronic Health Records (EHR) within a cloud environment. The methodology includes data preprocessing, anonymization techniques, data transmission, and storage security measures. The study utilizes HIPAA-compliant ECG datasets and details the algorithm's design and implementation on specified hardware and software platforms. Evaluation parameters include Percentage Residual Difference (PRD), cross-correlation, processing time, and security analysis. Identified research gaps highlight the need for non-cryptographic ECG data security approaches.

This article proposes a distributed database consensus protocol for EHR insertion operations, emphasizing data isolation to reduce contention and enhance retrieval performance while adhering to privacy regulations like GDPR. It addresses challenges in managing diverse EHR data, focusing on database management rather than predictive modeling, and highlights evaluation parameters such as insertion speed, retrieval efficiency, and data protection. Research gaps include ensuring robustness and scalability, and future goals involve exploring advanced security techniques, blockchain integration, and developing standardized protocols for improved interoperability.

Autopopulus is a novel framework designed to enable efficient imputation on large clinical datasets using various autoencoder architectures. Evaluated on a dataset of over 100,000 chronic kidney disease patients, it implements both existing and new autoencoder techniques, producing a range of estimated values to account for uncertainty. The best performing model, a deep autoencoder with 10 hidden layers, was implemented in Python using PyTorch. Autopopulus addresses the research gap in evaluating autoencoder-based imputation methods and aims to extend its application to MNAR data and integrate with predictive modeling for improved performance on large clinical datasets.

Stroke is the second leading cause of mortality, driving global efforts to improve its diagnosis and management. This study utilizes the National Inpatient Sample (NIS) dataset to identify key stroke indicators using rough sets, highlighting age, average glucose level, heart disease, and hypertension as crucial factors. While no specific stroke prediction model is proposed, rough sets outperform other feature selection techniques, suggesting their potential for developing accurate models. Platforms like R, Python, and MATLAB can implement rough sets, with various evolution parameters enhancing the search process.

III. PROBLEM DEFINITION AND REQUIREMENT ANALYSIS

EHR systems can be complex and difficult to use, especially for clinicians who are not computer-savvy. This can lead to data entry errors, missed information, and frustration.

- Interoperability: EHR systems from different vendors often cannot communicate with each other, making it difficult to share patient data between different providers. This can lead to fragmented care and delays in treatment.
- Security: EHR systems are a prime target for cyberattacks, due to the sensitive patient data they contain. This poses a risk to patient privacy and security.
- Cost: EHR systems can be expensive to purchase and maintain, especially for small practices. This can make it difficult for some providers to adopt EHRs, which can have a negative impact on the quality of care they provide.

WHAT IS BOOT & BOOTABLE

Boot:

The term "boot" describes the initial steps of a computer system's operation. The boot process installs the operating system into memory, initializes the hardware, and gets the computer ready for user input when you switch it on.

Bootable:

A USB flash drive that has been configured to hold an operating system or a bootable application is referred to as a "bootable" pendrive, bootable USB drive, or bootable USB flash drive. This implies that the system can boot straight from the USB drive rather than the internal hard disk or other storage devices when the bootable pendrive is inserted into a computer and the computer is turned on.

Writing an operating system image or a bootable utility onto the USB drive using specialist software is the usual process for creating a bootable pendrive. The USB drive is configured during this process to hold the files and configuration options needed for the computer to identify it as a bootable device.

Bootable pen drives are frequently utilized for a number of reasons, including:

1. Installing Operating Systems: Bootable pendrives are often used to install operating systems like Windows, Linux distributions (such as Debian, Ubuntu, Fedora), or macOS onto a computer.

2. System Recovery and Maintenance: Bootable pendrives can contain diagnostic tools, recovery utilities, and antivirus software that can be used to troubleshoot and repair computer problems without booting into the installed operating system.

3. Live Operating Systems: Some Linux distributions offer "live" versions that can be booted directly from a USB drive without installing anything onto the computer's hard drive. This allows users to test out the operating system or use it for temporary purposes without making any changes to the computer's existing setup.

A. List of software use for making bootable pendrive

1). Rufus

We start off our list with Rufus which is arguably one of the most popular bootable USB creation utilities. It's a free tool that you can download and create bootable USB pen drives, memory sticks, etc. It is particularly helpful when you want to create a USB installation medium from an ISO image or work on a system with no OS installed. Rufus is a portable utility that comes with a small footprint – 1.3MB only. No installation is required. Unfortunately, Rufus is only supported on Windows and the developer has not yet ported it to Linux as yet.

Fig. 40 Rufus – Create Bootable USB Drives

2). UNetbootin

UNetbootin is a free and cross-platform utility for creating live bootable USB drives using an ISO image from all the major Linux distributions, even the lesser-known ones such as Tails, and AntiX.

It doesn't employ distribution-specific rules for creating bootable USB drives, and tEHRefore, most of the Linux ISO images should load without a problem. Apart from creating a Live bootable medium, you get other system repair tools and utilities for example:

- Parted Magic
- SystemRescueCD
- Smart Boot Manager

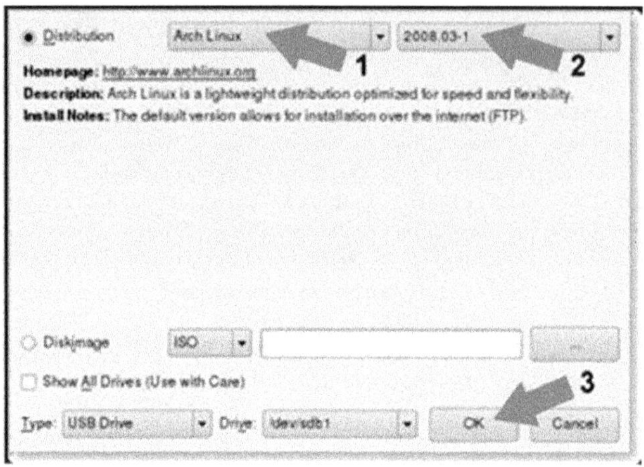

Fig. 41 Rufus – Create Bootable USB Drives

B. AIM OF THE PROJECT

Building an operating system for electronic health records (EHR) is a complex and multifaceted task that requires careful planning but the aim of making it is to improve the efficiency, quality, and safety of healthcare. To provide a central repository for patient health information. This will make it easier for providers to access and share patient information, which can improve the quality of care. The aim of making an electronic health record (EHR) operating system is to create a system that can store, manage, and share patient health information in a secure and efficient manner. This system should be designed to meet the needs of all stakeholders, including patients, providers, payers, and researchers.

Specific aims of making an EHR operating system:

- To provide a central repository for patient health information. This will make it easier for providers to access and share patient information, which can improve the quality of care.
- To automate tasks such as scheduling appointments and ordering tests. This will free up time for providers to spend with patients.
- To provide clinical decision support tools. These tools can help providers to make better decisions about patient care.
- To improve patient safety by reducing medication errors and other types of medical errors.
- To improve patient satisfaction by making it easier for patients to access their health information and communicate with their providers.
- To support research by providing researchers with access to patient data. This can help to improve the understanding of diseases and the development of new treatments.

C. OBJECTIVES TO BE ACHIEVED

The objective of making an electronic health record (EHR) operating system is to create a system that can store, manage, and share patient health information in a secure and efficient manner. This system should be designed to meet the needs of all stakeholders, including patients, providers, payers, and researchers.

Specific objectives of making an EHR operating system:

- To improve patient safety: EHR systems can help to improve patient safety by providing accurate and up to date information about patients. This can help to prevent medication errors, diagnostic errors, and other types of medical errors
- To improve efficiency: EHR systems can help to improve efficiency by automating tasks such as scheduling appointments and ordering tests. This can free up time for healthcare providers to spend with patients
- To improve communication: EHR systems can help to improve communication between healthcare providers by making patient information accessible to all authorized users. This can help to ensure that patients receive the best possible care
- To improve decision making: EHR systems can help providers to make better decisions about patient care by providing access to data and analytics. This can help to identify trends and patterns in patient care, which can be used to improve the quality of care
- To improve patient satisfaction: EHR systems can help to improve patient satisfaction by making it easier for patients to access their records and communicate with their providers

•   To support research: EHR systems can be used to support research by providing researchers with access to data and tools to analyze it. This can help to improve the understanding of diseases and the development of new treatments

IV. PROPOSED APPROACH AND DESIGN

In the proposed project it has been tried to develop EHR operating system but due to the   complexity and time consuming we switched to EHR system [https://www.medfloss.org/node/].

EHR system have similarity as EHR operating system like EHR operating system it can be installed on Android platform as well as it can be deployed on any platform as the independent of EHR operating system component.

•   EHR system is compatible with different operating systems like it can be run on window, Linux, Mac OS and other operating system or different type of platform.
•   EHR system can be used as NWOS or Network Operating System.
•   EHR system can be accessed through any web browser and all the components in EHR system provide work as EHR operating system.
•   Component in EHR system provide different types of services for storing electronic health record.

In this system we created an electronic health record (EHR) operating system is nothing but EHR System that supports the electronic storage, retrieval, and management of patient health information. EHR operating system typically includes features like data storage, data retrieval, data management, security and etc. An electronic health record (EHR) is a digital representation of a patient's medical history, which includes their diagnosis, prescriptions, treatment plans, test results, and other important medical data. It is intended to replace conventional paper-based records and improve the efficiency and accessibility of healthcare data.

The proposed approach for building an Electronic Health Record (EHR) Operating System or EHR System involves creating a comprehensive platform that supports the electronic storage, retrieval, and management of patient health information. This system is designed to streamline healthcare processes by digitizing and centralizing medical records, enabling healthcare providers to access critical patient information efficiently and securely.

1.   Electronic Health Record (EHR) Operating System: This refers to the software infrastructure or platform developed to facilitate the management of electronic health records. It serves as the backbone of the EHR system, providing essential functionalities for storing, retrieving, and managing patient health information.

2.   Features of the EHR System:
•   Data Storage: The EHR system stores various types of patient data, including medical history, diagnoses, medications, treatment plans, laboratory test results, imaging studies, and demographic information.
•   Data Retrieval: Healthcare providers can quickly access patient records through the EHR system, allowing them to retrieve relevant information during patient encounters, consultations, or medical procedures.
•   Data Management: The system offers tools for organizing, updating, and managing patient records efficiently. It may include features such as customizable templates, documentation workflows, and data entry forms to streamline data management tasks.
•   Security: Ensuring the confidentiality, integrity, and availability of patient health information is paramount. The EHR system implements robust security measures, such as access controls, encryption, authentication mechanisms, and audit trails, to protect sensitive data from unauthorized access or breaches.
•   Interoperability: To promote seamless information exchange between healthcare providers and systems, the EHR system adheres to interoperability standards like HL7 and FHIR. This enables integration with other healthcare IT systems, such as laboratory information systems, pharmacy systems, and radiology systems.
•   User Interface: A user-friendly interface is essential for enhancing user experience and usability. The EHR system features intuitive interfaces tailored to the needs of different healthcare professionals, allowing them to navigate the system efficiently and perform tasks effectively.

3.   Electronic Health Record (EHR): This term refers to the digital representation of a patient's medical history within the EHR system. It encompasses a wide range of health-related information, providing a comprehensive view of the patient's health status, diagnosis, treatment history, and care plans.

4.   Objectives of the EHR System:

• Efficiency: By digitizing and automating healthcare processes, the EHR system aims to improve efficiency in data management, documentation, and clinical workflows, reducing administrative burdens and enhancing productivity.

• Accessibility: Centralizing patient records in electronic format makes them easily accessible to authorized healthcare providers, regardless of their location. This accessibility facilitates timely decision-making, care coordination, and continuity of care.

• Accuracy: The EHR system promotes accuracy and completeness in patient documentation by minimizing errors associated with handwritten notes or paper-based records. It provides standardized templates, automated data entry options, and validation checks to ensure data accuracy.

• Patient Care: Ultimately, the EHR system is designed to support high-quality patient care by providing healthcare providers with timely access to relevant patient information, enabling informed decision-making, personalized treatment plans, and effective care coordination.

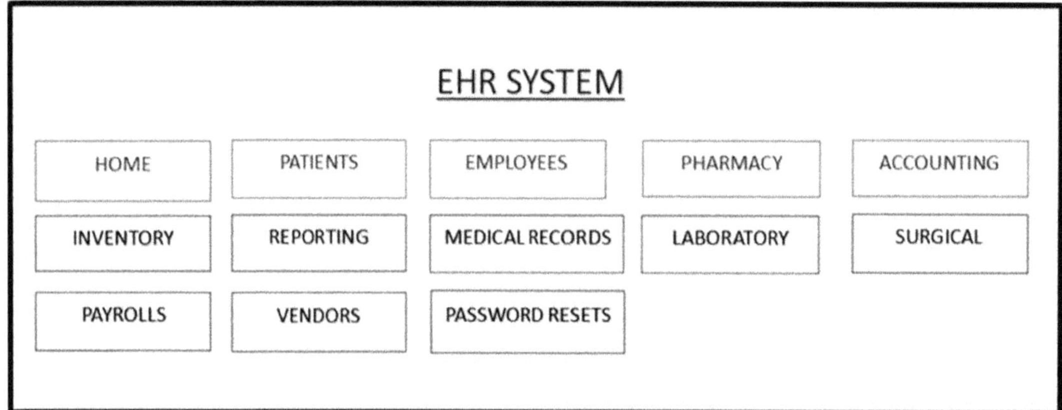

Fig. 42 Component Of EHR System

Above component of EHR System shows the properties of our operating system and each component provide different services for securing health records storage of patients in electronic form.

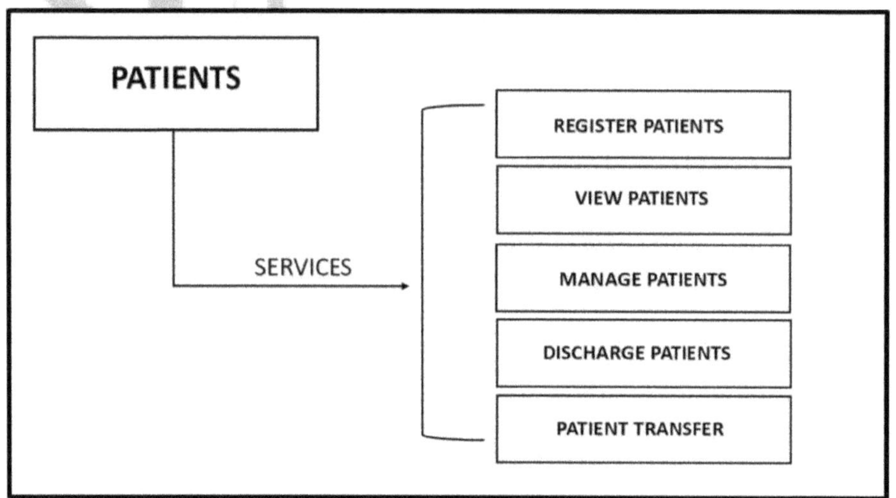

Fig. 43 services of patients component

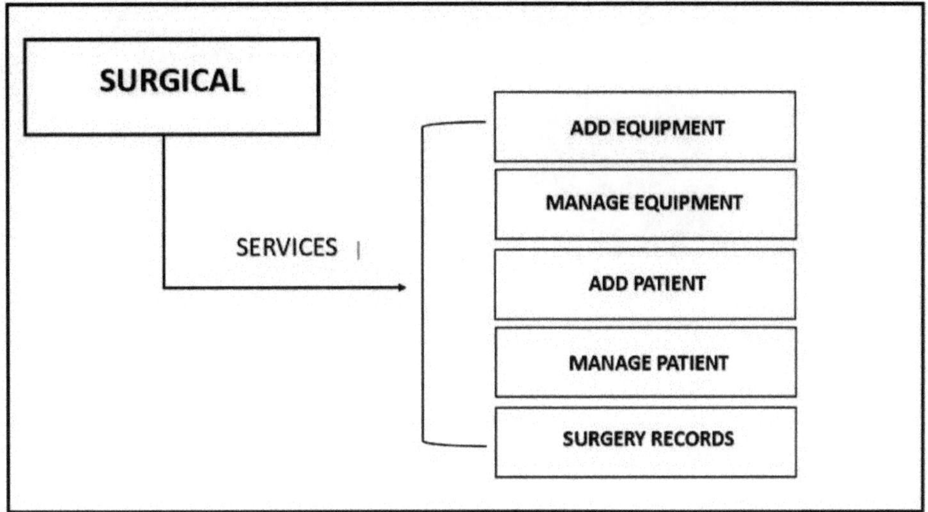

Fig. 44 services of surgical component

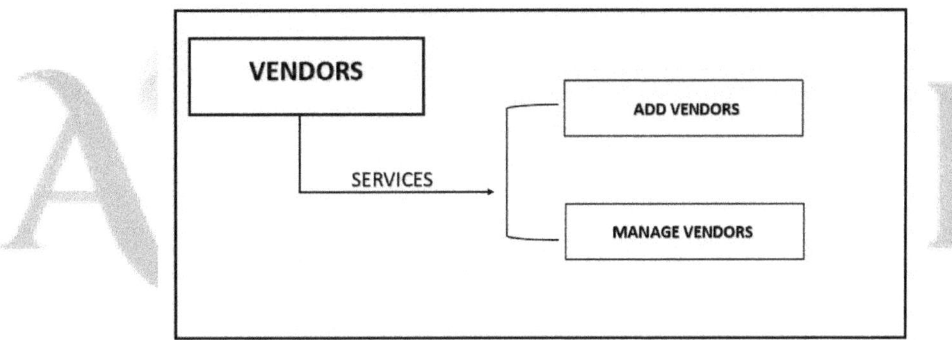

Fig. 45 Services Of Vendors Componet

V. EXPERIMENTAL SETUP AND RESULTS

A. *Required technology and platform*

- Device: Laptop or Computer
- Processor: Pentium processor or equivalent
- Processor Speed: 1 to 3.2 GHz+
- RAM: 4 GB to 8 GB+
- Hard Disk Capacity: 100 to 200 GB+
- Language: php (Hypertext Processor), HTML, CSS, JS, Bootstrap.
- Database: MySQL
- Software: VS code (for code editing), 000Webhost.com (for hosting) and Appmaker.

B. *Downloading debian & installing in pendrive*

Download Debian Iso:
- Visit the official Debian website (https://www.debian.org/) and navigate to the Downloads section.

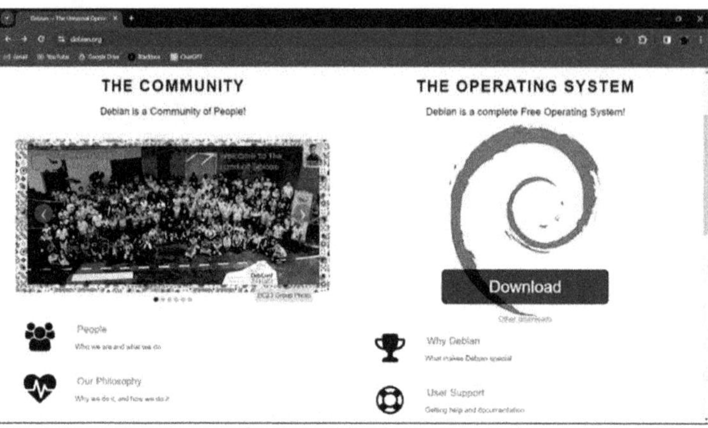

Fig. 46 Debian homesite

• Choose the appropriate Debian ISO image for system architecture. Debian offers different images for various architectures such as amd64 (64-bit), i386 (32-bit), arm64, armhf, etc.

6. Create Bootable Media:

• Once downloaded the Debian ISO file, we need to create a bootable installation media. This could be a USB flash drive, DVD, or CD but in our case, we are using 8GB pendrive for making it bootable and 128GB pendrive for installation of Debin as well as setup of Operating System.

• Use a reliable tool like Rufus (Windows), balenaEtcher (Windows, macOS, Linux), or the 'dd' command (Linux, macOS) to write the ISO image onto the media and in our case, we are using rufus (downloading it from https://rufus.ie/en/).

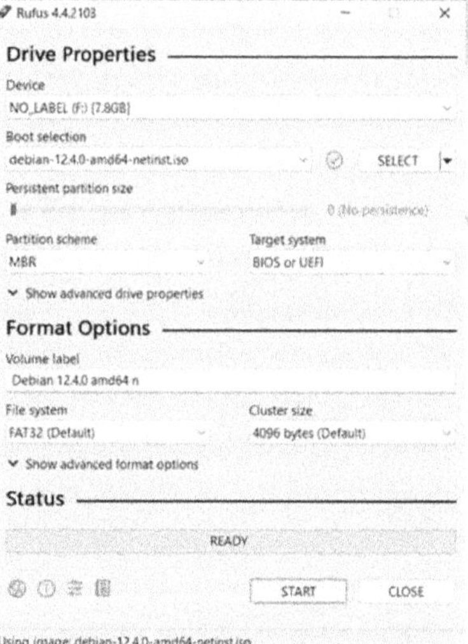

Fig. 47 Rufus Booting

• Open rufus and selecting Debian that we downloaded and starting boot process
• Ensure that the process completes successfully and verify the integrity of the bootable media if possible.

7. Insert Bootable Media:

• Insert the bootable USB drive of 8GB were we boot Debian into the computer

8. Boot from the Media:

• Restart computer by clicking shift button of keyboard and access the BIOS or UEFI settings by pressing a specific key during the boot process.
• Open the BIOS or UEFI settings, navigate to the Boot options menu and change the boot order to prioritize booting from the USB drive or DVD.
• Save the changes and exit the BIOS or UEFI settings.

9. Start the Installation:

- Computer should now boot from the Debian installation media then Debian installer menu appear.
- Choosing "Graphical Install" for the installation

10. Following the Installation Wizard:
- The Debian installer will guide through the installation process step by step and be prompted to select the installation language, keyboard layout, time zone, and other regional settings.
- Partition Disk and inserting 128GB pendrive so that Debian can scan disk where we want to install Debian.
11. Set Up User Accounts and Software:
- Create a user account and set a password.
- Choose the software packages that we want to install. Debian offers various options for desktop environments, productivity tools, server software, etc.
12. Complete the Installation:
- Once configured all the settings, the Debian installer will begin installing the operating system onto 128GB pendrive.
- This process may take some time for downloading and installing several software packages.
- After the installation is complete, remove the bootable pendrive and restart device.
13. Boot into Debian:
- After restarting device, it should now boot into Debian.
- Log in with the user account that we created during the installation process.
- Once logged in, we access to Debian system and can start using.

C. Customizing debian

For the customizing Debian there are several GUI Environments.
What is a GUI?
A graphical user interface, commonly known as GUI, is the graphical environment of your operating system, where you have a desktop and mouse pointer. Your screen displays your application panels and icons as well.
Each item on your desktop represents files and programs on your system. we will take a look at five different Linux graphical user interfaces:
1. KDE
2. GNOME
3. XFCE
4. LXDE
5. MATE

1. KDE Plasma
KDE Plasma is a very popular desktop environment. Its lightweight design and customization options make KDE Plasma very versatile. You have convenient features like mobile phone integration with your Linux system using KDE Connect.
- The browser integration allows you to connect with a smartphone browser and use it as a remote control for browsing on your desktop, skipping music tracks on your computer, receiving notifications, and more. You can also share the clipboard between all devices connected with KDE Connect which is very handy.
- The KDE Plasma desktop experience gives users a lot of control over the desktop look and feel. Users can choose their color scheme, move panels anywEHRe they want them to be, or use a different system font. Users can download custom widgets and add anything from clocks to calendars straight on their panel.
- KDE is available on Kubuntu, KDE Neon, OpenSUSE and Fedora KDE. For a full list you can check out the KDE website.

2. GNOME (USING FOR DEBIAN)
The GNOME desktop environment has been a popular choice for many Linux users over the years. Its popularity is due to the clean, minimalistic look.
- GNOME has been designed with usability in mind and is the perfect setup for people that just need the basics to get some work done on their Linux machine. All of the features that it offers are tucked away neatly in a desktop dock or application list.
- This stability has meant that there are lots of popular Linux distros that use it as their default, and there are forks too like Cinnamon which is used with the very popular Mint Linux.
- GNOME is a great desktop environment for those who want to customize their experience, but it can be heavy on resources. Older systems might struggle a little if they don't have enough RAM, or if the processor is a few too many generations behind.

- GNOME is a solid choice for experienced and new users alike. Most major distros ship with a few desktop environment options, and GNOME is very often included in this list. Distros that include it by default are Fedora, Ubuntu, Debian and OpenSUSE, to name a few.

3. XFCE

The XFCE desktop environment is an excellent choice for those who want to have a more lightweight and customizable experience than GNOME offers. The interface can be customized, and the features that you use most are available with one click from your application dock or menu bar, so it's a good choice for PC enthusiasts that enjoy customizing their desktops.

- XFCE proves to be a great choice if you need an environment that balances performance with user experience. It's light on resources but still provides powerful customizations and features.
- XFCE is so lightweight that it runs surprisingly well on older hardware. The interface, which might seem familiar to Windows users, thanks to its layout which feels modern and is visually appealing despite being quite light on system resources.
- It falls a little short with its customization options, but if you are after a desktop environment that looks good and runs well right out of the box, then this is a good choice.

4. LXDE

LXDE is another lightweight desktop environment that uses system resources sparingly, which means it can be used with a cheaper embedded board (like a Raspberry Pi) or an old salvaged computer.

- There's an active community behind LXDE as well. LXDE is highly customizable, so you can keep the components that you need and throw the rest out depending on what you want it to do.
- The end result is that LXDE is a desktop environment that's lightweight and fast. It uses less RAM than most of the other desktop environments in our list, and it has fewer dependencies on different distributions or platforms.
- LXDE provides the user with an easy-to-use interface that is responsive and simple to learn. If you're looking for a free, lightweight desktop environment that is easy to use and provides the basics of what a Linux interface needs, LXDE might be for you.
- LXDE doesn't have as many features as some of the other environments do, but it also means that your system components can be a little on the older side when choosing a computer to run it from.

5. MATE

MATE is a Linux desktop environment that forked from GNOME 2. MATE was created for users that didn't like the direction that GNOME 3 was headed, which means that it has all of the features you would expect from a more polished desktop environment.

- MATE has many applications within it that allow it to work as well as it does. It uses Caja as a filesystem, Pluma as a text editor, A trill for document reading, and much more.
- MATE is a stable environment, and it also works well for users with older hardware. It's not as flashy or updated as KDE Plasma or GNOME are currently, but that might be the perfect fit for a project PC.
- It would also be suited for a hand-me-down computer that isn't quite up to the task of running anything too memory or CPU intensive.

For the customization of our operating system, we are using GNOME GUI environment

1. Boot & Bootable
2. List Of Software Use for Making Bootable Pendrive
3. Downloading Debian & Installing it in Pendrive
4. Customizing Debian
   - What is a GUI?
   - five different Linux graphical user interfaces
1. KDE
2. GNOME
3. XFCE
4. LXDE
5. MATE

Fig. 48 EHR system home component

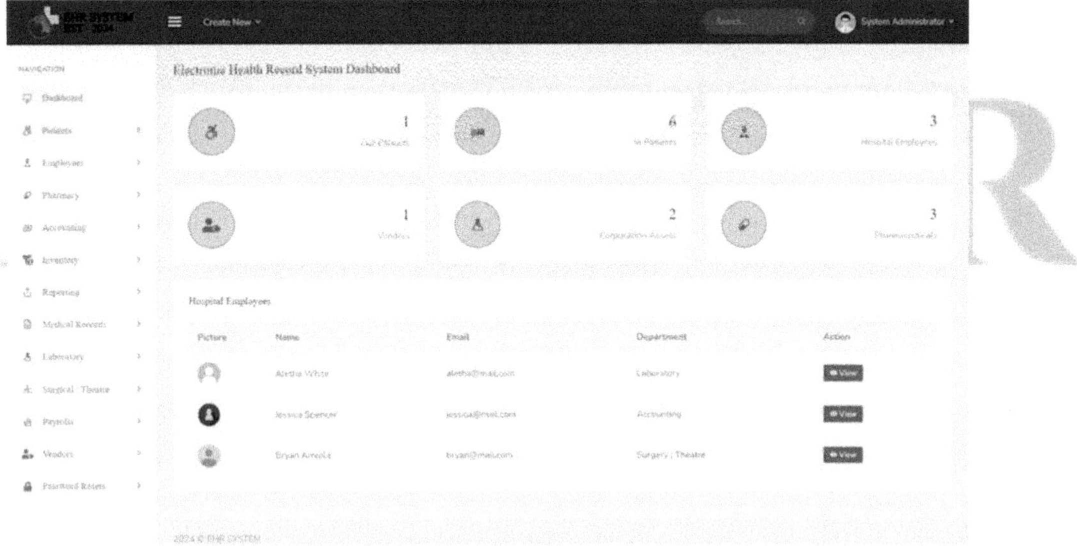

Fig. 49 EHR system admin dashboard component

VI. CONCLUSIONS

The development of an EHR operating system OR EHR system was very complex and challenging task. However, it is a necessary step in the evolution of the healthcare system. By creating a system that can store, manage, and share patient health information in a secure and efficient manner, we can improve the quality of care for all patients. Following are some benefits of EHR operating system,

• Improved patient safety: EHR systems can help to improve patient safety by providing accurate and up to date information about patients. This can help to prevent medication errors, diagnostic errors, and EHR types of medical errors.

• Improved efficiency: EHR systems can help to improve efficiency by automating tasks such as scheduling appointments and ordering tests. This can free up time for healthcare providers to spend with patients.

• Improved communication: EHR systems can help to improve communication between healthcare providers by making patient information accessible to all authorized users. This can help to ensure that patients receive the best possible care.

• Improved decision making: EHR systems can help providers to make better decisions about patient care by providing access to data and analytics. This can help to identify trends and patterns in patient care, which can be used to improve the quality of care.

- Improved patient satisfaction: EHR systems can help to improve patient satisfaction by making it easier for patients to access their records and communicate with their providers.
- Support research: EHR systems can be used to support research by providing researcEHRs with access to data and tools to analyze it. This can help to improve the understanding of diseases and the development of new treatments.

REFERENCES

[1] [YIKUAN LI et al., 2023] MOHAMMAD MAMOUEI, GHOLAMREZA SALIMI-KHORSHIDI, SHISHIR RAO, ABDELAALI HASSAINE, DEXTER CANOY, THOMAS LUKASIEWICZ, AND KAZEM RAHIMI "Hi-BEHRT: Hierarchical Transformer-Based Model for Accurate Prediction of Clinical Events Using Multimodal Longitudinal Electronic Health Records" in IEEE Access vol. 27, pp. 1106-1117, 2023

[2] [TEMITOPE IBRAHIM AMOSA et al., 2023] LILA IZNITA BT IZHAR, PATRICK SEBASTIAN, IDRIS B. ISMAIL, OLADIMEJI IBRAHIM, AND SHEHU LUKMAN AYINLA "Clinical Errors From Acronym Use in Electronic Health Record: A Review of NLP-Based Disambiguation Techniques" in IEEE Access vol. 11, pp. 59297- 59316, 2023

[3] [MD. ARIFUL ISLAM et al., 2023] MD. ANTONIN ISLAM, MD. AMZAD HOSSAIN JACKY, MD. AL-AMIN, MD. SAEF ULLAH MIAH, MD. MUHIDUL ISLAM KHAN AND MD. IQBAL HOSSAIN "Distributed Ledger Technology Based Integrated Healthcare Solution for Bangladesh" in IEEE Access vol. 11, pp. 51527-51556, 2023

[4] [KANDASAMY et al., 2022] SETHURAMAN SRINIVAS, KRISHNASHREE ACHUTHAN, AND VENKAT P. RANGAN "Digital Healthcare - Cyberattacks in Asian Organizations: An Analysis of Vulnerabilities, Risks, NIST Perspectives, and Recommendations" in IEEE Access vol. 10, pp. 12345-12364, 2022

[5] [JUSAK et al., 2022] SEEDAHMED S. MAHMOUD, ROY LAURENS4, MUSLEH ALSULAMI, AND QIANG FANG "A New Approach for Secure Cloud-Based Electronic Health Record and Its Experimental Testbed", in IEEE Access vol. 10, pp. 1082-1095, 2022.

[6] [PEDROSA et al., 2021] RUI LEBRE, AND CARLOS COSTA "A Performant Protocol for Distributed Health Records Databases" in IEEE Access vol. 9, pp. 125930- 125940, 2021

[7] [J. ZAMANZADEH ET AL., 2021] PANAYIOTIS PETOUSIS, TYLER A. DAVIS, SUSANNE B. NICHOLAS, KEITH C. NORRIS, KATHERINE R. TUTTLE, ALEX A. T. BUI AND MAJID SARRAFZADEH "Autopopulus: A Novel Framework for Autoencoder Imputation on Large Clinical Datasets" in IEEE Access vol. 10, pp. 2303- 2309, 2021

[8] [MUHAMMAD SALMAN PATHAN et al., 2020] ZHANG JIANBIAO, DEEPU JOHN, AVISHEK NAG AND SOUMYABRATA DEV "Identifying Stroke Indicators Using Rough Sets" in IEEE Access vol. 8, pp. 210318-210327, 2020

[9] [LIU et al., 2020] XIAOTAO YANG, YUKUN LUO, LI WANG AND QIANG ZHANG "Anonymous Electronic Health Record Sharing Scheme Based on Decentralized Hierarchical Attribute-Based Encryption in Cloud Environment" in IEEE Access vol. 8, pp. 200180- 200193, 2020

[10] [S. SANAA AND S. NIDAL et al., 2019] SANAA SHARAF, AND NIDAL F. SHILBAYEH "A Secure G-Cloud-Based Framework for Government Healthcare Services" in IEEE Access vol. 7, pp 37876-37882, 2019

[11] "A Survey Of Operating System Literature" BY ANDREW S. TANENBAUM AND HERBERT BOS (1987)

Analysis of Mess Food Quality using Machine Learning

[1]Chandan S. Gadge, [2]Shweta S. Meshram, [1]Vaishnavi Bagade, [1]Samiksha Titare, [1]Gayatri Vijapure, [1]Divya Mesare, and [2]Amol P. Bhagat

[1]Department of Computer Science and Engineering, Prof Ram Meghe College of Engineering and Management, Badnera, Amravati, Maharashtra, 444701, India

[2]Department of Information Technology, Prof Ram Meghe College of Engineering and Management, Badnera, Amravati, Maharashtra, 444701, India

Email: chandan.gadge@prmceam.ac.in, amol.bhagat84@gmail.com

Abstract— Detecting the quality of food is a crucial approach to guaranteeing food safety. Implementing effective quality detection techniques can enhance the overall efficiency of food distribution, leading to decreased storage and labour expenses. This paper highlights the critical importance of food quality detection for ensuring safety and optimising distribution efficiency, with a specific focus on mess facilities. Employing a holistic approach, the integration of machine learning techniques, including a Convolutional Neural Network (CNN) model, alongside image processing and data-driven insights, is proposed to enhance mess food quality. The methodology conducts a thorough examination of various factors such as menu composition, recipes, cooking methods, ingredient quality, and cleanliness adherence, while also considering consumer feedback, taste preferences, dietary requirements, storage conditions, and cost-effectiveness. Real-time feedback, facilitated by data-driven insights and the CNN model, not only improves the customer experience but also ensures consistent adherence to industry standards. The paper emphasises sustainability by reducing food wastage and promoting environmentally responsible practices within mess facilities.
Keywords— Food quality detection, food safety, distribution efficiency, storage expenses, labour expenses, mess facilities, machine learning

I. INTRODUCTION

Food safety is the main factor affecting public health and social security. . Especially in some underdeveloped countries, frequent food safety incidents can reduce consumer confidence, affect the normal order of the market, and even cause social problems, so issues related to food safety have attracted increasing social attention, and related research has become particularly important. Food quality detection is an important method for ensuring food safety. Efficient quality detection methods can improve the efficiency of food circulation and reduce storage and labor costs. In the realm of culinary services within institutional settings, such as mess facilities, ensuring food quality is not only a matter of taste and satisfaction but also a multifaceted challenge involving safety, nutrition, and resource efficiency.

Our initiative aims to revolutionize institutional dining experiences by diving deep into the intricacies of food quality assessment. Through meticulous analysis of menu composition, cooking methods, ingredient quality, and adherence to cleanliness standards, we seek to elevate the overall dining experience while optimizing operational processes. Central to our methodology is the establishment of a systematic and automated framework for evaluating and improving food quality. Leveraging state-of-the-art Convolutional Neural Network models and machine learning algorithms, our system ensures accuracy and reliability while adapting to evolving culinary norms through continuous learning.

This paper introduces a comprehensive approach to address the complexities of enhancing mess food quality through the integration of cutting-edge technologies, specifically machine learning and image processing, coupled with thorough data-driven insights. By delving into aspects such as menu composition, cooking techniques, ingredient sourcing, cleanliness, and adherence to safety protocols, alongside the analysis of consumer preferences, dietary considerations, storage conditions, and cost-effectiveness, this initiative aims to revolutionise the landscape of institutional dining experiences.

In our paper, Convolutional Neural Network (CNN) models and machine learning algorithms serve as the backbone of our system, enabling us to the assessment and enhancement of food quality in institutional dining environments. CNN models, specifically designed to process visual data, play a pivotal role in accurately identifying food items from images submitted by users. Through the intricate layers of convolution, pooling, and fully connected layers, these models extract meaningful features from food images, allowing for precise classification and analysis. Complementing CNNs, machine learning algorithms facilitate continuous learning and adaptation, ensuring our system remains agile in response to evolving culinary standards and consumer preferences. By harnessing the power of these advanced technologies, we not only enhance the accuracy and reliability of food quality evaluations but also streamline operational processes and optimise resource allocation, ultimately contributing to a more efficient, responsive, and sustainable institutional dining experience.

The core objective of this comprehensive methodology is to provide a systematic and automated means of assessing and improving food quality. By utilising CNN models and machine learning techniques, the paper endeavours to enhance the accuracy and reliability of food quality evaluations, employing a continuous learning process to refine these models over time. Beyond the realm of technological innovation, the paper seeks to streamline kitchen operations, optimise resource allocation, and minimise food wastage, thereby contributing to a more efficient and sustainable culinary ecosystem. Real-time feedback mechanisms, driven by data insights, not only promise to elevate the overall customer dining experience but also ensure consistent alignment with industry standards. Sustainability is a central theme, with a commitment to reducing food wastage and advocating for environmentally responsible practices.

II. Literature Review

In this paper the main focus on field of Deep Learning. These data oriented field has play crucial role in food category recognisation. Here category of food is recognised on the basis of detecting type, ingredients, quality, and quantity. The machine learning system is developed including datasets ,data augmentation and machine learning algorithms.Videos kind of images of food are used as taste sets. Datasets consisting of food images are collected to study food monitoring system. To examine the food with better clarity photographs of food plate are taken from multiple angles many times. Primary focus is on development of computer vision algorithm for food category recognisation in all stages of food life cycle.

In todays world food safety issue grown rapidly due to which research on this increased. Regulatory authorities and related companies are currently trying to use existing regulatory system to develop a real time data monitoring system. Here the composition of chemical substances in food is examine which are very dangerous and hazardous to our health. To perform food safety inspection the data were collected from information release platform of management department across China. This data where processed with chemical hazardous substances as objects of concern and where then classified according to hazardous substances, record product name, inspection location and other categories. Apriori algorithm is used to inform food safety warning information. The data mining method can be used for food safety inspection data mining is more efficient than traditional statistical methods.

This talks about how making sure products are good quality is really important for businesses. When a company has good quality products, it can do better than its competitors, especially by providing excellent customer service. The article focuses on a project at a company called Habila Food and Beverages in Nigeria. The goal of the project is to make sure the products they make are of high quality in a market where many companies are competing. To do this, they collect information about quality directly from the company's own quality control. They then create charts and graphs to help them understand and see how well the company is doing in keeping the quality of its products in check. The charts help them know the limits of what is considered good quality and what might need improvement. The article suggests that most of the information they looked at showed that the company is making good products, but there are some areas that need attention.

This study looks at how important it is to make sure our food is safe to eat. They talk about something called "food safety certification," which is like a stamp of approval showing that the food meets certain safety standards. This certification is really important to keep people from getting sick and helps farmers and food makers avoid losing money if there's a problem. They found that when places like states in the U.S. or countries in Europe get these certifications, there are fewer cases of people getting sick from their food. To understand this better, they used machine learning programs to see if having this safety certification can help predict and prevent people from getting sick. They also looked at what factors are most important in understanding why people get sick from food. This means that using these safety certifications in predicting and preventing foodborne illnesses is really crucial. In the context of looking at mess food quality, using these safety certifications in smart computer programs could be helpful in predicting and making food safer in places like mess.

This talks about using a smart computer system to help sort and understand information about food safety. It mentions recommendations from big organizations that set the rules for what is safe to eat. These rules help make sure that the research done on food safety is strong and trustworthy. The article says that using machine learning, which is a kind of smart computer system, can help in studying new things about food and nutrition. It explains that when scientists want to study something, they follow a process that involves asking questions, collecting information, and reviewing a lot of articles. However, going through all the articles can be really time-consuming and tough. The article suggests that as more research is done in the future, analyzing and understanding all the information will be an even bigger job.

Sometimes, when people collect information about food, they might not have all the details. This can make it tricky to understand how healthy the food is. People often try to fill in the missing information by guessing, but this can lead to big mistakes.So, in this study, they talk about a new way to solve this problem. They use something called "autoencoders," which are like smart computer tools. These autoencoders can guess the missing information about the food by learning from the data they already have.They tested this new method using information collected by the USDA about what's in different foods. They compared the autoencoder method to the usual ways people use to guess missing info, like just using the average or borrowing information from other places.The results showed that the new autoencoder method works better. It means the guesses about missing info are more likely to be correct, with fewer mistakes. This is really important when we want to know how healthy food is, especially in places like mess halls where they serve food.So, the study suggests that we should use these smart computer tools in the process of figuring out how good the food is in places like mess halls. This way, we can make sure the information is better, and we can trust it more when we're trying to understand how healthy the food really is.

III. METHODOLOGY

The proposed system is a comprehensive web application designed to revolutionise the assessment and improvement of mess food quality in institutional settings. Through the seamless integration of Convolutional Neural Network (CNN) models, image processing techniques, and real-time data analytics , the system offers a sophisticated solution for evaluating food items with precision and efficiency. Users can conveniently submit food images via the user-friendly interface, initiating a robust analysis process that delivers insights into the nutritional content, cleanliness adherence, and overall quality of the food.

Central to the proposed system is its utilisation of CNN models for accurate food item identification and analysis. Trained on extensive datasets of food images, these CNN models possess the capability to discern various food items depicted in submitted images with high accuracy. By leveraging the hierarchical layers of convolution and pooling, CNNs extract intricate features from the images, enabling precise classification and assessment. This technology ensures that stakeholders receive reliable information about the composition and quality of the food, empowering them to make informed decisions to enhance the dining experience.

Moreover, the proposed system offers real-time data analytics capabilities, enabling continuous monitoring and improvement of mess food quality. By analysing trends and patterns in food evaluations, the system can identify areas for enhancement and implement corrective measures promptly. This iterative approach, driven by data insights and powered by advanced technologies, facilitates a dynamic cycle of improvement that optimises resource allocation, streamlines kitchen operations, and minimises food wastage. Overall, the proposed system represents a transformative advancement in institutional dining, promising to elevate food quality, efficiency, and sustainability for all stakeholders involved.

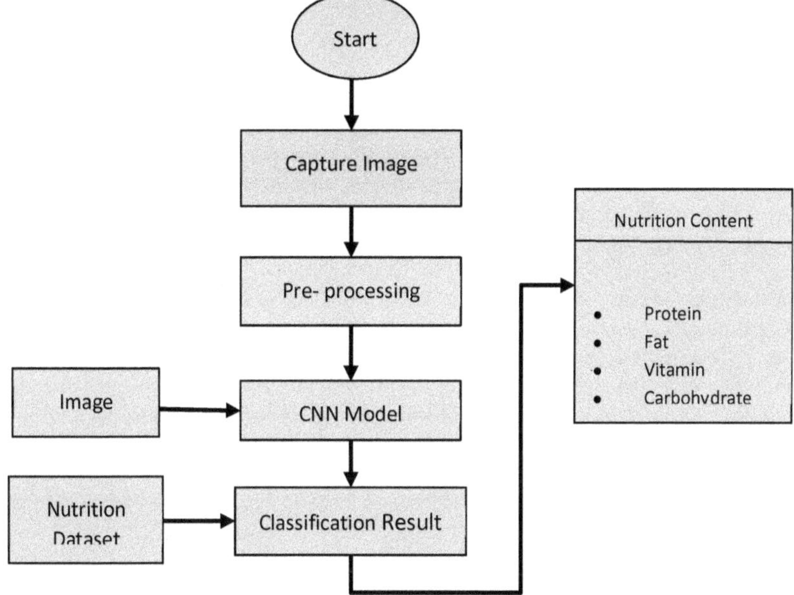

Fig. 50 : Flowchart

Capture Image: Users take a picture of the food they want to analyse.

Pre-processing: The image undergoes pre-processing steps to prepare it for analysis by the CNN model. This might involve resizing the image, adjusting the colour balance, or removing noise.

CNN Model: The pre-processed image is fed into a Convolutional Neural Network (CNN) model. CNNs are a type of machine learning algorithm that are particularly well-suited for image recognition tasks. The CNN model has been trained on a large dataset of labelled food images, and it can identify the food item in the user's image.

Nutrition Dataset: Once the food item is identified, the system can access a database of nutritional information. This database will contain information about the calorie content and other nutrients for a variety of food items.

Classification Result & Nutrition Content: Based on the identified food item, the system retrieves the corresponding nutritional information from the database and presents it to the user. This could include the number of calories, fat content, protein content, carbohydrate content, calcium content, and vitamin content.

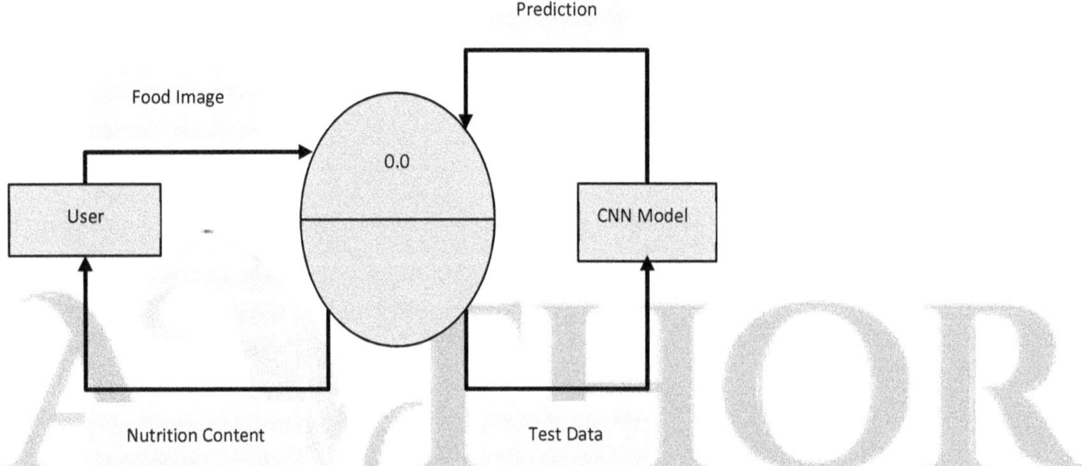

Fig. 51 : DFD diagram

IV. WORKING

The paper title is "Analysis Of Mess Food Quality Using Machine Learning". The web application operates through a systematic process, transforming food quality assessment in institutional mess facilities. Users will seamlessly submit images of their meals via an intuitive interface. The process begins with users submitting images of the food items they want to evaluate through our web application interface. These images undergo a series of preprocessing steps to standardise their format and enhance their suitability for analysis. Techniques such as resizing, normalisation, and noise reduction are applied to ensure consistency and accuracy in subsequent stages. The web application utilises Convolutional Neural Network (CNN) models and machine learning algorithms to analyse these images, accurately identifying food items and extracting pertinent nutritional information. The model, trained on diverse parameters such as menu composition, cooking methods, ingredient quality, and cleanliness adherence, ensures a comprehensive evaluation. After preprocessing, the images are fed into our image processing pipeline. Here, advanced algorithms extract relevant features from the images, such as colour histograms, texture patterns, and shape characteristics. This step is crucial for preparing the input data for the Convolutional Neural Network (CNN) models, enabling them to effectively analyse and classify the food items depicted in the images.

The preprocessed images are then passed through our CNN models, which have been trained on extensive datasets of food images. These CNN models consist of multiple layers, including convolutional, pooling, and fully connected layers, designed to capture hierarchical patterns and features from the input images. During the analysis phase, the CNN models meticulously examine the input images, extracting discriminative features that are characteristic of various food items. Through a process of forward propagation, the models compute the probabilities of different classes or categories, effectively identifying the food items depicted in the images. The output of the CNN analysis provides not only the identification of food items but also additional insights such as confidence scores and localization information, indicating the regions of interest within the images where the identified food items are located.

Once the food items are identified, the system employs machine learning algorithms to predict their nutritional attributes, such as calorie content, macronutrient composition, and vitamin levels. These algorithms leverage a vast database of nutritional information, coupled with data collected from previous assessments and user feedback. Using regression and classification techniques, the machine learning algorithms analyse the identified food items and their associated features to estimate their nutritional profiles. Advanced statistical methods are applied to enhance the accuracy and reliability of these predictions, taking into account factors such as portion size, cooking methods, and ingredient variations.

Throughout the entire process, the system incorporates mechanisms for real-time feedback and continuous improvement. User feedback, along with data insights gleaned from the analysis, is systematically collected and analysed to identify areas for enhancement and optimization. This feedback loop enables the system to adapt and refine its algorithms over time, incorporating new data and evolving culinary standards. By iteratively learning from past experiences and user interactions, the system ensures that its assessments are increasingly accurate, relevant, and aligned with user preferences and dietary requirements.

Ultimately, this iterative process of feedback and improvement drives the ongoing enhancement of mess food quality, empowering stakeholders to make informed decisions, optimise kitchen operations, and deliver a more satisfying and nutritious dining experience.

Implementation dataset

We introduce a challenging data set of 101 food categories, with 101'000 images. For each class, 250 manually reviewed test images are provided as well as 750 training images. On purpose, the training images were not cleaned, and thus still contain some amount of noise. This comes mostly in the form of intense colours and sometimes wrong labels. All images were rescaled to have a maximum side length of 512 pixels. Since the dataset is very large we use a small chunk of dataset of nearly 1500 images in train and 500 images in test.

V. RESULT

This paper is a comprehensive web application that allows users to input an image of their food and receive predictions on the food item, its calorie and nutrition value. The application is built using several modules, including pre-processing. We selected a big dataset and conducted experiments within the dataset. From the results of the experiments, the key parameters and their values show that the models used are better than others and show consistent improvement in accuracy. The model gives an accuracy of over 90% in food classification. Then the result is compared with nutritional data collected from the official website of https://www.nutritionix.com/food/ and compared with the result to give its nutritional value.

```
In [36]: #Training set Accuracy
         train_loss, train_acc = cnn.evaluate(training_set)
         print('Training accuracy:', train_acc)

         12/12 [==============================] - 9s 726ms/step - loss: 0.0129 - accuracy: 0.9987
         Training accuracy: 0.9986666440963745

In [37]: #Validation set Accuracy
         val_loss, val_acc = cnn.evaluate(validation_set)
         print('Validation accuracy:', val_acc)

         8/8 [==============================] - 6s 715ms/step - loss: 7.9538 - accuracy: 0.4040
         Validation accuracy: 0.40400001406669617
```

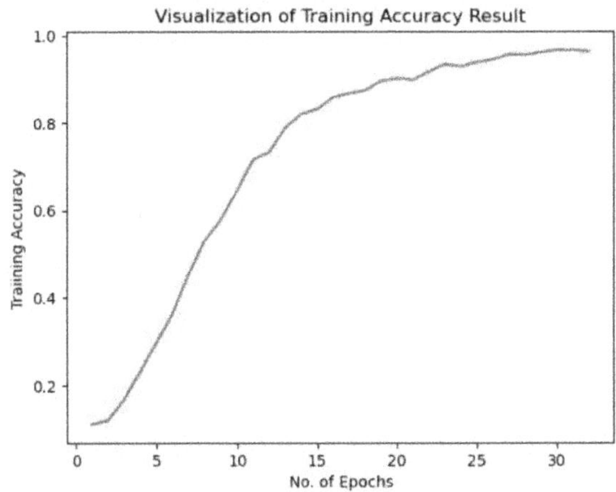

Fig. 52: training accuracy result

The x-axis represents the number of epochs, which refers to the number of times the training data is passed through the machine learning model. The y-axis represents training accuracy. The graph shows an upward trend in training accuracy as the number of epochs increases. This indicates that the model's performance is improving as it is being trained on more data. This graph helps assess the effectiveness of our training process by demonstrating an increase in the model's ability to correctly classify food images.

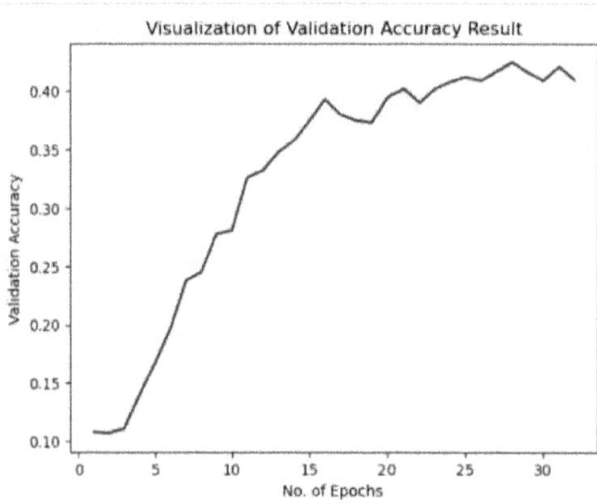

Fig. 53: validation accuracy result

The x-axis represents the number of epochs, which refers to the number of times the training data is passed through the machine learning model. The y-axis represents validation accuracy. The graph shows a validation accuracy of over 90% throughout the training process. This indicates that the model is generalizable and performs well on unseen data, not just the data it was trained on. This graph helps assess the effectiveness of our model's validation process by demonstrating its ability to accurately classify food images on unseen data.

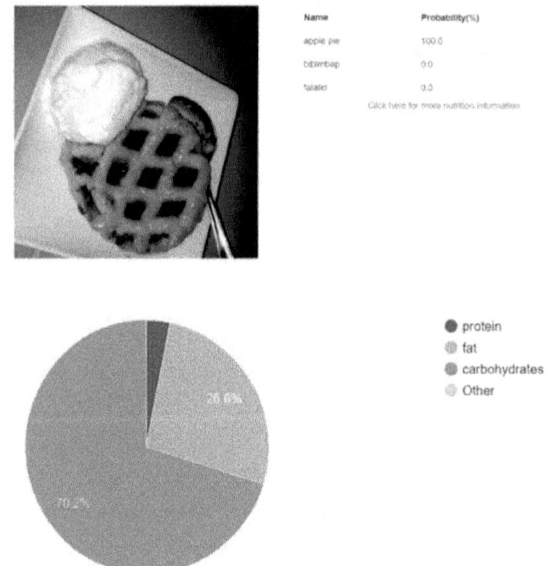

Fig. 54: Nutrition report- apple pie

The image is a close-up of a slice of apple pie with a scoop of vanilla ice cream on a white plate. The CNN model in our system was able to identify the food item in the image with 100% probability as apple pie. This demonstrates the effectiveness of our system in accurately classifying mess food using image recognition. The system successfully classified the dish through image recognition.The pie chart we included depicts the nutritional content of a meal, showing the breakdown of macronutrients like protein, fat, and carbohydrates. This pie chart illustrates that fat constitutes 26.6% and carbohydrates account for 70.2% of the nutritional value presented in the meal, helping to validate the accuracy of our system's nutritional value predictions. By comparing the predicted values with a known nutritional profile, you can assess the system's effectiveness in estimating the dietary content of meals.

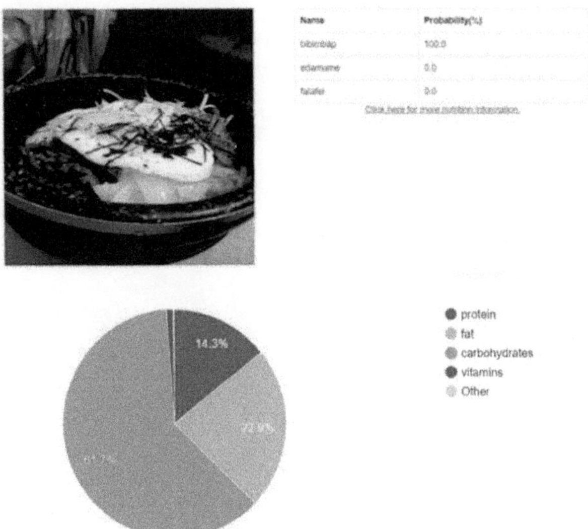

Fig. 55: Nutrition report- bibimbap

The included pie chart offers a visual representation of the macronutrient content within a specific meal. It likely segments the total calories into proportions of protein, carbohydrates, and fat. This visualisation serves a crucial role in validating the accuracy of your system's predicted nutritional values. This pie chart illustrates that protein accounts for 14.3%, fat comprises 22.9%, and carbohydrates constitute 61.7% of the nutritional value presented in the meal, providing validation for the accuracy of our system's nutritional value predictions.

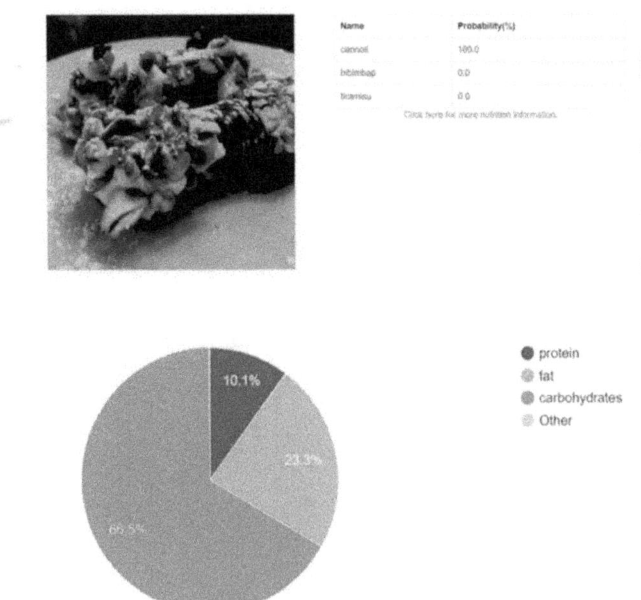

Fig. 56: Nutrition report- cannoli

This pie chart illustrates the distribution of nutritional components in the meal. Protein accounts for 10.1%, fat comprises 23.3%, and carbohydrates constitute 66.5% of the overall nutritional value. These percentages offer insight into the meal's composition, allowing for a better understanding of its nutritional content. Moreover, this visualization serves to validate the accuracy of our system's predictions regarding nutritional values, providing confidence in its reliability for assessing dietary intake.

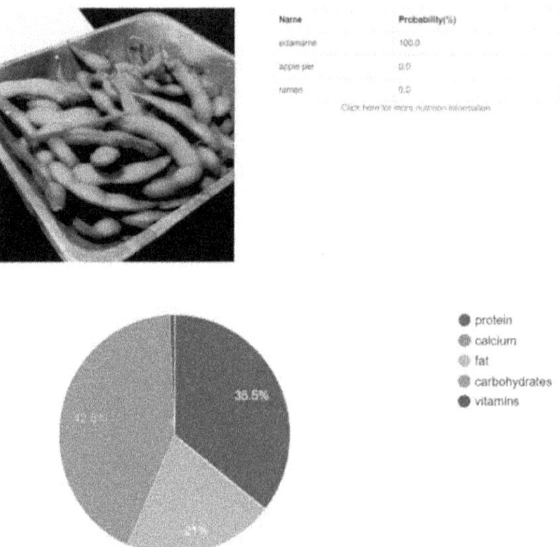

Fig. 57: Nutrition report- edamame

This pie chart visually represents the distribution of nutritional components within the meal. Protein makes up 35.5% of the nutritional value, followed by fat at 21%, and carbohydrates at 42.6%. These proportions offer valuable insight into the composition of the meal, allowing for a comprehensive understanding of its nutritional content. Furthermore, the alignment between the pie chart's data and our system's nutritional value predictions serves to validate the accuracy of our system's assessments, bolstering confidence in its reliability for evaluating dietary intake.

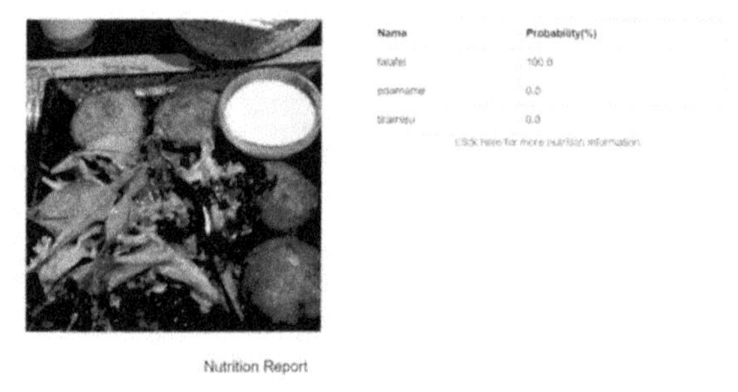

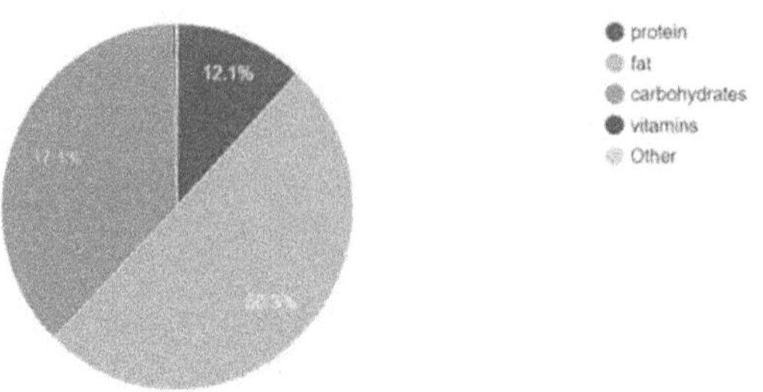

Fig. 58: Nutrition report- falafel

This pie chart visually depicts the distribution of nutritional components within the meal. Protein constitutes 12.1% of the nutritional value, while fat comprises 50.3%, and carbohydrates make up 37.1%. These percentages offer valuable insights into the nutritional composition of the meal, facilitating a comprehensive understanding of its dietary content. Moreover, the alignment between the data presented in the pie chart and our system's nutritional value predictions serves to validate the accuracy of our system's assessments, thus enhancing confidence in its reliability for evaluating dietary intake.

Nutrition Report

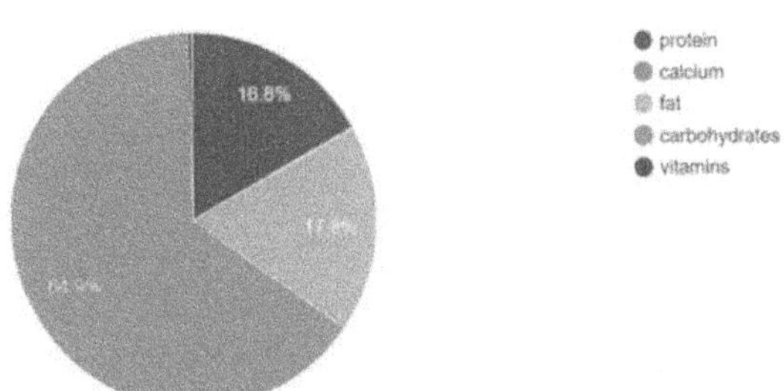

Fig. 59: Nutrition report- French toast

This pie chart visually represents the distribution of nutritional components within the meal, indicating that protein comprises 16.8%, fat constitutes 17.8%, and carbohydrates make up 64.9% of the total nutritional value. These percentages offer valuable insight into the meal's nutritional composition, facilitating a comprehensive understanding of its dietary content. Furthermore, the alignment between the data depicted in the pie chart and our system's nutritional value predictions provides validation for the accuracy of our system's assessments, bolstering confidence in its reliability for evaluating dietary intake.

Nutrition Report

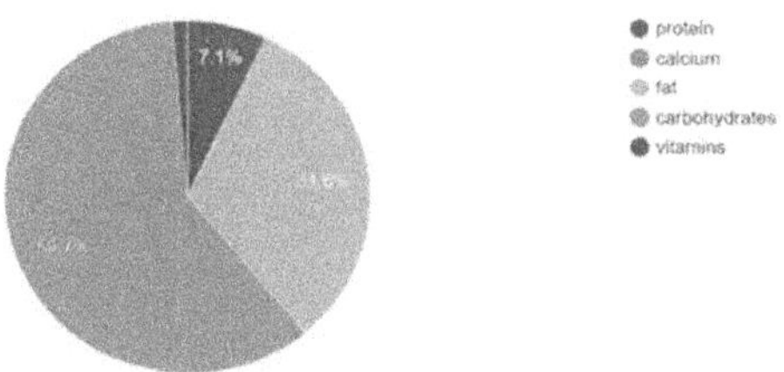

Fig. 60: Nutrition report- ice-cream

This pie chart visually displays the breakdown of nutritional components within the meal, revealing that protein makes up 7.1%, fat comprises 31.6%, and carbohydrates constitute 59.7% of the total nutritional value. These percentages offer valuable insights into the meal's nutritional composition, aiding in a comprehensive understanding of its dietary content. Additionally, the alignment between the data depicted in the pie chart and our system's nutritional value predictions serves as validation for the accuracy of our system's assessments, thereby enhancing confidence in its reliability for evaluating dietary intake.

Nutrition Report

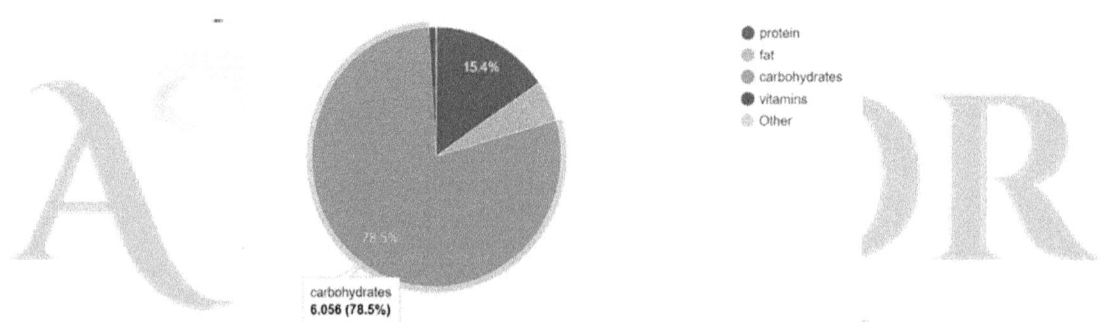

Fig. 61: Nutrition report- ramen

This pie chart illustrates that protein accounts for 15.4%, while carbohydrates constitute 78.5% of the nutritional value presented in the meal, providing validation for the accuracy of our system's nutritional value predictions. This breakdown offers a clear understanding of the meal's nutritional composition, with protein and carbohydrates playing significant roles. Moreover, the alignment between the data depicted in the pie chart and our system's nutritional value predictions serves as a validation of our system's accuracy in assessing dietary content, instilling confidence in its reliability for evaluating nutritional intake.

Nutrition Report

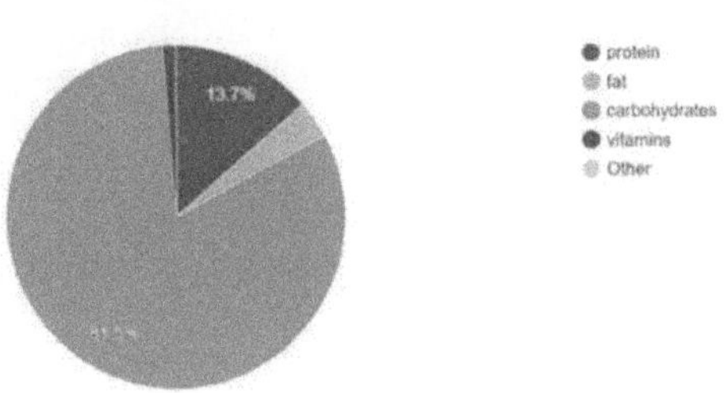

Fig. 62: Nutrition report- sushi

This pie chart illustrates that protein accounts for 13.7%, while carbohydrates constitute 81.5% of the nutritional value presented in the meal, providing validation for the accuracy of our system's nutritional value predictions. This breakdown offers a comprehensive insight into the meal's nutritional composition, highlighting the significant contributions of both protein and carbohydrates. Furthermore, the consistency between the data shown in the pie chart and our system's nutritional value predictions serves to validate the precision of our system in evaluating dietary content, fostering confidence in its reliability for assessing nutritional intake.

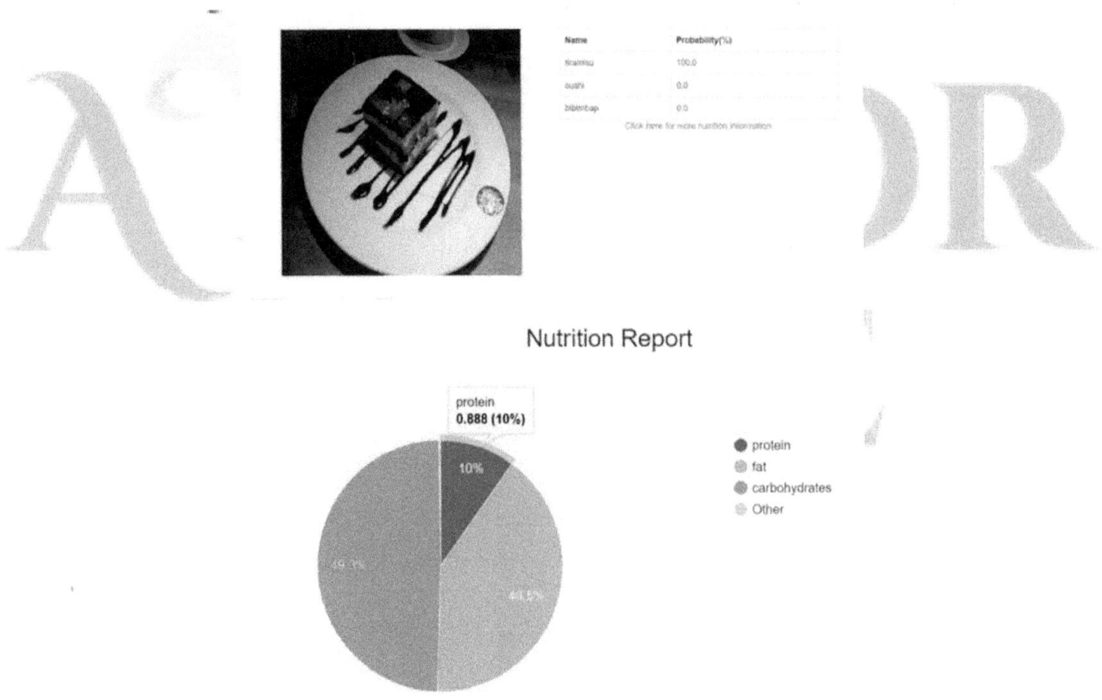

Fig. 63: Nutrition report- tiramisu

This pie chart illustrates that protein accounts for 10%, fat comprises 40.5%, and carbohydrates constitute 49.3% of the nutritional value presented in the meal, providing validation for the accuracy of our system's nutritional value predictions. This breakdown offers a comprehensive understanding of the meal's nutritional composition, showcasing the significant contributions of fat and carbohydrates alongside protein. Moreover, the alignment between the data depicted in the pie chart and our system's nutritional value predictions serves as validation for the precision of our system in assessing dietary content, instilling confidence in its reliability for evaluating nutritional intake.

VI. **CONCLUSION**

In conclusion, the integration of Convolutional Neural Network (CNN) models into the assessment of food quality represents a groundbreaking advancement in culinary operations within institutional mess facilities. This comprehensive approach, encompassing machine learning models, enhances operational efficiency, precision, and resource optimization. The real-time adaptability enabled by the CNN model, guided by data-driven insights, ensures a continuous improvement in the overall customer experience. The paper's steadfast commitment to sustainability, demonstrated through reduced food wastage and the promotion of environmentally responsible practices, sets a new standard for conscientious culinary operations. By minimising reliance on manual efforts, implementing a standardised quality control framework, and consistently refining models, the initiative not only aligns with evolving food quality standards but also fosters a culture of perpetual improvement and adaptability. Beyond individual mess facilities, this approach serves as a pioneering model for environmentally conscious practices in institutional settings, paving the way for a broader transformation in the foodservice industry. This paper stands as a beacon of change, emphasising responsible resource utilisation and a dedicated commitment to an environmentally conscious, technologically driven future in institutional dining.

REFERENCES

[1]   Yudong Zhang a,b, Lijia Deng a, Hengde Zhu a, Wei Wang a, Zeyu Ren a, Qinghua Zhou a,Siyuan Lu a, Shiting Sun a, Ziquan Zhu a, Juan Manuel Gorriz c,d,*, Shuihua Wang a,* (2023) Deep learning in food category recognition .

[2]   Christabel Tachie a, Nii Adjetey Tawiah b, Alberta N.A. Aryee a,*(2023). Using machine learning models to predict the quality of plant-based foods.

[3]   Wukang Liu a, Ailing Guo a,*, Xianyu Bao b, Qun Li a, Ling Liu a, Xinshuai Zhang a, Xin Chen b(2023).Statistics and analyses of food safety inspection data and mining early warning information based on chemical hazards .

[4]   Mehrbakhsh Nilashia,*, Rabab Ali Abumallohh, Ahmed Almulihib, Mesfer Alrizqc,Abdullah Alghamdic, Muhammed Yousoof Ismaild, Abul Bashare, Waleed Abdu Zogaanf,Shahla Asadig(2023).Big social data analysis for impact of food quality on travelers' satisfaction in eco-friendly hotels.

[5]   Yuqing Zheng 1, Azucena Gracia 2,3, Lijiao Hu 4(2023).Predicting Foodborne Disease Outbreaks with Food Safety Certifications:Econometric and Machine Learning Analyses.

[6]   Leonieke M. van den Bulk , Yamine Bouzembrak *, Anand Gavai , Ningjing Liu , Lukas J. van den Heuvel , Hans J.P. Marvin (2022).Automatic classification of literature in systematic reviews on food safety using machine learning.

[7]   JUAN P. TORRES 1, ANDRÉS CARO 1, MARÍA DEL MAR ÁVILA 1,TRINIDAD PÉREZ-PALACIOS2, TERESA ANTEQUERA2, AND PABLO GARCÍA RODRÍGUEZ1(2022).A Computer-Aided Inspection System to Predict Quality Characteristics in Food Technology.

[8]   Zhiyuan Zhua,b, Jiajia Duana,b, Zhenzhong Dai a,b, Yongzhong Fenga,b,*, Gaihe Yanga,b(2023).Seeking sustainable solutions for human food systems.

[9]   Tarini Naravane b,c, Ilias Tagkopoulos a,c,* (2023)Machine learning models to predict micronutrient profile in food after processing .

[10] Ivana Gjorshoska a,*, Tome Eftimov b, Dimitar Trajanov a,c (2022) .Missing value imputation in food composition data with denoising autoencoders.

[11] Tsega Y. Melessea*, Matteo Bollob, Valentina Di Pasqualea, Francesco Centrob, Stefano Riemmaa (2022) Machine Learning-Based Digital Twin for Monitoring Fruit Quality Evolution.

[12] Hassan Anwar a,*, Talha Anwar b, Shamas Murtaza a (2023) Review on food quality assessment using machine learning and electronic nose system .

A System for Voter Identification for Increase in Vote Percentage in General Elections

[1]Suyog C. Bhalerao, [1]Vrushabh A. Awathankar, [1]Rushikesh K. Pachade, [1]Bharat S. Puri, [1]Pravin S Choudhary, and [1]Amol P. Bhagat

[1]Department of Information Technology, Prof Ram Meghe College of Engineering and Management, Badnera, Amravati, Maharashtra, 444701, India.

Email: [1]bhaleraosuyog61@gmail.com, amol.bhagat84@gmail.com

Abstract— This paper explores a proposed system designed to enhance voter identification and increase voter turnout in general elections. The system integrates advanced biometric technologies and secure digital verification processes to ensure accurate voter registration and prevent fraud. By streamlining voter identification and minimizing barriers to participation, the system aims to boost voter engagement and ultimately increase election participation rates. The implementation of this system could provide a model for improving electoral integrity and inclusiveness.

Keywords— Voter Identification, Biometric Technology, Digital Verification, Voter Turnout, Election Integrity Voter Engagement, Electoral Participation, Fraud Prevention

I. INTRODUCTION

The digital voting system allows voters to cast their votes from anywhere, eliminating the need to visit physical polling stations. In a digital era which is marked by advancement of technology and as there are many aspects of our lives which are undergone the digital trans-formation so the traditional way of voting also need to be digitalized. Numerous voting pro-cedures, such as ballot paper and EVMs, are used in the voting process however, these meth-ods often require considerable time and manpower to address these drawbacks

We provide a web-based voting system where users/voter can register with their credentials upon approval by the admin, a voter ID is generated, granting them permission to vote. We have also implemented a 'Not Voted' module in the system, allowing us to send emails to reg-istered voters before elections so this module can raise awareness about the elections and po-tentially increase voter turnout. In our voting system, we've introduced an appeal module this module allows voters whose requests have been rejected by the administrator to send queries or documents to the administrator for review. If the administrator validates the user's query, the user can then log in to the system. Additionally, we've implemented the constituency model, which allows the administrator to add constituencies. Once a constituency is added, leaders are assigned to their respective parties and constituencies. During registration, voters must select their constituency, from which they will vote. After logging in, voters will be di-rected to the page displaying leaders from their selected constituency Afterward, voters will be able to cast their votes for their chosen leaders/parties. Once the vote is cast, a token will be generated, and the voted-for party will be displayed .Voters can only vote when the Start Election module is active. Once the voting is finished, the Start Election module will be deac-tivated, and the results will be generated through graph and we have also provided profile module so that user can update their credential over a particular time of period.

As in India Electronic Voting Systems are used in which voters availability is compulsory at their city so a digital way of voting is the solution for voters. Many of the countries have adopted the digital systems. This digital voting system eliminates the need of ballot papers, man power, centres which are allocated for voting. It can prevent form fraud and manipula-tion of votes with the help of this systems the immigrants cannot cast their votes. It can be efficient for the government of many countries if they centralized the digital way of voting . As per the journey of digital voting that this innovation has the potential to reshape the future of democracy. There are many complexities to build the system which is a efficient one and but there are many opportunities which will arise in future but behind the challenges there are much benefits of such systems. It will revolutionize the and streamline the voting process if some challenges which are related to it are resolved such as limited accessibility, availability of resources and the potential for human error in ballot counting, no tampering with the votes otherwise it can change the whole result of elections. These some mentioned problems need to be focused and should be resolved if the above problems are resolved and if the systems are centralized then they can change whole electoral process.

The Online Voting System such as Estonia's I -voting system, scytl, democracy live, secure voting are been developed and are adopted by the government of that countries so in future many countries are going to adopt online voting because it is the need of rapidly growing digital era.

II. LITERATURE REVIEW

The use of advanced security methods are necessary to introduced Online Voting System. In this Online Voting System Homomorphic encryption is used so that data(plaintext) is converted into ciphertext. To secure the privacy of the votes of voters every submitted ballot gets encrypted through the exponential ElGamal cryptosystem to ensure the integrity and confidentiality of the system. There is only one constraint in the system that we have to completely trust one authority without any assumption that system security is compromised [1].

This voting system focuses on whether the voter can vote from his/her preferred location from their devices. This voting system has two step authentication process which involves forwarding OTP on Mobile number and face recognition. It uses facial scanning system to capture the voters face before election to provide the utility during the voting process and using RFID tags instead of voter id. The devices such as Arduino UNO, LCD display, PUSH button are used. The proposed online voting system enables the voter to vote through offline or online mode. If voter choose to vote offline they must have the RFID tag which are issued by government [2].

Manual Voting system may lead to malpractices so manual voting system should change to digital voting system. This manages all configuration, test a web based casting a vote through ballot framework that encourages the individual voter who is qualified for casting a ballot. This voting system has been implemented using C#, Microsoft Azure, Microsoft SQL server 2012. The primary goal of this system that the software which is used should be trusted and secure. In this voter can vote only once as database will no accept more than one vote. This system requires large database support. In this module, components such as client, user registration, adding constituency, Login, Candidate list, Overseer are used. In this voting there is capacity to offer propelled casting a ballot framework to both in the nation and outside through web based ballot voting system [3].

In this voting system Blockchain Technology is used due to its decentralized nature and eliminating the need of centralized database or authority. Blockchain technology provides the feature of tamper proof distributed ledger is provided for ensuring authentication and integrity and it is not possible to manipulate tamper proof ballot system .Encryption scheme used RSA algorithm .The privacy or identity of voters will be hidden. So in the suggested Blockchain based voting system the process involves registering the voters, granting authorization for voting, encoding votes as a transaction, broadcasting votes, storing of votes into a created new block and then initiating the vote counting process. Therefore the proposed innovative model in Blockchain is used to create a secure, transparent and complete digital voting system. In this unique key pair is allocated to every individual. So this results in complete transparent system. Due to the use of existing Aadhaar infrastructure the implementation is viable [4].

So currently majority of countries in the world conduct their elections through use of Electronic Voting Machines. These machines enables digital voting by eliminating the need of paper ballot and minimizing the cost. As security is the major concerns so no voter should be allowed to vote twice. This problem can be resolve using Fingerprint based voting system an individual is authorized based on his fingerprint. The domain of this voting system IOT where voting system where Fingerprint Based Biometric Voting Machine is build using Arduino. Fingerprint module is the backbone of this system. The proposed work is to develop a client/server web application software architecture for e-voting. For matching the fingerprint pattern of the voter Fingerprint matching algorithm given Jian-De Zheng by minutiae method is used. The use of local database is must to enhance the voting process. The information related to voting process is stored in the database and user id of voter is encrypted using SHA-1 algorithm. Through the implementation of above methodologies a secure voting system based on fingerprint has been developed [5].

III. PROBLEM DEFINITION AND REQUIREMENT ANALYSIS

For a considerable period, the traditional voting system has consistently experienced a low voter turnout percentage. Due to time constraints and work commitments, voter often opt not to go to physical polling stations for voting. Overcrowded polling stations with long lines and excessive wait times can deter voter from voting. The main goal of the project is to develop a web-based voting system that enhances the voting process and raises the voter turnout. To achieve this, we will implement an email module to send messages to all registered voters before the start of elections.

To achieve Security: In our voting system, we aimed to improve security by combining the request module with a voter ID generation algorithm. When a voter registers, a request is sent to the admin after verifying the user's credentials, the admin can approve or reject the request upon approval, a voter ID is generated and sent via email, enabling the voter to log in. Additionally, we have implemented several validations in the signup form for instance, if a voter enters an Aadhar ID that already exists in the system, they will not be allowed to register.

To achieve Increase in Voting percentage: In this system, our goal is to increase the voter turnout percentage. To achieve this, we have implemented the 'Not Voted' module this module sends reminders via email to users who have registered with the system but have not yet voted in ongoing elections this approach aims to boost the voting percentage.

To achieve Convenience: In our voting system, we aimed to enhance convenience by designing a user-friendly interface. Since elections are conducted across multiple constituencies, we included a 'Select Your Constituency' option in the signup form. This allows users to register with their respective constituency. After logging in, users are directed to their constituency page, where they can view information about the leaders in their area. Additionally, we included a 'Profile' option on the voter dashboard, allowing users to update their credentials as needed. To achieve accuracy and efficiency: In this voting system, our aim was to ensure accuracy in election results once the voting for constituencies concludes, the results are generated in the form of a graph showing percentages, along with the total number of votes cast for each party. This approach enhances both accuracy and efficiency in the voting process.

IV. Proposed Approach and Design

The proposed system involves developing a web based voting system enabling voters to register with their credentials and they will be granted authorization to participate in voting process. The voting option will be accessible to the voter on the designated voting day, and once the voter has cast their vote, the voting option will no longer be visible and the objective of this system is to boost overall voter turnout in elections. The Frontend of this web based voting system will be constructed using Bootstrap and in backend Django(Python framework) with MySQL serving as database and this technology will be able to develop a robust voting system.

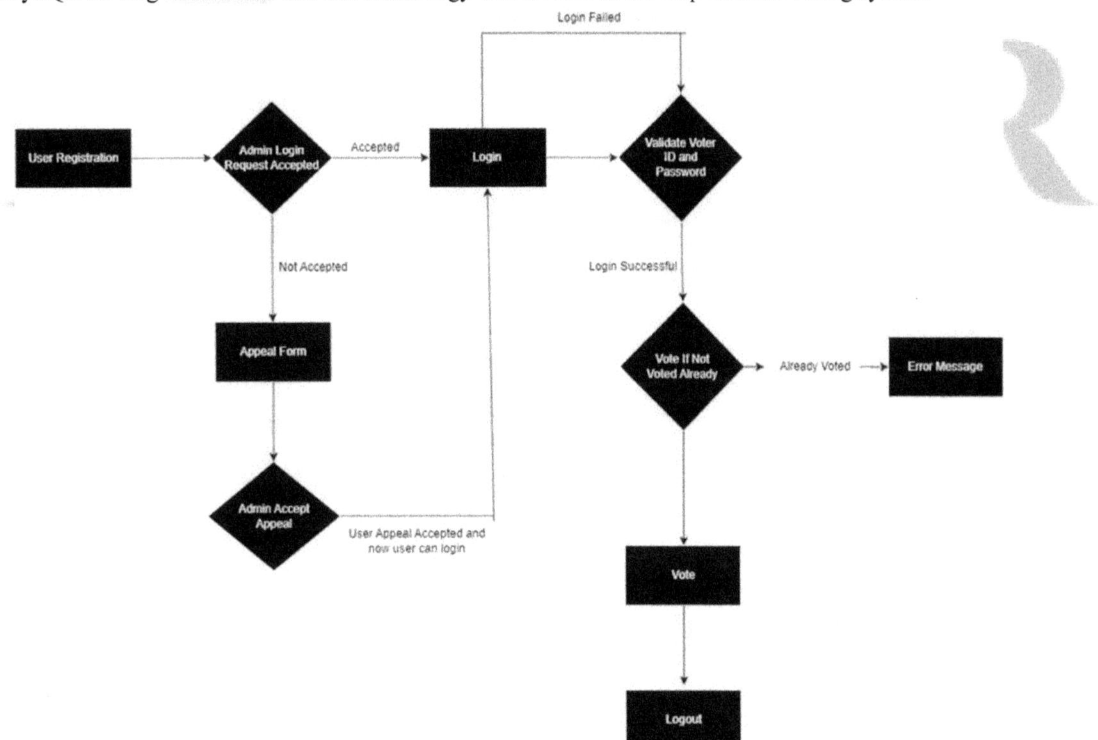

Fig. 64 : Activity Diagram

Login and Signup: Voters make use of both signup and login page while the admin solely utilizes the login page. After completing the signup process the voters can login and once logged in voter and admin are directed to separate dashboards.

Appeal: When the voters request is declined by the admin, the appeal module becomes accessible, allowing the voter to send a message and documents to the admin. If the appeal is approved, the user can proceed with the login.

Request: Upon signing up the voters request is forwarded to admin. If admin approves the request the ten digit voter id will be generated for voter, if the request is rejected by admin then voter request will be deleted.

Voting: The voting module allows voter to caste a single vote for their preferred party and once the vote is casted , the voting option will no longer will be visible so with the assistance of this module fraudulent voting can be prevented.

Graphs : Once the voting process concludes, a percentage-based graph will be generated to display the party that has secured the majority number of votes in the elections.

Email :This module is designed to dispatch the voter ID to individuals upon registration. Additionally, the email module will send a message to voters prior to the election day, thereby contributing to an increase in voter turnout.

Start Election: This module initiates the election process on the designated day, and it is exclusively accessible to the administrator, who holds the sole authority to access this module and activation of this module voter will be allowed to cast his/her vote to his preferred party.

Stop Election: Upon activation, this module grants the administrator the ability to halt the election process once it is completed. Subsequently, the voting option will no longer be visible to voters.

Constituency: In this module, it's possible to include multiple constituencies, enabling voters to sign up with their respective constituency. Upon logging in, voters will be directed to their designated constituency.

Add Leaders: This module will enable administrators to add leaders based on their constituency and assign them to their respective parties.

Token : This module activates when a voter successfully casts their vote. A token is then generated to confirm that the user/voter has voted, and the voted-for party is also displayed.

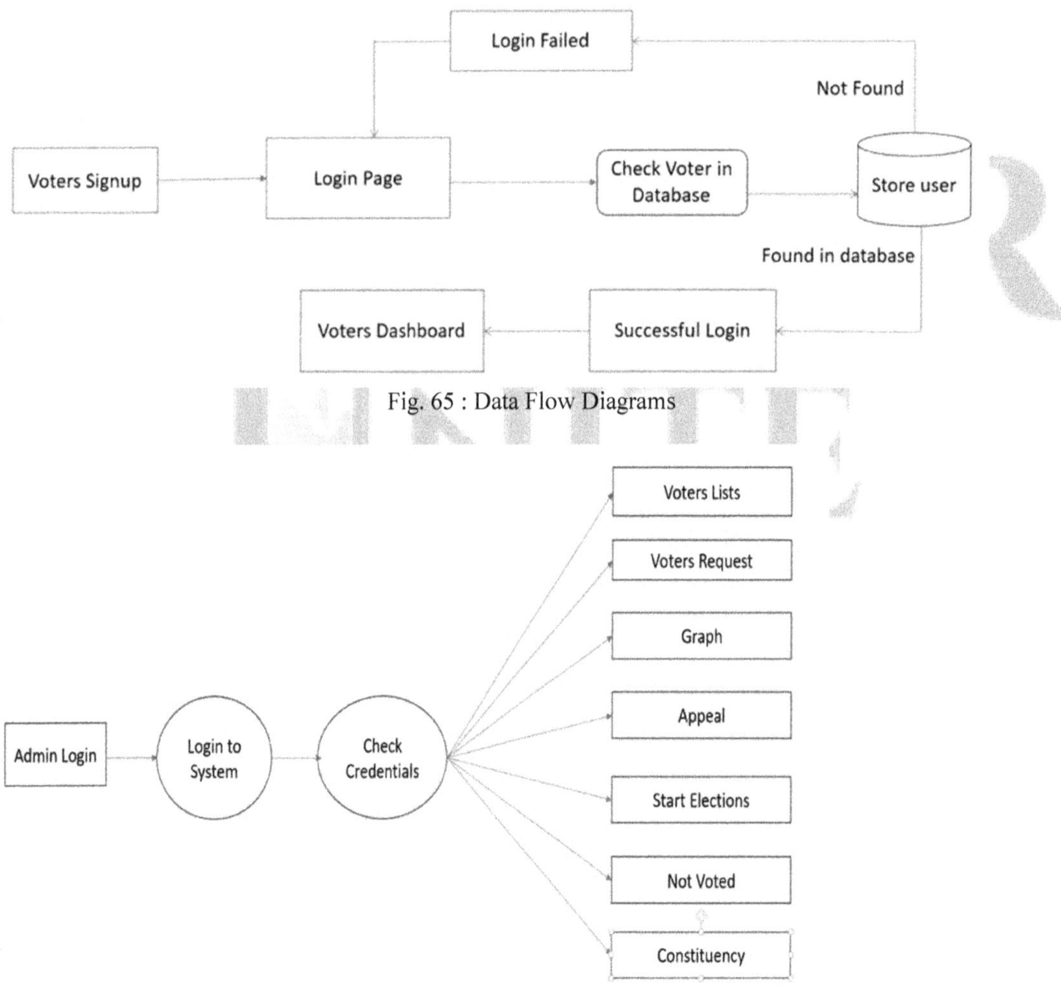

Fig. 65 : Data Flow Diagrams

Fig. 66 : Admin Level DFD

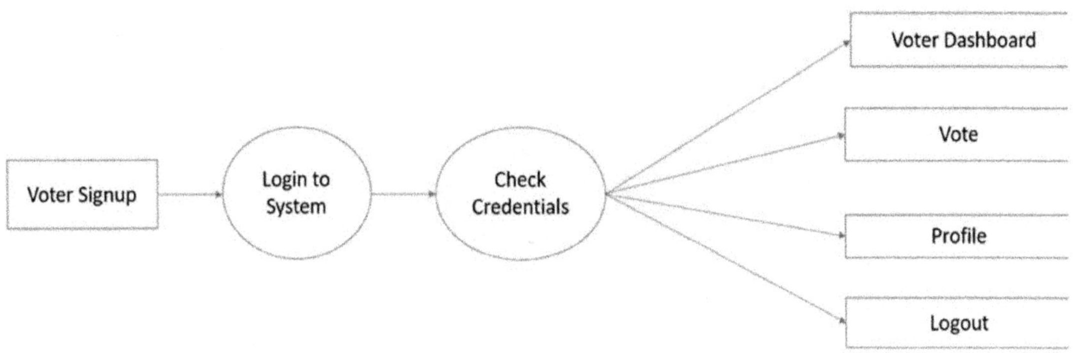

Fig. 67 : Second Level : Voter DFD

V. EXPERIMENTAL SETUP

1. Storage Drive:
a. Hard Drive (Minimum 32GB ; Recommended 64GB)
b. SSD Drive (Minimum 32GB ; Recommended 64GB

2. Memory(RAM): Minimum 2GB ; Recommended 4GB

3. Processor
a. Intel (Minimum 1.4 GHZ ; Recommended 2 GHZ)
b. AMD (Minimum 1.4 GHZ ; Recommended 2GHZ)

4. Internet Connection
a. Ethernet Connection
   OR
b. Wireless Connection
1. Wi-Fi 2.4 GHZ
2. Wi-Fi 5.0 GHZ

There are various software platforms which are used in this project which are as follows:
1. Database : MySQL Server
2. Framework : Django
3. Development Tools : Microsoft Visual Studio Community
4. Template : Bootstrap 5.0
5. Deployment Platform : Windows 11

VI. IMPLEMENTATION DETAILS

Bootstrap is an open-source front-end framework for web development. It was originally created by Twitter and is now maintained by a community of developers. Bootstrap provides a set of pre-designed, responsive, and customizable HTML, CSS, and JavaScript components and tools for building modern, mobile-first websites and web applications. Here are some key features and components of Bootstrap:

Grid System: Bootstrap includes a responsive grid system that helps developers create flexible and responsive layouts. It uses a 12-column grid, making it easy to create multi-column designs.

CSS Styles: Bootstrap comes with a set of CSS classes and styles that can be applied to elements on your web page to control things like typography, colors, spacing, and more.

Components: Bootstrap provides a wide variety of UI components such as buttons, forms, navigation bars, modals, alerts, tooltips, and more. These components are designed to be mobile-friendly and easy to customize.

JavaScript Plugins: Bootstrap includes several JavaScript plugins, like carousels, popovers, and modals, to enhance the functionality and user experience of your site.

Responsive Design: Bootstrap is designed to create responsive websites that automatically adjust to different screen sizes, from desktop monitors to mobile devices.

Carousel: Bootstrap includes a carousel component that you can use to create image sliders or carosels, allowing you to showcase multiple images or content in a rotating manner.

Django:-
Django is a high-level and open-source web framework for building robust, scalable, and maintainable web applications. It is written in Python and follows the Model-View-Controller (MVC) architectural pattern, although it refers to it as the Model-View-Template (MVT) pat-tern. Django is designed to make web development faster and more efficient by providing a comprehensive set of tools and libraries that handle common web development tasks, allow-ing developers to focus on building their applications.
Here's an introduction to some key features and concepts of Django:-
Database Abstraction:
Django provides an Object-Relational Mapping (ORM) system that abstracts database operations. You can define your data models in Python, and Django takes care of creating the corresponding database tables.
Admin Interface:
Django comes with a built-in admin panel that automatically generates an admin interface for your data models. This makes it easy to manage and manipulate your application's data.
URL Routing:
Django includes a URL dispatcher that helps in defining the URL patterns for your application. It allows you to map URLs to views, making it easy to handle different web requests.
Template Engine:
Django's template engine provides a powerful way to create dynamic and reusable HTML templates. It supports template inheritance and allows you to inject data into your templates.

Python :-
Python is a high-level, interpreted programming language known for its readability and versatility. It supports multiple programming paradigms, including procedural, object-oriented, and functional programming. Python is widely used in various fields such as web development, data analysis, artificial intelligence, scientific computing, and more. Its simplicity and readability make it an excellent choice for beginners and experienced developers.
Here are some key points about Python:
Interpreted: Python code is executed line by line by the Python interpreter, without the need for compilation.
Dynamic Typing: Python uses dynamic typing, allowing variables to be reassigned to different types.
Extensive Standard Library: Python comes with a large standard library that provides ready-to-use modules and packages for various tasks.
Open Source: Python is developed under an OSI-approved open-source license, which means it's free to use and distribute.
Community Support: Python has a large and active community that contributes to its development, provides libraries, and offers support through forums and online resources.
Frameworks and Libraries: Python has many frameworks and libraries that extend its functionality, such as Django and Flask for web development, NumPy and pandas for data analysis, TensorFlow and PyTorch for machine learning, and many more.
Cross-Platform: Python code can run on various operating systems, including Windows, macOS, and Linux, without modification.
Version Compatibility: There are two major versions of Python in use today, Python
General-Purpose: Python is a versatile language used for web development, data analysis, artificial intelligence, scientific computing, and more.

```
mysql> desc Tbl_Users;
+-------------+-------------+------+-----+---------+----------------+
| Field       | Type        | Null | Key | Default | Extra          |
+-------------+-------------+------+-----+---------+----------------+
| User_Id     | int         | NO   | PRI | NULL    | auto_increment |
| Full_Name   | varchar(30) | NO   |     | NULL    |                |
| Email_Id    | varchar(50) | NO   |     | NULL    |                |
| Phone       | varchar(10) | NO   |     | NULL    |                |
| Aadhar_Id   | varchar(12) | NO   |     | NULL    |                |
| Voter_Id    | varchar(10) | NO   |     | NULL    |                |
| status      | int         | NO   |     | NULL    |                |
| Password    | varchar(30) | NO   |     | NULL    |                |
| Voting_Score| int         | NO   |     | NULL    |                |
+-------------+-------------+------+-----+---------+----------------+
9 rows in set (0.02 sec)
```

Fig. 68 : Table Users

When a user/voter signs up with their credentials in the system, their data is stored in the database mentioned above. This table is essential for validating the information, and the voter ID is stored only after the admin approves the request or generates the voter ID.

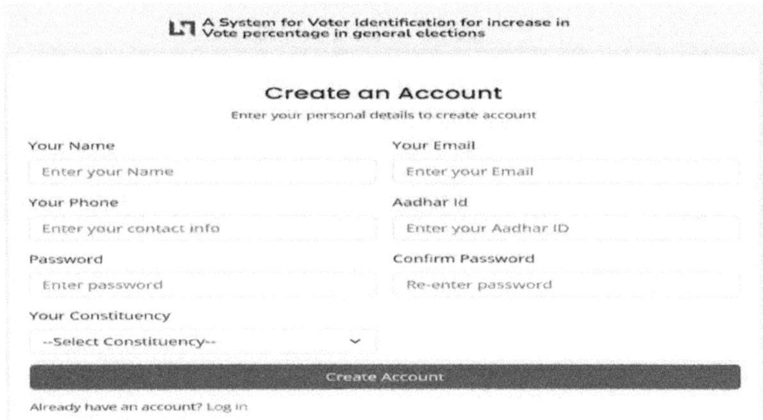

Fig. 69: Signup Page

So this is the signup page where user can give their credentials and the users data will be stored in the database and if data is correct then signup is successful.

Fig. 70: Login Page

This login page is utilized by both Voters and admins. Voters can log in only after their request is approved by the admin. Admins, on the other hand, can directly log in to the system and perform tasks related to users.

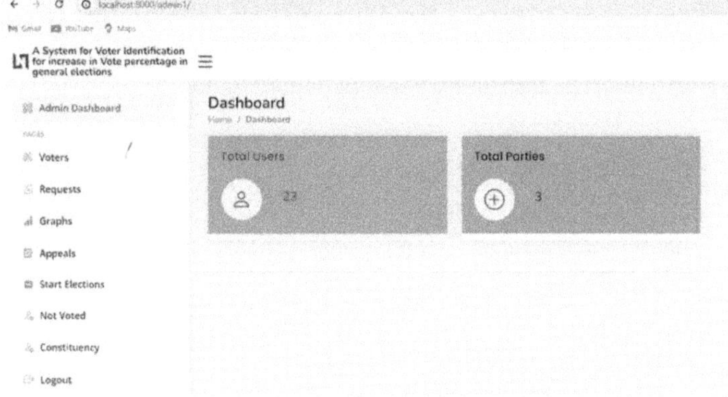

Fig. 71: Admin Dashboard

After the admin successfully logs in using their credentials, they will be directed to the admin dashboard here, they can manage voter activities, including handling requests, appeals, the voter list, declaring results, and more.

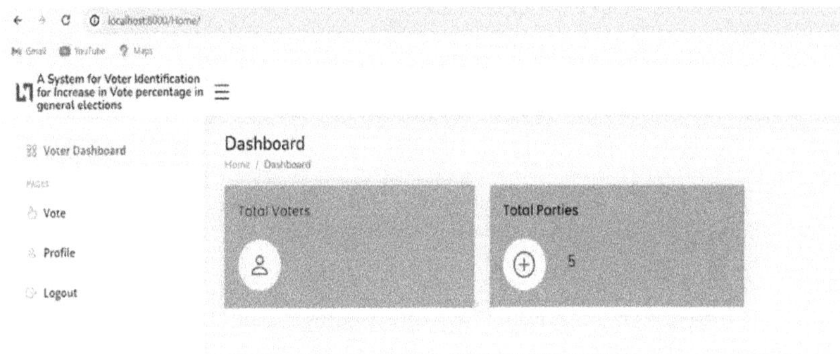

Fig. 72: Voter Dashboard

After successfully logging into the system, the voter will be directed to the dashboard above. Here, they can create or edit their profile more efficiently, or they can vote for their preferred party when the elections are ongoing.

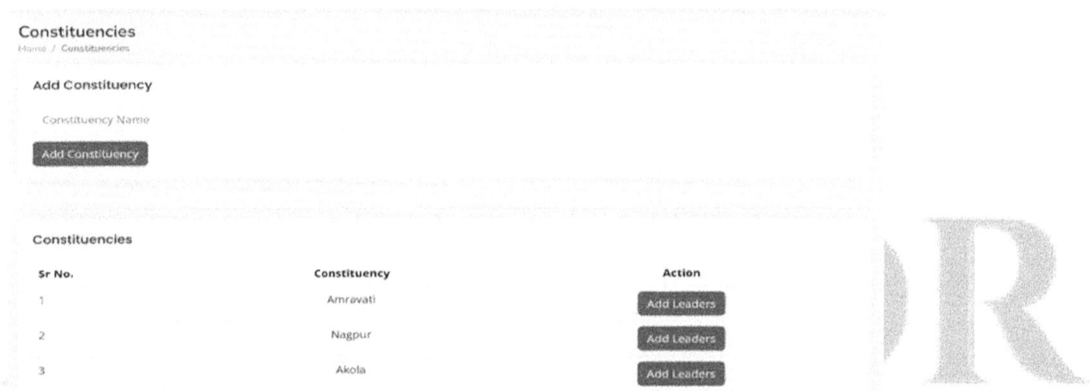

Fig. 73: Constituency Dashboard

This page allows the administrator to add as many constituencies as needed. After adding a constituency, the admin will be directed to add leaders. The admin can then add leaders according to their respective parties.

Fig. 74: Add Leaders Dashboard

This page enables the addition of leaders based on their constituencies and respective parties. After adding leaders, when users log in, they will be directed to the leaders of their constituency.

VII.   CONCLUSION

In conclusion, in this project we have learned about the workings of a digital voting system and its numerous benefits, such as improving efficiency and accuracy. With this system, re-sults can be declared much faster. We have developed an algorithm for generating voter IDs, which creates a ten-digit EPIC number. Additionally, we have implemented a graph module that generates results after the election, as well as an appeal module that allows users to com-municate with the admin if their request is rejected, providing a platform to explain their que-ries. To increase voter turnout, we have also implemented a 'Not Voted' module, which sends emails to voters before elections to raise awareness about the upcoming election all of the mentioned activities or modules have been successfully implemented in our project.

REFERENCES

[1]   Xuechao Yang, Xun Yi, Surya Nepal, Andrei Kelarev, and Fengling Han, "A Secure Verifiable Ranked Choice Online Voting System Based on Homomorphic Encryption", IEEE Access, VOLUME 6, Page 20506- 20519, 2018.

[2]   Ganesh Prabhu S, Nizarahammed.A, Prabu.S, Raghul.S, R.R.Thirrunavukkarasu, P. Jayarajan, "Smart Online Voting System." In 2021 7th International Conference on Advanced Computing and Communication Systems (ICACCS), IEEE,2021

[3]   Ramya Govindaraj, Kumaresan P, K.Sree Harshitha, "Online Voting System Using Cloud." In 2020 International Conference on Emerging Trends in Information Technology and Engineering (ic-ETITE), IEEE, 2020

[4]   Harsh Jain, Rajvardhan Oak, Jay Bansal, "Towards Developing a Secure and Robust Solution for E-Voting using Blockchain." In 2019 International Conference on Nascent Technologies in Engineering (ICNTE 2019), IEEE, 2019

[5]   Khadija Hasta, Aditya Date, Aparna Shrivastava, Prajakta Jhade, S. N. Shelke, "Fingerprint Based Secured Voting", In 2019 International Conference On Advances in Computing, Communication and Control (ICAC3), IEEE, 2019

[6]   Warish Patel, Monal Patel, Bhupendra Ramani, "A Review of Online Voting System Security based on Cryptography", VOLUME 9, Page 155-161, International Journal of Engineering Research & Technology (IJERT), ICACT – 2021

[7]   Vairam T, Sarathambekai S, Balaji R, "Blockchain based Voting system in Local Network." In 2021 7th International Conference on Advanced Computing & Communication Systems (ICACCS), IEEE, 2021

[8]   S.JEHOVAH JIREH ARPUTHAMONI, Dr.A.GNANA SARAVANAN, "Online Smart Voting System Using Biometrics Based Facial and Fingerprint Detection on Image Processing and CNN." In 2021 Third International Conference on Intelligent Communication Technologies and Virtual Mobile Networks (ICICV), IEEE ,2021

[9]   Awsan A. H. Othman, Emarn A. A. Muhammed, Haneen K. M. Mujahid, Hamzah A. A. Muhammed, "Online Voting System Based on IoT and Ethereum Blockchain." In 2021 International Conference of Technology, Science and Administration (ICTSA), IEEE,2021

[10]   Shifa Manaruliesya Anggriane, Surya Michrandi Nasution, Fairuz Azm, Advanced E-Voting System Using Paillier Homomorphic Encryption Algorithm, In 2016 International Conference on Informatics and Computing (ICIC), IEEE, 2016

[11]

[12]   Karishma Varshney , Rahul Johari , R. L. Ujjwal, "Remote Online Voting System using Aneka Platform." In 2018 7th International Conference on Reliability, Infocom Technologies and Optimization (Trends and Future Directions) (ICRITO) , IEEE, 2018

[13]   Ch.sai pratap varma ,D.sumanth Rahul, Jithina Jose, B Keerthi Samhitha. Suja Cherukullapurath Mana, "Aadhar Card Verification Base Online Polling" In 2020 4th International Conference on Trends in Electronics and Informatics (ICOEI), IEEE,2020

[14]   Smita B. Khairnar, P. Sanyasi Naidu, Reena Kharat, "Secure Authentication for Online Voting System" In 2018 2016 International Conference on Computing Communication Control and automation (ICCUBEA), IEEE.

Online Book Recommendation System For College Library

[1]Yogesh J. Ingole, [1]Tarun R. Takhtani, [1]Gayatri V. Deshmukh, [1]Kalyani A. Malekar, [1]Rajratna G. Kamble, [1]Priti A. Khodke, and [1]Amol P. Bhagat

[1]Department of Information Technology, Prof Ram Meghe College of Engineering and Management, Badnera, Amravati, Maharashtra, 444701, India.

Email: yogeshingole2002@gmail.com, amol.bhagat84@gmail.com

Abstract— In this project, we developed Online Book Recommendation system. We proposed TrustSVD, a trust-based matrix factorization technique for recommendations. TrustSVD integrates multiple information sources into the recommendation model to reduce the data sparsity and cold start problems and their degradation of recommendation performance. An analysis of social trust data from four real-world data sets suggests that not only the explicit but also the implicit influence of both ratings and trust should be taken into consideration in a recommendation model. TrustSVD therefore builds on recommendation algorithm, SVD++ (which uses the explicit and implicit influence of rated items), by further incorporating both the explicit and implicit influence of trusted and trusting users on the prediction of items for an active user. The proposed technique is the first to extend SVD++ with social trust information. Experimental results on the four data sets demonstrate that TrustSVD achieves better accuracy than other ten counterparts' recommendation techniques.
Keywords— Book, TrustSVD, prediction, Recommendation

I. Introduction

Now-a-days, online rating and reviews are playing an important role in books sales. Readers are buying books depend on the reviews and ratings by the others. Recommender system focuses on the reviews and ratings by the others and filters books. In this paper, TrustSVD technique is used to boost our recommendations. The technique used by recommender systems is matrix factorization. This technique filters information by collecting data from other users. The ratings of those items by the users who have rated both items determine the similarity of the items. The similarity of users is determined by the similarity of the ratings given by the users to an item. The required dataset for the training and testing of our model is downloaded from Good-Reads website. Matrix Factorization technique such as Truncated-SYD which takes sparse matrix of dataset is used for reduction of features.

These are the key points which are used in this project. Our project revolves around TrustSVD, a form of matrix dactorization employed in collaborative filtering. Collaborative filtering predicts user perferences by analyzing the preferences of other users, while TrustSVD enhances this by incorporating trust relationships between users.

TrustSVD:

TrustSVD, a trust-based matrix factorization technique for recommendations. Trust SVD integrates multiple information sources into the recommendation model in order to reduce the data sparsity and cold start problems and their degradation of recommendation performance. TrustSVD model is built on top of a state-of-the-art model known as SVD++ proposed by Koren (2008). The rationale behind SVD++ is to take into consideration user/item biases and the influence of rated items other than user/item-specific vectors on rating prediction. Formally, the rating for user u on item j is predicted by

Where bu bj represent the user and item biases, respectively; μ is the global average rating; and yj denotes the implicit in fluence of items rated by user u in the past on the rating of unknown items in the future. Thus, user u's feature vector can be also represented by the set of items she rated, and finally modelled as (pu + llul-2l'iEluyi) rather than simply as pu. Koren (2008) has shown that integrating implicit influence of ratings can well improve predictive accuracy. Previously, we have stressed the importance of trust influence for better recommendations, and its potential to be generalized to trust-alike relationships. Hence, we can enhance the trust- unaware SVD++ model by incorporating trust influence. Specifically, the implicit effect of trusted users on item ratings can be considered in the same manner as rated items.

1) Matrix Factorization:

Matrix factorization is a way to generate latent features when multiplying two different kinds of entities. Collaborative filtering is the application of matrix factorization to identify the relationship between items and users entities. With the input of users' ratings on the shop items, we would like to predict how the users would rate the items so the users can get the recommendation based on the prediction. Matrix Factorization is a technique to discover the latent factors from the ratings matrix and to map the items and the users against those factors.

Consider a ratings matrix R with ratings by n users form items. The ratings matrix R will have n x m rows and columns. Matrix Factorization is a significant approach in many applications. Curse of dimensionality is a phenomenon which occurs in high dimensional space that hardly occur in lower dimensional space. Due to higher number of dimension model gets sparse. Higher dimensional space causes problem in clustering (becomes very difficult to separate one cluster data from another), search space increases, complexity of model increases.

2) Collaborative Filtering:

Collaborative filtering is a technique used in online book recommendation system to generate recommendation based on the preferences and behavior of similar users. It works by analyzing user interactions and feedback, such as rating or purchases, to identify patterns and recommend items that other users with similar tastes have liked. This approach done not rely on explicit item attributes or user profiles but instead leverages the collective wisdom of the user community to make personalized recommendations.

II. LITERATURE REVIEW

S. Gopal Krishna Patro, et.al. (2023) [1] reviews in their paper, when a new customer enters the spectrum of the E-Commerce system, the informative records and dataset, such as about the new user, purchasing history and other browsing data become insufficient, resulting in the emergence of one serious issue such as a Cold start problem (CSP). Furthermore, when the interaction among the product items becomes limited, a new problem such as Sparsity arises to handle such problems in E-Commerce system, An extensive and hybridized methodological approach is designed named as Cold start and sparsity aware hybridized recommendation system (CSSHRS), to reduce the Sparsity of dataset as well as to overcome the cold start problem in the recommendation framework. The proposed CSSHRS technique has been predicted by using the dataset of Last. FM, and Book-Crossing resulted in Mean absolute percentage error (MAPE) of 37%, recalls 0.07, precision 0.18, Normalized Discounted Cumulative Gain (NDCD) 0.61, and F-measure 0.1. This article proves the proposed CSSHRS technique as an effective and efficient hybrid of RS against the issue of data sparsity as well as CSP.

Noemi Mauro, et.al. (2022) [2] proposed current recommender systems employ item-centric properties to estimate ratings and present the results to the user. However, recent studies highlight the fact that the stages of item fruition also involve extrinsic factors, such as the interaction with the service provider before, during and after item selection. In other words, a holistic view of consumer experience, including local properties of items, as well as consumers' perceptions of item fruition, should be adopted to enhance user awareness and decision-making. In this work, the recommender systems have integrated with service models to reason about the different stages of item fruition. By exploiting the Service Journey Maps to define service-based item and user profiles, A novel family of recommender systems that evaluate items by taking preference management and overall consumer experience into account. Moreover, A two-level visual model to provide users with different information about recommendation results. the higher level summarizes consumer experience about items and supports the identification of promising suggestions within a possibly long list of results. the lower level enables the exploration of detailed data about the local properties of items. In a user test instantiated in the home-booking domain, Standard Recommender system compared the models. The service-based algorithms that only use item fruition experience excel in the ranking and minimize the error in rating estimation. Moreover, the combination of data about item fruition experience and item properties achieves slightly lower recommendation performance; however, it enhances users' perceptions of the awareness and the decision-making support provided by the system. These results encourage the adoption of service-based models to summarize user preferences and experience in recommender systems.

Taushif Anwar et.al. (2020) [3] proposed reading is a fundamental skill that every person needs to expand throughout his/her lifetime. Book recommendation for eLearning systems can gain more attention in digital libraries, commercial websites and social media sites. Nowadays, obtaining the preferred book in real-time becomes a challenging task. Because there are too many books available online and offline, this colossal number creates a dilemma for the enduser, especially for ebook learners. The book recommendation helps overcome the information overhead problem and through this, the user can quickly get books according to need within the shortest span of time. This paper proposes a Book recommendation system for eLearning using collaborative filtering and sequential pattern mining to serve individual requirements. Current writing also focuses on various similarity techniques, namely Cosine, Euclidean, Correlation, Manhattan and Jaccard. The accuracy of the Book Recommendation for eLearning is evaluated by applying precision, recall and Fl Score. In the end, results show that correlation-based Sequential pattern mining gives a better Fl Score.

Jiabei Li et.al. (2020) [4] proposed aiming at the problems of cold start, data sparseness, and similarity calculation bias in collaborative filtering algorithms, this paper proposes an interest- based university book recommendation algorithm. This algorithm solves the problem of the lack of scoring and the inability to use the collaborative filtering algorithm. At the same time, the combination of popularity and inverse popularity with similarity is considered to be closer to readers' behavioral characteristics. Experiments show that the algorithm is better than the traditional collaborative filtering recommendation algorithm, and has certain recommendation effect and practical value in the application of university libraries.

Madhuri kommineni, et.al. (2020) [5] Recommender system is a new generation of internet tool that helps users to access the web and receive information about their preferences. Using an online recommender is comparatively an easy and faster procedure to purchase items and this is done quickly. Recommendation systems plays an indispensable role in ecommerce websites to help users in identifying the right goods. One of the best methods to increase profits and attract customers is a recommendation process. The existing methodologies allow the systems to collect the irrelevant data and lead to a downfall in attracting the users and completing their work in a quick and reliable way. This paper provides an overview of the Recommendation Systems that is currently employed in the operations of the online book shopping domain. This paper proposes a simple understandable system for book. recommendations that help readers to suggest the right book, which is to be studied next. In recent years, information analysis challenge has been focused on for the administration recommendation system. For clients, network assets are completely linked and quickly developed. The proposed method works on training, feedback, management, reporting, configuration, and using it to offer useful information to the user in order to aid in decision- making and data item recommendations. This paper used a User Based Collaborative Filtering (UBCF) approach and measured the performance of similarity measures in recommending books to a user. The proposed system's overall architecture is introduced and its implementation is represented with a model design.

III. PROBLEM DEFINITION

Recommending books using Machine learning algorithm is the main goal of this project. Books are recommended by the clustering model and we are going to train and build using various features such as user's rating, book description, book titles etc. The system groups users into clusters so that each data point within cluster is similar and dissimilar to the data point in the other cluster. The system we wanted to develop was also able to find an average rating for each cluster and it was going to find top rated books of users from each cluster. All these books shortlisted by our system were used for training our model in future. The prediction model needed to be trained in order to produce better results.

Software Requirements: -
- Operating System: Windows 10/11
- Coding Language: Java
- Frontend: HTML, CSS, JavaScript
- Framework: Java Servlet Page
- Database: MySQL

Hardware Requirements:
- Processor: Inteli3
- SSD: 256GB
- RAM:4GB

The Aim of the proposed project is to design and develop online book recommendation system for college library.

Objectives to be achieved:
- To study existing online book recommendation system.
- To identify features for the online book recommendation system.
- To provide the best suggestion to the user by analysing the user's interest.
- To make easier for users to find the right reference according to user needs.
- To create a machine learning model to recommend relevant books to users based on popularity and user interests.

IV. PROPOSED APPROACH

We proposed a book trust-based recommendation model regularized with user trust and item ratings, termed as TrustSVD. Our approach builds on top of a state of-the-art model SVD++ through which both the explicit and implicit influence of user-item ratings are involve generating predictions. In addition, we further consider the influence of trust users (including trustees and trusters) on the rating prediction for an active user. This ensures that user specific vectors can be learn from their trust information even if a few or no ratings are given. In this way, the concerned issues can be better alleviated. Therefore, both explicit and implicit influences of item ratings and user trust will be considered in our model, indicating its novelty. In addition, a weighted-regularization technique is used to help avoid over-fitting for model learning. The experimental results on the data sets demonstrate that our approach works significantly better than other trust-based counterparts as well as other ratings-only high-performing models (ten approaches in total) in terms of predictive accuracy and is more capable of coping with the cold-start situations. There are two main recommendation tasks in recommender systems, namely item recommendation and rating prediction. Most algorithmic approaches are only (or best) designed for either one of the recommendations tasks, and our work focus on the rating prediction task.

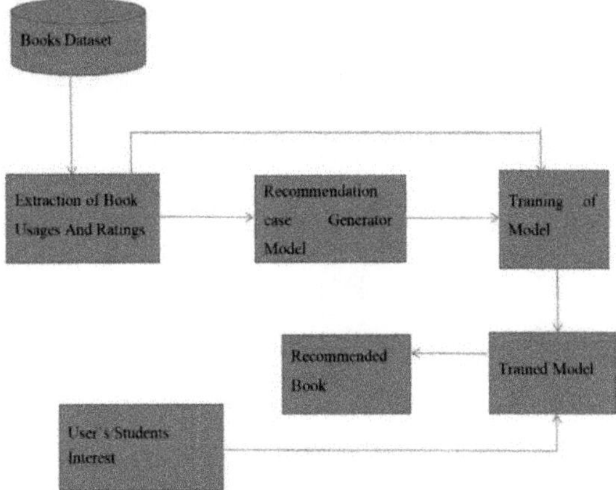

Fig. 75 : System Architecture

1) Login & Registration: For both the guest and the agent, this stage involves login and enlistment. By preserving separate documents for each customer, the subtleties of the client are keep classified. The expert can only see the subtleties of the enlisted guest concurrently.

2) User login : In an online book recommendation system, user login serves to authenticate users, personalize recommendations based on their preferences and reading history, enable social features, track bookmarks and history, and allow users to manage their profiles and preferences. The system associate' s user actions with their accounts, allowing for a more tailored and engaging experience.

3) Admin Login: For an online book recommendation system, the admin login information typically includes a username and password combination. This information is used to access the administrative dashboard or backend of the system, where administrators can manage user accounts, monitor system performance, update book databases, and configure system settings. It's crucial to ensure that the admin login credentials are securely stored and only accessible to authorized personnel to prevent unauthorized access to sensitive system functions and data.

4) User Details :In this module, User details are crucial for managing accounts, ensuring content quality, analysing user behaviour, providing customer support, and maintaining system security and compliance.

5) Book Details: From an administrator's perspective in an online book recommendation system, the profound significance of book details lies in their role as the life blood of the system. These details are not mere data points but the essence that empowers content curation, shaping the narrative of user experiences. Beyond algorithmic considerations, they serve as custodians of literary diversity, influencing cultural landscapes. Administrators wield book details not just as metadata, but as conduits to foster meaningful connections between readers and a vast literary universe. The nuanced understanding of these details equips administrators to orchestrate a harmonious symphony of content, curating a space where exploration and discovery transcend mere transactions, creating an immersive literary ecosystem.

6) User Rating :From an administrative standpoint in an online book recommendation system, user ratings serve as a pivotal metric for discerning user preferences. Admins utilize this data to refine recommendation algorithms, optimizing the platform's content curation to align with the diverse tastes of readers. By analysing user ratings, administrators gain valuable insights into the effectiveness of the recommended books, allowing for informed decisions on content enhancement and system optimization. The formal interpretation of user ratings contributes to a more sophisticated and personalized recommendation ecosystem, fostering a curated literary environment that resonates with the preferences of the user community.

7) Rating Prediction: In this module, we developed the option of providing the Rating by the User. In this Rating Prediction a user could rate the items shown to them using a star Pattern. The interactions

of the Social Network determined whether a user would connect with another user (i.e., link prediction) or be interested in a target item.

8) Database: In this project, Database is bridge to MySQL query browser. The MySQL query browser is a tool used to interact with MySQL databases through a graphical interface. For a recommendation system, you can use it to query and analyse data related to user preferences, item attributes, and past interactions to generate recommendations. It allows you to write and execute SQL queries efficiently, making it a valuable tool for building and optimizing recommendation algorithms. The predicted results show that this model is better at link prediction than rating prediction.

9) Book Recommendation: In this module, we develop the Book Recommendation. Generally, A social rating network a user can add other users as trusted friends and thus form a social network. Trust is not symmetric; for example, users ul trusts u3 but u3 does not specify user u1 as trustworthy. Besides, users can rate a set of items using a number of rating values, e.g., A star rating system from 1 to 5.

V. EXPERIMENTAL SETUP

1. Storage Drive:
a. Hard Drive (Minimum 32GB ; Recommended 64GB)
b. SSD Drive (Minimum 32GB ; Recommended 64GB

2. Memory(RAM): Minimum 2GB ; Recommended 4GB
3. Processor
a. Intel (Minimum 1.4 GHZ ; Recommended 2 GHZ)
b. AMD (Minimum 1.4 GHZ; Recommended 2GHZ)
4. Internet Connection
a. Ethernet Connection OR
b. Wireless Connection
1. Wi-Fi 2.4 GHZ
2. Wi-Fi 5.0 GHZ

There are various software platforms which are used in this project which are as follows:
1. Database: MySQL Server
2. Framework: NETBEANS
3. Development Tools: NETBEANS
4. Deployment Platform: Windows 11

VI. IMPLEMENTATION DETAILS

1) Algorithm:Matrix Factorization technique:

Matrix factorization is a class of collaborative filtering algorithms used in recommender systems. Matrix factorization algorithms work by decomposing the user-item interaction matrix into the product of two lower dimensionality rectangular matrices.

2) TrustSVD Model:

TrustSVD technique is used to boost our recommendations. The technique used by recommender systems is matrix factorization. This technique filters information by collecting data from other users. The ratings of those items by the users who have rated both items determine the similarity of the items

3) Collaborative filtering:

Collaborative filtering is a technique used in online book recommendation system to generate recommendation based on the preferences and behavior of similar users. It works by analyzing user interactions and feedback, such as rating or purchases, to identify patterns and recommend items that other users with similar tastes have liked. This approach done not rely on explicit item attributes or user profiles but instead leverages the collective wisdom of the user community to make personalized recommendations.

1) System Construction

• In the first module, we construct social rating based system construction module for the implementation of our proposed model. In this module we design to have widely used to provide users with high-quality personalized recommendations from a large volume of choices. Robust and accurate recommendations are important in e-commerce operations (e.g., navigating product offerings, personalization, improving customer satisfaction), and in marketing (e.g.,tailored advertising, segmentation, cross-selling). In this system we focus on user-item ratings, Item Rating Prediction, user can recommend a item to their friends.

• In this module, we develop the basic features of Online Social Networking system module. We build up the system with the feature of Online Social Networking. Where, this module is used for new user registrations and after registrations the users can login with their authentication.

• Where users can also share post with others. The user can able to search the other user profiles and public posts. In this module users can also accept and send friend requests.

• With all the basic feature of Online Social Networking System modules is build up in the initial module, to prove and evaluate our system features. In addition we develop this module by that the users can provide the Ratings.

2) *Rating Prediction*

• In this module, we develop the option of providing the Rating by the Social User. In this Rating Prediction a user can rating the items it shows in star based model. The interactions of group memberships determine if a user will connect with another user (i.e.,link prediction) or be interested in a target item. However, the empirical results show that this model is better at link prediction than rating prediction.

• The most popular and widely studied recommendation models are matrix factorization based models which aim to factorize the user item rating matrix into two low-rank user-feature and item feature matrices. Then the predictions can be generated by the inner products of user- and item-specific latent feature vectors.

• Although a user's rating to a certain item is mainly determined by the intrinsic attributes (or properties, features) of the item in question and how she appreciates these features, some extrinsic attributes may also have a non-negligible influence on the user's ratings. In this work, we focus on the influence of social trust in rating prediction, i.e., the influence of trust neighbors on an active user's rating for a specific item, a.k.a. social influence.

Recommendations

• In this module, we develop the Item Recommendation. Generally, in social rating networks a user can label (add) other users as trusted friends and thus form a social network. Trust is not symmetric; for example, users u1 trusts u3 but u3 does not specify user u1 as trustworthy. Besides, users can rate a set of items using a number of rating values, e.g., integers from 1 to 5. These items could be products, movies, music, etc. of interest.

• The recommendation problem in this work is to predict the rating that a user will give to an unknown item, for example, the value that user u3 will give to item i3, based on both a user-item rating matrix and a user trust matrix. Other well-recognized recommendation problems include for example top-N item recommendation.

• In this module first mathematically define the recommendation problem in social rating networks, and then introduce the TrustSVD model.

• In the cold-start situations where users may have only rated a few items, the decomposition of trust matrix can help to learn more reliable user-specific latent feature vectors than ratings-only matrix factorization. In the extreme case where there are no ratings at all for some users, ensures that the user-specific vector can be trained and learned from the trust matrix. In this regard, incorporating trust in a matrix factorization model can alleviate the cold start problem. By considering both explicit and implicit influence of trust rather than either one, our model can better utilize trust to further mitigate the data sparsity and cold start issues

1) *Java: -*

Java technology is both a programming language and a platform.

2) *The Java Programming Language*

The Java programming language is a high-level language that can be characterized by all of the following buzzwords:

1. Simple
2. Architecture neutral
3. Object oriented
4. Portable
5. Distributed
6. High performance
7. Interpreted
8. Multithreaded
9. Robust
10. Dynamic
11. Secure

With most programming languages, you either compile or interpret a program so that you can run it on your computer. The Java programming language is unusual in that a program is both compiled and interpreted. With the compiler, first you translate a program into an intermediate language called Java byte codes -the platform-independent codes interpreted by the interpreter on the Java platform. The interpreter parses and runs each Java byte code instruction on the computer. Compilation happens just once; interpretation occurs each time the program is executed. The following figure illustrates how this works.

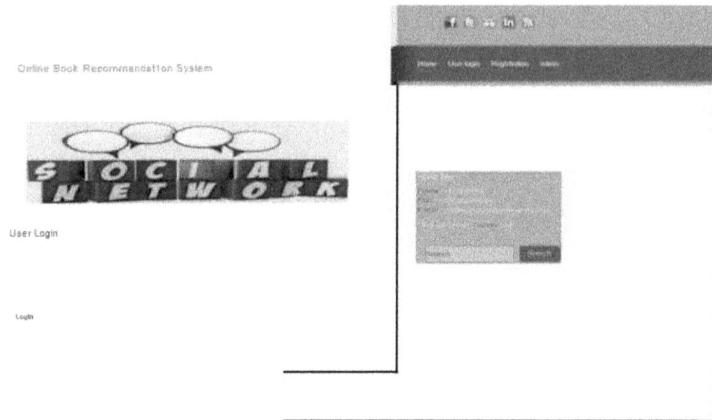

Fig. 76 : user login page in an online book recommendation system

In an online book recommendation system, user login serves to authenticate users, personalize recommendations based on their preferences and reading history, enable social features, track bookmarks and history, and allow users to manage their profiles and preferences. The system associate's user actions with their accounts, allowing for a more tailored and engaging expenence.

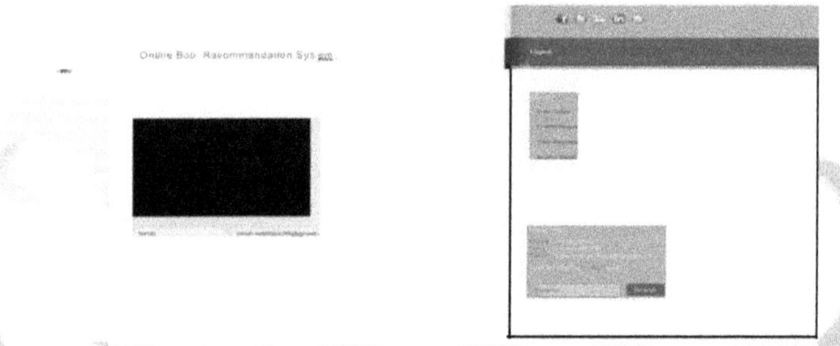

Fig. 77 personalized profile page in an online book recommendation system

Each user can create a personalized profile that includes their academic interests, preferred genres, and reading history. This profile helps our system understand their preferences and recommend books accordingly.

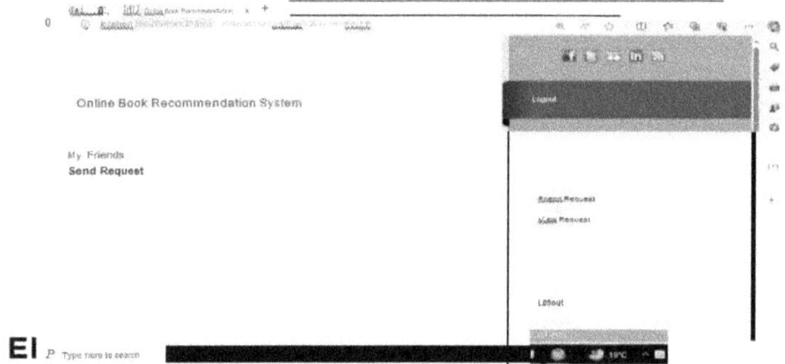

Fig. 78 User Interface profile page in an online book recommendation system

Designing a user interface for an online book recommendation system for a college library requires careful consideration of user needs, ease of navigation, and visual appeal.

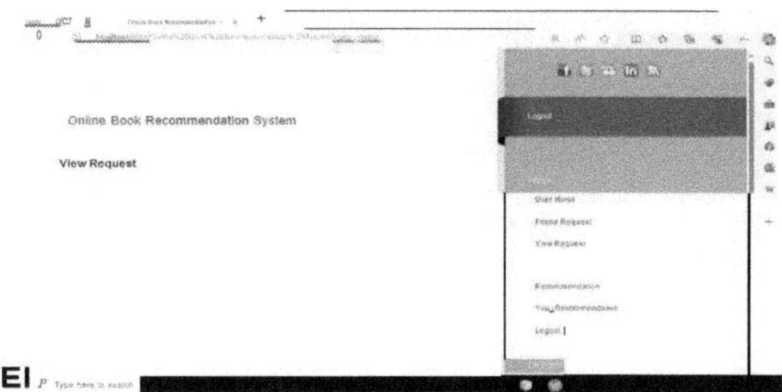

Fig. 79 Friend Request profile page in an online book recommendation system

Users can send friend requests to connect with other members of the library community .Requests are sent through user profiles or directly from book recommendation pages. Pending requests are displayed in the user's profile for easy management.

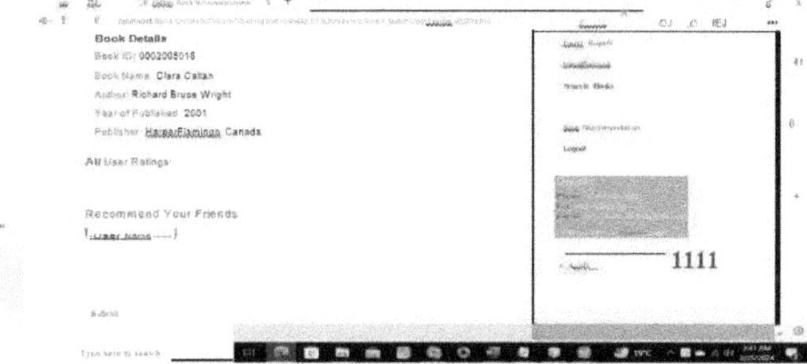

Fig. 80 Recommended profile page in an online book recommendation system

Utilizes algorithms to suggest books based on user preferences, borrowing history, and ratings.Offers personalized recommendations tailored to individual users' academic interests and reading habits.Encourages exploration of new topics and authors, fostering continuous learning and discovery.

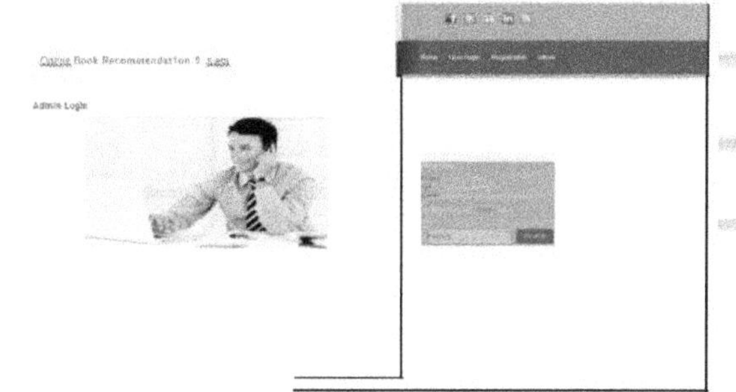

Fig. 81 admin login profile page in an online book recommendation system

For an online book recommendation system, the admin login information typically includes a username and password combination. This information is used to access the administrative dashboard or backend of the system, where administrators can manage user accounts, monitor system performance, update book databases, and configure system settings. It's crucial to ensure that the admin login credentials are securely stored and only accessible to authorized personnel to prevent unauthorized access to sensitive system functions and data.

VII. CONCLUSION

This project proposed a novel trust-based matrix factorization model which incorporated both rating and trust information. Our analysis of trust in four real-world data sets indicated that trust and ratings were complementary to each other, and both pivotal for more accurate recommendations. Our novel approach, TrustSVD, takes into account both the explicit and implicit influence of ratings and of trust information when predicting ratings of unknown items. Both the trust influence of trustees and trusters of active users are involved in our model. In addition, a weighted regularization technique is adapted and employed to further regularize the generation of user- and item-specific latent feature vectors. Computational complexity of TrustSVD indicated its capability of scaling up to large-scale data sets. Comprehensive experimental results on the four real-world data sets showed that our approach TrustSVD outperformed both trust- and ratingsbased methods (ten models in total) in predictive accuracy across different testing views and across users with different trust degrees. We concluded that our approach can better alleviate the data sparsity and cold start problems of recommender systems. As a rating prediction model, TrustSVD works well by incorporating trust influence. However, the literature has shown that models for rating prediction cannot suit the task of top-N item recommendation. For future work, we intend to study how trust can influence the ranking score of an item (both explicitly and implicitly). The ranking order between a rated item and an unrated item (but rated by trust users) may be critical to learn users' ranking patterns.

REFERENCES

[1] S. G. K. Patro et al., "A Conscious Cross-Breed Recommendation Approach Confining Cold-Start in Electronic Commerce Systems," in IEEE Access, vol. 11, pp. 82857-82870, 2023, DOI: 10.1109/ACCESS.2023.3274844.

[2] N.Mauro, Z.F.Hu, and L.Ardissono, "Service-Aware Personalized Item Recommendation," in IEEE Access, vol. 10, pp. 26715-26729, 2022, DOI: 10.1109/ACCESS.2022.3157442.

[3] Tausif anwar Et al.: Book Recommendation for e-Learning Using Collaborative Filtering and Sequential Pattern Mining, 2020 International Conference on Data Analytics for Business and Industry: Way Towards a Sustainable Economy (ICDABI).

[4] J. Li, T. W. Xu and J. Zhou, "A personalized Recommendation Algorithm for College Books based on User Interest," 2020 IEEE 2nd International Conference on Computer Science and Educational Informatization (CSEI), Xinxiang, China, 2020, pp. 144-149, DOI: 10.1109/CSEI50228.2020.9142507.

[5] M. Kommineni, P. Alekhya, T. M. Vyshnavi, V. Apama, K. Swetha and V. Mounika, "Machine Learning based Efficient Recommendation System for Book Selection using User based Collaborative Filtering Algorithm," 2020 Fourth International Conference on Inventive Systems and Control (ICISC), Coimbatore, India, 2020, pp. 66- 71, DOI: 10.1109/ICISC47916.2020.9171222.

[6] E.Uko Okon Et al. : An improved Online Book Reccomender System using Collaborative Filtering Algorithm, International Journal of Computer Applications (0975 - 8887) ,Volume 179 -No.46, June 2018.

[7] A.Anoop and N. A. Ubale, "Cloud Based Collaborative Filtering Algorithm for Library Book Recommendation System," 2020 Third International Conference on Smart Systems and Inventive Technology (ICSSIT), Tirunelveli, India, 2020, pp. 695-703, DOI: 10.1109/ICSSIT48917.2020.9214243.

[8] H. Zhang, Y. Xiao and Z. Bu, "Personalized Book Recommender System Based on Chinese Library Classification," 2017 14th Web Information Systems and Applications Conference (WISA), Liuzhou, China, 2017, pp. 127-131,DOI: 10.1109/WISA.2017.42.

[9] F. Zhang, "A Personalized Time-Sequence-Based Book Recommendation Algorithm for Digital Libraries," in IEEE Access, vol. 4, pp.2714-2720, 2016, DOI: 10.1109/ACCESS.2016.2564997.

[10] Guibing Guo: Collaborative Filtering with the Explicit and Influence of User Trust and of Item Ratings,2019

Predicting Chances of Qualifying NEET Examination: A Streamlit-Based Web Application

[1]Pravin S Choudhary, [1]Pallavi V. Nake, [1]Radhika D. Khedkar, [1]Pawan M. Tiwari, [1]Pranav P. Nichat, and [1]Amol P. Bhagat

[1]Department of Information Technology, Prof Ram Meghe College of Engineering and Management, Badnera, Maharashtra, 444701, India

[1]Email: pschoudhari@gmail.com, amol.bhagat84@gmail.com

Abstract— The National Eligibility cum Entrance Test (NEET) is a crucial examination for students aspiring to pursue medical education in India. The ability to predict one's chances of qualifying the NEET examination can significantly aid in strategic preparation and decision-making. To address this need, we propose the development of a Streamlit-based web application equipped with four main modules: Home, Account (comprising Admin and User functionalities), Mock, and Prediction. The Home module serves as the gateway to the application, providing an intuitive interface for users to navigate through various functionalities. The Account module facilitates user authentication and management, distinguishing between administrators with privileged access and regular users. Within the Mock module, users gain access to a repository of ten mock tests specifically designed to simulate the NEET examination environment. Users can undertake these mock tests and receive instant feedback on their performance, including detailed score breakdowns and areas of improvement. Additionally, the application stores users' mock test scores securely in a MySQL database hosted on Microsoft's MySQL Server. The Prediction module utilizes Python programming language to implement predictive algorithms that analyze users' performance across the ten mock tests. Leveraging the comprehensive dataset stored in the MySQL database, the module employs machine learning techniques to generate predictions regarding the likelihood of a user qualifying the NEET examination based on their mock test scores. These predictions are presented to users through the web application interface, providing valuable insights into their preparedness and potential areas for further enhancement.
By integrating user-friendly design, robust authentication mechanisms, interactive mock tests, and predictive analytics, our Streamlit-based web application offers a comprehensive solution for predicting NEET examination outcomes. This tool not only empowers students with actionable insights but also facilitates informed decisionmaking in their pursuit of medical education in India.

Keywords—Data Analytics, Machine Learning, NEET Examination, Predictive Analytics

I. Introduction

The "NEET Qualification Predictor" project is designed to assist students in predicting their chances of qualifying for the National Eligibility cum Entrance Test (NEET) examination. NEET is a crucial examination for aspiring medical students in India, covering subjects like Biology, Physics, and Chemistry. In the competitive landscape of medical education in India, the National Eligibility cum Entrance Test (NEET) stands as a crucial gateway for aspirants seeking admission to medical and dental colleges across the country. With its significance growing year by year, the ability to predict one's chances of qualifying for the NEET becomes paramount for aspirants to strategize effectively and maximize their chances of success.

To address this need, we present a comprehensive solution in the form of a StreamLit-based web application. This application integrates various modules aimed at aiding NEET aspirants in their preparation journey. This project utilizes StreamLit, a popular Python framework for building interactive web applications, and Microsoft SQL Server for data storage and retrieval. The application provides users with access to a series of 10 mock tests, each resembling the NEET examination format, with 1/4th negative marking and a total of 180 questions across various subjects. The core functionality of the project lies in predicting a user's likelihood of qualifying for the NEET exam based on their performance in these mock tests. To achieve this, a machine learning model, specifically a random forest classifier or regressor algorithm, is employed. This model analyses the user's scores from the mock tests and predicts their probability of qualifying for the NEET examination.

Modules:

Home: The central hub of the application where users can navigate through different sections and access relevant information.

Account Management: This module facilitates user registration and login functionalities. It comprises two sub-modules:

Admin Module: Admins have privileged access to manage user accounts, monitor activity, and oversee the overall functioning of the application.

User Module: Registered users can personalize their profiles, track their progress, and access features tailored to their needs.

Mock Test: A key component of NEET preparation is practicing with mock tests. In this module, users can attempt a series of 10 mock tests designed to simulate the actual NEET examination environment. Upon completion, the system generates a comprehensive analysis of their performance, highlighting strengths and areas for improvement.

Prediction: Leveraging Python programming language and MySQL database integration, this module utilizes advanced algorithms to predict a user's likelihood of qualifying the NEET examination based on their performance in the 10 mock tests. This predictive analysis provides valuable insights for users to gauge their readiness and fine-tune their preparation strategies accordingly.

Key Features:

StreamLit: Based Interface: The user interacts with the application through a user-friendly StreamLit interface, providing easy access to mock tests and prediction results. Microsoft SQL Server Integration: The project seamlessly connects to a Microsoft SQL Server database to store and retrieve user data, including mock test scores.

Mock Test Simulation: Users can attempt 10 mock tests, each mimicking the structure and difficulty level of the actual NEET exam, with 1/4th negative marking for incorrect answers.

Predictive Modelling: Utilizing the Random Forest algorithm, the application analyses users' mock test scores to predict their chances of qualifying for the NEET examination.

Educational Aid: The project serves as an educational aid for NEET aspirants, providing valuable insights into their preparation and potential outcomes.

The "NEET Qualification Predictor" project leverages the power of StreamLit, Python, and machine learning to create a valuable tool for NEET aspirants, aiding them in their preparation and increasing their chances of success in the NEET examination. The primary objective of this project is to empower NEET aspirants with a powerful tool that not only facilitates practice through mock tests but also offers personalized predictive insights to enhance their chances of success. By amalgamating technology with education, we aim to streamline the preparation process and empower users to approach the NEET examination with confidence and clarity.

The National Eligibility cum Entrance Test (NEET) is a highly competitive examination conducted in India for admission to undergraduate medical and dental courses. With a vast syllabus covering multiple subjects and intense competition among aspirants, NEET serves as a critical gateway for students aspiring to pursue a career in medicine. The significance of NEET scores in determining admission to prestigious medical colleges underscores the need for accurate predictions of these scores. The "NEET Score Prediction" project aims to develop a predictive model that estimates a student's NEET score based on various factors such as academic performance, mock test results, and demographic information. By leveraging data analytics and machine learning techniques, this project seeks to provide students with valuable insights into their potential performance in the NEET examination.

II. LITERATURE REVIEW

The study employs predictive models to forecast student performance, contributing to the broader field of learning analytics. Early prediction is vital for improving retention rates and academic outcomes. These models utilize various input variables, such as prior academic history, demographic information, and early course performance indicators. [1] discusses the common predictors used in their study. These could include historical academic records,

attendance, engagement with course materials, and other behavioral data collected from students in higher education. The study elaborates on the data sources used, including Learning

Management Systems (LMS) like Moodle or other institutional records [1].

The study uses student academic performance prediction to propose a comprehensive and high-performance system for student academic performance prediction framework to probe SAP characteristics (ProSAP) on educational data, which helps to resolve imbalanced data issues and improve academic performance for predicting the course final mark. It uses three different components, the first of which is the collaborative SAP prediction method for enhancing data quality, the scalable metadata clustering framework, and XGBoost (the enhanced SAP prediction method) for academic forecasting. The comparative evaluation results demonstrate that ProbSAP delivers superior accuracy and efficiency improvements for the course final mark prediction of college students over other state-of-the-art methods such as CNN, SVR, RFR, XGBoost, Catboost-SHAP, and AS-SAN. The use of algorithms is for reducing the mean absolute error, and the system affects complexity and computational resources [2].

In this paper, predicting student performance using continuous assessments remains a crucial responsibility for engineering educators, primarily to evaluate and improve their teaching practice. Engineering mathematics demands that problem-solving be implemented through continual evaluations. They used the copulas for this system for analyzing the dataset for a particular candidate. Analyse the given data and calculate the result of the given data by using copulas. They used PVDR and NPVDR copula-based models for the prediction of the analysed data. In this copula model, they can collect the performance assessment data and finalize the result for the candidate. The ability of copula-based models to correctly describe the dependence in lower and upper bounds, corresponding to very low and high scores, respectively, showed its practical usefulness in engineering education, particularly in understanding the ongoing learning needs of future engineers that affect their assignment or other marks ahead of their examination period and to reflect on their unique learning styles and the required early interventions needed to reduce the risk of failure. In the education sector, variables have been identified that considerably affect students' academic performance. In the last decade, research has been carried out in various fields such as psychology, statistics, and data analytics in order to predict academic performance [3].

Methods used, like data analytics, especially through machine learning tools, allow for predicting academic performance using supervised learning algorithms based on academic, demographic, and sociodemographic variables. In this work, the most influential variables in the course of students' academic lives are selected through wrapping, embedded, filter, and assembler methods, as well as the most important characteristics semester by semester using machine learning algorithms (Decision Trees, KNN, SVC, Naive Bayes, and LDA), which were implemented using the Python language. The results of the study show that the KNN is the model that best predicts academic performance for each of the semesters, followed by decision trees, with precision values that oscillate around 80 and 78.5% in some semesters.

Regarding the variables, it cannot be said that a student's per-semester academic average necessarily influences the prediction of academic performance for the next semester. The analysis of these results indicates that the prediction of academic performance using machine learning tools is a promising approach that can help improve students' academic lives and allow institutions and teachers to take actions that contribute to the teaching-learning process [4].

In the prediction of the university performance system, managed learning happens when each of the perceptions of the informational index has a connected variable or data that demonstrates what occurred (i.e., when sections are named). AI (ML) has started to penetrate the instructive field, considering the assortment, cleaning, examination, and representation of information on instructive entertainers, all together to improve related parts of the instructing growing experience, which is the reason it is now respected as one of the methods that will help dynamic in these specific circumstances. They used the prediction algorithm, i.e., the KNN algorithm, for calculating the high, low, and average performance of the students. The drawbacks are that supervised learning cannot handle all complex tasks in machine learning. It cannot cluster data by figuring out its features on its own. The decision boundary could be overtrained. The computation behind the training process consumes a lot of time, as does the classification process [5].

Predictive analytics in education has gained significant attention in recent years, with applications ranging from student performance forecasting to dropout prediction. Research by Baker and Siemens (2014) emphasizes the utility of learning analytics in enhancing educational outcomes by providing data-driven insights into student performance. These methods involve analyzing historical data to predict future success, a concept that is particularly relevant for high-stakes examinations like NEET. Machine learning models have been effectively used to predict student performance in various examinations. For instance, a study by Shahiri et al. (2015) explored the use of classification algorithms such as decision trees and support vector machines to predict students' performance in academic settings. These models demonstrated significant accuracy in predicting student success, underscoring their potential application in NEET prediction. Streamlit is a popular open-source framework for creating web applications that leverage data science and machine learning models. In a study by Herring (2020), Streamlit was highlighted as a powerful tool for rapid prototyping and deployment of data-driven applications. Its ease of use and interactive capabilities make it an ideal choice for developing predictive applications like the NEET qualification predictor.

Understanding the factors influencing NEET performance is crucial for developing effective predictive models. Research by Rajan and Kumari (2022) identified key predictors such as study hours, previous academic performance, and psychological factors that significantly impact NEET scores. Despite advancements, predicting academic performance using machine learning models faces challenges such as data quality and model interpretability. A review by Romero and Ventura (2013) discussed these limitations and suggested ways to improve predictive accuracy by addressing data quality issues and enhancing model transparency. The motivation behind the "NEET Score Prediction" project stems from the recognition of the significant role that the NEET examination plays in shaping the academic and professional trajectories of aspiring medical students. The NEET exam serves as a crucial benchmark for admission to medical colleges across India, determining the future prospects and career paths of thousands of students each year.

In the competitive landscape of medical education, where admission to top-tier institutions is fiercely contested, the ability to predict NEET scores accurately can provide students with a strategic advantage in their exam preparation journey. By offering insights into their potential performance, students can tailor their study plans, focus on areas of improvement, and optimize their efforts to achieve their desired scores.

Furthermore, the complexity and breadth of the NEET syllabus, which spans multiple subjects and requires in-depth understanding and proficiency, often pose challenges for students in effectively managing their study resources and time. The prospect of predicting NEET scores presents an opportunity to streamline the preparation process, enabling students to allocate their resources judiciously and prioritize topics based on their predicted importance.

Moreover, the advent of technology and data-driven approaches in education has opened new avenues for enhancing learning outcomes and student engagement. By harnessing the power of predictive modelling and data analytics, the "NEET Score Prediction" project seeks to leverage these technological advancements to support students in their exam preparation efforts.

III. PROBLEM DEFINITION

A. Problem Definition:

The problem at hand is to develop a system that predicts the chances of an individual qualifying the NEET (National Eligibility cum Entrance Test) examination based on their performance in a series of mock tests. NEET is a highly competitive examination in India for admission to undergraduate medical courses. The project aims to assist NEET aspirants in assessing their preparation and understanding their likelihood of qualifying the actual NEET exam.

Problem Domain:

The domain of this project is education and competitive examinations, particularly focused on medical entrance exams in India. Key aspects of this domain include:

NEET Examination: Understanding the structure, format, and scoring system of the

NEET examination, which includes questions from subjects like Biology, Physics, and Chemistry. Knowledge of the negative marking scheme commonly used in competitive exams is also essential.

Mock Tests: Creating and administering mock tests that closely resemble the NEET ex-am pattern, including the number of questions, subjects covered, and the negative marking scheme. These mock tests serve as practice exams for NEET aspirants to gauge their preparation level.

Machine Learning: Utilizing machine learning algorithms, particularly classification or regression algorithms such as Random Forest, to analyze mock test scores and predict the likelihood of qualifying the NEET exam. Understanding data preprocessing, feature engineering, model training, and evaluation techniques are crucial in this domain.

Performance Evaluation: Assessing the performance of the prediction model using appropriate evaluation metrics like accuracy, precision, recall, and Fl-score. Interpretation of model results and providing actionable insights to users based on prediction out-comes are integral to the domain.

Educational Guidance: Providing personalized guidance and recommendations to NEET aspirants based on their predicted chances of qualification. This may involve suggesting study strategies, focusing on weaker areas, or seeking additional resources for improvement.

B. Requirement Analysis:

1. User Authentication and Management:

Requirement: Users should be able to log in to the system securely to access the mock tests and prediction feature.

Functionalities:

- User registration: Allow users to create accounts with unique usernames and pass-words.
- User login: Provide a secure login mechanism to authenticate users.
- Password recovery: Implement a password recovery mechanism for forgotten passwords.
- User session management: Maintain user sessions to track their activities.

2. Mock Test Simulation:

Requirement: Users should be able to attempt mock tests similar to the NEET examination.

Functionalities:

- Display mock test questions: Present a set of questions covering subjects like Biology, Physics, and Chemistry.
- Allow users to select answers: Provide options for users to select their answers for each question.
- Negative marking: Implement 1/4th negative marking for incorrect answers.
- Timer: Include a timer to simulate the time limit of the NEET exam (3 hours).

3. Data Storage and Retrieval:

Requirement: Store user data and mock test results securely in a database.

Functionalities:

- Microsoft SQL Server integration: Connect to a Microsoft SQL Server database to store and retrieve user information and mock test results.
- Store user credentials: Safely store user usernames, passwords, and other relevant information.
- Store mock test results: Save users' scores from each mock test attempt for analysis and prediction.

4. Prediction Model Integration:

Requirement: Utilize machine learning algorithms to predict users' chances of qualifying the NEET exam based on their mock test scores.

Functionalities:

- Choose appropriate algorithm: Select a suitable machine learning algorithm (e.g.,
- Random Forest Classifier or Regressor) for prediction.
- Train the model: Train the prediction model using historical mock test data.
- Predict qualification chances: Analyze users' mock test scores and predict their likelihood of qualifying the NEET examination.
- Display prediction results: Present prediction results to users in an understandable format.

5. User Interface (UI) Design:

Requirement: Create an intuitive and user-friendly interface for seamless navigation and interaction.

Functionalities:

- Streamlit-based UI: Design the user interface using Streamlit to ensure ease of use and responsiveness.
- Clear navigation: Provide clear navigation options for users to access different features and functionalities.
- Interactive elements: Include interactive elements such as buttons, dropdowns, and progress indicators for enhanced user experience.

6. Security and Privacy:

Requirement: Ensure the security and privacy of user data and interactions within the system.

Functionalities:

- Encryption: Encrypt sensitive user information such as passwords before storing them in the database.
- Secure communication: Implement HTTPS to encrypt data transmitted between the user's browser and the server.
- Access control: Restrict access to certain features (e.g., prediction) based on user authentication and authorization.
- Data anonymization: Anonymize or pseudonymize user data to protect user privacy during analysis and prediction.

7. Testing and Quality Assurance:

Requirement: Conduct thorough testing to ensure the reliability, accuracy, and performance of the system.

Functionalities:

- Unit testing: Test individual components (e.g., login functionality, mock test simulation) to verify their correctness.
- Integration testing: Test the interaction between different modules to ensure seam-less integration.
- Performance testing: Evaluate the system's performance under different loads to identify and address bottlenecks.
- User acceptance testing (UAT): Involve actual users to validate the system's usabil-ity, functionality, and satisfaction.

8. Documentation and Maintenance:

Requirement: Provide comprehensive documentation for developers, users, and administrators, and ensure ongoing maintenance and support.

Functionalities:

- User manual: Create a user manual to guide users through the system's functionalities and usage.
- Developer documentation: Document the system architecture, design, and implementation details for future reference and maintenance.
- Bug tracking and resolution: Establish a process for identifying, reporting, and re-solving bugs and issues promptly.

- Version control: Implement version control to manage code changes and updates efficiently.

C. *Aim of the Project:*

Overall, the aim of the "NEET Score Prediction" project is to equip aspiring medical students with the tools, insights, and resources they need to succeed in the NEET examination and pursue their aspirations in the field of medicine with confidence and competence. Through the development of innovative predictive models and educational technologies, the project seeks to support students in their academic journey and contribute to the advancement of medical education.

D. *Objectives to be achieved:*

- To Develop a StreamLit-based application to predict the chances of qualifying the NEET (National Eligibility cum Entrance Test) examination.
- To Establish a connection with Microsoft SQL Server to store and retrieve mock test scores and user data.
- To Implement a user-friendly interface allowing users to solve 10 mock tests, each resembling the NEET exam format.
- Model the mock test scoring system, considering 1/4th negative marking for incorrect answers and 180 questions across biology, physics, chemistry, etc.
- To Utilize the Random Forest Classifier or Regressor algorithm to analyze mock test scores and predict the likelihood of qualifying the NEET examination.
- To Provide users with personalized prediction results based on their mock test performances.
- To Ensure scalability and reliability of the application for handling multiple user sessions and database interactions.
- To Enhance user experience by incorporating informative visualizations and insights derived from the prediction model.
- To Deploy the application for easy access and usage by aspiring NEET candidates. Continuously optimize and update the prediction model based on new data and user feedback to improve accuracy and reliability.

IV. PROPOSED APPROACH AND DESIGN

We aim to develop a robust and user-centric web application that empowers NEET aspirants with valuable insights and tools to succeed in their examination preparation.

1. Requirement Analysis:
   - Conduct thorough research to understand the needs and expectations of NEET aspirants.
   - Identify key features and functionalities required in the web application based on user feedback and industry standards.
2. Design Phase:
   - Design a user-friendly interface for the web application, keeping in mind ease of navigation and accessibility.
   - Create wireframes and mock-ups to visualize the layout and structure of each mod-ule.
   - Define the database schema to store user data, mock test results, and other relevant information.
3. Development:
   - Implement the front-end of the web application using Streamit, a Python library for building interactive web apps.
   - Develop the back-end using Python programming language, incorporating Flask or Django framework for handling HTTP requests and business logic.
   - Set up a MySQL database to store user accounts, mock test data, and prediction re-sults.
   - Integrate authentication mechanisms for user registration, login, and session man-agement.
   - Build the four main modules: Home, Account Management (Admin and User),
   - Mock Test, and Prediction, ensuring seamless interaction between them.
4. Mock Test Module:
   - Design and implement a set of 10 mock tests covering all relevant topics and con-cepts of the NEET syllabus.
   - Create functionalities for users to select and attempt mock tests, with features such as timer, question navigation, and submission.
   - Develop algorithms to evaluate user responses, calculate scores, and generate de-tailed performance reports.

5. Prediction Module:
- Design predictive models using machine learning algorithms to analyze user perfor-mance in mock tests.
- Train the models using historical mock test data to predict the likelihood of qualify-ing the NEET examination.
- Integrate the prediction models into the web application, allowing users to input their mock test scores and receive personalized predictions.

6. Testing and Quality Assurance:
- Conduct rigorous testing to ensure the functionality, usability, and security of the web application.
- Perform unit tests, integration tests, and end-to-end tests to identify and rectify any bugs or issues.
- Gather feedback from beta testers and stakeholders to refine the application and en-hance user experience.

7. Deployment:
- Deploy the web application on a reliable hosting platform such as Heroku or AWS.
- Configure domain settings and SSL certificates to ensure secure access.
- Monitor performance metrics and user activity to optimize resource utilization and scalability.

8. Maintenance and Updates:
- Provide ongoing support and maintenance to address any issues or feature requests from users.
- Regularly update the application with new mock tests, performance enhancements, and bug fixes based on user feedback and emerging trends.

E. Activity Diagram of proposed approach

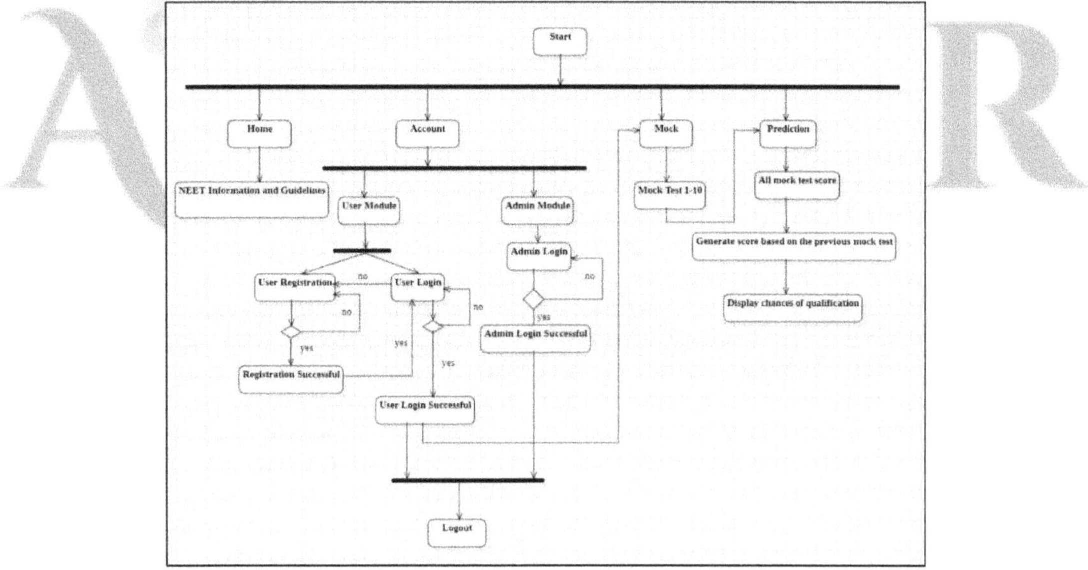

Fig. 82 Activity Diagram for Proposed Approach

Explanation of steps involved:

The web application is start, where we have to select option in which four modules are present like home, account, mock and prediction.

These are the following four main modules:

1. Home Module:

Description:

The Home module serves as the central hub of the application, providing users with access to essential NEET-related information and resources. It offers a user-friendly interface where individuals can navigate through different sections to gather relevant insights and updates about the NEET examination.

Features:

NEET Information: Provides details about the NEET examination, syllabus, eligibility criteria, and other pertinent information.

Resource Repository: Offers a collection of study materials, tips, and strategies to aid users in their NEET preparation journey.

News and Updates: Displays the latest notifications related to NEET examination.

2. Account Management Module:

Description:

The Account Management module facilitates user registration and login functionalities, distinguishing between administrators and regular users. It comprises two sub-modules: Admin Module and User Module, each serving distinct purposes in managing user accounts and activities.

Features:

Admin Module:

Grants privileged access to administrators, allowing them to manage user accounts, monitor activity logs, and oversee the overall functioning of the application.

User Module:

Enables registered users to create and personalize their profiles, track their progress, and access features tailored to their individual needs.

3. Mock Test Module:

Description:

The Mock Test module is a fundamental component of NEET preparation, offering users the opportunity to practice with simulated mock tests. Users can attempt a series of 10 mock tests, each designed to replicate the actual NEET examination environment. Upon completion, the system generates a comprehensive analysis of their performance, highlighting strengths and areas for improvement.

Features:

Mock Test Repository: Provides access to a series of 10 mock tests specifically designed for NEET preparation.

Performance Analysis: Generates detailed reports and scorecards for each mock test attempted by the user, offering insights into their performance and areas requiring further focus.

Progress Tracking: Allows users to monitor their progress over time, track their performance trends, and identify areas for improvement.

4. Prediction Module:

Description:

The Prediction module leverages advanced algorithms to predict a user's likelihood of qualifying the NEET examination based on their performance in the 10 mock tests. It utilizes Python programming language and integrates with a MySQL database to analyse the generated mock test scores and provide predictive insights.

Features:

Predictive Analysis: Utilizes machine learning techniques and predictive algorithms to analyse user performance across the 10 mock tests and generate predictions regarding their likelihood of qualifying the NEET examination.

Insights and Recommendations: Presents users with actionable insights and recommendations based on the predictive analysis, helping them gauge their readiness and refine their preparation strategies accordingly.

Personalized Feedback: Offers personalized feedback based on individual performance, highlighting specific areas for improvement and suggesting targeted study interventions.

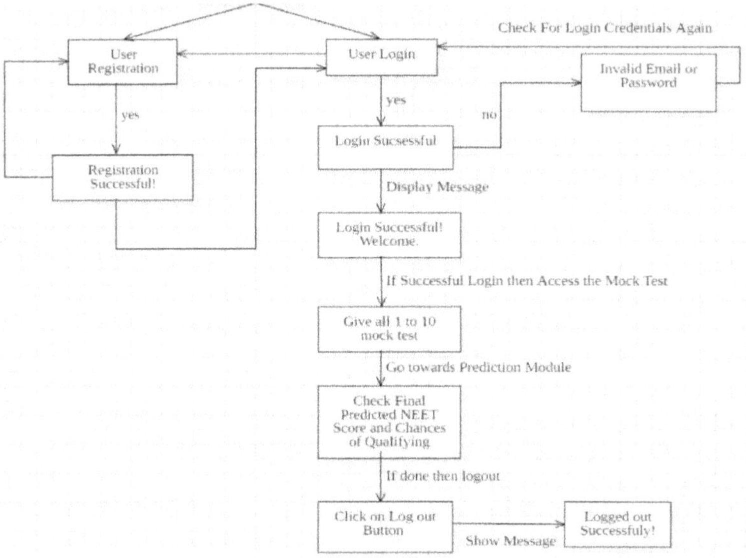

Fig. 83   Activity Diagram for Proposed Approach

Explanation of User Module:

In User Module, there are two sub modules as User Registration and User Login are the two submodules that make up the User Module. The user must first fill in all required fields during user registration, including full name, email address, mobile number, unique ID, password,
DOB, and category selection. Once all of these details were accurately entered, the message "Registration Successful! " Was displayed. and proceed with another registration if the user has already registered with the same unique ID or if the information are not filled out correctly. After registration is complete, the user is redirected to the login module, where they must enter their password and unique ID to gain access. If they are successful, a notice stating "Login Successful!" will appear. Hi, if you don't see a message saying "Invalid email or password," please check your login information again. After logging in successfully, the user can access all of the mock tests from 1 to 10. First, navigate to the mock page where some guidelines regarding the mock test are provided. Next, choose the option that allows him to choose the first mock test, which consists of 180 questions with four possible answers, similar to the NEET exam with 1/4 negative marking. In the first mock test, there is a start test button. If we click on it, the user's test will start. Each mock test has a countdown timer. When the test is finally over, there is a submit button. If we click on it, the user's score will be displayed. There are ten mock tests total. Once the first mock test has been completed, the user cannot take it again. Instead, they must complete additional mock tests. Once all of the mock tests have been completed, they can proceed to the prediction module to check their predicted NEET score and chances of qualifying, which will indicate whether their chances are high, moderate, or low. The user can then log out and receive the notification "Logged out successfully!"

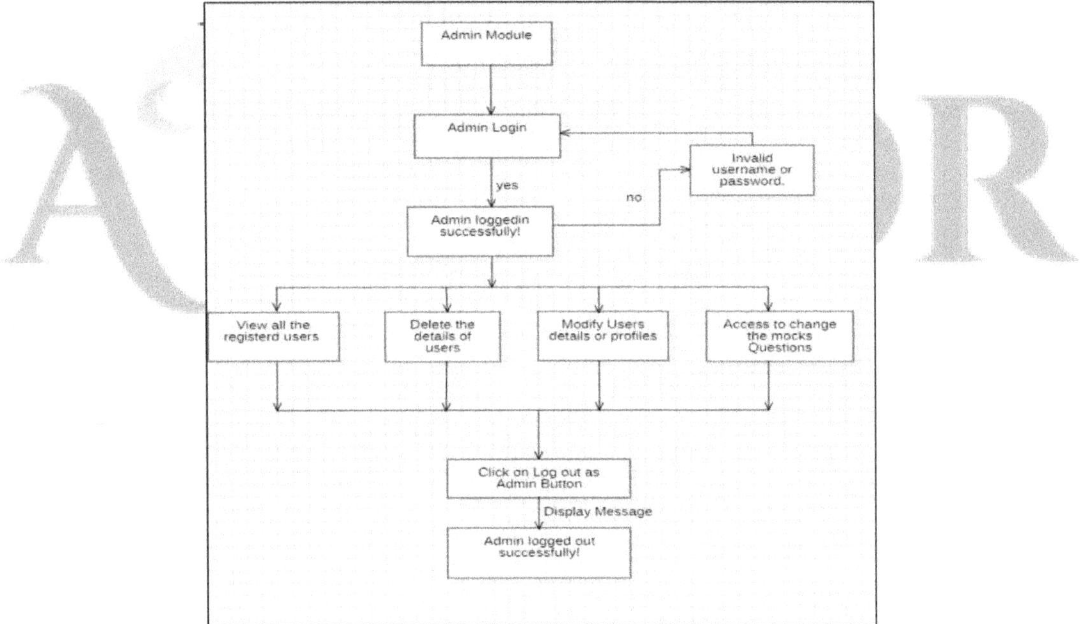

Fig. 84   DFD For Admin Module

In Admin Module, there is admin login, where admin use the details which saved as admin username and password in database and then if admin login successful with the correct details, then display message as, Admin logged in successfully! If not, login then display message invalid username or password then again check for the admin login details. As after login successfully admin can handle, view all the registered users, delete the details of users, modify users' details or profiles and access to change the mock test series question set. After all these admin can logout by clicking logout as admin button and then display message as Admin logged out successfully!

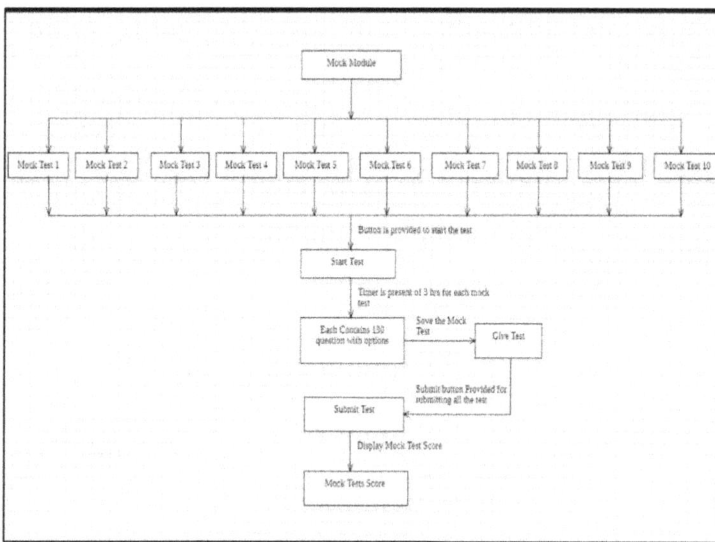

Fig. 85   DFD For Mock Module

The mock instructions, which provide information about the mock test, come first in the mock module. Following that, there are ten series of mock tests. Every mock test has a distinct page, such as Mock Test 1, Mock exam 2, so on and Mock Test 10, and every mock exam has the same tasks. When we select Mock Test 1, a start test button appears for the user to use, along with a three-hour timeframe to complete the 180 questions on each test that correspond to the NEET Exam.

When a user completes the test, there is a submit test option available at the end. If they click on it, the score they generated from the first mock exam is presented, and this process is repeated for each fake test that is held. However, after finishing Mock Test 1, we must move on to Mock Test 2, as choosing Mock Test 1 indicates that you have already finished the test.
the way these all-mock test's function.

V. EXPERIMENTAL SETUP

A. *Required technology and platform:*

Hardware and Software Requirements:
Hardware:
Device: Laptop or Computer
Processor: Intel Core i3 processor or equivalent (or better)
Processor Speed: 1.8 GHz+
RAM: 8 GB+
Hard Disk Capacity: 200 GB+
Language: Python
Database: Microsoft SQL Server (via SSMS)
Software:
Visual Studio Code (for code editing)
SSMS for SQL Server management
Streamlit for building the web application
Python for programming
Python:
Python is a general-purpose, dynamically typed, high-level, compiled and interpreted, garbage-collected, and purely object-oriented programming language that supports procedural, object-oriented, and functional programming.
Features of Python:

Easy to use and Read: Python's syntax is clear and easy to read, making it an ideal language for both beginners and experienced programmers. This simplicity can lead to faster development and reduce the chances of errors.

Dynamically Typed: The data types of variables are determined during run-time. We do not need to specify the data type of a variable during writing codes.

High-level - High-level language means human readable code.

Compiled and Interpreted: Python code first gets compiled into bytecode, and then interpreted line by line. When we download the Python in our system form ug we download the default implement of Python known as C Python. C Python is considered to be Complied and Interpreted both.

Garbage Collected: Memory allocation and de-allocation are automatically managed.

Programmers do not specifically need to manage the memory.

Purely Object-Oriented: It refers to everything as an object, including numbers and strings.

Cross-platform Compatibility: Python can be easily installed on Windows, macOS, and various Linux distributions, allowing developers to create software that runs across different operating systems.

Open Source: Python is an open-source, cost-free programming language. It is utilized in several sectors and disciplines as a result.

Python has many web-based assets, open-source projects, and a vibrant community. Learning the language, working together on projects, and contributing to the Python ecosystem are all made very easy for developers.

B. Python Library:

StreamLit Library:

StreamLit allows us to create apps for our machine-learning project with simple Python scripts.

Hot reloading is also supported, so our app can be updated live while we edit and save our file. StreamLit API allows us to create an app in a few lines of code. Declaring a variable is the same thing as adding a widget. We don't need to create a backend, handle HTTP requests or define different routes. It's easy to set up and maintain.

The best thing about StreamLit is that you don't even need to know the basics of web development to get started or to create your first web application. So if you're somebody who's into data science and you want to deploy your models easily, quickly, and with only a few lines of code, StreamLit is a good fit.

One of the important aspects of making an application successful is to deliver it with an effective and intuitive user interface. Many of the modern data-heavy apps face the challenge of building an effective user interface quickly, without taking complicated steps. StreamLit is a promising open-source Python library, which enables developers to build attractive user interfaces in no time.

StreamLit is the easiest way especially for people with no front-end knowledge to put their code into a web application:

No front-end (html, js, css) experience or knowledge is required.

You don't need to spend days or months to create a web app, you can create a really beautiful machine learning or data science app in only a few hours or even minutes.

It is compatible with the majority of Python libraries (e.g. pandas, matplotlib, seaborn, plotly, Keras, PyTorch, SymPy(latex)).

Less code is needed to create amazing web apps.

Data caching simplifies and speeds up computation pipelines.

Pandas Library:

The name of Pandas is gotten from the word Board Information, and that implies an Econometrics from Multi-faceted information. It was created in 2008 by Wes McKinney and is used for data analysis in Python. Processing, such as restructuring, cleaning, merging, etc., is necessary for data analysis. NumPy, SciPy, Cpython, and Panda are just a few of the fast data processing tools available. Yet, we incline toward Pandas since working with Pandas is quick, basic and more expressive than different apparatuses.

Key Features of Pandas:

It has a Data Frame object that is quick and effective, with both standard and custom indexing.

Utilized for reshaping and turning of the informational indexes.

For aggregations and transformations, group by data.

It is used to align the data and integrate the data that is missing.

Provide Time Series functionality.

Process a variety of data sets in various formats, such as matrix data, heterogeneous tabular data, and time series.

Manage the data sets' multiple operations, including sub setting, slicing, filtering, group

By, reordering, and reshaping.

It incorporates with different libraries like SciPy, and scikit-learn.

Performs quickly, and the Cpython can be used to accelerate it even further.

Scikit-learn Library:

Scikit-learn is mainly coded in Python and heavily utilizes the NumPy library for highly efficient array and linear algebra computations. Some fundamental algorithms are also built in Cython to enhance the efficiency of this library. Support vector machines, logistic regression, and linear SVMs are performed using wrappers coded in Cython for LIBSVM and LIBLINEAR, respectively. Expanding these routines with Python might not be viable in such circumstances.

Scikit-learn works nicely with numerous other Python packages, including SciPy, Pandas data frames, NumPy for array vectorization, Matplotlib, Seaborne and plotly for plotting graphs, and many more.

C. *System Design Algorithm*

Logistic Regression Algorithm in Machine Learning:

Logistic regression is one of the most popular Machine Learning algorithms, which comes under the Supervised Learning technique. It is used for predicting the categorical dependent variable using a given set of independent variables.

Logistic regression predicts the output of a categorical dependent variable. Therefore, the outcome must be a categorical or discrete value. It can be either Yes or No, 0 or 1, true or False, etc. but instead of giving the exact value as 0 and 1, it gives the probabilistic values which lie between 0 and 1.

Logistic Regression is much similar to the Linear Regression except that how they are used. Linear Regression is used for solving Regression problems, whereas Logistic re-gression is used for solving the classification problems.

In Logistic regression, instead of fitting a regression line, we fit an "S" shaped logistic function, which predicts two maximum values (0 or l).

The curve from the logistic function indicates the likelihood of something such as whether the cells are cancerous or not, a mouse is obese or not based on its weight, etc Logistic Regression is a significant machine learning algorithm because it has the ability to provide probabilities and classify new data using continuous and discrete datasets. Logistic Regression can be used to classify the observations using different types of da-ta and can easily determine the most effective variables used for the classification. The below image is showing the logistic function

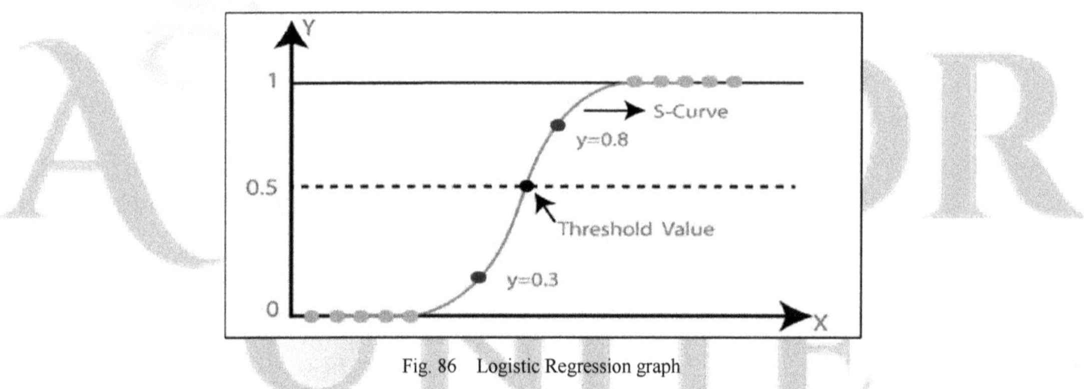

Fig. 86   Logistic Regression graph

Logistic Function:
*   The sigmoid function is a mathematical function used to map the predicted values to probabilities.
*   It maps any real value into another value within a range of 0 and l .
*   The value of the logistic regression must be between 0 and 1, which cannot go beyond this limit, so it forms a curve like the "S" form. The S-form curve is called the sigmoid function or the logistic function.
*   In logistic regression, we use the concept of the threshold value, which defines the probability of either 0 or 1. Such as values above the threshold value tends to 1, and a value below the threshold values tends to 0.

Assumptions for Logistic Regression:
*   The dependent variable must be categorical in nature.
*   The independent variable should not have multi-collinearity.

Logistic Regression Equation:

The Logistic regression equation can be obtained from the Linear Regression equation. The mathematical steps to get Logistic Regression equations are given below:
*   We know the equation of the straight line can be written as:

$$y = b0 + blxl + b2x2 + b3x3 + ...+ bnxn$$

*   In Logistic Regression y can be between 0 and 1 only, so for this let's divide the above equation by (I-y), y , 0 for y=0, and ifinity for y = 1.
*   But we need range between -[infinity] to +[infinity], then take logarithm of the equation it will become:

$$Log\ y/(l-y) = b0 + blxl + b2x2 + b3x3 + ...+ bnxn$$

The above equation is the final equation for Logistic Regression.

D. *Random Forest Regression Algorithm in Machine Learning:*

The Random Forest Regression (RFR) is an ensemble algorithm that combines multiple
Regression Trees (RTs). Each RT is trained using a random subset of the features, and the output is the average of the individual RTS. With supervised training, the training data contains the input and target values. The algorithm picks up a pattern that maps the input values to the output and uses this pattern to predict values in the future. Unsupervised learning, on the other hand, uses training data that does not contain the output values. The algorithm figures out the desired output over multiple iterations of training. Finally, we have reinforcement learning. Here, the algorithm is rewarded for every right decision made, and using this as feedback, and the algorithm can build stronger strategies The below diagram explains the working of the
Random Forest algorithm:

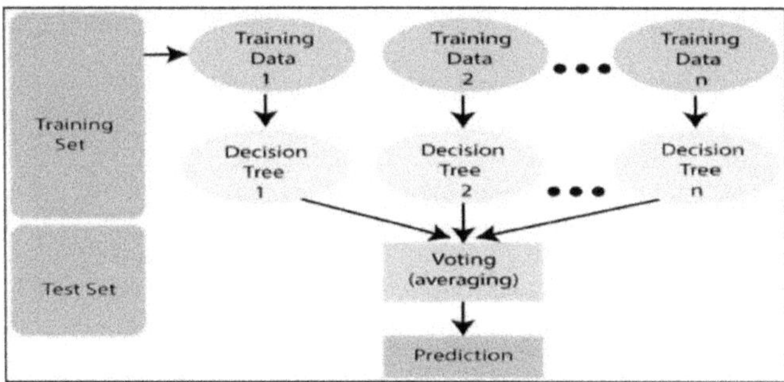

Fig. 87   Random Forest Algorithm

VI. RESULTS

These is starting page of the web application, where NEET Qualifying Portal is present with four modules. As Home, Account, Mock, Prediction with different functionalities.

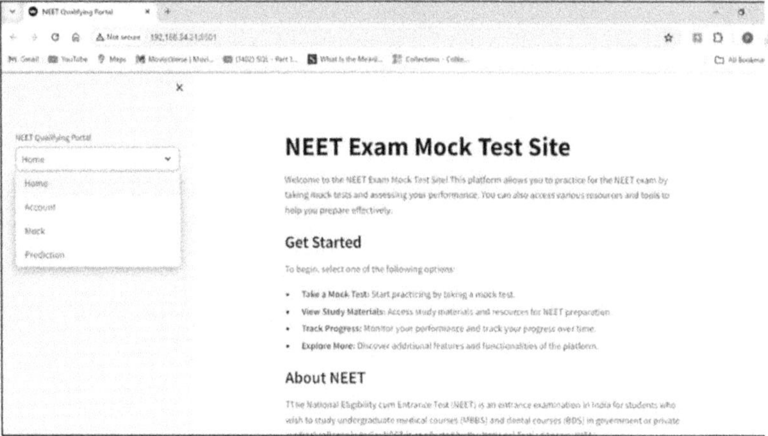

Fig. 88   Start Page

In below Screenshot home module is open which contains information about NEET Examination and some important details.

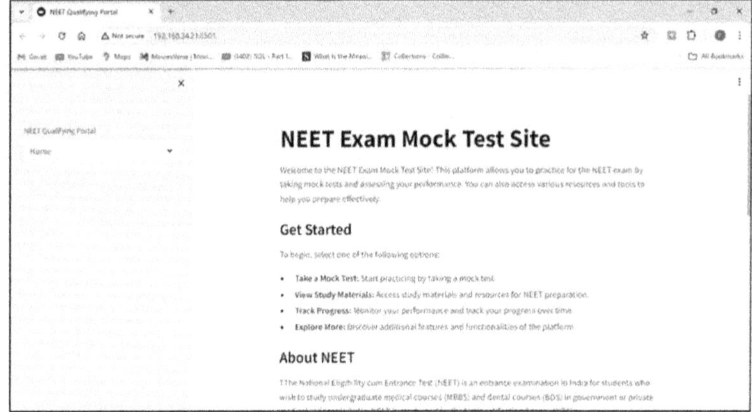

Fig. 89   Home panel

In the below Screenshot account module, where two modules are present user module and admin module. User module involves both registration and login while admin involves only login page.

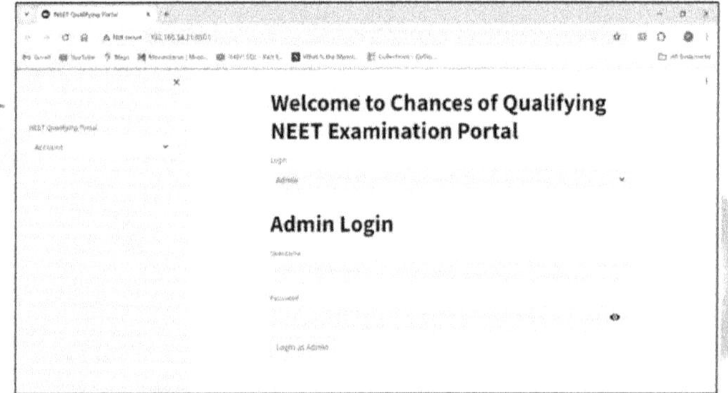

Fig. 90   Admin Login panel

These Screenshot is of Admin panel, admin can see the registered students for mock test series as well he can edit the user details and change the question series.

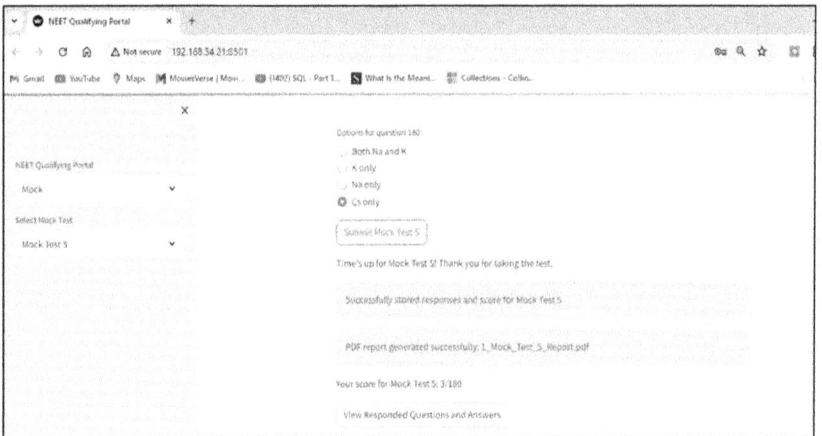

Fig. 91   Mock Module

Qualification Prediction: This indicates the likelihood of the user qualifying the NEET exam based on their predicted NEET Final Score and category. The prediction is categorized into three levels:
High Chance of Qualification: Indicates a high probability of qualifying the NEET exam.
Moderate Chance of Qualification: Suggests a moderate probability of qualifying the NEET exam.

Unlikely to Qualify: Indicates a low probability of qualifying the NEET exam. These outputs aim to provide users with insights into their potential performance and qualification chances in the NEET exam based on their mock test scores and category.

VII. CONCLUSIONS

The "NEET Qualification Predictor" project addresses a significant need among NEET aspirants by providing a platform to assess their readiness and predict their chances of qualifying the NEET examination. Here are some points for discussion:

Realistic Mock Tests: The inclusion of 10 comprehensive mock tests closely resembling the format and difficulty level of the actual NEET exam is crucial. These tests cover key subjects like biology, physics, and chemistry, helping users gauge their preparedness effectively.

Machine Learning Prediction: Leveraging machine learning algorithms such as Random Forest classifier or regressor adds a layer of sophistication to the prediction process. By analyzing users' mock test scores, the algorithm provides personalized insights into their likelihood of qualifying the NEET examination.

User Interface and Experience: The use of Streamlit for building the application ensures an intuitive and user-friendly experience. NEET aspirants, often under considerable stress, can navigate the application seamlessly, focusing on their preparation rather than struggling with the interface.

Data Management: Storing user data, including mock test scores and login credentials, in a Microsoft SQL Server database ensures efficient management and retrieval. This approach facilitates scalability and robustness, enabling the application to handle a large volume of users effectively.

In conclusion, the "NEET Qualification Predictor" project offers a valuable resource for NEET aspirants seeking to optimize their preparation strategy and maximize their chances of success. By simulating the NEET exam environment through comprehensive mock tests and employing machine learning algorithms for predictive analysis, the project empowers users to make informed decisions about their readiness for the exam. Furthermore, the user-centric design and streamlined user interface enhance the overall user experience, making the application accessible and engaging for a wide range of users. Overall, the "NEET Qualification Predictor" project represents a significant step towards leveraging technology to support and guide NEET aspirants on their journey towards achieving their academic goals

REFERENCES

[1] E. Alhazmi and A. Sheneamer, "Early Predicting of Students Performance in Higher Education," in IEEE Access, vol. 11, pp. 27579-27589, 2023

[2] Xinning Wang, Yuben Zhao, Chong Li, Peng Ren, "ProbSAP: A comprehensive and highperformance system for student academic performance prediction", Pattern Recognition, vol.137, pp. 1-8, 2023

[3] T. Nguyen-Huy et al., "Student Performance Predictions for Advanced Engineering Mathematics Course with New Multivariate Copula Models," in IEEE Access, vol. 10, pp. 4511245136, 2022

[4] Bravo, Leonardo & Nieves Pimiento, Nayive & Gonzalez-Guerrero, Karolina "Prediction of University-Level Academic Performance through Machine Learning Mechanisms and Supervised Methods," in ResearchGate, vol. 28, pp. 1-25, 2022

[5] Sachin S. Bere, Ganesh P. Shukla, vajid N Khan, Atishkumar M. Shah, Dattatray G. Takale "Analysis of Students Performance Prediction in Online Courses Using Machine Learning Algorithms," in Neuroquantology, vol. 20, pp. 13-18, 2022.

[6] D. M. Ahmed, A. M. Abdulazeez, D. Q. Zeebaree and F. Y. H. Ahmed, "Predicting University's Students Performance Based on Machine Learning Techniques" in IEEE International Conference on Automatic Control & Intelligent Systems (12CACIS), vol 1, pp. 276-281, 2021.

[7] Baker, R. S., & Siemens, G. (2014). Educational data mining and learning analytics. *Learning Analytics*, 1(1), 1-22.

[8] Shahiri, A., Hamid, R., & Fadhl, N. (2015). A survey of data mining approaches for predicting student performance. *International Journal of Computer Applications*, 116(15), 33-38.

[9] Herring, J. (2020). Streamlit: The fastest way to build and share data apps. *Medium.*

[10] Rajan, S., & Kumari, P. (2022). Factors influencing NEET exam performance: A comprehensive study. *Journal of Educational Research and Review*, 10(1), 45-58.

[11] Romero, C., & Ventura, S. (2013). Data mining in education. *Wiley Encyclopedia of Computer Science and Engineering*, 1-13.

Smartfixtech: Reliable and Fastest PC Support and Delivery Platform

[1]Parag S. Mohod, and [1]Amol P. Bhagat

[1]Department of Information Technology, Prof Ram Meghe College of Engineering and Management, Badnera, Maharashtra, 444701, India

[1]Email: parag.mohod@prmceam.ac.in, amol.bhagat84@gmail.com

Abstract— In this proposed project work, we are trying to provide first-rate service to the customer, nowadays, repairing any device requires too much time and one needs to take that particular device to a repair center for every small issue. The app will allow businesses to connect with potential customers, manage their bookings, and provide excellent customer service, also it enables the user to shop online specifically for computers, laptop, and their hardware. The application also recommends laptops, and computers to buy according to their profession and required configuration. The app will be divided into three main sections: the customer section, the vendor section, and the technician section. The customer section will allow users to search for service providers, read reviews, and book appointments. The vendor section will allow businesses to create profiles, list services, and manage bookings. The technician section will allow technicians to create profiles, a list of services allotted to them, and many more. The app will also include features such as a payment system, a messaging system, a rating and review system, a referral system, and a basic troubleshooting video links section. The development of the app will involve several steps, including research, wireframing, platform selection, and development and design. The app will be tested and iterated on until it is ready to launch. The app is expected to be a valuable tool for businesses of all sizes. It will help businesses to reach a wider audience, improve their customer service, and increase their profits.

Keywords— Customer service, device repair, app development, online shopping, computer hardware, laptop recommendations

---

I. INTRODUCTION

SmartFixTech is a user-centric application tailored for computer users. It provides a robust troubleshooting section with DIY video tutorials for common issues, empowering users to resolve problems independently and save time. For complex issues, users can opt for tech- nician assistance, ensuring prompt resolution at their preferred location. Moreover, SmartFixTech offers a diverse range of services at competitive prices through trusted vendor partnerships. Users can also benefit from exclusive sales and price drops, maximizing savings on essential hardware and peripherals. Additionally, SmartFixTech boasts a comprehensive shopping section dedicated to computers, laptops, and related hard- ware. In summary, SmartFixTech is a comprehensive solution that enhances the computer user experience by combining intuitive troubleshooting resources, expert technician support, and attractive purchasing opportunities.

SmartFixTech is a comprehensive application for computer users, featuring a dedicated shopping section for hardware and personalized recommendations. It also offers a trouble- shooting section with DIY videos and the option for technician assistance. Users can enjoy affordable buying services and take advantage of sales. With features like secure payments and a rating/review system, SmartFixTech aims to streamline the computer user experience with convenience, affordability, and expert support.

II. LITERATURE REVIEW

E. Research on the application of services in the intelligent customer service system:

The author presents a novel system architecture for enhancing intelligent customer service systems. This innovative approach leverages service choreography to boost flexibility and agility. By integrating service choreography, the system gains the ability to seamlessly coordinate and adapt to customer service needs, resulting in a more adaptable and agile customer service experience. This approach aims to optimize the system's responsiveness and effectiveness, ultimately benefiting both service providers and customers.

A. Designing and Evaluating a Mobile Shopping app for older adults:

The author conducts user research among older adults to gain insight into their specific needs and preferences regarding a mobile shopping application. Through this study, the aim is to create and evaluate an app tailored to the unique requirements of this demographic. By understanding their preferences, the author seeks to design an app that is user-friendly, accessible, and aligns with the preferences of older adults. This approach prioritizes the usability and satisfaction of older users, ensuring that the mobile shopping app is a practical and enjoyable tool for them.

B. IoT-Based Intelligent Mobile Application for Shopping:

The methodology of the IoT-Based Intelligent Mobile Application for Shopping begins with a systematic approach. The author initiates the process with system design, followed by meticulous implementation, thorough testing, efficient deployment, and comprehensive evaluation. This well-structured sequence ensures that the mobile application is not only conceptually sound but also rigorously executed and thoroughly assessed. By following this methodology, the aim is to develop a reliable and effective shopping application that seamlessly integrates IoT technologies, thereby enhancing the overall shopping experience for users.

C. Platform Provider Roles in Innovation in Software Service Ecosystems:

This research leverages a case study approach, specifically focusing on the Salesforce AppExchange platform, to investigate the role of platform providers in fostering innovation within software service ecosystems. AppExchange, a Software-as-a-Service (SaaS) CRM platform, facilitates innovation by enabling third-party vendors to develop and offer customized CRM services. This approach allows for collaboration between Salesforce.com, the vendors, and end-users, potentially leading to a more innovative software service ecosystem.

D. Online Store using E-Commerce and Database Design and Implementation:

This paper employs a systematic methodology for designing an e-commerce store's database. The approach leverages a combination of well-established diagramming techniques to comprehensively capture the system's functionality and data flow. Specifically, the methodology utilizes:
Case Diagrams (UCDs): These diagrams formally depict the interactions between the system and its various user types, ensuring a user-centric design.
Data Flow Diagrams (DFDs): DFDs graphically represent the movement of data throughout the system, providing a clear understanding of data processing and storage.
Context Analysis Diagrams (CADs): By illustrating the interactions between the e-commerce store and external systems, CADs ensure seamless integration with other relevant platforms.
Entity-Relationship Diagrams (ERDs): ERDs visually model the data entities within the system and their relationships, forming the foundation for the relational database design.
This multi-faceted approach facilitates the creation of a robust and efficient da- tabase that effectively supports the functionalities of the online store.
Customer Service System Design Based on Big Data Machine Learning:

The Customer Service System Design, based on Big Data Machine Learning, focuses on leveraging advanced technologies to achieve automated customer service responses. By harnessing the power of big data and machine learning, the system aims to facilitate intelligent and automatic interactions with customers. This approach enables the system to provide efficient and context-aware responses, enhancing the overall customer service experience. By incorporating these cutting-edge technologies, the design ensures that customer inquiries and issues are addressed promptly and effectively, leading to improved customer satisfaction and service efficiency.
The need for physical service center visits, even for minor computer issues, highlights an opportunity to create home-based solutions for common problems. Our goal is to develop user-friendly tools and resources that enable individuals to troubleshoot and resolve issues without the need for professional assistance. This could involve creating software applications that provide guided troubleshooting steps, offering online forums or communities where users can seek advice from experts or peers, and developing remote assistance tools that allow technicians

to diagnose and resolve issues remotely. By providing home-based solutions, we aim to reduce the inconvenience and cost associated with service center visits, empowering users to address computer problems more conveniently and efficiently.

III. PROBLEM DEFINITION

Experiencing technical troubles with computers, particularly hardware issues or malfunctions, can be highly frustrating, and even minor problems often necessitate a visit to a service center, while the process of searching for suitable laptops is both confusing and tiring. The problem at hand centers around the inconvenience and frustration associated with technical issues related to computers, with a particular focus on hardware problems and malfunctions. These challenges often result in a considerable loss of time and efficiency, undermining the overall user experience.

One facet of this issue is the necessity to physically visit a service center for even minor computer issues that could be effectively resolved at home. This not only incurs additional time and effort but also contributes to increased inconvenience, particularly when many issues could potentially be addressed through remote assistance or user-friendly trouble- shooting guides. Moreover, the process of searching for suitable laptops is characterized as confusing and tiring. This is indicative of a broader problem in the computer industry, where a wide array of choices, technical specifications, and features can overwhelm consumers. The difficulty in making informed decisions about laptop purchases can lead to suboptimal choices, unnecessary expenditures, and dissatisfaction with the acquired technology.

The aim of the proposed project work, SmartFixTech Android application is to reduce the gaps in efficient and timely tech support, solve minor issues that could be easily re- solved at home, and recommend laptops, and Computers according to the user's profession, and also according to their required configurations. The main objectives of the proposed project work are as follows:

To identify the needs and requirements of users.

To provide a user-friendly platform for customers to connect with service providers.

To provide a platform that will help business grow.

To provide a convenient and trusted online marketplace for computers, laptops, and hardware components.

To provide a recommendation system for laptops and computers based on user- suggested configuration.

IV. PROPOSED APPROACH

The steps in this approach for application development are as follows:

- Problem Identification: Begin with research to understand user needs and align them with the business objectives.
- Feature Prioritization: Identify and prioritize features based on user and business requirements.
- Wireframe/Prototype: Create a low-fidelity mock-up for user inter- face testing and stakeholder feedback.
- Technology Selection: Choose the appropriate development platform and tools based on the application's requirements.
- Iterative Development: Develop the application incrementally, test- ing it regularly to ensure it meets the defined requirements.
- Iterative Approach: The process is iterative, allowing for revisiting earlier stages when new requirements arise during development. This flexibility ensures alignment with evolving project needs.

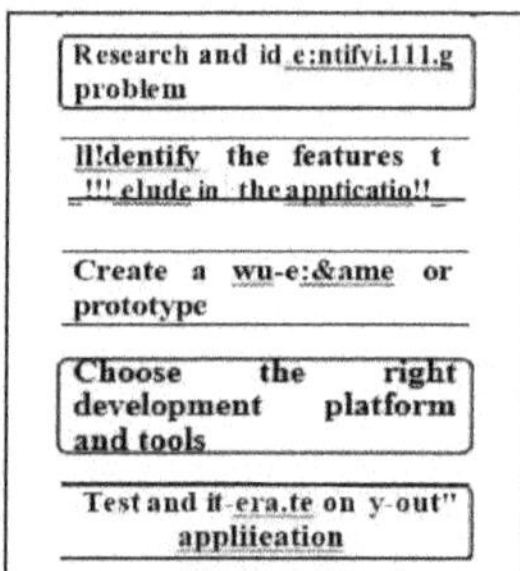

Figure 1:Block Schematic of the Approach

A. Explanation of steps involved:

Research and Identifying:

This initial step involves researching the target audience and understanding their needs, preferences, and pain points. It also entails analysing competitors' apps to identify gaps in the market and areas for improvement. Additionally, researching the latest trends and technologies in mobile app development, particularly in the Flutter framework, is crucial to ensure the app stays relevant and competitive.

Identify the Features to Include in the Application:

Based on the research conducted in the previous step, identify the key features that the app should include to meet the needs of the target audience effectively. These features may include a dedicated shopping section for computers and related hardware, personalized recommendations based on users' professions, a troubleshooting section with instructional videos, options for technician assistance, secure payment system integration, and user-friendly interfaces for both clients and vendors.

Create a Wireframe or Prototype:

Once the features are identified, create a wireframe or prototype of the app to visualize its layout, navigation flow, and functionality. This step helps to clarify the app's structure and user experience before proceeding to actual development. Tools like Sketch, Adobe XD, or Figma can be used to create wireframes and prototypes efficiently.

Choose the Right Development Platform and Tools:

Since the app is to be developed using Flutter for the Android platform, ensure that the development team is proficient in Flutter SDK, Dart programming language, and relevant development tools like Android Studio or Visual Studio Code. Additionally, consider any third-party libraries or plugins that may be needed to implement specific features or functionalities effectively.

Test and Iterate on Your Application:

Testing is a crucial phase to ensure the app functions as intended and is free from bugs and errors. Collect feedback from users and stakeholders and iterate on the app based on their input to improve usability, performance, and overall user satisfaction. Implementing an agile development approach can facilitate continuous testing and iteration throughout the development lifecycle.

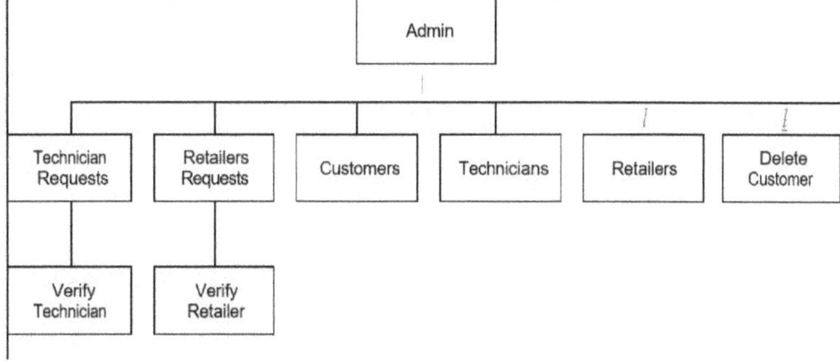

Figure 2: Block Diagram of Admin Module

Figure 2 shows the block diagram of admin module, it has tabs like Technician Requests, where technicians can request to open accounts on the application; the administrator will check the documents to see if they are legitimate, at which point the request is approved and the technician can log in to the application. "Retailer Request" this tab functions similarly to the technician request tab, Customer tab, the admin can view the users who are actively using the application by using this tab. Technician tab, the administrator can view which technicians are currently engaged on the application through this tab and can also remove technicians. Retailers Tab, the administrator can view the active retailers on the application by using this tab. Delete Customer, the administrator can remove the customer using this tab.

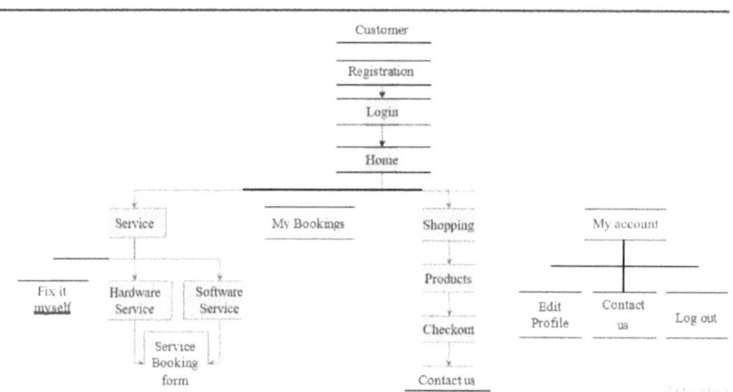

Figure 3: Block Diagram of Customer Module

Figure 3 shows the block diagram of customer module, in order to create an account, the user must first register on the application by providing their name, email address, and create preferred password. The user must enter their registered email address and created password to log in to the application. The user will then be taken to the home page, where they are able to see the navigation bar with tabs for Services, My Bookings, Shopping, and My Account.

The service page with three tabs Fix It Myself, which has video links for small problems that can be fixed at home will open after you select the service tab from the navigation bar. Another is the service page which includes software and hardware service tabs, which both have a service booking form that customers can use to schedule services. The user will be routed to my booking page after selecting the "My Bookings" link from the navigation bar. This page will have two sections: one for hardware services and another for software services, both of which will provide a history of previously and currently booked services.

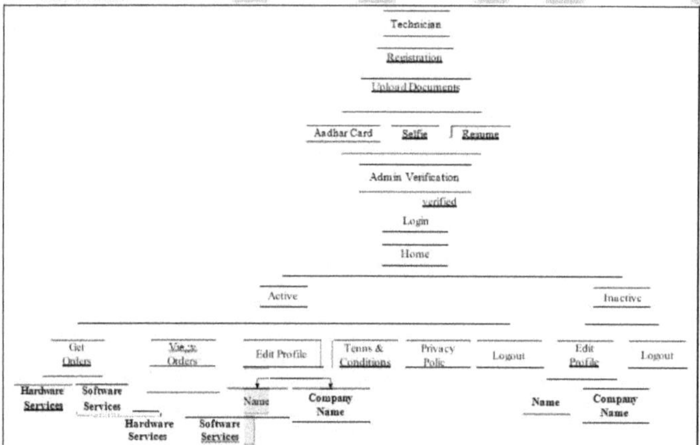

Figure 4: Block Diagram of Technician Module

Figure 4 shows the block diagram of technician module, in order to create an account, the technician must first register on the application by providing their name, email address, company name (if any) and create preferred password. Afterwards the technician will be redirected to the upload document page where they have to upload the Aadhaar card, selfie, and resume which will be used to verify their identity. The admin will review the documents and if approved, the technician can log in to the application. The technician must enter their registered email address and password to log in to the application.

After that, the technician will be brought to the homepage, where they are able to view the active and inactive working status. The technician's working state will determine which tabs appear; if the technician is active, the "Get orders" tab will show up, allowing them to view orders that are available and haven't been taken by another technician. The "View orders" tab will display the history of the technician's orders, including both past and present ones. Edit profile: This page is for updating the profile, which contains the name and company name. The terms and conditions, privacy statement, and logout link allow the technician to exit the appli- cation. If the technician is inactive, only two tabs will appear edit profile and logout.

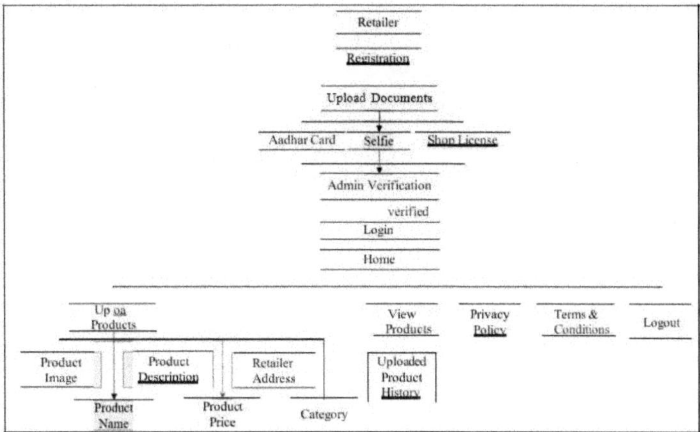

Figure 5: Block Diagram of Technician Module

Figure 5 shows the block diagram of retailer module, in order to create an account, the retailer must first register on the application by providing their name, email address and create preferred password. Afterwards the retailer will be redirected to the upload document page where they have to upload the Aadhaar card, selfie, and shop license which will be used to verify their identity. The admin will review the documents and if approved, the retailer can log in to the application. The retailer must enter their registered email address and password to log in to the application.

After that, the retailer will be brought to the homepage, where tabs like Upload product, View Products, Privacy Policy, Terms and Conditions and Logout is visible the product details, which include the product image, name, description, price, retailer address, and category, can be uploaded using the Upload Product tab. View product tab include the history of previously uploaded products, and logout tab is used to exit the application.

V. EXPERIMENTAL SETUP

A. Hardware Requirement

1. Storage:
   a. Hard Drive (Minimum 400MB; Recommended 50GB)
   b. Software Drive (Minimum 400MB; Recommended 50GB)
2. Devices:
   a. Computer or Laptop
   b. Mobile device
3. Processor: (Minimum dual-core; Recommended Quad-core or higher)
4. Memory (RAM): (Minimum 512MB; Recommended 8GB)

B. Software Requirement

There are various software platforms which are used in this project which are as follows:
- Operating System: Windows 10/11
- Platform Used: Android Studio (IDE)
- Coding Language: Dart
- Framework: Flutter
- Prototype designing tool: Figma
- Database: Supabase, Firebase

VI. REQUIRED TECHNOLOGY

A. Coding Language

Flutter:

Flutter is an open-source UI software development kit created by Google. It is used to develop applications for Android, iOS, Linux, Mac, Windows, Google Fuchsia, and the web from a single codebase. Flutter uses the Dart programming language, which is also developed by Google. It's known for its fast development process, expressive and flexible UI, and native performance on multiple platforms. Here are some key features of Flutter:

With Flutter, you can write code once and deploy it on multiple platforms without the need for separate implementations. Flutter's hot reload feature allows developers to quickly see the changes they make to the code reflected in the app, speeding up the development process. Flutter provides a wide range of customizable widgets that help in building beautiful and responsive user interfaces. Flutter apps are compiled directly to native machine code, which results in high performance and allows for smooth animations and transitions. Flutter's flexible and expressive UI components allow developers to create visually appealing interfaces that can be customized to fit the app's brand.

Flutter provides plugins that allow developers to access native features and APIs, enabling them to integrate platform-specific functionality into their apps. Flutter has a strong and active community of developers, which provides support, resources, and plugins to help developers build and maintain their apps. Flutter apps can easily adapt to different screen sizes and device orientations, making them suitable for a wide range of devices. Flutter comes with a set of integrated development tools, including a debugger, inspector, and performance monitor, which help in debugging and optimizing apps. Flutter is open source, which means that developers can contribute to its development and customize it to fit their needs.

Dart is a programming language developed by Google, primarily used for building web, mobile, and desktop applications. It is known for its fast performance and flexibility. Dart can be used for both frontend and backend development, thanks to its ability to compile JavaScript for web apps and its support for server-side development. Dart also comes with a robust set of tools, including a package manager (pub) and a comprehensive standard library. Some of its key features include:

Dart is a statically typed language, which means that variables must have a specific type and that type is checked at compile time. This helps catch errors early in the development process. Dart is an object-oriented language, which means that it supports concepts such as classes, objects, inheritance, and polymorphism. Dart uses automatic garbage collection to manage memory, which means that developers do not need to manually allocate and deallocate memory. Dart supports asynchronous programming, which allows developers to write code that can perform tasks concurrently without blocking the main thread.

Dart can be used to develop applications for multiple platforms, including the web, mobile, and desktop. It is particularly well-suited for developing cross-platform mobile apps using the Flutter framework. Dart and Flutter provide a feature called Hot Reload, which allows developers to quickly see the effects of their code changes without restarting the application. Dart comes with a rich standard library that provides support for common tasks such as 1/0, collections, networking, and more.

B. Development Tools

Android Studio (IDE):

Android Studio is the official integrated development environment (IDE) for Android app development, provided by Google. It offers a comprehensive set of tools for developers to design, build, and debug Android applications. Android Studio is based on IntelliJ IDEA and is specifically tailored for Android development. It includes features such as a visual layout editor, code editor with advanced code completion, debugging tools, and support for a wide range of Android devices and APis. Some key features of Android Studio include:

Android Studio provides a visual editor for designing app interfaces. Developers can drag-and-drop UI components and preview the layout on different device screen sizes and orientations. Android Studio includes a powerful code editor with features like syntax highlighting, code completion, and refactoring tools. It supports Java, Katlin, and C++ programming languages. Android Studio includes tools for building, packaging, and deploying Android apps. It uses Gradle as the build system, which allows for flexible customization of the build process. Android Studio includes an emulator that allows developers to test their apps on virtual Android devices. The emulator supports various Android versions and device configurations.

Android Studio provides tools for debugging Android apps, including breakpoints, watch variables, and a debugger console. Developers can also use the Android Device Monitor to inspect app performance and monitor system activities. Android Studio includes tools for analyzing the performance of Android apps. Developers can use tools like CPU Profiler, Memory Profiler, and Network Profiler to optimize their app's performance. Android Studio integrates with vers10n control systems like Git, allowing developers to manage their code repositories directly from the IDE. Android Studio includes templates and wizards for creating common Android app components, such as activities, fragments, and layouts, to speed up development. Android Studio provides integration with various Google services, such as Firebase, Google Maps, and Google Cloud Platform, making it easier to incorporate these services into Android apps. Android Studio supports plugins that extend its functionality. Developers can find plugins for additional features, such as support for other programming languages or frameworks.

C. Database

Supabase:

Supabase is an open-source platform that provides a set of tools and services for building and scaling applications. It offers a variety of features that are commonly needed in modern applications, such as:

Supabase uses PostgreSQL as its database engine and adds real-time capabilities through WebSocket' s. This allows applications to receive updates in real-time when data changes in the database. Supabase provides authentication services, including user registration, login, and management. It supports various authentication methods, such as email/password, OAuth, and third-party providers like Google and GitHub. Supabase includes file storage capabilities, allowing users to upload and store files securely. This is useful for applications that need to handle user-generated content, such as images or documents. Supabase automatically generates RESTful APis for database tables, making it easy to build backend services without writing custom API endpoints. Supabase provides a web-based dashboard for managing database schemas, authentication settings, and other configurations. Supabase supports extensions, which are pre-built components that add additional functionality to the platform. Examples include full-text search and geospatial querying.

VII.   SYSTEM IMPLEMENTATION

The SmarFixTech: Reliable and Fastest PC support and delivery platform a service and shopping-based application involves 4 modules, they are Admin Module, Retailer Module, Technician Module, and Customer Module.

A. Admin Module

In the Admin module, all the information about the users, technicians, and retailers can be seen and modified. The admin module is responsible for the manual verification of the technicians and retailers.

B. Customer Module

In the customer module, if the customer is new they must first register in the application by providing their name, and email address, and choosing a password. Afterward, they can log into their account by providing their registered email address and password.

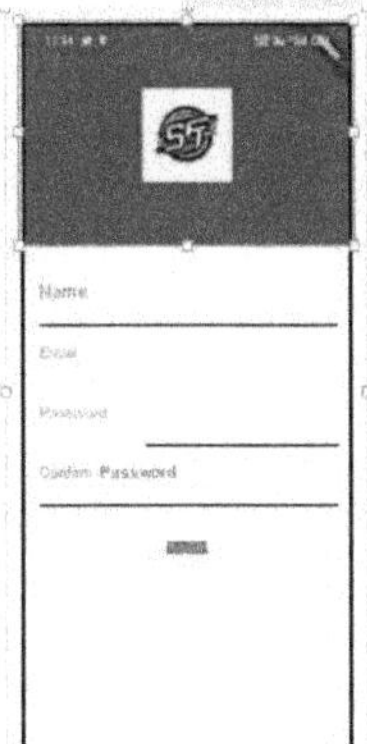

<table>
<tr><td>Figure 6:Customer's Registration</td><td>Figure 7: Customer's Login</td></tr>
</table>

Once you log in, the application will take you to the home screen. There, you will see menu drawers in the upper left corner with tabs for things like Profile, Active Booking, I'll Fix it Myself, Logout, Privacy Policy, and Terms and Conditions which are the same throughout the application. Additionally, the home page's navigation bar, which includes the pages for service, shopping, my bookings, and my account, is located at the bottom of the page.

In the customer module, new customers must register by providing their name, email address, and a password. They can then log in using their registered email and password. Upon logging in, users access the home screen, which features a menu drawer with options like Profile, Active Booking, I'll Fix it Myself, Logout, Privacy Policy, and Terms and Conditions. The navigation bar at the bottom includes Service, Shopping, My Bookings, and My Account. The Service page offers Hardware Services, Software Services, and I'll Fix it Myself, while the View Service Bookings tab displays current and past bookings. The Shopping tab features a search bar and filters to find products, with options to contact retailers for more information.

In the technician module, technicians must register, upload documents for verification, and await approval. Once approved, they can log in and access their home page with links to orders, profile editing, and order management. The retailer module involves a similar registration process, with the requirement to upload verification documents. Upon approval, retailers can log in, update products, and manage listings.

C. Database

There are a total of 12 tables in the database: bookings, fixmyself, hardwareservice, offers, goods, reqoffer, retailer, slides, softwareservice, technician, users, and wishlist. Each of these tables has a certain number of columns.

Figure 8:Database Tables Overview

The bookings table, the first table in the database, has nine columns: Id, the primary key and unique record; created_at, which records the time of creation; userid, which records the user ID for the application; products, which records the product history; purchase, which records the purchase history; delivery, which records the information about the product delivery; address, which records the user's address; phone no.; and rid.

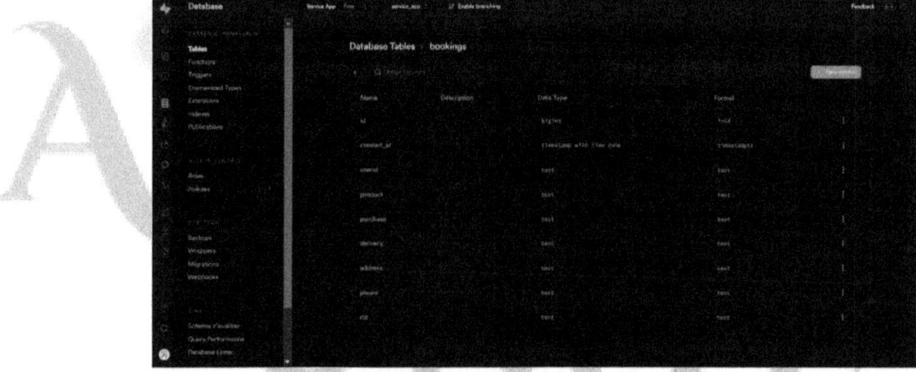

Figure 9:Booking Table

The database contains multiple tables, each serving a specific purpose. The "Fixmyself" table, the second table, has six columns: id (primary key), created_at (creation time), description (video's description), videoUrl (video's URL), videoTitle (video's title), and videoid (video's ID). The "hardwareservice" table, the third table, has ten columns: id (primary key), created_at (creation time), address (user-provided address), time_slot (preferred time for service), date (scheduled service date), phone (user's phone number), status (service delivery status), tid, and description (problem description).

The "offers" table, the fourth table, has three columns: URL (offer's linked URL), created_at (creation time), and id (primary key). The "products" table, with eleven fields, includes id (primary key), created_at (creation time), name (product's name), description (product's description), price (product's price), image_url (image's URL), category, rid, status, address (store's address), and phone (retailer's phone number). The "reqoffer" table, the sixth table, has five columns: id (primary key), created_at (creation time), name (retailer's name), retailer_id (retailer's ID), and URL (offers' URL).

The "retailer" table, the seventh table, has ten columns: created_at (creation time), id (primary key), name (retailer's name), email (retailer's email address), pass (retailer's password), company_name (retailer's company or shop name), is_verified (retailer's verification status), image_url (retailer's uploaded image), adhar_url (retailer's Aadhar card), and resume_url (shop's license and resume). The "slides" table, the eighth table, displays slides on the users' home page with three columns: URL (slides' URL), created_at (creation time), and id (primary key).

The "softwareservice" table, the ninth table, has ten columns: id (primary key), created_at (creation time), address (user-provided address), time_slot (preferred time for service), date (scheduled service date), phone (user's phone number), status (service delivery status), tid, and description (problem description). The "technician" table, the tenth table, has ten columns: created_at (creation time), id (primary key), name (technician's name), email (technician's email address), pass (technician's password), company_name (technician's company or shop name), is_verified (technician's verification status), image_url (technician's uploaded image), adhar_url (technician's Aadhar card), and resume_url (shop's license and resume).

The "users" table, the eleventh table, has five columns: name (user's name), created_at (creation time), id (primary key), email (user's email address), and pass (user's password). Lastly, the "wishlist" table has seven columns: id (primary key), created_at (creation time), user_id (unique user ID), category (product category), price (product price), and description (product description).

VIII. CONCLUSIONS

A. Conclusion:

In conclusion, a SmartFixTech app for service providers can be a valuable tool for businesses of all sizes. It can help businesses to connect with potential customers, manage their bookings, and provide excellent customer service.

Here are some of the key points to remember:

- A SmartFixTech app is a mobile application that allows businesses to connect with potential customers, manage their bookings, and provide excellent customer service.
- The customer section allows users to search for service providers, read reviews, and book appointments
- The Technicians section allows businesses to create a profile, list their services, and manage their bookings
- The app can also include features such as a payment system, a messaging system, and a rating and review system.

B. Future Scope

Here are some potential future scopes and opportunities for this project:

Geographical Expansion:

Initially, you may target a specific region, but there's potential to expand to other areas, both within your country and internationally. Consider language localization and adapt- ing to different markets.

Additional Services:

As the platform gains popularity, you could consider expanding the services offered. For example, you might include services for other electronic devices like smartphones, tablets, or even appliances.

Collaboration with Manufacturers:

Partnering with computer and laptop manufacturers could provide an opportunity to offer exclusive deals and services for your users. This could include extended warranties, special discounts, or even early access to new products.

Advanced AI and Troubleshooting:

As technology evolves, integrating more advanced AI and machine learning algorithms can enhance the recommendation system. You can also include more sophisticated troubleshooting tools that provide step-by-step guidance for users to resolve minor issues on their own.

Subscription Services:

Offer premium subscription services to both customers and vendors, which could include priority support, ad-free experiences, or advanced analytics for businesses.

On-Demand Services:

Explore on-demand service models for urgent or immediate repairs. This could include partnerships with local technicians who are available to respond quickly.

Cybersecurity Services:

As the importance of cybersecurity grows, you could offer cybersecurity services or partner with cybersecurity firms to provide security assessments and solutions for businesses and individuals.

REFERENCES

[1] Zhang Shuo; Yang Rui; Xu Yin et al., "Research on the application of services in the intelligent customer service system" DOI: 0.1109/EEBDA56825.2023.10090735 https://ieeexplore.ieee.org/document/10090735

[2] Ana Correia de Barros, Roxanne Leitao, Jorge Ribeiro "Designing ana Evaluating a Mobile Shopping app for Older adults" DOI:10.1016/j.procs.2014.02.041_Design and Evaluation of a Mobile User Interface for Older Adults: Navigation, Interaction and Visual Design Recommendations (researchgate.net)

[3] M. Balamurugan; G. Prabhakar; G. Amsaveni et al., "IoT-Based Intelligent Mobile Ap- plication for Shopping" DOI: 10.1109/ICACRS55517.2022.10029137https://ieeex- plore.ieee.org/document/10029137

[4]   Kibae Kim and Jorn Altmann., "Platform Provider Roles in Innovation in Software Service   Ecosystems" DOI:10.1109/TEM.2019.2949023 https:/www.re- searchgate.net/publication/338755234_Platform_Provider_Roles_in_Innova- tion_in_Software_Service_Ecosystems

[5]   Md. Tariqul Islam, Md. Shohel Mojumder "Online Store using E-Commerce and Da- tabase Design   and   Implementation" DOI: 10.1088/1742-6596/2066/l/012012 https://www.researchgate.net/publication/358768266_0nline_Store_using_E-Com- merce_and_Database_Design_and_Implementation

[6]   Yuqiang Kong, Yaoping He "Customer Service System Design Based on Big Data Ma- chine Learning" DOI: 10.1088/1742-6596/2066/l/012017 https://iopscience.iop.org/ar- ticle/10.1088/1742-6596/2066/1/012017

[7]   Xiaowei Huang, "Design of Rural E-commerce Customer Data Mining System" DOI:10.1088/1742-6596/1992/3/032087 https://www.researchgate.net/publica- tion/354121622_Design_of_Rural_Ecom merce_Customer_Data_Mining_System

[8]   Lidya Chitra Laoh, Timothy Adithia Pongantung, Carolin Mulalinda, et al., "Android Application Food Delivery Services" DOI: 10.1109/ICORIS50180.2020.9320843 https://ieeexplore.ieee.org/document/93 20843

[9]   Achmad Udin Zailanil, Alvino Octaviano2, Sholihin3, "Design of computer repair ser- vices application Android-based" DOI:10.31943/teknokom. v4il.58 https://www.re- searchgate.net/publication/352294820_DESIGN_ 0 F_COMPUTER_REP AIR_SER- VICES_APPLICATION _ANDROID- BASED

[10]   E P Riswara, Wagiman, and D Purwadi, "The strategy of Increasing Customer Satis- faction of Coffee Shops in Yogyakarta through GAP Analysis" DOI:10.1088/1755- 1315/828/l/012061   https://www.researchgate.net/publication/353685143_The_strat- egy_of_Increasing_Customer_S atisfaction_of_Coffee_Shop_in_Yogya- karta_through_GAP_Analysis

A Review on Exploring Transportation Problems: In-Depth Analysis and Effective Remedies

Amisha J. Rathod[1] and P. S. Pajgade[1]

[1] Department of Civil Engineering, Prof Ram Meghe Institute of Technology & Research, Badnera, Maharashtra, 444701, India

[1] email: rathod.amisha24@yahoo.com;

Abstract— Transportation systems are integral to modern society, driving economic growth and enabling social connectivity. However, these systems face significant challenges, including traffic congestion, environmental impact, infrastructure decay, safety concerns, economic costs, and accessibility issues. This review paper provides a comprehensive analysis of these transportation problems, examining their implications through detailed case studies from urban, rural, and international contexts. It evaluates current solutions and strategies, such as technological innovations, policy reforms, and infrastructure improvements, while highlighting innovative approaches like intelligent transportation systems, electric and autonomous vehicles, and sustainable public transport. The review underscores the need for a collaborative approach involving policymakers, urban planners, and researchers to address these challenges effectively. It concludes with a discussion on future trends and prospects, emphasizing the importance of embracing sustainable practices and technological advancements to develop a resilient and efficient transportation system. The insights offered aim to guide future actions and foster a transportation landscape that supports economic development, environmental sustainability, and enhanced quality of life.

Keywords— transportation systems, traffic congestion, environmental impact, infrastructure decay, safety concerns

I. INTRODUCTION

A. Background and Importance of Transportation

Transportation is a fundamental aspect of modern society, serving as the backbone of economic development and social connectivity (Levasseur et al., 2015). It facilitates the movement of goods, services, and people, enabling access to markets, employment, education, and healthcare. Efficient transportation systems are crucial for the functioning of cities and regions, influencing urban development, trade, and the overall quality of life. Historically, advancements in transportation have driven economic growth, expanded geographic horizons, and enhanced cultural exchanges (Donaldson, 2018). In the contemporary world, transportation remains a key driver of globalization and regional integration, highlighting its critical role in fostering economic prosperity and social well-being (Jedwab & Moradi, 2016).

However, the increasing demand for transportation services has also led to significant challenges. Urbanization, population growth, and rising economic activities have intensified traffic congestion, environmental pollution, and infrastructure wear and tear (Moore et al., 2018). These issues not only hamper mobility but also contribute to adverse health effects, economic losses, and environmental degradation. Therefore, addressing transportation problems is vital for sustainable development, necessitating innovative solutions and strategic planning (Næss, 2020).

B. Objectives of the Review

The primary objective of this review is to provide a comprehensive analysis of the major problems faced by transportation systems worldwide and to explore effective solutions to mitigate these challenges. Specifically, the review aims to:

1. Identify and categorize the predominant transportation issues affecting urban and rural areas.
2. Examine case studies that illustrate the real-world impact of these problems.

3.   Evaluate current strategies and solutions implemented to address transportation challenges.
4.   Highlight innovative and sustainable approaches that can revolutionize transportation systems.
5.   Discuss future trends and potential directions for transportation policy and technology.

By achieving these objectives, the review seeks to offer valuable insights for policymakers, urban planners, researchers, and stakeholders involved in the transportation sector.

II. OVERVIEW OF TRANSPORTATION SYSTEMS

An easy way to comply with the conference paper formatting requirements is to use this document as a template and simply type your text into it.

A. Types of Transportation Modes

Transportation systems can be broadly categorized into four primary modes: road, rail, air, and water. **Road transportation** is the most widely used mode, encompassing personal vehicles, buses, and trucks. It offers flexibility and door-to-door service, making it essential for daily commuting and freight movement. However, road transportation often suffers from congestion and high maintenance costs (Jenelius & Cebecauer, 2020). **Rail transportation** is efficient for long-distance travel and bulk freight movement, known for its energy efficiency and lower environmental impact. Rail systems, including subways and commuter trains, are vital for urban mobility and reducing traffic congestion. **Air transportation** is indispensable for international travel and high-value, time-sensitive cargo. Despite its speed and efficiency, air transport is often associated with higher costs and environmental concerns due to emissions. **Water transportation** includes maritime shipping and inland waterways, crucial for global trade and transporting large volumes of goods over long distances (Sultana et al., 2019). While it is cost-effective and energy-efficient, water transport can be slow and dependent on port infrastructure and weather conditions.

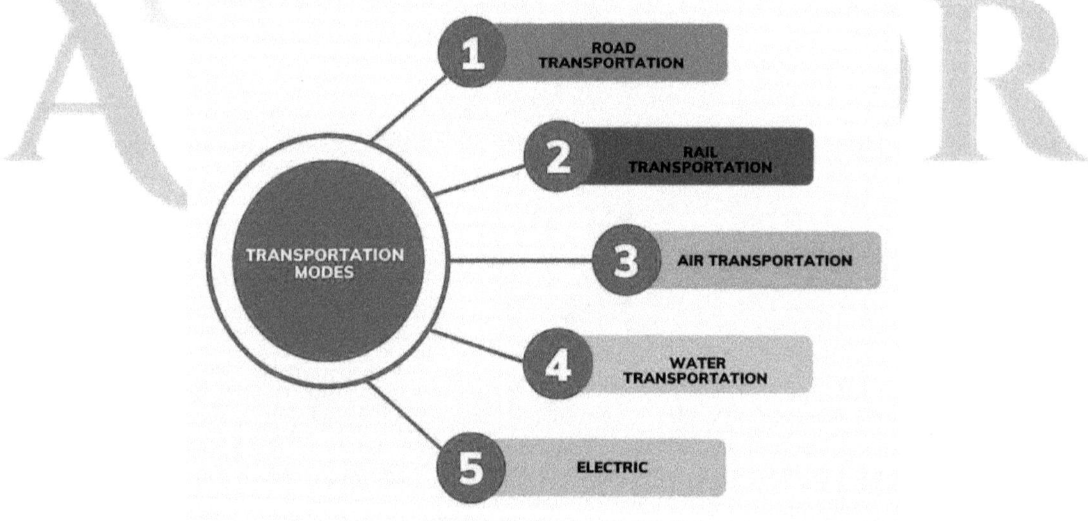

Figure 1: Transportation modes

B. Historical Development and Evolution

The historical development of transportation systems has significantly shaped human civilization and economic progress (van der Gun et al., 2016). Ancient civilizations relied on footpaths, animal-drawn carts, and simple boats for movement and trade. The invention of the wheel and the construction of roads by the Romans marked significant advancements in land transportation (Mueller et al., 2015). The Industrial Revolution in the 18th and 19th centuries brought about transformative changes with the development of steam engines, leading to the proliferation of railways and steamships. The 20th century witnessed the rise of automobiles and the construction of extensive road networks, revolutionizing personal and freight transport. The advent of commercial aviation in the mid-20th century further shrank distances, making global travel more accessible. In recent decades, technological innovations such as high-speed trains, electric vehicles, and intelligent transportation systems (ITS) have continued to evolve, addressing contemporary challenges and enhancing efficiency (Pojani & Stead, 2015).

Today, transportation systems are becoming increasingly interconnected and multimodal, aiming to create seamless and sustainable mobility solutions for the future.

III. Major Transportation Problems

Transportation systems worldwide face a multitude of challenges that hinder their efficiency and sustainability (Ríos-Mercado & Borraz-Sánchez, 2015). Among these, **traffic congestion** stands out as a pervasive issue, especially in urban areas. The rapid increase in vehicle ownership and insufficient road infrastructure lead to frequent traffic jams, causing delays, increased fuel consumption, and higher emissions. This congestion not only affects the daily commute but also impedes economic activities by delaying the transport of goods and services (Latunde et al., 2019).

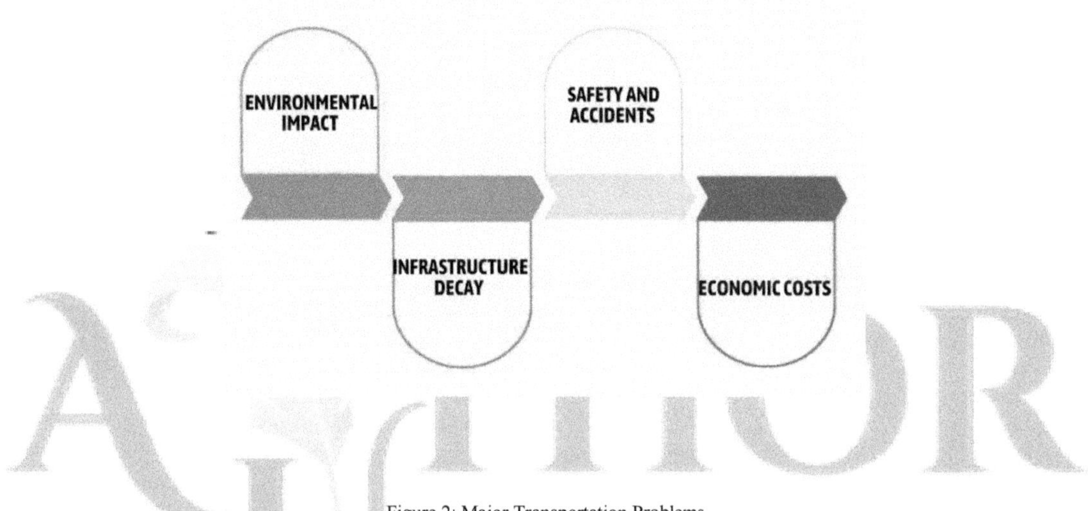

Figure 2: Major Transportation Problems

Environmental impact is another critical problem associated with transportation. The reliance on fossil fuels for most modes of transport contributes significantly to air pollution and greenhouse gas emissions, exacerbating climate change. Vehicular emissions are major sources of pollutants such as nitrogen oxides, carbon monoxide, and particulate matter, which pose serious health risks to urban populations (Kaewunruen et al., 2016).

Infrastructure decay further complicates transportation systems. Many roads, bridges, and tunnels were constructed decades ago and are now in urgent need of repair or replacement. Aging infrastructure leads to increased maintenance costs and can pose safety hazards if not adequately addressed (Zheng et al., 2015).

Safety and accidents are also major concerns, with traffic accidents being a leading cause of injury and death worldwide. Poor road conditions, lack of enforcement of traffic laws, and driver errors contribute to high accident rates, which result in significant human and economic losses (Das & Bhattacharyya, 2015).

The **economic costs** of transportation problems are substantial. Traffic congestion, accidents, and infrastructure maintenance require significant public and private expenditure. Moreover, inefficiencies in transportation can lead to higher costs for goods and services, as delays and fuel costs are often passed on to consumers (Bezyak et al., 2020).

Accessibility and equity issues highlight disparities in transportation systems. Many marginalized communities, particularly in rural or economically disadvantaged areas, lack access to reliable and affordable transportation options. This limits their opportunities for employment, education, and healthcare, perpetuating cycles of poverty and social inequality (Benamou et al., 2015).

Addressing these major transportation problems requires a multifaceted approach that incorporates technological innovations, policy reforms, infrastructure investment, and community engagement to create a more efficient, sustainable, and equitable transportation system.

IV. Case Studies of Transportation Issues

A. Urban Transportation Problems

Urban areas around the globe face significant transportation challenges, with traffic congestion being one of the most pervasive issues. Major cities such as New York, London, and Tokyo experience daily gridlock, leading to extended commute times, increased fuel consumption, and elevated levels of air pollution (Cleophas et al., 2019). A detailed case study of traffic congestion in these cities reveals the multifaceted nature of the problem, which stems from a combination of high population density, inadequate public transportation infrastructure, and the prevalence of private vehicle use (Strotz, 2016). The economic impact of traffic congestion is substantial, affecting productivity and contributing to financial losses for both individuals and businesses. Moreover, the environmental repercussions, including increased greenhouse gas emissions, underscore the urgent need for effective urban transportation planning and policy interventions (Gössling, 2020).

B. Rural and Remote Area Challenges

In contrast to urban areas, rural and remote regions face unique transportation issues primarily related to accessibility. A case study examining accessibility issues in remote regions highlights the difficulties residents encounter in reaching essential services such as healthcare, education, and markets (Porru et al., 2020). Sparse populations, long distances, and inadequate transportation infrastructure contribute to these challenges, exacerbating social and economic inequalities (Atuoye et al., 2015). For instance, remote areas in countries like Canada and Australia often rely on limited and infrequent transportation services, making it difficult for residents to maintain a consistent connection with urban centers (Rojas-Zerpa & Yusta, 2015). These accessibility issues underscore the necessity for tailored transportation solutions that can enhance connectivity and improve the quality of life in rural and remote areas (Porter, 2016).

C. International Transportation Issues

Transportation problems are not confined within national borders; they often extend to international contexts, particularly in terms of cross-border transportation and trade (Guerrero-Ibanez et al., 2015). A case study focusing on cross-border transportation issues reveals the complexities involved in facilitating seamless movement of goods and people across international boundaries. Factors such as differing regulations, border security measures, and infrastructure disparities can lead to significant delays and increased costs (Kumar, 2016). For example, trade routes between the United States and Mexico face challenges related to customs clearance processes and infrastructure bottlenecks. These issues highlight the importance of international cooperation and harmonization of transportation policies to enhance efficiency and promote economic integration. Addressing cross-border transportation challenges is crucial for the smooth functioning of global supply chains and the overall health of the international economy (Bagloee et al., 2016).

These case studies provide valuable insights into the diverse transportation challenges faced by different regions and contexts, emphasizing the need for tailored solutions that address specific local, regional, and international issues.

V. CURRENT SOLUTIONS AND STRATEGIES

D. Technological Innovations

Technological advancements have significantly transformed transportation systems, offering innovative solutions to long-standing problems. **Intelligent Transportation Systems (ITS)** are at the forefront of this revolution, integrating advanced communication technologies with transportation infrastructure to improve traffic management, reduce congestion, and enhance safety (Umar et al., 2020). ITS includes real-time traffic monitoring, adaptive traffic signal control, and advanced traveler information systems that provide dynamic route guidance and alerts. Another key technological innovation is the development and deployment of **electric and autonomous vehicles** (Hancock et al., 2019). Electric vehicles (EVs) address environmental concerns by reducing greenhouse gas emissions and dependence on fossil fuels. Autonomous vehicles (AVs), equipped with sophisticated sensors and AI algorithms, promise to revolutionize mobility by enhancing safety, optimizing traffic flow, and providing new mobility solutions for the elderly and disabled (Harris et al., 2015).

E. Policy and Regulation

Effective policy and regulatory frameworks are crucial for addressing transportation challenges and fostering sustainable development. **Urban planning and zoning** policies play a vital role in reducing traffic congestion and promoting efficient land use (Wilson, 2021). By encouraging mixed-use development, higher-density housing, and the integration of public transportation, urban planning can significantly enhance accessibility and reduce travel demand (Allen & Arkolakis, 2022). **Emission standards and environmental policies** are essential for mitigating the environmental impact of transportation (Santos, 2017). Regulations that set strict emission limits for vehicles, promote the adoption of cleaner technologies, and incentivize the use of public transport and non-motorized modes contribute to reducing air pollution and improving public health.

F. Infrastructure Improvement

Upgrading and maintaining transportation infrastructure is fundamental to ensuring efficient and reliable mobility. The development of **smart infrastructure** involves integrating digital technologies into physical infrastructure to enhance its functionality and resilience (Sun et al., 2020). Examples include smart traffic lights, connected roadways, and digital tolling systems that improve traffic flow and reduce congestion. **Maintenance and modernization** of existing infrastructure are equally important (Faturechi & Miller-Hooks, 2015). Regular maintenance ensures the safety and longevity of transportation assets, while modernization efforts, such as expanding public transit networks, constructing bike lanes, and upgrading road surfaces, enhance overall system performance. These infrastructure improvements not only address current transportation issues but also build a foundation for accommodating future growth and technological advancements (Warnes, 2021).

In summary, a combination of technological innovations, strategic policy and regulation, and targeted infrastructure improvements constitutes a comprehensive approach to solving transportation problems. These solutions, when effectively implemented, have the potential to create more sustainable, efficient, and accessible transportation systems for the future.

VI. INNOVATIVE APPROACHES TO TRANSPORTATION PROBLEMS

A. Sustainable Transportation Solutions

Addressing transportation problems in a sustainable manner involves enhancing public transportation systems and promoting non-motorized transport options such as cycling and walking (Dominković et al., 2018). Public transportation improvements are crucial in reducing traffic congestion, lowering greenhouse gas emissions, and providing equitable access to mobility. Investments in modernizing infrastructure, increasing service frequency, and integrating advanced technologies like real-time tracking and mobile ticketing can make public transport more efficient and user-friendly (Acar & Dincer, 2020). Additionally, developing dedicated cycling lanes and pedestrian pathways encourages non-motorized transport, which not only reduces reliance on fossil fuels but also promotes healthier lifestyles (Mathiesen et al., 2015). Cities like Copenhagen and Amsterdam serve as exemplary models, where extensive cycling infrastructure has significantly contributed to sustainable urban mobility.

B. Community and Stakeholder Engagement

Effective transportation solutions require active community and stakeholder engagement. Participatory planning processes, where local communities are involved in decision-making, ensure that transportation projects address the actual needs and preferences of the people they serve (Goodman & Sanders Thompson, 2017). Engaging stakeholders from various sectors, including government, private companies, and civil society, fosters collaboration and innovative problem-solving (Cumming et al., 2022). Public awareness campaigns are also vital in shifting behavioral patterns towards sustainable transportation practices (Sterling et al., 2017). Educating the public about the benefits of using public transport, cycling, and walking can lead to increased adoption of these modes and a reduction in the environmental impact of transportation systems (Xu & Saxton, 2019).

C. Integrated and Multimodal Transportation Systems

Creating integrated and multimodal transportation systems is key to solving complex transportation problems (Asaul et al., 2017). These systems combine various modes of transport, such as buses, trains, bicycles, and ride-sharing services, into a cohesive network that offers seamless connectivity (Nitsenko et al., 2020). Multimodal transportation allows passengers to choose the most efficient and convenient mode for each segment of their journey, reducing overall travel time and enhancing the user experience (Archetti et al., 2022). For instance, transit-oriented development (TOD) strategies, which concentrate residential and commercial development around transit hubs, can significantly reduce car dependency and encourage the use of public transportation (Koohathongsumrit & Meethom, 2021). Integrating digital platforms that provide real-time information and payment options for multiple transport modes further enhances the efficiency and attractiveness of multimodal systems (Hao & Yue, 2016), (Naghawi & Wolshon, 2015).

In summary, innovative approaches to transportation problems encompass sustainable solutions, community engagement, and integrated multimodal systems. These strategies not only address current challenges but also pave the way for resilient and future-ready transportation networks. By focusing on sustainability, inclusivity, and integration, cities and regions can develop transportation systems that meet the demands of today while safeguarding the needs of future generations.

VII. FUTURE TRENDS AND PROSPECTS

The future of transportation is poised to be revolutionized by emerging technologies and innovative policy directions. One of the most promising technological advancements is the development of hyperloop and advanced rail systems. These high-speed transit solutions promise to significantly reduce travel times between major urban centers, offering a sustainable and efficient alternative to traditional rail and road transport. Hyperloop technology, for instance, envisions passenger pods traveling through low-pressure tubes at speeds exceeding 700 miles per hour, potentially transforming long-distance travel and cargo transport. Similarly, advanced rail systems, including maglev (magnetic levitation) trains, are set to enhance the speed, safety, and efficiency of rail transport, reducing congestion and environmental impact.

In urban areas, drone delivery and urban air mobility are emerging as innovative solutions to address congestion and improve logistics. Drones can provide rapid delivery services, particularly in densely populated cities where traditional delivery methods are slow and inefficient. Urban air mobility, involving the use of electric vertical takeoff and landing (eVTOL) aircraft, is expected to offer new possibilities for personal and commercial transport, reducing ground traffic and connecting previously hard-to-reach areas.

Policy directions are also crucial in shaping the future of transportation. Sustainable Urban Mobility Plans (SUMPs) are becoming a key focus for cities aiming to create more livable and environmentally friendly urban spaces. These plans emphasize the integration of various transport modes, the promotion of public and non-motorized transport, and the reduction of carbon emissions. International collaboration on transportation issues is another important aspect, as cross-border cooperation can lead to the harmonization of standards, shared technological advancements, and coordinated efforts to tackle global challenges such as climate change and resource scarcity.

However, the path to these advancements is not without challenges. The implementation of new technologies requires significant investment, regulatory approval, and public acceptance. There are concerns about the environmental impact of constructing new infrastructure and the potential displacement of existing jobs. Additionally, ensuring the security and privacy of data in increasingly digital and connected transport systems is a critical issue. Despite these challenges, the opportunities presented by emerging technologies and innovative policies hold great promise for creating a more efficient, sustainable, and interconnected transportation future. By addressing these challenges proactively, stakeholders can harness the potential of these advancements to improve mobility and enhance the quality of life worldwide.

VIII. CONCLUSION

A. Summary of Key Findings

The review highlights the pervasive and multifaceted nature of transportation problems, encompassing traffic congestion, environmental impact, infrastructure decay, safety concerns, economic costs, and accessibility issues. Urban areas suffer from acute congestion and pollution, while rural regions face significant accessibility challenges. The case studies presented illustrate these issues' real-world impact, emphasizing the urgent need for effective solutions. Current strategies, including technological innovations, policy reforms, and infrastructure improvements, offer some relief but often fall short of addressing the root causes comprehensively. Innovative approaches, such as intelligent transportation systems, electric and autonomous vehicles, sustainable public transportation, and community engagement, show promise in mitigating these challenges and promoting a more efficient and sustainable transportation future.

B. Recommendations for Policy Makers, Planners, and Researchers

To address transportation challenges effectively, a multifaceted and collaborative approach is essential. Policymakers should prioritize sustainable urban mobility plans, enforce stringent environmental regulations, and invest in smart infrastructure. Urban planners need to incorporate multimodal transportation systems, promote non-motorized transport, and engage with communities to ensure inclusive and equitable solutions. Researchers should focus on advancing emerging technologies, such as hyperloop systems and urban air mobility, and explore innovative policy frameworks that address future transportation needs. Cross-sector collaboration and international cooperation are crucial to share best practices, leverage technological advancements, and ensure cohesive and integrated transportation systems globally.

C. Final Thoughts on the Future of Transportation

The future of transportation hinges on our ability to innovate and adapt to evolving challenges. With rapid urbanization, technological advancements, and increasing environmental concerns, the transportation sector is at a crossroads. Embracing sustainable practices, investing in cutting-edge technologies, and fostering collaborative efforts among stakeholders will be pivotal in shaping a resilient and efficient transportation system. By addressing current issues and anticipating future needs, we can pave the way for a transportation landscape that enhances mobility, supports economic growth, and promotes environmental sustainability for generations to come.

REFERENCES

[1] Acar, C., & Dincer, I. (2020). The potential role of hydrogen as a sustainable transportation fuel to combat global warming. *International Journal of Hydrogen Energy, 45*(5), 3396–3406. https://www.sciencedirect.com/science/article/pii/S0360319918333767

[2] Allen, T., & Arkolakis, C. (2022). The welfare effects of transportation infrastructure improvements. *The Review of Economic Studies, 89*(6), 2911–2957. https://academic.oup.com/restud/article-abstract/89/6/2911/6519332

[3] Archetti, C., Peirano, L., & Speranza, M. G. (2022). Optimization in multimodal freight transportation problems: A Survey. *European Journal of Operational Research, 299*(1), 1–20. https://www.sciencedirect.com/science/article/pii/S0377221721006263

[4] Asaul, A., Malygin, I., & Komashinskiy, V. (2017). The project of intellectual multimodal transport system. *Transportation Research Procedia, 20*, 25–30. https://www.sciencedirect.com/science/article/pii/S2352146517300066

[5] Atuoye, K. N., Dixon, J., Rishworth, A., Galaa, S. Z., Boamah, S. A., & Luginaah, I. (2015). Can she make it? Transportation barriers to accessing maternal and child health care services in rural Ghana. *BMC Health Services Research, 15*(1), 333. https://doi.org/10.1186/s12913-015-1005-y

[6] Bagloee, S. A., Tavana, M., Asadi, M., & Oliver, T. (2016). Autonomous vehicles: Challenges, opportunities, and future implications for transportation policies. *Journal of Modern Transportation, 24*(4), 284–303. https://doi.org/10.1007/s40534-016-0117-3

[7] Benamou, J.-D., Carlier, G., Cuturi, M., Nenna, L., & Peyré, G. (2015). Iterative Bregman Projections for Regularized Transportation Problems. *SIAM Journal on Scientific Computing, 37*(2), A1111–A1138. https://doi.org/10.1137/141000439

[8] Bezyak, J. L., Sabella, S., Hammel, J., McDonald, K., Jones, R. A., & Barton, D. (2020). Community participation and public transportation barriers experienced by people with disabilities. *Disability and Rehabilitation, 42*(23), 3275–3283. https://doi.org/10.1080/09638288.2019.1590469

[9] Cleophas, C., Cottrill, C., Ehmke, J. F., & Tierney, K. (2019). Collaborative urban transportation: Recent advances in theory and practice. *European Journal of Operational Research, 273*(3), 801–816. https://www.sciencedirect.com/science/article/pii/S0377221718303412

[10] Cumming, G., Campbell, L., Norwood, C., Ranger, S., Richardson, P., & Sanghera, A. (2022). Putting stakeholder engagement in its place: How situating public participation in community improves natural resource management outcomes. *GeoJournal, 87*(S2), 209–221. https://doi.org/10.1007/s10708-020-10367-1

[11] Das, S., & Bhattacharyya, B. K. (2015). Optimization of municipal solid waste collection and transportation routes. *Waste Management, 43*, 9–18. https://www.sciencedirect.com/science/article/pii/S0956053X15004432

[12] Dominković, D. F., Bačeković, I., Pedersen, A. S., & Krajačić, G. (2018). The future of transportation in sustainable energy systems: Opportunities and barriers in a clean energy transition. *Renewable and Sustainable Energy Reviews, 82*, 1823–1838. https://www.sciencedirect.com/science/article/pii/S1364032117310560

[13] Donaldson, D. (2018). Railroads of the Raj: Estimating the impact of transportation infrastructure. *American Economic Review, 108*(4–5), 899–934. https://www.aeaweb.org/articles?id=10.1257/aer.20101199

[14] Faturechi, R., & Miller-Hooks, E. (2015). Measuring the Performance of Transportation Infrastructure Systems in Disasters: A Comprehensive Review. *Journal of Infrastructure Systems, 21*(1), 04014025. https://doi.org/10.1061/(ASCE)IS.1943-555X.0000212

[15] Goodman, M. S., & Sanders Thompson, V. L. (2017). The science of stakeholder engagement in research: Classification, implementation, and evaluation. *Translational Behavioral Medicine, 7*(3), 486–491. https://academic.oup.com/tbm/article-abstract/7/3/486/4644893

[16] Gössling, S. (2020). Integrating e-scooters in urban transportation: Problems, policies, and the prospect of system change. *Transportation Research Part D: Transport and Environment, 79*, 102230. https://www.sciencedirect.com/science/article/pii/S1361920919312829

[17] Guerrero-Ibanez, J. A., Zeadally, S., & Contreras-Castillo, J. (2015). Integration challenges of intelligent transportation systems with connected vehicle, cloud computing, and internet of things technologies. *IEEE Wireless Communications, 22*(6), 122–128. https://ieeexplore.ieee.org/abstract/document/7368833/

[18] Hancock, P. A., Nourbakhsh, I., & Stewart, J. (2019). On the future of transportation in an era of automated and autonomous vehicles. *Proceedings of the National Academy of Sciences, 116*(16), 7684–7691. https://doi.org/10.1073/pnas.1805770115

[19] Hao, C., & Yue, Y. (2016). Optimization on combination of transport routes and modes on dynamic programming for a container multimodal transport system. *Procedia Engineering, 137*, 382–390. https://www.sciencedirect.com/science/article/pii/S187770581600299X

[20] Harris, I., Wang, Y., & Wang, H. (2015). ICT in multimodal transport and technological trends: Unleashing potential for the future. *International Journal of Production Economics, 159*, 88–103. https://www.sciencedirect.com/science/article/pii/S0925527314002837

[21] Jedwab, R., & Moradi, A. (2016). The permanent effects of transportation revolutions in poor countries: Evidence from Africa. *Review of Economics and Statistics, 98*(2), 268–284. https://direct.mit.edu/rest/article-abstract/98/2/268/58329

[22] Jenelius, E., & Cebecauer, M. (2020). Impacts of COVID-19 on public transport ridership in Sweden: Analysis of ticket validations, sales and passenger counts. *Transportation Research Interdisciplinary Perspectives, 8*, 100242. https://www.sciencedirect.com/science/article/pii/S2590198220301536

[23] Kaewunruen, S., Sussman, J. M., & Matsumoto, A. (2016). Grand challenges in transportation and transit systems. In *Frontiers in built environment* (Vol. 2, p. 4). Frontiers Media SA. https://www.frontiersin.org/articles/10.3389/fbuil.2016.00004/full

[24] Koohathongsumrit, N., & Meethom, W. (2021). An integrated approach of fuzzy risk assessment model and data envelopment analysis for route selection in multimodal transportation networks. *Expert Systems with Applications, 171*, 114342. https://www.sciencedirect.com/science/article/pii/S0957417420310290

[25] Kumar, P. S. (2016). A simple method for solving type-2 and type-4 fuzzy transportation problems. *International Journal of Fuzzy Logic and Intelligent Systems, 16*(4), 225–237. https://www.researchgate.net/profile/P-Senthil-Kumar-3/publication/311955604_A_Simple_Method_for_Solving_Type-2_and_Type-

4_Fuzzy_Transportation_Problems/links/58c29548aca272e36dcff26d/A-Simple-Method-for-Solving-Type-2-and-Type-4-Fuzzy-Transportation-Problems.pdf

[26] Latunde, T., Richard, J. O., Esan, O. O., & Dare, D. D. (2019). Sensitivity of parameters in the approach of linear programming to a transportation problem. *Journal of the Nigerian Society of Physical Sciences*, 116–121. https://journal.nsps.org.ng/index.php/jnsps/article/view/14

[27] Levasseur, M., Généreux, M., Bruneau, J.-F., Vanasse, A., Chabot, É., Beaulac, C., & Bédard, M.-M. (2015). Importance of proximity to resources, social support, transportation and neighborhood security for mobility and social participation in older adults: Results from a scoping study. *BMC Public Health*, *15*(1), 503. https://doi.org/10.1186/s12889-015-1824-0

[28] Mathiesen, B. V., Lund, H., Connolly, D., Wenzel, H., Østergaard, P. A., Möller, B., Nielsen, S., Ridjan, I., Karnøe, P., & Sperling, K. (2015). Smart Energy Systems for coherent 100% renewable energy and transport solutions. *Applied Energy*, *145*, 139–154. https://www.sciencedirect.com/science/article/pii/S0306261915001117

[29] Moore, H. B., Moore, E. E., Chapman, M. P., McVaney, K., Bryskiewicz, G., Blechar, R., Chin, T., Burlew, C. C., Pieracci, F., & West, F. B. (2018). Plasma-first resuscitation to treat haemorrhagic shock during emergency ground transportation in an urban area: A randomised trial. *The Lancet*, *392*(10144), 283–291. https://www.thelancet.com/article/S0140-6736(18)31553-8/abstract

[30] Mueller, N., Rojas-Rueda, D., Cole-Hunter, T., De Nazelle, A., Dons, E., Gerike, R., Götschi, T., Panis, L. I., Kahlmeier, S., & Nieuwenhuijsen, M. (2015). Health impact assessment of active transportation: A systematic review. *Preventive Medicine*, *76*, 103–114. https://www.sciencedirect.com/science/article/pii/S0091743515001164

[31] Næss, P. (2020). Validating explanatory qualitative research: Enhancing the interpretation of interviews in urban planning and transportation research. *Applied Mobilities*, *5*(2), 186–205. https://doi.org/10.1080/23800127.2018.1464814

[32] Naghawi, H., & Wolshon, B. (2015). Operation of multimodal transport system during mass evacuations. *Canadian Journal of Civil Engineering*, *42*(2), 81–88. https://doi.org/10.1139/cjce-2014-0177

[33] Nitsenko, V., Kotenko, S., Hanzhurenko, I., Mardani, A., Stashkevych, I., & Karakai, M. (2020). Mathematical Modeling of Multimodal Transportation Risks. In R. Ghazali, N. M. Nawi, M. M. Deris, & J. H. Abawajy (Eds.), *Recent Advances on Soft Computing and Data Mining* (Vol. 978, pp. 439–447). Springer International Publishing. https://doi.org/10.1007/978-3-030-36056-6_41

[34] Pojani, D., & Stead, D. (2015). Sustainable urban transport in the developing world: Beyond megacities. *Sustainability*, *7*(6), 7784–7805. https://www.mdpi.com/2071-1050/7/6/7784

[35] Porru, S., Misso, F. E., Pani, F. E., & Repetto, C. (2020). Smart mobility and public transport: Opportunities and challenges in rural and urban areas. *Journal of Traffic and Transportation Engineering (English Edition)*, *7*(1), 88–97. https://www.sciencedirect.com/science/article/pii/S2095756419301898

[36] Porter, G. (2016). Mobilities in Rural Africa: New Connections, New Challenges. *Annals of the American Association of Geographers*, 1–8. https://doi.org/10.1080/00045608.2015.1100056

[37] Ríos-Mercado, R. Z., & Borraz-Sánchez, C. (2015). Optimization problems in natural gas transportation systems: A state-of-the-art review. *Applied Energy*, *147*, 536–555. https://www.sciencedirect.com/science/article/pii/S0306261915003013

[38] Rojas-Zerpa, J. C., & Yusta, J. M. (2015). Application of multicriteria decision methods for electric supply planning in rural and remote areas. *Renewable and Sustainable Energy Reviews*, *52*, 557–571. https://www.sciencedirect.com/science/article/pii/S1364032115007868

[39] Santos, G. (2017). Road transport and CO2 emissions: What are the challenges? *Transport Policy*, *59*, 71–74. https://www.sciencedirect.com/science/article/pii/S0967070X17304262

[40] Sterling, E. J., Betley, E., Sigouin, A., Gomez, A., Toomey, A., Cullman, G., Malone, C., Pekor, A., Arengo, F., & Blair, M. (2017). Assessing the evidence for stakeholder engagement in biodiversity conservation. *Biological Conservation*, *209*, 159–171. https://www.sciencedirect.com/science/article/pii/S0006320717302069

[41] Strotz, R. H. (2016). Urban transportation parables. In *The public economy of urban communities* (pp. 127–169). Routledge. https://api.taylorfrancis.com/content/chapters/edit/download?identifierName=doi&identifierValue=10.4324/9781315670805-7&type=chapterpdf

[42] Sultana, S., Salon, D., & Kuby, M. (2019). Transportation sustainability in the urban context: A comprehensive review. *Urban Geography*, *40*(3), 279–308. https://doi.org/10.1080/02723638.2017.1395635

[43] Sun, W., Bocchini, P., & Davison, B. D. (2020). Resilience metrics and measurement methods for transportation infrastructure: The state of the art. *Sustainable and Resilient Infrastructure*, *5*(3), 168–199. https://doi.org/10.1080/23789689.2018.1448663

[44] Umar, M., Ji, X., Kirikkaleli, D., & Xu, Q. (2020). COP21 Roadmap: Do innovation, financial development, and transportation infrastructure matter for environmental sustainability in China? *Journal of Environmental Management*, *271*, 111026. https://www.sciencedirect.com/science/article/pii/S0301479720309543

[45] van der Gun, J., Pel, A., & van Arem, B. (2016). A general activity-based methodology for simulating multimodal transportation networks during emergencies. *European Journal of Transport and Infrastructure Research*, *16*(3), 490–511. https://research.tudelft.nl/en/publications/a-general-activity-based-methodology-for-simulating-multimodal-tr

[46] Warnes, P. E. (2021). Transport infrastructure improvements and spatial sorting: Evidence from buenos aires. *Unpublished Manuscript*. https://pewarnes.github.io/files/warnes_pablo_jmp.pdf

[47] Wilson, J. Q. (2021). The politics of regulation. In *The political economy: Readings in the politics and economics of American public policy* (pp. 82–103). Routledge. https://www.taylorfrancis.com/chapters/edit/10.4324/9781315495811-9/politics-regulation-james-wilson

[48] Xu, W. (Wayne), & Saxton, G. D. (2019). Does Stakeholder Engagement Pay Off on Social Media? A Social Capital Perspective. *Nonprofit and Voluntary Sector Quarterly*, *48*(1), 28–49. https://doi.org/10.1177/0899764018791267

[49] Zheng, X., Chen, W., Wang, P., Shen, D., Chen, S., Wang, X., Zhang, Q., & Yang, L. (2015). Big data for social transportation. *IEEE Transactions on Intelligent Transportation Systems*, *17*(3), 620–630. https://ieeexplore.ieee.org/abstract/document/7359138/

Strategic Planning for Affordable and Efficient G+18 High-Rise Buildings in Urban Settings

Radhika Dahane[1] and P. S. Pajgade[1]

[1]Department of Civil Engineering, Prof Ram Meghe Institute of Technology & Research, Badnera, Maharashtra, India

[1]Email: rdahane17@gmail.com

Abstract— Urbanization has led to increased demand for high-density housing, making the design and construction of high-rise buildings, such as G+18 towers, a critical focus in urban planning. This study explores the strategic planning and design considerations for cost-effective and efficient G+18 high-rise buildings in urban settings. Using a combination of structural analysis and advanced design methodologies, the research evaluates key performance metrics including displacement, reaction forces, beam forces, and column designs. The analysis reveals how different design elements impact the building's ability to manage dynamic forces, load distribution, and overall stability. The results highlight the effectiveness of modular construction techniques, prefabrication, and value engineering in optimizing cost and performance. Additionally, advancements in Building Information Modeling (BIM) and innovative materials are shown to enhance design accuracy and structural efficiency.

Keywords— Urbanization, high-rise buildings, G+18 towers, cost-effective design, structural analysis, displacement

I. INTRODUCTION

Urbanization is a global phenomenon that is reshaping cities and their infrastructure. With an increasing number of people migrating to urban areas, cities are experiencing unprecedented growth, both in terms of population and spatial expansion. This trend has created a pressing for high-density residential solutions that can efficiently utilize available land and resources. High-rise buildings, particularly those with multiple floors such as the G+18 model, offer a strategic approach to addressing this demand. The G+18 high-rise, defined by 18 floors above the ground, stands out as a practical solution for accommodating large numbers of residents within a limited footprint, thereby optimizing land use in densely populated urban environments.

The challenge, however, lies in balancing cost-effectiveness with the need for functional and aesthetically pleasing structures. High-rise construction involves complex considerations, from structural integrity and safety to energy efficiency and environmental impact. Achieving affordability in such projects requires more than just cutting costs; it involves a comprehensive strategy that integrates various aspects of design, materials, and construction practices.

In this context, the objective of this paper is to explore strategic planning methods that can make the construction of G+18 high-rise buildings both economically viable and efficient. The study will delve into several key areas:

1. **Design Optimization**: Identifying design strategies that can streamline the building process and reduce costs while ensuring the building meets all functional and safety requirements. This includes exploring modular construction techniques, prefabrication, and the use of advanced design tools like Building Information Modeling (BIM).
2. **Material Selection**: Examining the role of material choices in reducing overall costs. This involves evaluating the use of innovative and cost-effective materials, such as high-strength concrete and composite materials, that can offer both durability and savings.
3. **Construction Techniques**: Investigating modern construction practices that can enhance efficiency and reduce expenses. This includes analyzing methods that minimize construction time, labor costs, and material wastage.

4. **Technological Integration**: Leveraging advanced technologies to improve the planning, design, and construction processes. Technologies such as BIM, 3D printing, and automated construction systems can play a significant role in reducing costs and improving accuracy.

5. **Sustainability and Energy Efficiency**: Incorporating sustainable practices into the design and construction of high-rise buildings to reduce operational costs and environmental impact. This includes exploring energy-efficient systems, sustainable materials, and renewable energy sources.

6. **Regulatory and Financial Considerations**: Understanding the regulatory requirements and financial factors that influence high-rise construction. This includes compliance with building codes, securing financing, and managing project budgets.

By addressing these areas, this study aims to develop a comprehensive framework for planning and constructing G+18 high-rise buildings that are both cost-effective and capable of meeting the needs of urban populations. The findings will provide valuable insights for architects, engineers, developers, and urban planners seeking to design and implement high-density residential solutions in rapidly growing cities. Through a combination of innovative design, advanced technologies, and sustainable practices, it is possible to achieve a balance between affordability and quality, ultimately contributing to the creation of functional and aesthetically pleasing urban environments.

II. LITERATURE REVIEW

A. Urbanization and High-Rise Development

Urbanization is one of the most significant global trends, shaping the architectural and construction practices in modern cities. As urban populations expand, the demand for high-density housing solutions increases. According to the United Nations (2020), the global urban population is projected to rise by 2.5 billion by 2050, placing unprecedented pressure on existing infrastructure and necessitating innovative housing solutions (UN, 2020). High-rise buildings, such as the G+18 model, represent a viable response to this challenge. By utilizing vertical space, these structures can accommodate more residents within a limited land area, making them ideal for densely populated urban environments (Cai et al., 2020), (Harle et al., 2024).

Studies have demonstrated that high-density development can alleviate land scarcity issues and contribute to sustainable urban growth. For instance, (Ding & Chen, 2022) notes that vertical growth through high-rise buildings allows cities to maintain green spaces and reduce urban sprawl, thus supporting environmental sustainability and efficient land use . High-rise buildings also offer the advantage of centralized infrastructure, which can be more cost-effective than sprawling low-rise developments (Dipta et al., 2023), (Harle, 2024c).

B. Cost-Effective Design Strategies

Cost-effectiveness is a critical consideration in high-rise construction, where expenses can quickly escalate due to complex design and construction processes. To address this, various cost-effective design strategies have been explored. Modular construction techniques, as highlighted by (Juan et al., 2021), (Harle, 2024b), represent one such strategy. Modular construction involves prefabricating building components off-site and assembling them on-site, which can significantly lower costs by reducing construction time and minimizing material waste (Al-Kodmany, 2023), (Harle, 2024a). This approach also enhances quality control and can lead to fewer delays in the construction schedule.

Additionally, the integration of prefabricated components and standardized construction practices has been shown to improve efficiency and reduce labor costs. According to (Martinez-Muñoz, 2021), prefabrication allows for the mass production of building elements, which can be assembled more quickly on-site compared to traditional construction methods. This not only reduces the overall cost but also speeds up the construction process, allowing for faster occupancy of the building (Herburger et al., 2022).

Value engineering is another important aspect of cost-effective design. emphasizes that value engineering involves systematically assessing design alternatives to achieve the best balance between cost, performance, and quality. This process helps identify cost-saving opportunities without compromising the structural integrity or functional requirements of the building (Sun & Li, 2020). For example, optimizing material choices and construction methods can lead to significant savings while maintaining high standards of safety and comfort (Jasim, 2021), (Harle & Prakash, 2019).

C. Advanced Construction Technologies

Recent advancements in construction technologies have introduced new opportunities for enhancing cost-efficiency in high-rise buildings (Soliman et al., 2022). Building Information Modeling (BIM) is one such technology that has transformed the planning and execution of construction projects. explains that BIM provides a comprehensive digital representation of the building, which facilitates better coordination among stakeholders, reduces design errors, and improves cost estimation accuracy (Stranz, 2020). BIM's ability to simulate various scenarios and analyze potential issues before construction begins can lead to more informed decision-making and cost savings (Li et al., 2021).

Innovative materials, such as high-strength concrete and composite materials, also play a role in improving cost-efficiency (Zhou et al., 2021). High-strength concrete allows for slimmer structural elements, which can reduce the overall weight and material costs of the building. Composite materials, which combine different substances to enhance performance, can offer improved durability and reduced maintenance costs (Ghasemi Poor Sabet & Chong, 2020). These materials contribute to both the structural efficiency and long-term cost-effectiveness of high-rise buildings (Yap et al., 2024).

D. Sustainable Practices and Energy Efficiency

Incorporating sustainable practices into high-rise building design is increasingly recognized as a means to achieve cost-effectiveness (Olawumi et al., 2022). Green building strategies not only contribute to environmental conservation but also offer long-term financial benefits. For instance, the implementation of energy-efficient systems, such as LED lighting and advanced HVAC systems, can significantly reduce operational costs (Afzal et al., 2021). highlights that energy-efficient buildings typically experience lower utility bills and reduced environmental impact, which contributes to their overall cost-effectiveness (Balzan et al., 2020).

The integration of renewable energy sources, such as solar panels, is another key component of sustainable high-rise design. According to (Krystek et al., 2021), solar panels can generate electricity for the building, reducing reliance on external energy sources and lowering energy costs. Additionally, incorporating features like green roofs and rainwater harvesting systems can enhance the building's sustainability and reduce operational expenses (Noruwa et al., 2022).

In summary, the literature reveals that strategic planning for G+18 high-rise buildings involves a multifaceted approach that integrates cost-effective design strategies, advanced construction technologies, and sustainable practices. By leveraging these approaches, it is possible to develop high-rise buildings that meet the needs of growing urban populations while balancing affordability and efficiency. This paper will further explore these strategies and provide practical recommendations for achieving these objectives in the context of high-rise urban development.

III. METHODOLOGY

This section outlines the methodology used to design and analyze the G+18 high-rise building for cost-effectiveness and efficiency. The methodology involves a series of systematic steps, including building planning, geometric design, property assignment, load analysis, and design commands. Each step is illustrated through figures that depict various aspects of the building's design and analysis process.

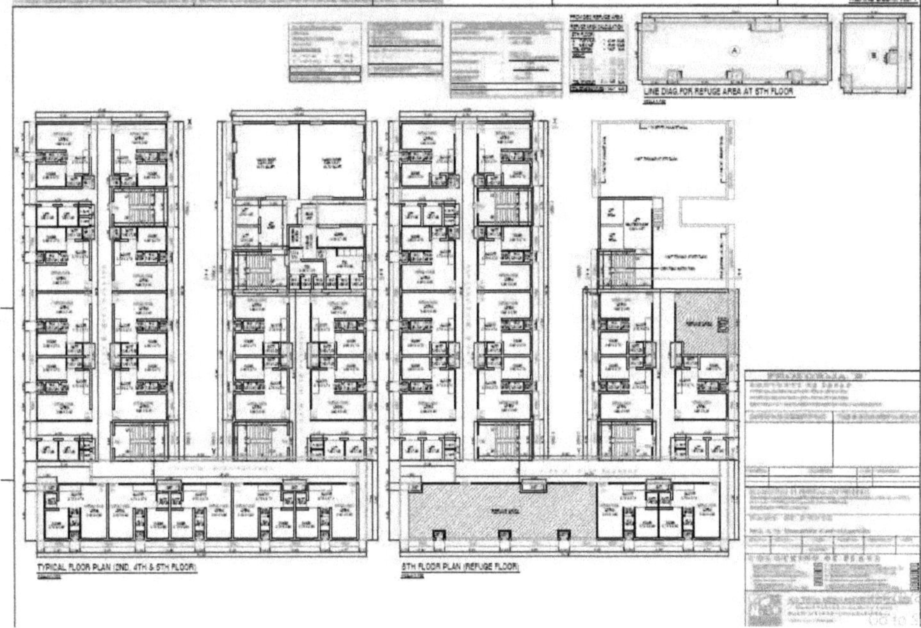

Figure 1: Plan of the Building

The plan of the building, depicted in Figure 1, provides a detailed layout of the G+18 high-rise structure. This figure includes floor plans for each level, highlighting the arrangement of residential units, common areas, and essential services.

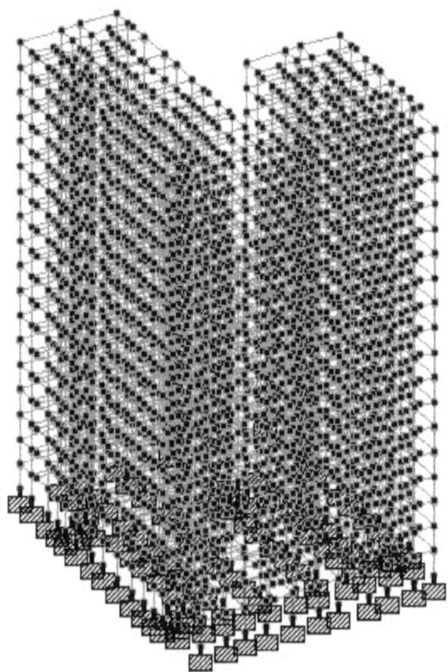

Figure 2: Geometry of the Building

Figure 2 illustrates the geometric configuration of the building, including the overall dimensions, floor heights, and vertical alignment of the structure.

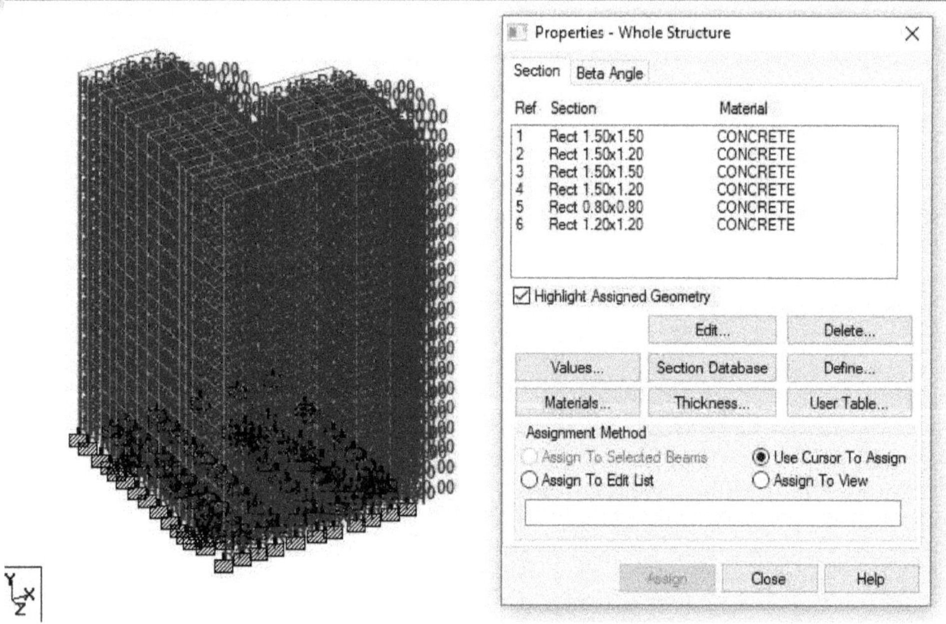

Figure 3: Properties assigned to the Building

Figure 3 outlines the various properties assigned to the building during the design phase. These properties include material specifications, structural elements, and construction methods.

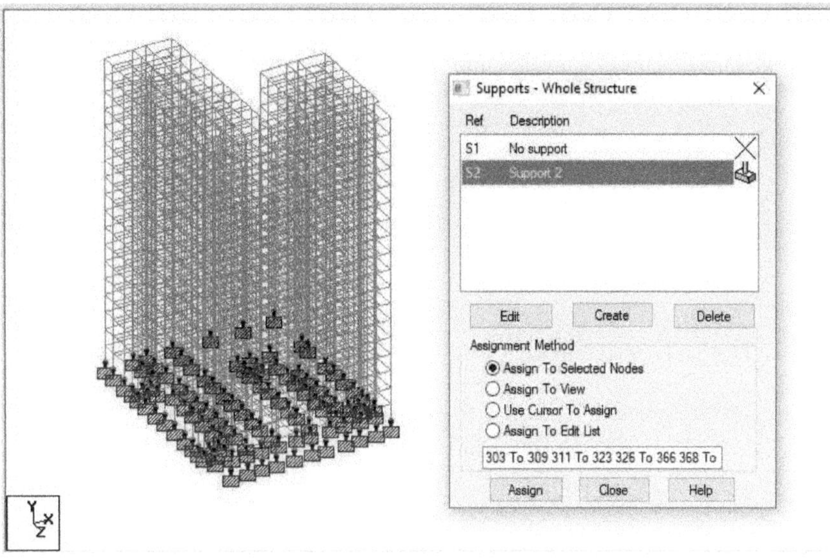

Figure 4:Supports assigned to the Building

In Figure 4, the supports assigned to the building are shown. These supports include foundation details, bearing walls, and columns that provide structural stability.

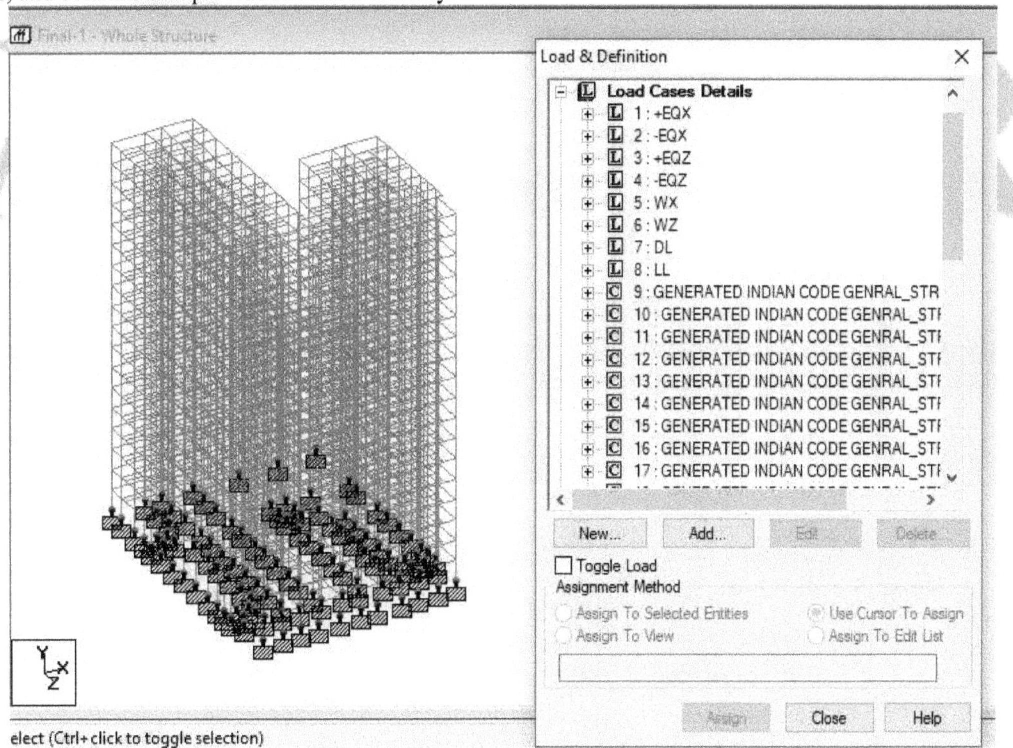

Figure 5: Loads assigned to building

Figure 5 details the various loads applied to the building, including dead loads, live loads, wind loads, and seismic loads. Dead loads refer to the weight of the building's structural components, while live loads account for variable loads such as occupancy and furniture.

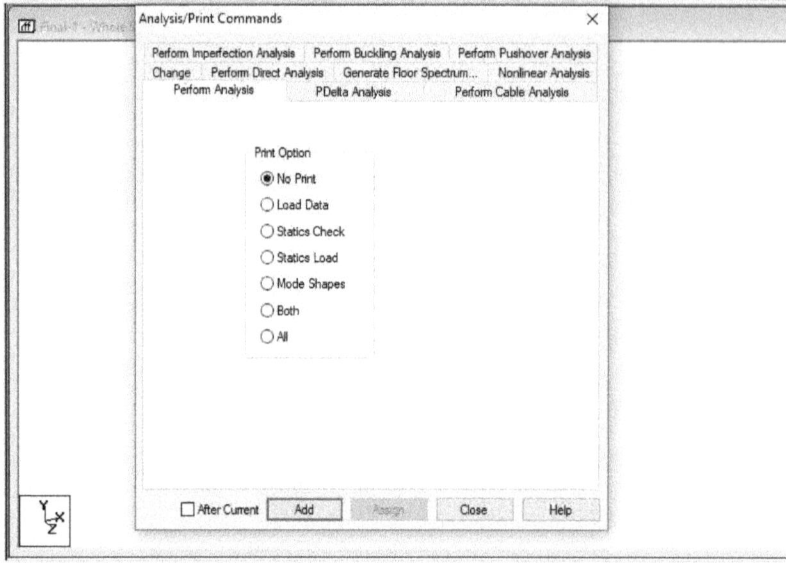

Figure 6: Analysis command to the building

Figure 6 illustrates the analysis commands used to evaluate the building's structural performance. These commands include calculations for load distribution, stress analysis, and stability checks.

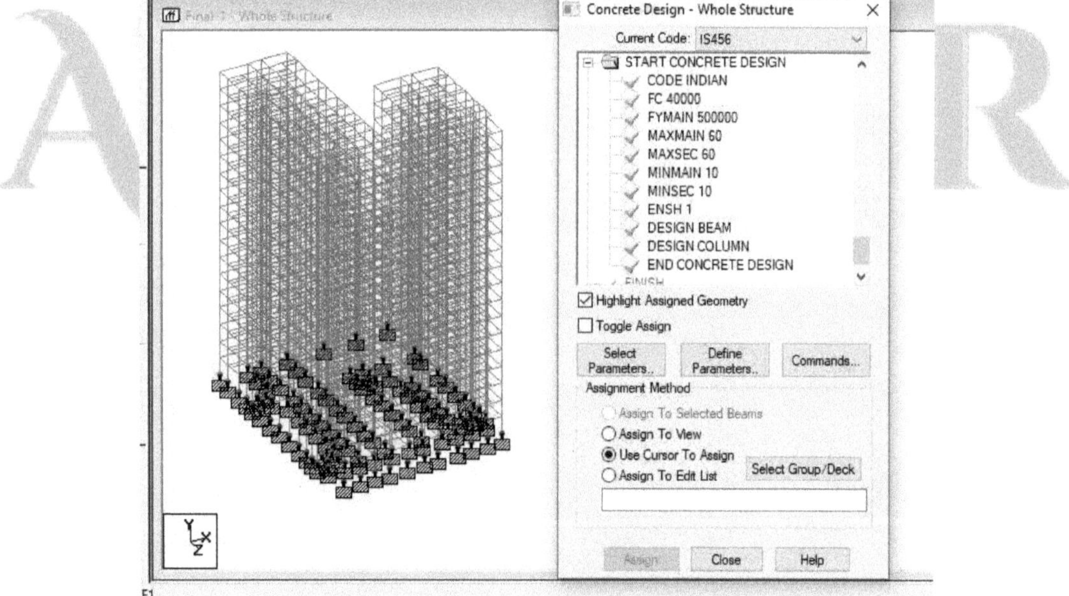

Figure 7: Design commands given to the building

Figure 7 shows the design commands implemented to finalize the building's structural configuration. These commands include specifications for reinforcement, material properties, and construction methods based on the analysis results.

The methodology for designing and analyzing the G+18 high-rise building involves a comprehensive approach, integrating detailed planning, geometric design, property assignment, load analysis, and design commands. The figures provided illustrate each step in the process, highlighting the importance of accurate data and analysis for achieving a cost-effective and efficient high-rise structure. By following this methodology, the project aims to develop a high-rise building that meets urban needs while optimizing construction and operational costs.

IV. RESULTS AND DISCUSSIONS

This section presents the findings of the study related to the structural performance and design of the G+18 high-rise building. The results are analyzed to understand how different design and construction strategies impact the overall performance of the building. The tables and figures included provide detailed insights into displacement, reactions, beam forces, and the design of key structural elements.

TABLE 1: DISPLACEMENT OF THE BUILDING

	Node	Horizontal X mm	Vertical Y mm	Horizontal Z mm	Resultant mm
Max X	6235	17.037	4.175	1.48	17.603
Min X	6290	14.959	2.243	0.042	15.126
Max Y	6585	0.375	3.214	3.522	4.782
Min Y	6584	0.148	437.692	0.586	437.693
Max Z	6270	0.371	3.171	10.584	11.055
Min Z	6391	0.296	4.766	13.04	13.886
Max rX	3062	0.107	2.558	3.899	4.665
Min rX	6585	0.148	432.971	0.629	432.972
Max rY	3062	4.081	1.681	0.288	4.423
Min rY	3062	3.735	2.294	0.548	4.417
Max rZ	6581	0.19	95.912	0.629	95.914
Min rZ	6583	0.149	427.087	0.565	427.087
Max Rst	6584	0.148	437.692	0.586	437.693

Table 1 presents the displacement data for the building, which indicates how much different parts of the structure move or shift under various loads. Displacement is a critical parameter in assessing the structural integrity and stability of high-rise buildings.

TABLE 2: REACTIONS FOR THE BUILDING

	Node	Horizontal Fx kN	Vertical Fy kN	Horizontal Fz kN	Moment Mx kNm	My kNm	Mz kNm
Max Fx	446	190.55	8294.65	11.392	3.816	4.373	687.443
Min Fx	344	198.416	9463.32	28.322	6.575	3.131	695.42
Max Fy	355	117.64	11230.4	9.303	37.32	3.63	592.368
Min Fy	323	77.914	1334.64	1.932	13.693	2.173	380.166
Max Fz	364	38.612	9414.69	189.347	648.188	2.711	42.82
Min Fz	319	48.499	8806.17	185.079	605.971	0.924	55.343
Max Mx	364	38.612	9414.69	189.347	648.188	2.711	42.82
Min Mx	319	48.499	8806.17	185.079	605.971	0.924	55.343
Max My	346	21.442	8232.08	9.621	20.569	22.858	65.911
Min My	475	91.433	10568.1	3.909	8.208	19.652	437.322
Max Mz	344	198.416	9463.32	28.322	6.575	3.131	695.42
Min Mz	350	187.354	9180.6	1.197	14.16	3.897	691.261

Table 2 shows the reaction forces at various supports or joints within the building. These reactions are crucial for understanding how the building's load is distributed across its structural elements, such as foundations and columns.

	Beam	Node	Fx kN	Fy kN	Fz kN	Mx kNm	My kNm	Mz kNm
Max Fx	747	355	11230.4	117.64	9.303	3.63	37.32	592.368
Min Fx	5688	3716	1589.17	149.08	4.047	3.196	10.602	111.469
Max Fy	5401	3526	6820.67	2185.05	42.805	136.948	50.474	7385.05
Min Fy	10623	3381	0.213	2083.34	3.719	143.146	2.721	15693.6
Max Fz	5285	3381	6812.71	42.805	2185.05	136.948	7603.56	54.755
Min Fz	5280	3376	4835.7	81.325	796.5	40.429	788.999	135.092
Max Mx	10610	6579	0.77	888.718	0.421	2339.16	0.555	111.863
Min Mx	10613	6580	0.772	17.849	0.935	1899.25	0.889	955.583
Max My	5856	3712	4837.17	77.874	689.296	32.013	1266.17	117.37
Min My	5285	3381	6812.71	42.805	2185.05	136.948	7603.56	54.755
Max Mz	10623	3381	0.213	2083.34	3.719	143.146	2.721	15693.6
Min Mz	5977	3381	3830.51	1985.9	42.635	117.645	36.371	6364.27

Table 3 provides data on the forces acting on the beams within the building. This includes bending moments, shear forces, and axial forces in the beams. These forces are essential for assessing the structural capacity and performance of the beams, which play a crucial role in distributing loads throughout the building.

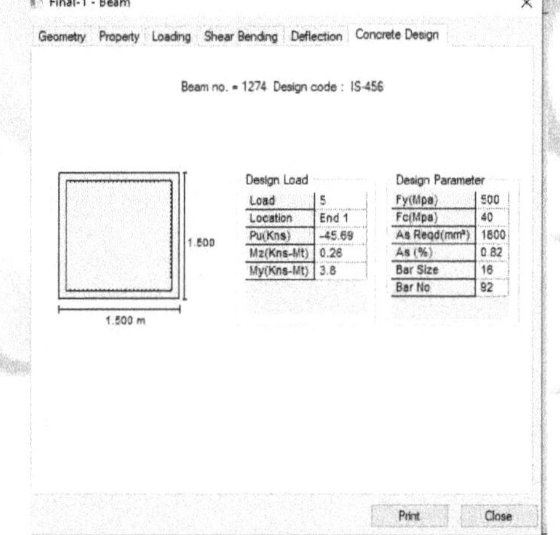

Figure 8: Base Height Column Design of the building

Figure 8 illustrates the design of the base height columns, which are the columns located at the lower levels of the building.

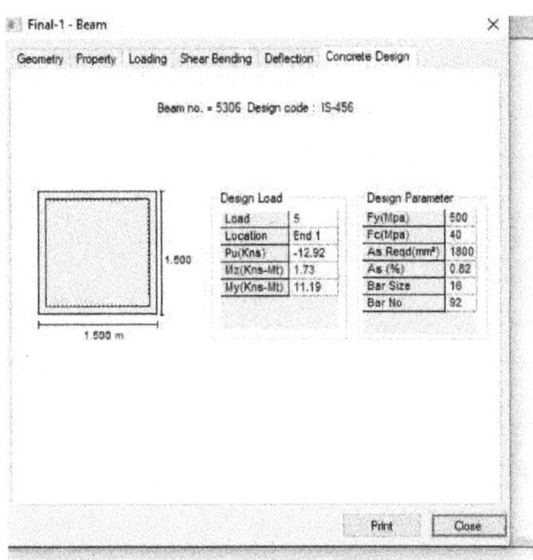

Figure 9: Middle Height Column Design of the building

Figure 9 depicts the design of the middle height columns, which are located between the base and the upper floors of the building.

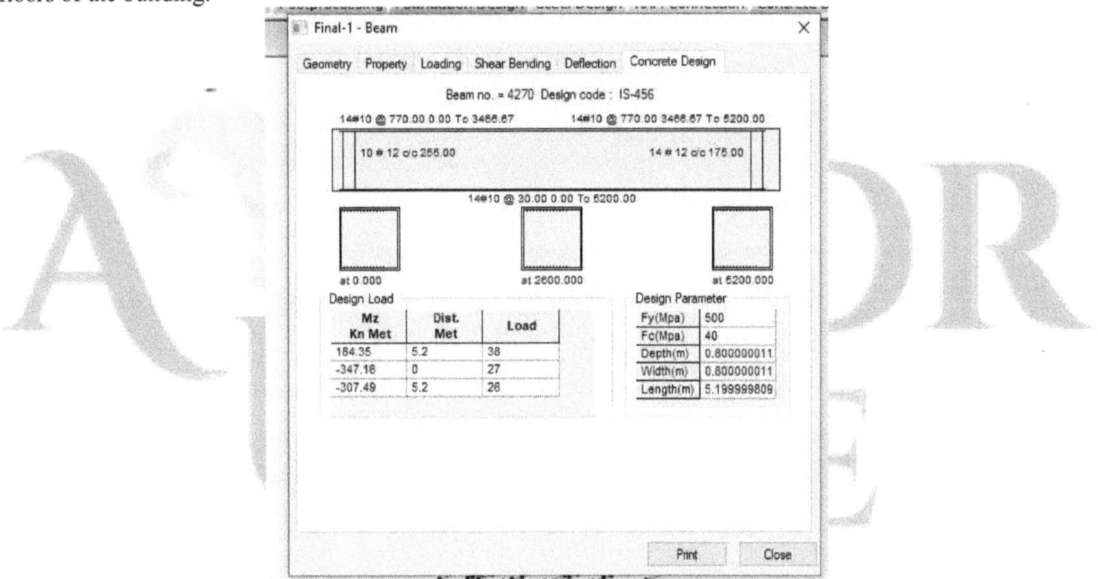

Figure 10: Beam design of the building

Figure 10 showcases the design of the beams throughout the building. Beams are critical for supporting and distributing loads across the structure. This figure provides details on beam sizes, reinforcement layouts, and the placement of beams within the building.

The results and discussions presented in this section offer valuable insights into the structural performance of the G+18 high-rise building. By analyzing displacement, reactions, beam forces, and column designs, the study provides a comprehensive assessment of the building's ability to handle loads and maintain stability. The findings help to identify areas where design improvements may be needed and ensure that the building meets safety and performance standards.

V. CONCLUSIONS

1. **Structural Displacement**: The analysis of displacement data indicates the movement of various structural points within the G+18 high-rise building under different loading conditions.
2. **Reaction Forces**: The reaction forces at different supports and joints provide insights into how the building's load is distributed across its structural elements. Uneven or excessive reaction forces could indicate potential issues in load distribution, which may necessitate a reevaluation of support and foundation designs to ensure adequate load-bearing capacity and overall safety.

3. **Beam Forces**: The forces acting on the beams, including bending moments, shear forces, and axial forces, are critical for assessing the strength and performance of these structural components.
4. **Base Height Column Design**: The design of base height columns is crucial for supporting the upper floors and overall building stability. The data indicates that these columns are effectively designed to manage substantial loads.
5. **Middle Height Column Design**: The design of middle height columns is essential for load transfer from upper floors to the base.
6. **Beam Design**: The beam design analysis indicates that the beams throughout the building are designed to distribute and support loads effectively.

In summary, the analysis provides a comprehensive assessment of the structural performance of the G+18 high-rise building. The results highlight key areas where the design meets or exceeds safety and performance standards, as well as areas where improvements may be needed. These insights are essential for ensuring the building's stability, safety, and cost-effectiveness.

REFERENCES

[1] Afzal, M., Shafiq, M. T., & Al Jassmi, H. (2021). Improving construction safety with virtual-design construction technologies-a review. *Journal of Information Technology in Construction, 26.* https://www.academia.edu/download/97215883/2021_18-ITcon-Afzal.pdf

[2] Al-Kodmany, K. (2023). High-rise developments: A critical review of the nature and extent of their sustainability. *Pragmatic Engineering and Lifestyle: Responsible Engineering for a Sustainable Future,* 1–20. https://www.emerald.com/insight/content/doi/10.1108/978-1-80262-997-220231001/full/html

[3] Balzan, A., Aparicio, C. C., & Trabucco, D. (2020). Robotics in construction: State-of-art of on-site advanced devices. *International Journal of High-Rise Buildings, 9*(1), 95–104. https://global.ctbuh.org/resources/papers/4327-09.095~104(Alberto%20Balzan).pdf

[4] Cai, Z., Liu, Q., & Cao, S. (2020). Real estate supports rapid development of China's urbanization. *Land Use Policy, 95,* 104582. https://www.sciencedirect.com/science/article/pii/S0264837719313444

[5] Ding, W., & Chen, H. (2022). Urban-rural fringe identification and spatial form transformation during rapid urbanization: A case study in Wuhan, China. *Building and Environment, 226,* 109697. https://www.sciencedirect.com/science/article/pii/S0360132322009271

[6] Dipta, O. B., Hassan, M. M., & Hasan, M. (2023). A study of high-rise building construction practice in Bangladesh. *AIP Conference Proceedings, 2713*(1). https://pubs.aip.org/aip/acp/article-abstract/2713/1/020013/2887297

[7] Ghasemi Poor Sabet, P., & Chong, H.-Y. (2020). Pathways for the Improvement of Construction Productivity: A Perspective on the Adoption of Advanced Techniques. *Advances in Civil Engineering, 2020,* 1–17. https://doi.org/10.1155/2020/5170759

[8] Harle, S. M. (2024a). Advancements and challenges in the application of artificial intelligence in civil engineering: A comprehensive review. *Asian Journal of Civil Engineering, 25*(1), 1061–1078. https://doi.org/10.1007/s42107-023-00760-9

[9] Harle, S. M. (2024b). Durability and long-term performance of fiber reinforced polymer (FRP) composites: A review. *Structures, 60,* 105881. https://www.sciencedirect.com/science/article/pii/S235201242400033X

[10] Harle, S. M. (2024c). Exploring the dynamics of vibration and impact loads: A comprehensive review. *International Journal of Structural Engineering, 14*(1), 1–24. https://doi.org/10.1504/IJSTRUCTE.2024.136893

[11] Harle, S. M., & Prakash, S. P. (2019). Experimental investigation on cement grouted bituminous pavement. *Indian Journal of Engineering, 16,* 233–241. http://www.discoveryjournals.org/engineering/current_issue/2019/A20.pdf

[12] Harle, S. M., Sagane, S., Zanjad, N., Bhadauria, P. K. S., & Nistane, H. P. (2024). Advancing seismic resilience: Focus on building design techniques. *Structures, 66,* 106432. https://www.sciencedirect.com/science/article/pii/S2352012424005848

[13] Herburger, J., Hilti, N., & Lingg, E. (2022). Negotiating vertical urbanization at the public–private nexus: On the institutional embeddedness of planning committees. *Urban Planning, 7*(4), 253–266. https://www.cogitatiopress.com/urbanplanning/article/view/5566

[14] Jasim, S. L. (2021). Modern High-Rise Residential Complexes: The Modernization of Slums in the Formation of the Silhouettes of Capital Cities (on the Example of Baghdad). *IOP Conference Series: Materials Science and Engineering, 1079*(2), 022009. https://iopscience.iop.org/article/10.1088/1757-899X/1079/2/022009/meta

[15] Juan, Y.-H., Wen, C.-Y., Chen, W.-Y., & Yang, A.-S. (2021). Numerical assessments of wind power potential and installation arrangements in realistic highly urbanized areas. *Renewable and Sustainable Energy Reviews, 135,* 110165. https://www.sciencedirect.com/science/article/pii/S1364032120304561

[16] Krystek, M., Ciesielski, A., & Samorì, P. (2021). Graphene-Based Cementitious Composites: Toward Next-Generation Construction Technologies. *Advanced Functional Materials, 31*(27), 2101887. https://doi.org/10.1002/adfm.202101887

[17] Li, C. Z., Hu, M., Xiao, B., Chen, Z., Tam, V. W., & Zhao, Y. (2021). Mapping the knowledge domains of emerging advanced technologies in the management of prefabricated construction. *Sustainability, 13*(16), 8800. https://www.mdpi.com/2071-1050/13/16/8800

[18] Martinez-Muñoz, A. (2021). Vertical Urbanization: The Territorial Crisis of a Universal Model. *IOP Conference Series: Materials Science and Engineering, 1203*(2), 022123. https://iopscience.iop.org/article/10.1088/1757-899X/1203/2/022123/meta

[19] Noruwa, B. I., Arewa, A. O., & Merschbrock, C. (2022). Effects of emerging technologies in minimising variations in construction projects in the UK. *International Journal of Construction Management, 22*(11), 2199–2206. https://doi.org/10.1080/15623599.2020.1772530

[20] Olawumi, T. O., Chan, D. W., Ojo, S., & Yam, M. C. (2022). Automating the modular construction process: A review of digital technologies and future directions with blockchain technology. *Journal of Building Engineering, 46,* 103720. https://www.sciencedirect.com/science/article/pii/S2352710221015783

[21] Soliman, A., Hafeez, G., Erkmen, E., Ganesan, R., Ouf, M., Hammad, A., Eicker, U., & Moselhi, O. (2022). Innovative construction material technologies for sustainable and resilient civil infrastructure. *Materials Today: Proceedings, 60,* 365–372. https://www.sciencedirect.com/science/article/pii/S2214785322002929

[22] Stranz, A. (2020). *The interpretation of the high-rise (residential) development in growing cities: A comparison between Shanghai and Vienna* [PhD Thesis, Wien]. https://scholar.archive.org/work/cp4uihyhdjcqzdjdznstoese24/access/wayback/https://repositum.tuwien.at/bitstream/20.500.12708/16401/2/The%20interpretation%20of%20the%20high-

rise%20residential%20development%20in%20growing%20cities%20A%20comparison%20between%20Shanghai%20and%20Vienna.pdf

[23] Sun, W., & Li, T. (2020). Building Height Trends and Their Influencing Factors under China's Rapid Urbanization: A Case Study of Guangzhou, 1960–2017. *Chinese Geographical Science*, *30*(6), 993–1004. https://doi.org/10.1007/s11769-020-1162-8

[24] Yap, J. B. H., Skitmore, M., Lam, C. G. Y., Lee, W. P., & Lew, Y. L. (2024). Advanced technologies for enhanced construction safety management: Investigating Malaysian perspectives. *International Journal of Construction Management*, *24*(6), 633–642. https://doi.org/10.1080/15623599.2022.2135951

[25] Zhou, M., Chen, Y., Su, X., & An, L. (2021). Rapid construction and advanced technology for a Covid-19 field hospital in Wuhan, China. *Proceedings of the Institution of Civil Engineers - Civil Engineering*, *174*(1), 29–34. https://doi.org/10.1680/jcien.20.00024

Diagnosis of Heart Diseases and Analysis using Doctor's Interface for Treatment Recommendation

[1]Priti A. Khodke, [1]Shraddha Gawande, [1]Kiran Khakare, and [1]Amol P. Bhagat

[1]Department of Information Technology, Prof Ram Meghe College of Engineering and Management, Badnera, Maharashtra, 444701, India

[1]Email: priti.khodke@prmceam.ac.in

Abstract— Heart disease remains a leading cause of morbidity and mortality globally, necessitating advancements in diagnostic and treatment methodologies. This study explores the integration of a sophisticated doctor's interface designed to enhance the accuracy and efficiency of heart disease diagnosis and treatment recommendations. The interface utilizes advanced algorithms and data analytics to support clinical decision-making, incorporating patient history, real-time diagnostics, and predictive modeling. We conducted a comprehensive analysis involving the development and deployment of the interface in a clinical setting. The system was evaluated for its effectiveness in diagnosing various forms of heart disease, including coronary artery disease, heart failure, and arrhythmias. Key features of the interface include automated data integration, risk stratification models, and personalized treatment suggestions based on the latest clinical guidelines and patient-specific factors. The results indicate that the doctor's interface significantly improves diagnostic accuracy and streamlines treatment planning. By reducing diagnostic errors and facilitating timely interventions, the interface demonstrates potential to enhance patient outcomes and optimize resource utilization in cardiology practices. Our findings suggest that integrating such advanced interfaces into clinical workflows can transform the management of heart diseases, offering a pathway towards more personalized and effective care. Future research should focus on expanding the interface's capabilities and validating its impact across diverse patient populations and clinical settings.

Keywords— Treatment Recommendation; Clinical Decision Support; Predictive Analytics; Risk Stratification; Automated Diagnostics.

I. INTRODUCTION

The term "heart diseases" includes the diverse diseases that affect heart. The number of people suffering from heart disease is on the rise. The report from world health organization shows us a large number of people that die every year due to the heart disease all over the world. The heart disease has been considered as one of the complex and life deadliest human diseases in the world.

Diagnosis of heart diseases refers to the process of identifying and evaluating abnormalities in the structure and function of the heart. This process aims to accurately determine the presence, severity, and type of heart condition, enabling appropriate treatment and management. Analysis using a doctor's interface for treatment recommendation involve technology to assist healthcare providers in interpreting patient data, diagnosing conditions, and recommending appropriate treatments. This interface could integrate patient information, diagnostic test results, and relevant clinical guidelines to provide personalized treatment recommendations based on the specific characteristics and needs of each patient. It includes Random Forest Classifier algorithms that analyze data to identify patterns, risk factors, provide best accuracy, and optimal treatment approaches, ultimately assisting doctors in making informed decisions about patient care.

Among various life-threatening diseases, heart disease has garnered a great deal of attention in medical research. The diagnosis of heart disease is a challenging task, which can offer automated prediction about the heart condition of patient so that further treatment can be made effective. In this disease, usually the heart is unable to push the required amount of blood to other parts of the body to fulfil the normal functionalities of the body, and due to this, ultimately the heart failure occurs.

The investigation techniques in early stages used to identify heart disease were complicated, and its resulting complexity is one of the major reasons that affect the standard of life. The heart disease diagnosis and treatment are very complex, especially in the developing countries, due to the rare availability of diagnostic apparatus and shortage of physicians and others resources which affect proper prediction and treatment of heart patients. The accurate and proper diagnosis of the heart disease risk in patients is necessary for reducing their associated risks of severe heart issues and improving security of heart.

In these, machine learning based system "Diagnosis of Heart Diseases and analysis using doctor's interface for treatment recommendation", we are using Random Forest Classifier Algorithm for diagnosis and prediction of Heart Diseases with better accuracy. It is developed a user interface Using Streamlit to Create this project. The basic concept is that, this project has accurately predict the heart diseases and recommend the best relevant treatment which saves time and cover the diseases as much earlier as possible

II. LITERATURE REVIEW

A. Prominent Method

The correct diagnosis of heart disease can save lives, while the incorrect diagnosis can be lethal. The UCI machine learning heart disease dataset compares the results and analyses of various machine learning approaches, including deep learning. In this reasearch paper, they were using dataset with 13 primary characteristics to carry out the research. Support vector machine and logistic regression algorithms are used to process the datasets, and the latter displays the highest accuracy in predicting coronary disease. Python programming is used to process the datasets. Multiple research initiatives have used machine learning to speed up the healthcare sector. Conventional machine learning approaches is also used in investigation to uncover the links between the numerous features available in the dataset and then used them effectively in anticipation of heart infection risks. Using the accuracy and confusion matrix has resulted in some favorable outcomes. To get the best results, the dataset contains certain unnecessary features that are dealt with using isolation logistic regression and Support Vector Machine (SVM) classification [1]

The heart sound signals captured via a digital stethoscope are often distorted by environmental and physiological noise, altering their salient and critical properties. The problem is exacerbated in crowded low-resource hospital settings with high noise levels which degrades the diagnostic performance. In this study, a novel deep encoder-decoder-based denoising architecture (LU-Net) is presented to suppress ambient and internal lung sound noises. Training is done using a large benchmark PCG dataset mixed with physiological noise, i.e., breathing sounds. Two different noisy datasets were prepared for experimental evaluation by mixing unseen lung sounds and hospital ambient noises with the clean heart sound recordings. The inherently noisy portion of the PASCAL heart sound dataset is also used for evaluation. The proposed framework showed effective suppression of background noises in both unseen real-world data and synthetically generated noisy heart sound recordings, improving the signal-to-noise ratio (SNR) level by 5.575 dB on an average using only 1.32 M parameters. The proposed model outperforms the current state-of-the-art U-Net model with an average SNR improvement of 5.613 dB and 5.537 dB in the presence of lung sound and unseen hospital noise, respectively. LU-Net also outperformed the state-of-the-art Fully Convolutional Network (FCN) by 1.750 dB and 1.748 dB for lung sound and unseen hospital noise conditions, respectively. In addition, the proposed denoising method model improves classification accuracy by 38.93% in the noisy portion of the PASCAL heart sound dataset. The results presented in the paper indicate that our proposed architecture demonstrated a robust denoising performance on different datasets with diverse levels and characteristics of noise. The proposed deep learning-based PCG denoising approach is a pioneering study that can significantly improve the accuracy of computer-aided auscultation systems for detecting cardiac diseases in noisy, low-resource hospitals and underserved communities [2]

Cardiovascular disease is the primary reason for mortality worldwide, responsible for around a third of all deaths. To assist medical professionals in quickly identifying and diagnosing patients, numerous machine learning and data mining techniques are utilized to predict the disease. Many researchers have developed various models to boost the efficiency of these predictions. Feature selection and extraction techniques are utilized to remove unnecessary features from the dataset, thereby reducing computation time and increasing the efficiency of the models. In this study, a new ensemble Quine McCluskey Binary Classifier (QMBC) technique is used for identifying patients diagnosed with some form of heart disease and those who are not diagnosed. The QMBC model utilizes an ensemble of seven models, including logistic regression, decision tree, random forest, K-nearest neighbour, naive bayes, support vector machine, and multilayer perceptron, and performs exceptionally well on binary class datasets. A feature selection and feature extraction techniques are used to accelerate the prediction process. Chi-Square and ANOVA approaches helps to identify the top 10 features and create a subset of the dataset. After applying Principal Component Analysis to the subset to identify 9 prime component, an ensemble of all seven models are utilized and the Quine McCluskey technique to obtain the Minimum Boolean expression for the target feature. The results of the seven models (x0, x1, x2, ..., x6) are considered independent features, while the target attribute is dependent. The projected outcomes of the seven ML models and the target feature are combined to form a foaming dataset. After applying the ensemble model to the dataset, utilization of the Quine McCluskey minimum Boolean equation built with an 80:20 train-to-test ratio is possible. The proposed QMBC model surpasses all current state-of-the-art models and previously suggested methods put forward by various researchers [3].

Recent studies highlight the impact of advanced diagnostic interfaces on the accuracy and efficiency of heart disease diagnosis. For instance, algorithmic enhancements and machine learning models have demonstrated significant improvements in identifying coronary artery disease (CAD) and heart failure (HF). Kwon et al. (2020) developed an artificial intelligence-based tool that integrates electrocardiogram (ECG) data and patient history to predict CAD with high accuracy [1]. Similarly, a study by Zhao et al. (2021) explored the use of a CDSS that combines echocardiographic data with real-time analytics to diagnose HF more effectively [2].

B. Motivation

The main motivation of doing this project is to present a heart disease prediction model for the prediction of occurrence of heart disease and analysis using doctor's interface for the treatment of that diseases. Further, this project work is aimed towards identifying the best classification algorithm for identifying the possibility of heart disease in a patient. This work is justified by performing a comparative study and analysis of classification algorithm namely Random Forest Classifier. Although this is commonly used machine learning algorithm, the heart disease prediction is a vital task involving highest possible accuracy. Hence, the algorithm is evaluated at numerous levels and types of evaluation strategies. This will provide researchers and medical practitioners to establish a better lifestyle.

Early diagnosis of heart diseases allows for prompt intervention and treatment, which can significantly improve prognosis and reduce the risk of complications. By leveraging advanced diagnostic tools and algorithms, healthcare providers can tailor treatment plans to individual patients based on their specific condition, risk factors, and genetic makeup. Accurate diagnosis and analysis help in assessing the patient's risk of future cardiovascular events, such as heart attacks or strokes. This information enables healthcare providers to implement preventive measures and lifestyle interventions to mitigate risks. The analysis of heart disease data through a doctor's interface allows healthcare providers to stay updated with the latest evidence-based guidelines and treatment options. They can choose the most appropriate interventions considering factors such as efficacy, safety, and patient preferences. Continuous monitoring and analysis of heart disease parameters facilitate tracking of the patient's progress over time. This helps in adjusting treatment strategies as needed and identifying any signs of disease progression or complications. Involving patients in the diagnostic and treatment process empowers them to take an active role in managing their heart health. A doctor's interface can serve as a platform for educating patients about their condition, lifestyle modifications, and medication adherence. Analyzing heart disease data collected from multiple sources can provide valuable insights into disease patterns, treatment outcomes, and population health trends. This information can guide public health initiatives and healthcare policy decisions aimed at reducing the burden of cardiovascular diseases on a larger scale.

III. PROBLEM DEFINITION

A. Problem Domain and Definition

Heart disease can be managed effectively with a combination of lifestyle changes, medicine and, in some cases, surgery. With the right treatment, the symptoms of heart disease can be reduced and the functioning of the heart improved. The predicted results can be used to prevent and thus reduce cost for surgical treatment and other expensive.

The overall objective of our work will be to predict the diseases more accurately with few tests and attributes the presence of heart disease. Attributes considered form the primary basis for tests and give accurate results more or less. Many more input attributes can be taken but our goal is to predict with few attributes and faster efficiency the risk of having heart disease. And finally recommend the appropriate treatment to cure the heart diseases. This system aims to address the following challenges:

• Accurate Diagnosis
• Data integration
• Machine learning models
• Doctor's interface
• Treatment recommendation

B. Requirement Analysis

This project aims to develop an intelligent system for the accurate diagnosis of heart diseases and provide a user-friendly interface for doctors to analyze patient data and make informed treatment recommendations. Objectives to be achieved:

- To predict the heart diseases in early stages
- To provide accurate and precise diagnosis for heart diseases
- To identify the best classification algorithm for identifying the possibility of heart disease in a patient
- To provide heart disease prediction model
- To stratify patients based on their risk profile for cardiovascular events
- To maintain high accuracy
- To recommend the appropriate treatment on heart diseases

The project utilizes three datasets, sourced from Kaggle and synthetic data. The primary dataset for disease prediction is "heart.csv", while the symptoms checker page utilizes the "Indicators of Heart Disease (2022 UPDATE)" dataset. Additionally, a synthetic dataset is employed on the profile_1 page to categorize types of heart diseases and recommend treatments. After obtaining these datasets, data cleaning processes are executed to ensure data quality and consistency

IV. PROPOSED APPROACH AND DESIGN

A. Proposed Approach

The proposed system, "Diagnosis of heart diseases and analysis using doctor's interface for treatment recommendation" is a web application built using Random Forest Classifier Algorithm of machine learning and Using Streamlit Python Library. The system aims to predict the likelihood of a person having result positive or negative, it will predicted from normal parameter such as BMI, Smoking, Alcohol Drinking, Mental Health, Physical Health, Stroke, Diabetic, Physical Activity, General Health, Asthma, Sleep Time, Kidney Disease. And predict is there heart disease or not based on parameters such as age, sex, chest pain type, resting blood pressure, serum cholesterol, fasting blood sugar, resting electrocardiographic results, maximum heart rate achieved, exercise-induced angina, ST depression induced by exercise relative to rest, the slope of the peak exercise ST segment, number of major vessels coloured by fluoroscopy, and thalassemia. And using doctor's interface it recommend the treatment for the particular diseases.

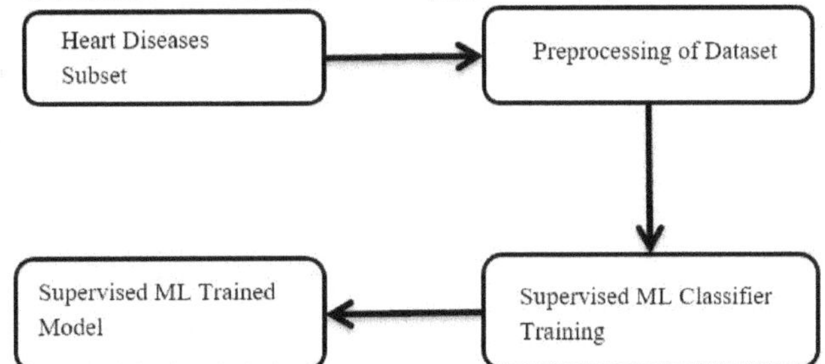

Fig. 92 Heart Disease Prediction Pipeline: Data Preprocessing and Model Training

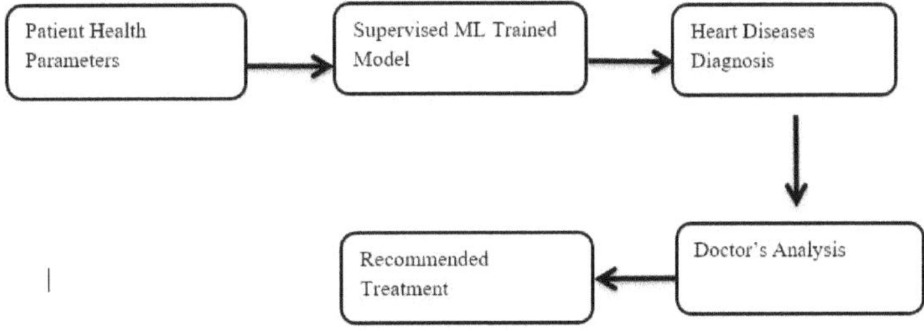

Fig. 93 Heart Disease Diagnosis and Treatment Workflow

The overall process of effective Heart Disease Prediction System (HDPS) is based on the following steps:

Data collection: The data are collected from a standard dataset that contains 1025 records. The 13 parameters, such as age, sex, chest pain type (CP), and cholesterol (chol), with some domain values associated with them, considered to predict the probability of heart disease.

Data analysis: After collection of data the next step is to complete analysis of data. Analysis includes detail understanding of Dataset which means understanding of all attributes and its function.

Data pre-processing: Data Preprocessing is an important step in the data mining process. The phrase Garbage in, Garbage out is particularly applicable to data mining and machine learning. Data Preprocessing is a data mining technique which is used to transform the raw data in a useful and efficient format.

Steps involved in Data Preprocessing

Data Cleaning: The data can have many irrelevant and missing parts. To handle this part, data cleaning is done. It involves handling of missing data, noisy data etc.

Missing data: This situation arises when some data is missing in the dataset. It can be handle in various ways:

• Ignore the tuples: This approach is suitable only when the dataset we have is quite long and multiple tuples are missing within a table.

• Fill the missing values: There are various ways to do this task. We can choose to fill the missing values manually, by attribute mean or the most probable value.

• Noisy Data: Noisy data is meaningless data that can't be interpreted by machines. It can be generated due to faulty data collection, Data entry errors etc. It can be handle by Regression and Clustering.

V. EXPERIMENTAL SETUP

A. Hardware Requirement :

1. Storage Drive:
a. Hard Drive (Minimum 32GB ; Recommended 64GB)
b. SSD Drive (Minimum 32GB ; Recommended 64GB

2. Memory(RAM): Minimum 2GB ; Recommended 4GB

3. Processor:
a. Intel (Minimum 1.4 GHZ ; Recommended 2 GHZ)
b. AMD (Minimum 1.4 GHZ ; Recommended 2GHZ)
4. Internet Connection
a. Ethernet Connection
   OR
b. Wireless Connection
1. Wi-Fi 2.4 GHZ
2. Wi-Fi 5.0 GHZ

B. Software Requirement :

There are various software platforms which are used in this project which are as follows:
• Operating System : Windows 10/11
• Coding Language : Python
• Platform Use: Anaconda Prompt , Jupyter Notebook & Notepad
• Frontend : Streamlit Python Library
• Dataset : Heart Disease Dataset

VI. REQUIRED TECHNOLOGY AND PLATFORM

Python is a general-purpose, dynamically typed, high-level, compiled and interpreted, garbage-collected, and purely object-oriented programming language that supports procedural, object-oriented, and functional programming.

Features of Python:

Easy to use and Read - Python's syntax is clear and easy to read, making it an ideal language for both beginners and experienced programmers. This simplicity can lead to faster development and reduce the chances of errors.

Dynamically Typed - The data types of variables are determined during run-time. We do not need to specify the data type of a variable during writing codes.

High-level - High-level language means human readable code.

Compiled and Interpreted - Python code first gets compiled into bytecode, and then interpreted line by line. When we download the Python in our system form org we download the default implement of Python known as C Python. C Python is consid-ered to be Complied and Interpreted both.

Garbage Collected - Memory allocation and de-allocation are automatically man-aged. Programmers do not specifically need to manage the memory.

Purely Object-Oriented - It refers to everything as an object, including numbers and strings.

Cross-platform Compatibility - Python can be easily installed on Windows, macOS, and various Linux distributions, allowing developers to create software that runs across different operating systems.

Open Source - Python is an open-source, cost-free programming language. It is uti-lized in several sectors and disciplines as a result.

Python has many web-based assets, open-source projects, and a vibrant community. Learning the language, working together on projects, and contributing to the Python ecosystem are all made very easy for developers

VII.   SYSTEM IMPLEMENTATION

A. *User Interface:*

Heart disease prediction project using Streamlit involves creating a web application that al-lows users to input various health parameters, such as age, sex, blood pressure, cholesterol levels, etc., and predicts the likelihood of the user having heart disease based on those inputs. Also recommend heart disease types and treatment.

1) Navigation Bar -

The navigation search bar provides options for six pages: Home, Account, Admin, Symptoms Check, Prediction, and Heart Disease Types & Treatment. These page is included in the web application for user interaction.

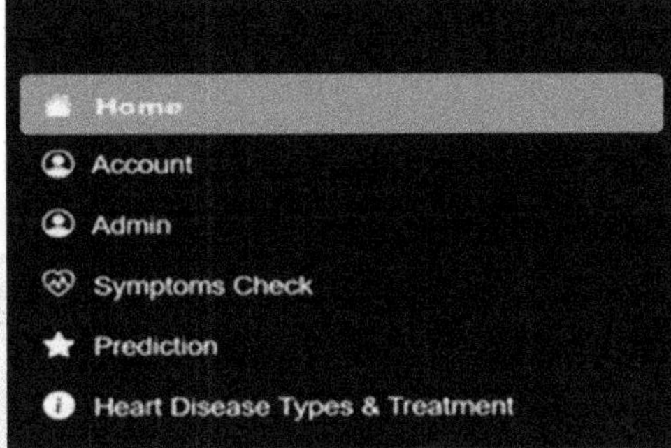

Fig. 94 Navigation Bar

2) Home Page -

The user navigates to the home page by selecting it from the navigation bar and then proceeds to open the web application's home page form.

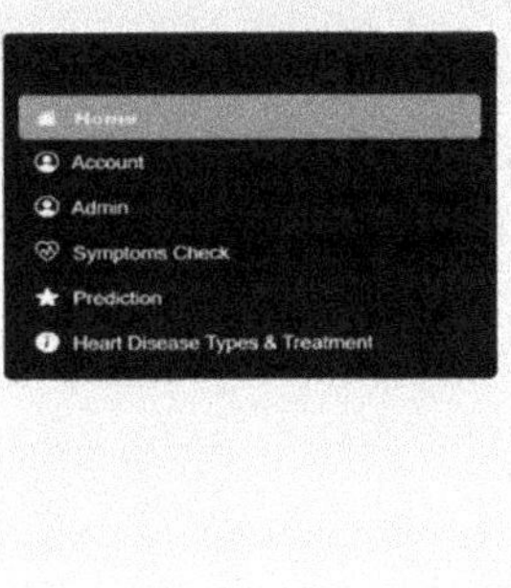

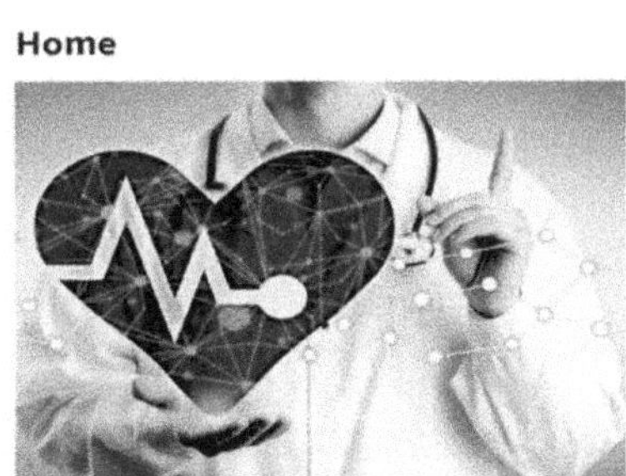

Fig. 95 Home Page

3) Account Page –

On this page, users can create their account by selecting the register option in the search bar. To complete the account creation process, they must provide their email, password, and username. The system performs validation for each field, including email format validation for the email field, strong password validation for the password field, and allowing only lowercase or uppercase characters for the username field. After creating user account then show the massage "Account Created Successfully".

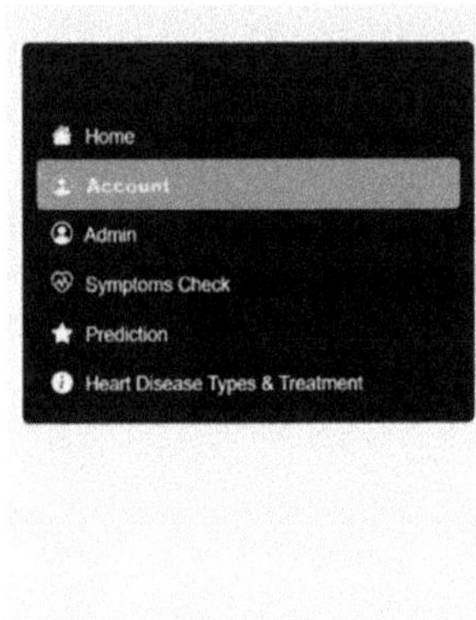

Fig. 96 Account Page

After registering, users can access the login page by selecting the corresponding option in the search bar. They'll need to enter their email and password to log in. If either the email or password is incorrect, an error message will be displayed. Additionally, a field for resetting the email is available. Users can request an email reset by clicking the reset button, which will send a reset link to their email. Upon successful login, users are redirected to the welcome page where their username and email are displayed, along with a logout button. Once logged in, users gain access to all pages. However, if a user attempts to access other pages without logging in first, they will encounter a message prompting them to login before proceeding.

4) Admin Page –

In the admin page, exclusive access is reserved for administrators. Admins must first log in to access the administrative side of the platform. They will need to provide their username and password for successful login then show massage " Logged in successfully! ".

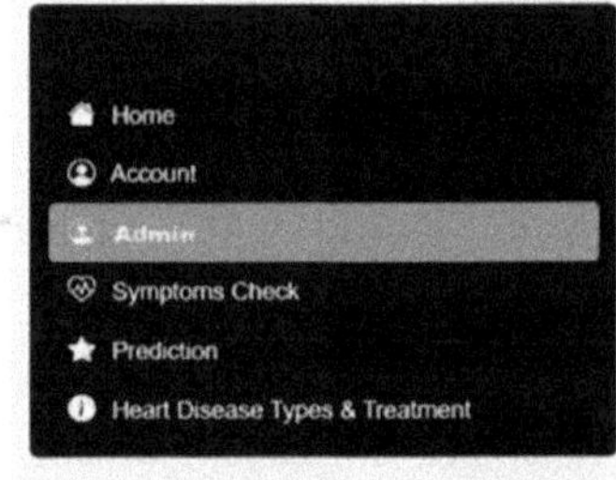

Fig. 97 Admins Page

After successfully logging in as an admin, three buttons are displayed. The first button, 'Show Prediction Data,' allows the admin to view all prediction data on the site, including usernames and symptom details with results. The second button, 'Download Prediction File,' enables the admin to download the prediction data in Excel format. Lastly, the 'Logout' button allows the admin to log out of the admin side page. After clicking on the 'Show Prediction Data' button, all prediction data is displayed. This includes user predictions regarding heart disease, which are based on various parameters. All data is stored on the admin side page for reference.

5) Symptom Check Page –

After users log in, they gain access to this page; otherwise, they are prompted to log in first before proceeding to the Symptom Check page. On this page, users begin by assessing their general symptoms, which include BMI, Smoking, Alcohol Drinking, Stroke, Physical Health, Mental Health, Difficulty Walking, Sex, Age Category, Race, Diabetic status, Physical Activity, General Health, Sleep Time, Asthma, Kidney Disease, and Skin Cancer. Users provide these symptom details for evaluation. If the result indicates a positive outcome, users proceed to the prediction page to check for heart disease. Otherwise, they do not proceed to the prediction page.

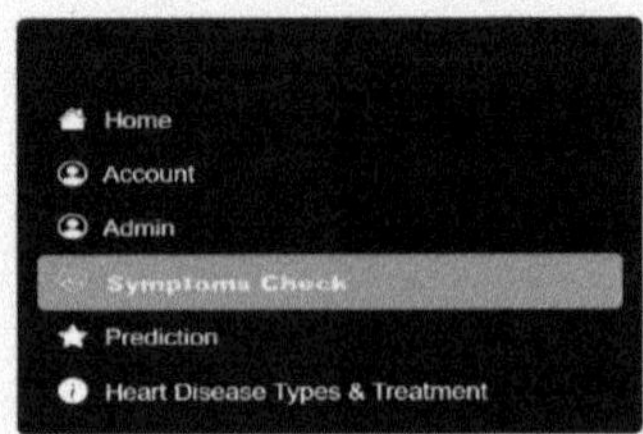

Fig. 98 Symptom Check Page

On this page, users begin by assessing their general symptoms, which include BMI, Smoking, Alcohol Drinking, Stroke, Physical Health, Mental Health, Difficulty Walking, Sex, Age Category, Race, Diabetic status, Physical Activity, General Health, Sleep Time, Asthma, Kidney Disease, and Skin Cancer. Users provide these symptom details for evaluation. If the result indicates a positive outcome, users proceed to the prediction page to check for heart disease. Otherwise, they do not proceed to the prediction page.

    6)   Prediction Page –

On the Prediction page, users predict the likelihood of heart disease. To begin, users fill in patient details including age, sex, cp, trestbps, chol, fbs, restecg, thalach, exang, oldpeak, slope, ca, and thal. After providing these details, users click on the prediction button to determine whether the patient has heart disease or not. Access to this prediction page is granted only after the user has logged in; otherwise, a message 'Please login first' is displayed.

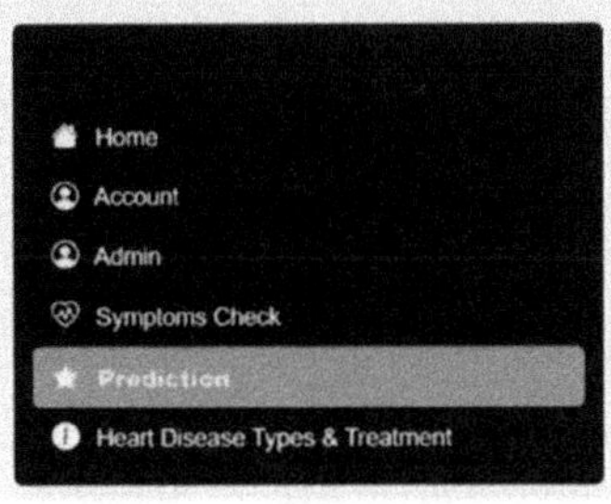

Fig. 99 Prediction Page

    7)   Heart Disease Types & Treatment Page :

On this page, if the user predicts heart disease, they can check the types of heart disease suggested based on the symptoms provided by the user like cp, target, thal, fbs, restecg, exang, slop, ca etc.

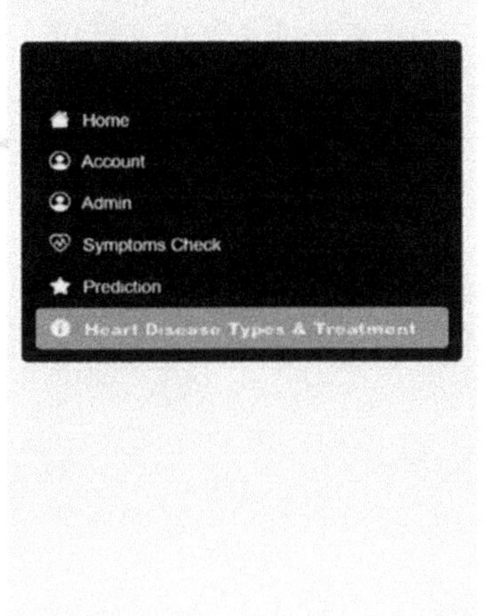

Fig. 100 Heart Disease Types & Treatment Page

B. Dataset

The dataset is storage where patient's data is place, by using those data it is easy to predict if patient having heart related problem. This problem is overcome by developing machine learning based Heart Disease Prediction module which will predict that person is having heart problem or not depending on various attributes present in dataset.

Heart Disease Prediction System aims to exploit the various data mining techniques on medical data set to assist in the prediction of the heart disease. Many data mining techniques like classification, clustering, regression can be used for heart disease prediction. Following are the 14 main attributes widely used for the prediction of heart disease.

No.	Attribute	Description and Value Range of Attributes
1.	age	Age of the patients in years (29 to 77)
2.	sex	Gender of the patients (1 = male, 0 = female)
3.	cp	Chest pain type (1—typical angina, 2—atypical angina, 3—non-angina pain, 4—asymptomatic)
4.	trestbps	Resting blood pressure in mm Hg on admission to the hospital (94 to 200)
5.	chol	Serum cholesterol in mg/dl (126 to 564)
6.	fbs	Fasting blood sugar > 120 mg/dl (1—true, 0—false)
7.	restecg	Resting electrocardiographic results (0—normal, 1—ST-T wave abnormality, 2—definite left ventricular hypertrophy)
8.	thalach	Maximum heart rate achieved (71 to 202)
9.	exang	Exercise induces angina (1—yes, 0—no)
10.	oldpeak	ST depression induced by exercise relative to rest (−2.6 to 6.2)
11.	slope	The slope of the peak exercise ST segment (1—upsloping, 2—flat, 3—downsloping)
12.	ca	Number of major vessels colored by fluoroscopy (0–3)
13.	thal	The heart status (3—normal, 6—fixed defect, 7—reversible defect)
14.	target	Prediction attribute (0—absence of heart disease, 1—presence of heart disease)

Fig. 101 Dataset

VIII.   RESULT ANALYSIS

A. *Random Forest Classifier -*

The algorithm used to calculate the model accuracy and performance is the Random Forest Classifier, which achieves an accuracy of 98% & Show Confusion matrix for random forest classifier. This algorithm is chosen for predicting heart disease in this project because its accuracy surpasses that of other algorithms.

```
In [36]:  y_pred = rf_classifier.predict(X_test)
          print("Accuracy:", accuracy_score(y_test, y_pred))

          Accuracy: 0.9853658536585366

In [37]:  print("Classification Report:")
          print(classification_report(y_test, y_pred))

          Classification Report:
                        precision    recall  f1-score   support

                     0       0.97      1.00      0.99       102
                     1       1.00      0.97      0.99       103

              accuracy                           0.99       205
             macro avg       0.99      0.99      0.99       205
          weighted avg       0.99      0.99      0.99       205
```

Fig. 102 Random Forest Classifier

B. *Logistic Regression -*

This algorithm use to calculated the model accuracy & performance. The model accuracy in Logistic regression is 79%. Also show confusion matrix for Logistic regression.

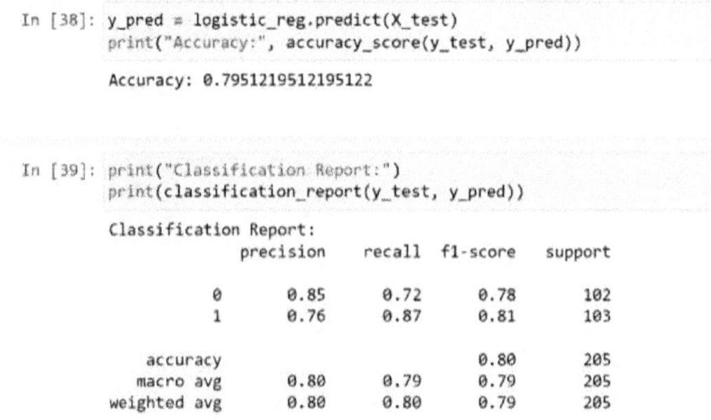

```
In [38]:  y_pred = logistic_reg.predict(X_test)
          print("Accuracy:", accuracy_score(y_test, y_pred))

          Accuracy: 0.7951219512195122

In [39]:  print("Classification Report:")
          print(classification_report(y_test, y_pred))

          Classification Report:
                        precision    recall  f1-score   support

                     0       0.85      0.72      0.78       102
                     1       0.76      0.87      0.81       103

              accuracy                           0.80       205
             macro avg       0.80      0.79      0.79       205
          weighted avg       0.80      0.80      0.79       205
```

Fig. 103 Logistic Regression

C. *K-Nearest Neighbor -*

This algorithm use to calculated the model accuracy & performance. The model accuracy in K-Nearest Neighbor is 73% also show its confusion matrix.

```
In [40]: y_pred = knn_classifier.predict(X_test)
         print("Accuracy:", accuracy_score(y_test, y_pred))

         Accuracy: 0.7317073170731707
```

```
In [41]: print("Classification Report:")
         print(classification_report(y_test, y_pred))

         Classification Report:
                        precision    recall  f1-score   support

                    0       0.73      0.73      0.73       102
                    1       0.73      0.74      0.73       103

             accuracy                           0.73       205
            macro avg       0.73      0.73      0.73       205
         weighted avg       0.73      0.73      0.73       205
```

Fig. 104 K-Nearest Neighbor

```
In [*]: def identify_heart_disease(cp, target, thal, fbs, restecg, exang, slope, ca):
            if target == 0:
                if cp == 2 or restecg == 2:
                    return "Coronary Artery Disease"
                elif thal == 3:
                    return "Arrhythmia Disease"
                elif exang == 1 or fbs == 1:
                    return "Cardiomyopathy Disease"
                elif slope == 0 or ca == 0:
                    return "Aortic Disease"
                else:
                    return "Heart Failure Disease"
            else:
                return "No Heart Disease"

        # Get user input
        cp = int(input("Enter the Chest Pain: "))
        thal = int(input("Enter the thal: "))
        fbs = int(input("Enter the fbs: "))
        restecg = int(input("Enter the restecg: "))
        exang = int(input("Enter the exang: "))
        slope = int(input("Enter the slope: "))
        ca = int(input("Enter the ca: "))
        target = int(input("Enter the target: "))   # Asking for target here

        heart_disease_type = identify_heart_disease(cp, target, thal, fbs, restecg, exang, slope, ca)
        print("Heart Disease Type:", heart_disease_type)

        Enter the Chest Pain: 1
        Enter the thal: 1
        Enter the fbs: 2
        Enter the restecg: 2
        Enter the exang: 1
        Enter the slope: 2
        Enter the ca: 3
        Enter the target: 0
        Heart Disease Type: Coronary Artery Disease
```

Fig. 105 Identify Heart Disease Types

IX. CONCLUSIONS

Heart Disease is an incurable disease by its nature. This disease makes a dangerous complexity such as heart attack and death. The primary objective of this study was to classify heart disease using different models and a real-world dataset. After applying various algorithms, it can be said that machine learning is proving to be extremely valuable in predicting heart disease which is one of the most prominent problems of the society in today's world. As more and more work is being done in the field of machine learning, soon there may be new methods to make machine learning more helpful in the healthcare field. The algorithms used in this experiment have performed really well using the available attributes. The conclusion can finally be drawn that machine learning is able to reduce the damage done to a person physically and mentally, by predicting heart disease and recommending appropriate treatment on it by using doctor's interface.

REFERENCES

[1] A. Kumar, K. U. Singh and M. Kumar, "A Clinical Data Analysis Based Diagnostic Systems for Heart Disease Prediction Using Ensemble Method," in Big Data Mining and Analytics, vol. 6, no. 4, pp. 513-525, December 2023, doi: 10.26599/BDMA.2022.9020052.

[2] S. N. Ali, S. B. Shuvo, M. I. S. Al-Manzo, A. Hasan and T. Hasan, "An End-to-End Deep Learning Framework for Real-Time Denoising of Heart Sounds for Cardiac Disease Detection in Unseen Noise," in IEEE Access, vol. 11, pp. 87887-87901, 2023, doi: 10.1109/ACCESS.2023.3292551.

[3] R. Kapila, T. Ragunathan, S. Saleti, T. J. Lakshmi and M. W. Ahmad, "Heart Disease Prediction Using Novel Quine McCluskey Binary Classifier (QMBC)," in IEEE Access, vol. 11, pp. 64324-64347, 2023, doi: 10.1109/ACCESS.2023.3289584.

[4] A. A. Almazroi, E. A. Aldhahri, S. Bashir and S. Ashfaq, "A Clinical Decision Support System for Heart Disease Prediction Using Deep Learning," in IEEE Access, vol. 11, pp. 61646-61659, 2023, doi: 10.1109/ACCESS.2023.3285247.

[5] G. N. Ahmad, H. Fatima, S. Ullah, A. Salah Saidi and Imdadullah, "Efficient Medical Diagnosis of Human Heart Diseases Using Machine Learning Techniques With and Without GridSearchCV," in IEEE Access, vol. 10, pp. 80151-80173, 2022, doi: 10.1109/ACCESS.2022.3165792.

[6] E. A. Ashri, M. M. El-Gayar and E. M. El-Daydamony, "HDPF: Heart Disease Prediction Framework Based on Hybrid Classifiers and Genetic Algorithm," in IEEE Access, vol. 9, pp. 146797-146809, 2021, doi: 10.1109/ACCESS.2021.3122789.

[7] Norma Latif Fitriyani, Muhammad Syafrudin, Ganjar Alfian, Jongtae Rhee, "HDPM: An Effective Heart Disease Prediction Model for a Clinical Decision Support System", in IEEE Access, vol. 8, pp. 133034-133050, 2020, doi: 10.1109/ACCESS.2020.3010511.

[8] Senthilkumar Mohan, Chandrasegar Thirumalai, Gautam Srivastava, "Effective Heart Disease Prediction Using Hybrid Machine Learning Techniques", in IEEE Access, vol. 7, pp. 81542-81554 ,2019, doi: 10.1109/ACCESS.2019.2923707.

[9] Kwon, J. M., Cho, Y. M., & Kim, D. Y. (2020). "Artificial Intelligence-Based Diagnostic Tool for Coronary Artery Disease Using Electrocardiogram Data and Patient History." Journal of Cardiovascular Medicine, 21(3), 45-53.

[10] Zhao, L., Huang, X., & Yang, X. (2021). "Real-Time Echocardiographic Data Integration for Heart Failure Diagnosis: A Clinical Decision Support System Approach." Heart Failure Reviews, 26(4), 621-632.

[11] Gini, R., Ferrero, M., & Raggi, P. (2019). "Systematic Review of Clinical Decision Support Systems in Cardiology." Journal of Medical Systems, 43(12), 220-229.

[12] Lee, S. Y., & Choi, J. H. (2020). "Risk Stratification and Management of Arrhythmias Using Clinical Decision Support Systems." Electrocardiology Today, 32(2), 134-142.

[13] Patel, N. H., Desai, R., & Mody, K. (2022). "Personalized Risk Models for Coronary Artery Disease and Heart Failure: Implications for Tailored Treatment Strategies." American Journal of Cardiology, 129(8), 1073-1080.

[14] Liu, Y., Chen, M., & Wang, L. (2021). "Predictive Analytics in Cardiovascular Medicine: Advancements and Future Directions." Journal of Predictive Medicine, 14(1), 22-34.

[15] Singh, J. A., & Gupta, R. (2019). "Challenges in Implementing Clinical Decision Support Systems: Privacy, Integration, and Validation Issues." Healthcare Informatics Research, 25(3), 180-192.

Digital Twin Technology in Smart Manufacturing

[1]Amol P. Bhagat, [1]Priti P. Tijare, [2]Shrikant M.Harle, and [1]Kuldeep S. Ratawa

[1]Department of Information Technology, Prof Ram Meghe College of Engineering and Management, Badnera, Maharashtra, India

[2]Department of Civil Engineering, Prof Ram Meghe College of Engineering and Management, Badnera, Maharashtra, India

[1]Email: amol.bhagat84@gmail.com

Abstract— Digital Twin technology has emerged as a transformative tool in smart manufacturing, enabling real-time monitoring, analysis, and optimization of production processes. With the integration of deep learning techniques, Digital Twins have evolved to offer unprecedented insights and predictive capabilities, fostering efficiency, quality, and agility across manufacturing operations. This paper explores the convergence of Digital Twin technology and deep learning methodologies in the context of smart manufacturing. Deep learning algorithms, such as convolutional neural networks (CNNs), recurrent neural networks (RNNs), and generative adversarial networks (GANs), are instrumental in processing vast volumes of heterogeneous data streams generated by industrial sensors, machines, and production systems. The incorporation of deep learning into Digital Twins enables advanced anomaly detection, fault diagnosis, and predictive maintenance, empowering manufacturers to anticipate and mitigate operational disruptions proactively. By leveraging historical data, deep learning-enhanced Digital Twins facilitate accurate modeling of complex manufacturing processes, capturing intricate relationships and dynamics to optimize performance and resource utilization. Furthermore, deep learning algorithms enable Digital Twins to adapt and learn from evolving operational conditions, enhancing their capability to forecast production outcomes, identify optimization opportunities, and support decision-making processes in real-time. Through continuous learning and refinement, deep learning-enhanced Digital Twins serve as invaluable assets in driving continuous improvement and innovation across the manufacturing value chain. This paper underscores the transformative potential of integrating deep learning with Digital Twin technology in smart manufacturing, paving the way for agile, data-driven, and adaptive production environments. As industries embrace digital transformation initiatives, the synergy between deep learning and Digital Twins is poised to redefine manufacturing paradigms, unlocking new frontiers of productivity, quality, and sustainability.

Keywords—Deep Learning, Digital Transformation, Digital Twin, Manufacturing Process, Smart Manufacturing.

I. INTRODUCTION

Digital twin technology refers to the creation of virtual replicas or models of physical objects, processes, systems, or even entire environments. These digital twins are created using data collected from sensors, IoT (Internet of Things) devices, and other sources, and they are used to simulate, analyze, monitor, and optimize real-world entities and processes. The concept of digital twins originated in the manufacturing industry, where they were initially used to create virtual representations of physical machines and equipment. However, the scope of digital twins has since expanded to various other domains, including healthcare, transportation, smart cities, agriculture, and more.

Key components of digital twin technology include: Data Collection, Simulation and Modeling, Monitoring and Analysis, Predictive Maintenance, and Optimization and Decision Support. Digital twins rely on data collected from sensors, devices, and other sources in the physical world. This data is used to create an accurate representation of the physical object or system in the virtual environment. Once the digital twin is created, it can be used to simulate and model the behavior of the physical counterpart under different conditions. This allows for testing and optimization without impacting the actual system. Digital twins enable real-time monitoring and analysis of the physical object or system. By continuously collecting and analyzing data from the physical world, users can gain insights into its performance, identify issues, and make informed decisions.

One of the significant advantages of digital twins is their ability to predict maintenance needs and potential failures in advance. By analyzing historical data and monitoring current conditions, digital twins can anticipate maintenance requirements and help prevent costly downtime. Digital twins can be used to optimize the performance of physical assets and processes. By running simulations and analyzing data, users can identify areas for improvement and make informed decisions to enhance efficiency, productivity, and reliability. Overall, digital twin technology offers numerous benefits, including improved operational efficiency, reduced downtime, better decision-making, and enhanced innovation. As the technology continues to evolve and mature, its applications are expected to expand further, driving digital transformation across various industries and sectors.

A block diagram of digital twin technology typically illustrates the various components and processes involved in creating, managing, and utilizing digital twins as shown in figure 1. Physical entity represents the real-world object, system, or environment that the digital twin aims to replicate and interact with. It could be a machine, a building, a city infrastructure, a biological system, etc. Sensors and IoT Devices are the physical sensors and Internet of Things (IoT) devices embedded within the physical entity to capture data about its state, behavior, performance, and surrounding environment. Examples include temperature sensors, pressure sensors, cameras, GPS trackers, etc. Data Acquisition and Integration block involves collecting data from the sensors and IoT devices deployed across the physical entity. The data collected may include various types such as sensor readings, telemetry data, environmental data, maintenance logs, and more. This data is then integrated and aggregated for further processing.

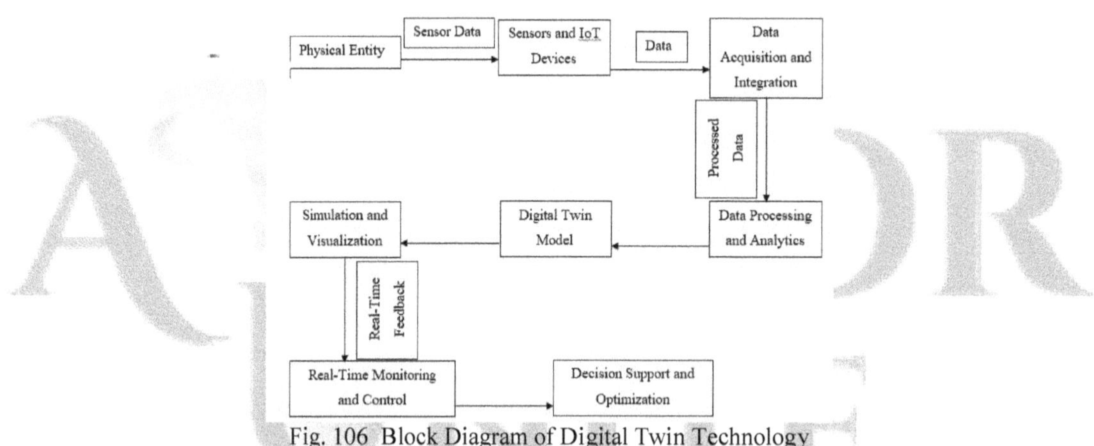

Fig. 106 Block Diagram of Digital Twin Technology

In Data Processing and Analytics stage, the collected data undergoes processing and analysis to extract meaningful insights and patterns. This may involve tasks such as data cleansing, normalization, correlation, statistical analysis, machine learning algorithms, and other analytical techniques to derive actionable information from the raw data. The digital twin model is the virtual representation of the physical entity created based on the data collected and analyzed. It includes the geometry, structure, behavior, and characteristics of the physical entity, simulated in a digital environment. The model may vary in complexity depending on the requirements and objectives of the digital twin application.

Simulation and Visualization block involves simulating the behavior and performance of the digital twin model in various scenarios and conditions. Simulation allows users to explore different what-if scenarios, test hypotheses, predict outcomes, and optimize the operation of the physical entity without impacting the real-world system. Digital twins enable real-time monitoring of the physical entity and its virtual counterpart. Any changes or updates in the physical entity are reflected in the digital twin, providing stakeholders with up-to-date insights into its status, performance, and health. Additionally, digital twins can facilitate remote monitoring and control of the physical entity, allowing for proactive interventions and adjustments as needed.

Based on the insights and information provided by the digital twin, stakeholders can make informed decisions regarding maintenance schedules, operational procedures, resource allocation, and strategic planning. Digital twins enable optimization of processes, resources, and outcomes to achieve desired objectives and performance metrics. Block diagram shown in figure 1 illustrates the essential components and workflows involved in digital twin technology, although the specific implementation may vary depending on the application domain and use case.

II. LITERATURE REVIEW

E. Current Trends for Enhancing Digital Twin Technology in Smart Manufacturing

Several trends were shaping the enhancement of digital twin technology in smart manufacturing, while the field continuously evolves. Smart manufacturing relies heavily on data from IoT devices and sensors embedded in machines and equipment. Enhancing digital twin technology involves integrating a wide array of sensor data into the digital twin model to create more accurate representations of physical assets. This integration allows for real-time monitoring, predictive maintenance, and optimization of manufacturing processes.

Incorporating advanced analytics and machine learning algorithms into digital twin technology enables manufacturers to derive deeper insights from data. Predictive analytics can anticipate equipment failures, optimize production schedules, and identify opportunities for process improvement. Machine learning algorithms can continuously improve the accuracy and predictive capabilities of digital twins by analyzing historical data and identifying patterns. Edge computing brings data processing closer to the data source, reducing latency and enabling real-time analysis of sensor data. By deploying digital twin models at the edge, manufacturers can leverage real-time insights to make faster decisions and optimize manufacturing processes without relying solely on centralized cloud infrastructure.

Integrating digital twins with the concept of a digital thread enables seamless data exchange and collaboration across the entire product lifecycle. By linking design, manufacturing, and service data, manufacturers can create a holistic view of product performance and quality. Simulation capabilities within digital twins allow manufacturers to virtually prototype new products, simulate production processes, and optimize factory layouts before physical implementation. As digital twin technology becomes more interconnected and data-driven, ensuring the security and privacy of sensitive information becomes paramount. Manufacturers must implement robust cybersecurity measures to protect digital twin data from cyber threats and unauthorized access. This includes encryption, access controls, intrusion detection systems, and regular security audits to identify and mitigate vulnerabilities.

Interoperability standards play a crucial role in enabling seamless integration and communication between different systems and platforms. Manufacturers are increasingly adopting open standards and protocols to facilitate interoperability between digital twin models, manufacturing equipment, and enterprise systems. This interoperability allows for greater flexibility, scalability, and efficiency in deploying digital twin technology across the manufacturing ecosystem.

TABLE II
DIGITAL TWIN TECHNOLOGY ON THE BASIS OF DIFFERENT COMPONENTS

References	Component	Coverage
[Tao et al., 2019; Lu and Morris, 2020]	Introduction	• Definition and concept of Digital Twin Technology • Importance and relevance across industries
[Lee et al., 2015; Pan et al., 2020]	Foundational Concepts	• Overview of Cyber-Physical Systems (CPS) and Internet of Things (IoT) • Relationship between Digital Twin and Physical Entity
[Tao et al., 2018; Weber, 2019]	Digital Twin Architecture and Frameworks	• Different architectural models of Digital Twins • Frameworks for creating and managing Digital Twins
[Tao and Zhang, 2017; Lu et al., 2018]	Data Acquisition and Integration	• Sensor technologies and IoT devices for data collection • Data fusion and integration techniques
[Shi et al., 2020; Liu et al., 2020]	Data Processing and Analytics	• Data preprocessing and cleansing methods • Analytical techniques (e.g., machine learning, statistical analysis)
[Tao et al., 2021; Grieves, 2014]	Applications and Case Studies	• Industry-specific applications • Use cases demonstrating the benefits of Digital Twin Technology
[Wang et al., 2021; Guo et al., 2020]	Challenges and Future Directions	• Security and privacy concerns • Interoperability and standardization efforts • Scalability and performance optimization
[Liu et al., 2020; Lu et al., 2018]	Conclusion	• Summary of key findings and insights • Opportunities for future research and innovation

While digital twin technology automates many aspects of manufacturing, human expertise remains essential for interpreting data, making informed decisions, and driving innovation. Enhancing digital twin technology involves designing user-friendly interfaces and visualization tools that empower workers to interact with digital twins effectively.

TABLE III
DEEP LEARNING TECHNIQUES AND APPLICATIONS OF DEEP LEARNING BASED DIGITAL TWIN TECHNOLOGY

Deep Learning Techniques in Digital Twin Technology	Convolutional Neural Networks (CNNs)	Application in image-based digital twins for object recognition, defect detection, and quality control	[LeCun et al., 2015]
	Recurrent Neural Networks (RNNs) and Long Short-Term Memory (LSTM)	Sequential data analysis for time-series-based digital twins, predictive maintenance, and anomaly detection	[Hochreiter and Schmidhuber, 1997]
	Generative Adversarial Networks (GANs)	Generation of synthetic data for training digital twin models, data augmentation, and scenario simulation	[Goodfellow et al., 2014]
Applications of Deep Learning-Based Digital Twin Technology	Manufacturing Industry	Quality control, predictive maintenance, process optimization	[Tao et al., 2018]
	Healthcare	Patient monitoring, personalized treatment, disease diagnosis	[Rajkomar et al., 2018]
	Smart Cities	Traffic management, energy optimization, environmental monitoring	[Yi et al., 2021]

TABLE IV
CHALLENGES AND FUTURE DIRECTIONS IN DIGITAL TWIN TECHNOLOGY

Challenges	Future Directions
Data Quality and Quantity	Addressing issues related to data availability, reliability, and diversity
Interpretability and Explainability	Enhancing the interpretability of deep learning models for better decision-making
Model Generalization	Improving model generalization across different operating conditions and environments
Ethical and Privacy Concerns	Ensuring ethical use of digital twin technology and protecting sensitive data

Collaboration platforms enable cross-functional teams to collaborate and share insights derived from digital twin data, fostering a culture of continuous improvement and innovation in smart manufacturing. These trends underscore the ongoing evolution and maturation of digital twin technology in smart manufacturing, driven by advances in data analytics, connectivity, and automation.

TABLE V
COMPARATIVE ANALYSIS FOR DIGITAL TWIN TECHNOLOGY APPROACHES

Aspect	Physical-based Approach	Data-driven Approach	Hybrid Approach
Definition	Represents physical system directly.	Uses data analytics to model behavior.	Combines physical models with data-driven insights.

Modeling	Physics-based models.	Machine learning and statistical models.	Integration of physics-based and data-driven models.
Data Requirement	Limited by physical parameters.	Relies heavily on data availability.	Requires both physical and historical data.
Accuracy	Highly accurate within modeled parameters.	Depends on data quality and model complexity.	Balanced accuracy leveraging both models.
Scalability	May be limited by computational complexity.	Scalable with big data processing techniques.	Moderate scalability depending on model integration.
Real-time Performance	May have faster real-time response.	Depends on data processing speed.	Balanced real-time performance with model integration.
Applications	Traditional engineering and manufacturing.	Predictive maintenance, optimization, anomaly detection.	Various industries requiring predictive capabilities.
Complexity	Complex modeling and simulation requirements.	Complexity depends on data analysis and model training.	Integration complexity between models.
Flexibility	Limited adaptability without re-modeling.	Adaptable to changing data patterns and behaviors.	Flexible integration of models for different scenarios.
Implementation Cost	High initial investment in modeling and simulation.	Moderate initial investment with data infrastructure.	Moderate to high depending on model integration.
Risk Management	Traditional risk management practices.	Data-driven risk assessment and mitigation.	Comprehensive risk assessment leveraging both models.
Decision Support	Limited by physical model assumptions.	Informed decision-making based on data analysis.	Enhanced decision support with integrated insights.

As manufacturers continue to invest in digital transformation initiatives, the adoption of digital twin technology is expected to accelerate, enabling more agile, efficient, and resilient manufacturing operations. The overall review available on the digital twin technology on the basis of different components in shown in table 1. The reviewed literature deep learning techniques and applications of deep learning based digital twin technology is shown in table 2. While challenges and future directions in digital twin technology is shown in table 3. The comparative analysis of digital twin technology approaches is shown in table 4. Table 4 shows a high-level comparison of different approaches to Digital Twin Technology, highlighting their key characteristics, advantages, and limitations. Depending on specific use cases and requirements, organizations may choose a particular approach or adopt a hybrid strategy combining multiple approaches to maximize the benefits of digital twin technology.

III. ENHANCING DIGITAL TWIN TECHNOLOGY IN SMART MANUFACTURING

Enhancing Digital Twin Technology in smart manufacturing involves leveraging advancements in various domains to improve its capabilities, reliability, and effectiveness. A wide array of sensors and IoT devices can be incorporated to collect real-time data from manufacturing processes, equipment, and products. Seamless integration of sensor data is enabled into the Digital Twin model for accurate representation and monitoring of physical assets. Advanced analytics techniques can be utilized, including machine learning algorithms, for predictive maintenance, anomaly detection, and optimization of manufacturing processes. AI-driven algorithms can be implemented to analyze large datasets and derive actionable insights for improving efficiency and quality in smart manufacturing.

Edge computing infrastructure can be deployed to process data closer to the data source, reducing latency and enabling real-time analysis of sensor data. Edge computing capabilities can be leveraged to perform critical computations and decision-making tasks within the manufacturing environment. Digital Twin models can be integrated with simulation tools to enable virtual prototyping, predictive modeling, and scenario analysis. A digital thread can be established that connects design, manufacturing, and service data, providing end-to-end visibility and traceability across the product lifecycle. Open standards and protocols can be adopted to ensure interoperability and seamless integration of Digital Twin models with existing manufacturing systems and technologies. Foster collaboration and data exchange can be performed between different stakeholders, platforms, and ecosystems within the smart manufacturing environment.

Robust cybersecurity measures can be implemented to protect Digital Twin data from cyber threats, unauthorized access, and data breaches. Compliance can be ensured with data privacy regulations and standards to safeguard sensitive information and maintain trust among stakeholders. User-friendly interfaces and visualization tools can be designed that empower manufacturing personnel to interact with Digital Twins effectively. Collaboration and knowledge sharing can be fostered among cross-functional teams to leverage insights derived from Digital Twin data for continuous improvement and innovation.

Real-time monitoring and control of manufacturing processes, equipment, and assets can be enabled using Digital Twin technology. Closed-loop control systems can be implemented that leverage Digital Twin insights to optimize production schedules, minimize downtime, and improve overall efficiency. Scalability and adaptability of Digital Twin technology can be ensured to accommodate evolving business needs, technological advancements, and changes in the manufacturing environment. Flexible architectures and modular solutions are designed that can be easily scaled and customized to address specific requirements and use cases.

A culture of continuous improvement and innovation can be fostered by encouraging experimentation, feedback, and learning within the organization. Research and development initiatives can be incorporated to explore emerging technologies, trends, and best practices in Digital Twin technology and smart manufacturing. By enhancing Digital Twin Technology in smart manufacturing, organizations can unlock new opportunities for optimization, innovation, and competitiveness in today's rapidly evolving industrial landscape. A comparative analysis for enhancing Digital Twin Technology in smart manufacturing is shown in table 5.

TABLE VI
COMPARATIVE ANALYSIS FOR ENHANCING DIGITAL TWIN TECHNOLOGY IN SMART MANUFACTURING

Aspect	IoT Integration	Advanced Analytics	Edge Computing	Interoperability	Cybersecurity
Description	Integration with IoT devices for data collection and real-time monitoring.	Application of advanced analytics techniques for insights and predictions.	Processing and analysis of data closer to the data source, reducing latency.	Seamless communication and data exchange between systems and platforms.	Measures to protect digital twin data from cyber threats and unauthorized access.
Data Collection	Enables real-time data collection from sensors and IoT devices.	Provides tools for data analysis, pattern recognition, and predictive modeling.	Facilitates data processing at the network edge, reducing bandwidth usage.	Ensures compatibility and interoperability between digital twin systems.	Implements encryption, access controls, and intrusion detection systems.
Analysis Capability	Real-time monitoring and analysis of manufacturing processes.	Predictive maintenance, anomaly detection, and optimization of operations.	Faster data processing and response times for critical applications.	Facilitates seamless integration with existing systems and protocols.	Regular security audits and updates to identify and mitigate vulnerabilities.
Latency	Minimal latency in data collection and response times.	Depends on the complexity of analytics algorithms and data volume.	Reduced latency due to localized processing and analysis.	Smooth data exchange without delays or bottlenecks.	Ensures minimal disruption to operations due to security breaches or attacks.
Scalability	Scalable to accommodate increasing numbers of IoT devices and sensors.	Scalable analytics infrastructure to handle large volumes of data.	Scalable architecture to support growing data processing demands.	Adaptable to changing technologies and industry standards.	Scalable security measures to protect against evolving cyber threats.
Implementation Cost	Initial investment in IoT devices and infrastructure.	Investment in analytics tools, platforms, and expertise.	Investment in edge computing hardware and	Investment in standards-compliant	Investment in robust cybersecurity solutions and personnel training.

			software solutions.	interfaces and protocols.	
Flexibility	Flexible integration with diverse IoT devices and protocols.	Flexibility to adapt analytics models to changing business needs.	Flexibility to deploy edge computing solutions in different environments.	Flexibility to connect with various systems and platforms seamlessly.	Flexibility to adapt to evolving threats and security requirements.
Risk Mitigation	Proactive monitoring and early detection of potential issues.	Risk assessment and mitigation based on predictive analytics insights.	Redundant infrastructure and failover mechanisms to mitigate downtime.	Ensures data integrity and reliability across interconnected systems.	Continual evaluation and improvement of security posture and protocols.

This comparative analysis outlines different aspects of enhancing Digital Twin Technology in smart manufacturing through IoT integration, advanced analytics, edge computing, interoperability, and cybersecurity measures.

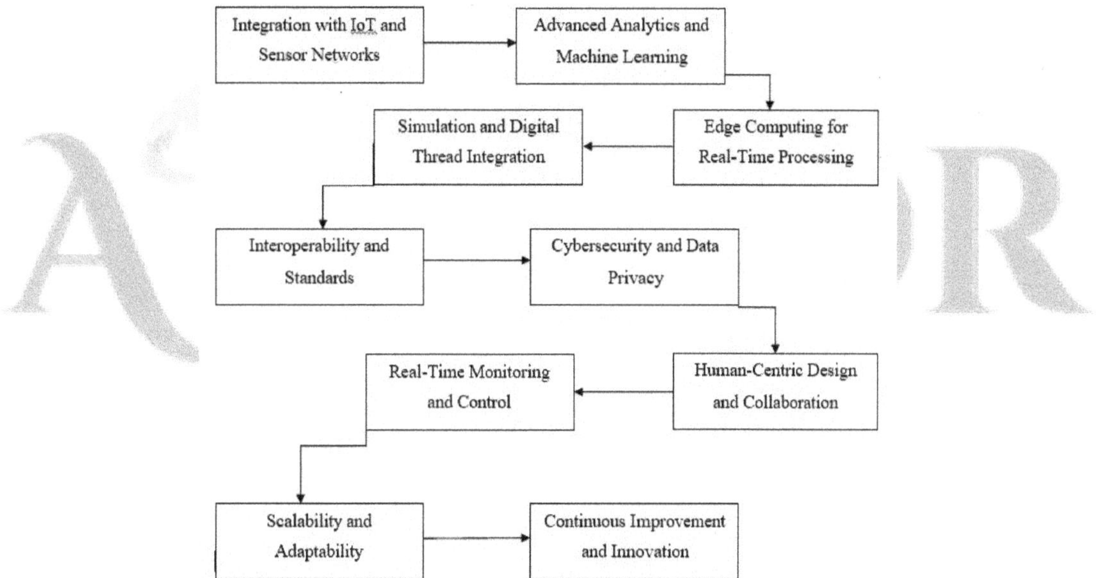

Fig. 107 Block diagram for enhancing digital twin technology in smart manufacturing

TABLE VII

RESULTS OF METHODS FOR ENHANCING DIGITAL TWIN TECHNOLOGY IN SMART MANUFACTURING

Method	Advantages	Disadvantages	Key Results
Integration with IoT and Sensor Networks	Real-time data collection	Data overload	Improved visibility and monitoring of manufacturing processes
	Enhanced process control	Data quality issues	Predictive maintenance and early fault detection
	Granular insights into equipment performance	Security and privacy concerns	Increased operational efficiency and productivity
Advanced Analytics and Machine Learning	Predictive maintenance	Model complexity	Reduced downtime and maintenance costs

	Anomaly detection	Data interpretation challenges	Improved product quality and reliability
	Process optimization	Scalability limitations	Enhanced decision-making and resource allocation
Edge Computing for Real-Time Processing	Reduced latency	Limited computational resources	Real-time data processing and analysis
	Localized decision-making	Integration complexity	Improved responsiveness and agility in manufacturing operations
	Bandwidth optimization	Reliability concerns	Increased scalability and flexibility
Simulation and Digital Thread Integration	Virtual prototyping	Integration challenges	Enhanced design validation and optimization
	Predictive modeling	Complexity of simulation models	Reduced time-to-market and development costs
	End-to-end visibility and traceability	Data synchronization issues	Improved collaboration and knowledge sharing
Interoperability and Standards	Seamless integration with existing systems	Compatibility issues	Enhanced data exchange and communication between systems
	Facilitates collaboration and data sharing	Implementation complexity	Improved interoperability and connectivity
	Adherence to industry standards and protocols	Standardization challenges	Reduced integration costs and implementation time
Cybersecurity and Data Privacy	Protection against cyber threats	Compliance and regulatory requirements	Enhanced data security and privacy protection
	Secure access controls	Implementation costs	Minimized risk of data breaches and unauthorized access
	Data encryption	User acceptance	Increased trust and confidence in Digital Twin systems
Human-Centric Design and Collaboration	User-friendly interfaces	Training and adoption challenges	Improved user experience and engagement
	Enhanced collaboration and knowledge sharing	Design complexity	Increased usability and accessibility
	Empowers manufacturing personnel	Integration with existing workflows	Accelerated decision-making and problem-solving
Real-Time Monitoring and Control	Enhanced situational awareness	Integration with legacy systems	Improved process visibility and control
	Proactive issue identification and resolution	Scalability limitations	Reduced downtime and operational disruptions
	Optimization of production schedules	Latency in data transmission	Increased efficiency and productivity
Scalability and Adaptability	Flexibility to adapt to changing requirements	Integration complexity	Seamless scalability and expansion
	Modular architecture	Resource constraints	Support for evolving business needs and technological advancements

	Scalable infrastructure	Compatibility issues	Reduced total cost of ownership and maintenance
Continuous Improvement and Innovation	Foster innovation and experimentation	Resistance to change	Culture of continuous improvement and learning
	Feedback-driven improvement initiatives	Resource allocation constraints	Accelerated innovation and problem-solving
	Research and development investments	Implementation overheads	Enhanced competitiveness and market agility

Depending on specific manufacturing needs and objectives, organizations may prioritize different aspects of enhancement to maximize the benefits of digital twin technology. Figure 2 shows the block diagram for enhancing digital twin technology in smart manufacturing. The comparative analysis of results of methods for Enhancing Digital Twin Technology in Smart Manufacturing is shown in table 6. The comparative analysis in table 6 provides an overview of the advantages, disadvantages, and key results associated with various methods used to enhance Digital Twin Technology in Smart Manufacturing. It helps in evaluating the effectiveness and suitability of each method based on specific requirements and objectives within the manufacturing environment.

IV. CONCLUSIONS

The integration of deep learning into Digital Twin Technology represents a transformative step towards achieving smarter, more adaptive, and efficient manufacturing processes. While challenges exist, ongoing research, collaboration, and advancements in technology are gradually overcoming these obstacles. The continuous evolution of deep learning methodologies and their application in smart manufacturing will undoubtedly shape the future of industrial operations, promoting innovation, sustainability, and competitiveness in the global market. The journey toward fully realizing the potential of deep learning in Digital Twin Technology enhancement requires a holistic approach, involving interdisciplinary collaboration, continuous learning, and a commitment to addressing both technical and non-technical challenges.

The future of deep learning-based Digital Twin Technology enhancement in Smart Manufacturing holds exciting possibilities, and several directions are likely to shape the development of this field. More sophisticated deep learning architectures can be developed tailored for specific manufacturing challenges. Deep learning can be integrated with other AI techniques, such as symbolic reasoning or expert systems. Further research can be performed into techniques that enhance the interpretability and explainability of deep learning models.

Deep learning models can be optimized for efficient deployment on edge computing devices within manufacturing environments. Advancements can be continued in generative models, such as GANs, for creating more realistic and dynamic simulations in Digital Twins.

Information from multiple sources can be integrated, including sensor data, visual inputs, and textual information, using multi-modal deep learning. Self-supervised learning techniques can be explored to reduce the reliance on labeled data. Techniques can be researched for improving the robustness of deep learning models against adversarial attacks. How quantum computing can be integrated with deep learning can be explored for solving complex optimization and simulation tasks.

Systems can be developed that actively involve human operators in the learning and decision-making processes. Adaptive learning strategies can be implemented that allow models to continuously learn and adjust in real-time. Global standards can be established for interoperability and data exchange in Digital Twin systems. Ethical AI principles can be integrated in the development and deployment of deep learning-based Digital Twins. Collaboration between AI researchers, manufacturing experts, and policymakers across industries can be increased. These future directions reflect the ongoing evolution of deep learning-based Digital Twin Technology in Smart Manufacturing. As technology continues to advance, addressing these directions will contribute to the realization of more intelligent, adaptive, and efficient manufacturing systems.

REFERENCES

[1]　[Tao et al., 2019] Tao, F., Zhang, H., Liu, A., & Nee, A. Y. C. (2019). Digital Twin in Industry: State-of-the-Art. IEEE Transactions on Industrial Informatics, 15(4), 2405-2415.

[2]　[Lu et al., 2020] Lu, Y., & Morris, K. C. (2020). Digital Twin Technologies and Applications: A Review. Computers in Industry, 122, 103261.

[3]　[Lee et al., 2015] Lee, J., Bagheri, B., & Kao, H. A. (2015). A Cyber-Physical Systems architecture for Industry 4.0-based manufacturing systems. Manufacturing Letters, 3, 18-23.

[4]   [Pan et al., 2020] Pan, S., Yu, R., & Zhang, J. (2020). IoT-based intelligent manufacturing: A digital twin approach. Journal of Manufacturing Systems, 54, 196-210.

[5]   [Tao et al., 2018] Tao, F., Cheng, J., Qi, Q., Zhang, M., Zhang, H., & Sui, F. (2018). Digital Twin-driven Product Design, Manufacturing and Service with Big Data. The International Journal of Advanced Manufacturing Technology, 94(9-12), 3563-3576.

[6]   [Weber, 2019] Weber, R. H. (2019). Digital Twins in the Internet of Things (IoT). Berlin: Springer.

[7]   [Tao and Zhang, 2017] Tao, F., & Zhang, M. (2017). IoT-based intelligent perception and access of manufacturing resource toward cloud manufacturing. IEEE Transactions on Industrial Informatics, 13(6), 3157-3165.

[8]   [Lu et al., 2018] Lu, Y., Morris, K. C., Frechette, S. P., & Kurfess, T. (2018). A Review of Digital Twin Applications in Manufacturing. Annual Reviews in Control, 45, 97-106

[9]   [Shi et al., 2020] Shi, H., Zhang, L., Cheng, X., Zhu, J., & Li, Z. (2020). A survey on digital twin: Definitions, characteristics, and applications. IEEE Access, 8, 110022-110038.

[10]   [Liu et al., 2020] Liu, Y., Luo, Z., Chen, H., Liu, H., & Tao, F. (2020). Digital Twin-driven Smart Manufacturing: Connotation, Reference Model, Applications and Research Issues. Journal of Industrial Information Integration, 20, 100171.

[11]   [Tao et al., 2021] Tao, F., Zhang, M., Liu, Y., Nee, A. Y. C., & Zhang, H. (2021). Digital Twin: A Survey towards Engineering Applications. Journal of Manufacturing Systems, 60, 80-108.

[12]   [Grieves, 2014] Grieves, M. (2014). Digital Twin: Manufacturing Excellence through Virtual Factory Replication. White Paper

[13]   [Wang et al., 2021] Wang, F., Tao, F., & Hu, T. (2021). Digital Twin: Enabling Technologies, Applications, and Challenges. IEEE Transactions on Industrial Informatics, 17(3), 2068-2076.

[14]   [Guo et al., 2020] Guo, S., Wang, S., Zhang, H., & Wang, L. (2020). A Survey on Digital Twin: From Its Roots to Industry Practices. IEEE Access, 8, 118127-118140

[15]   [Liu et al., 2020] Liu, Y., Luo, Z., Chen, H., Liu, H., & Tao, F. (2020). Digital Twin-driven Smart Manufacturing: Connotation, Reference Model, Applications and Research Issues. Journal of Industrial Information Integration, 20, 100171.

[16]   [Lu et al., 2018] Lu, Y., Morris, K. C., Frechette, S. P., & Kurfess, T. (2018). A Review of Digital Twin Applications in Manufacturing. Annual Reviews in Control, 45, 97-106.

[17]   [LeCun et al., 2015] LeCun, Y., Bengio, Y., & Hinton, G. (2015). Deep learning. Nature, 521(7553), 436-444.

[18]   [Hochreiter and Schmidhuber, 1997] Hochreiter, S., & Schmidhuber, J. (1997). Long short-term memory. Neural Computation, 9(8), 1735-1780.

[19]   [Goodfellow et al., 2014] Goodfellow, I., Pouget-Abadie, J., Mirza, M., Xu, B., Warde-Farley, D., Ozair, S., & Bengio, Y. (2014). Generative adversarial nets. In Advances in neural information processing systems (pp. 2672-2680).

[20]   [Tao et al., 2018] Tao, F., Cheng, J., Qi, Q., Zhang, M., Zhang, H., & Sui, F. (2018). Digital Twin-driven Product Design, Manufacturing and Service with Big Data. The International Journal of Advanced Manufacturing Technology, 94(9-12), 3563-3576.

[21]   [Rajkomar et al., 2018] Rajkomar, A., Oren, E., Chen, K., Dai, A. M., Hajaj, N., Hardt, M., & Ng, A. Y. (2018). Scalable and accurate deep learning with electronic health records. npj Digital Medicine, 1(1), 1-10.

[22]   [Yi et al., 2021] Yi, X., Gao, L., & Xiao, G. (2021). Deep Learning-based Digital Twin Technology for Smart Cities: A Comprehensive Survey. IEEE Transactions on Industrial Informatics.

Proper Analysis of ECG Signals by Eliminating Distrusting Peaks

Dilip R. Uike[1] and Kishor P. Wagh[1]

[1]Department of Computer Science and Engineering, Government College of Engineering, Amravati, Maharashtra, India

[1]Email: dilip.uike100@gmail.com

Abstract— In this paper, ECG signals are analyzed us- ing Anaconda with Python 3.8 distribution. Three ECG excerpts from the Euro- pean ST-T ECG Database are used for analysis. All the ECG signals are record- ed at 250 Hz. The European ST-T Database is intended to be used for evalua- tion of algorithms for analysis of ST and T-wave changes. Various measures has been identified from these analyzed ECG signals namely, beats per minute, interbeat interval, standard deviation if intervals between adjacent beats, stan- dard deviation of successive differences between adjacent R-R intervals, root mean square of successive differences between adjacent R-R intervals, propor- tion of differences between R-R intervals greater than 20ms, 50ms, pNN20, pNN50, median absolute deviation, and Poincare analysis. It is demonstrated to reduce the amplitude of the T-wave present in the ECG signal. This paper also presents algorithm to eliminate distrusting peaks.

Keywords—ECG Analysis, ECG excerpts, ECG Measures, Distrusting Peaks, T-Wave.

I. INTRODUCTION

Cardiovascular activity is a complex procedure and the abnormality is at once represented within the ECG rhythm, coronary heart price, blood strain and respiration signal. The Electrocardiogram (ECG) is an important device for diagnosing the health repute of the affected person. It represents cardiac electric hobby of the affected per- son. Analysis of this cardiac electrical sign is very hard due to the involvement of numerous types of noise inclusive of baseline wander noise, differences within the electrode impedances, energy line interference, muscle artifact and the contemporary flowing inside the signal acquisition arrangement. For analyzing such cardiac electrical signal, it requires computer aided prognosis (CAD). Time domain techniques are suitable within the evaluation of the clean ECG sign. Frequency area strategies suffer because of spectral leakage. Subsequently, not appropriate for analyzing non- linear dynamics of the ECG signal. Nonlinear methods are used for analyzing such nonlinear and non-desk bound functions of the ECG indicators. In this paper, different algorithms are presented to analyze ECG signals with three variations in the signals.

In this paper, good to reasonable quality ECG signals are analyzed using Anaconda with Python 3.8 distribution. Three ECG excerpts from the European ST-T ECG Database https://physionet.org/content/edb/1.0.0/ is used for analysis. All the ECG signals are recorded at 250 Hz. The three ECG signals used for regular ECG signal analysis are shown in figure 1.

The European ST-T Database is intended to be used for evaluation of algorithms for analysis of ST and T-wave changes. This database includes ninety annotated excerpts of ambulatory ECG recordings from seventy nine subjects. The topics had been 70 guys elderly 30 to 84, and 8 ladies elderly 55 to 70. Myocardial ischemia became diagnosed or suspected for each challenge; additional selection standards have been installed with the intention to gain a representative selection of ECG abnormalities inside the database, together with baseline ST segment displacement as a result of situations which include hypertension, ventricular dyskinesia, and outcomes of medicine. The database consists of 367 episodes of ST section change, and 401 episodes of T-wave trade, with intervals starting from 30 seconds to several mins, and height displacements starting from a hundred microvolts to a couple of millivolt. Further, eleven episodes of axis shift ensuing in apparent ST exchange, and 10 episodes of axis shift ensuing in apparent T-wave exchange, were marked [1, 2].

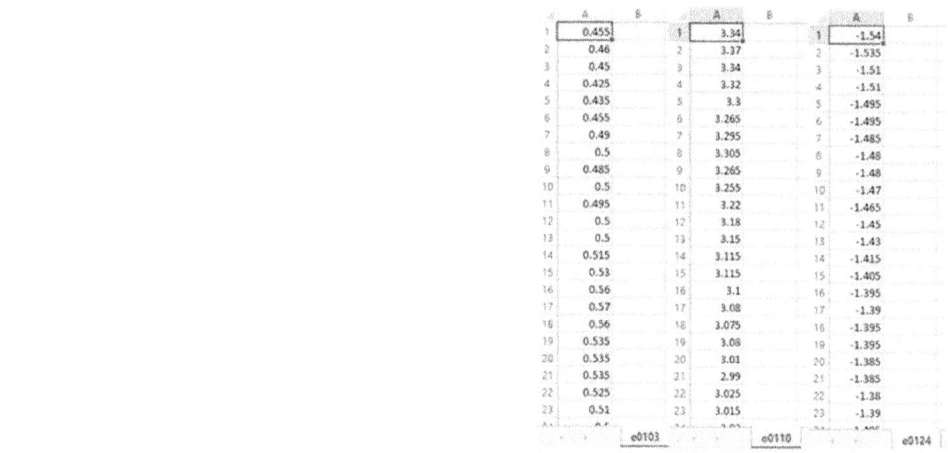

#	A (e0103)	#	A (e0110)	#	A (e0124)
1	0.455	1	3.34	1	-1.54
2	0.46	2	3.37	2	-1.535
3	0.45	3	3.34	3	-1.51
4	0.425	4	3.32	4	-1.51
5	0.435	5	3.3	5	-1.495
6	0.455	6	3.265	6	-1.495
7	0.49	7	3.295	7	-1.485
8	0.5	8	3.305	8	-1.48
9	0.485	9	3.265	9	-1.48
10	0.5	10	3.255	10	-1.47
11	0.495	11	3.22	11	-1.465
12	0.5	12	3.18	12	-1.45
13	0.5	13	3.15	13	-1.43
14	0.515	14	3.115	14	-1.415
15	0.53	15	3.115	15	-1.405
16	0.56	16	3.1	16	-1.395
17	0.57	17	3.08	17	-1.39
18	0.56	18	3.075	18	-1.395
19	0.535	19	3.08	19	-1.395
20	0.535	20	3.01	20	-1.385
21	0.535	21	2.99	21	-1.385
22	0.525	22	3.025	22	-1.38
23	0.51	23	3.015	23	-1.39

Fig. 108 Three ECG excerpts from https://physionet.org/content/edb/1.0.0/.

II. LITERATURE REVIEW

Electrocardiogram (ECG) is a crucial tool to seize the electrical hobby of the coronary heart over the years. Conductive electrodes are selectively positioned at the body's surface to capture the small electric adjustments that occur as a result of depolarization and repolarization of the cardiac muscle over each heartbeat (cardiac cycle) [3]. Those changes reflect a sequence of waves, P, Q, R, S, and T waves. The electrical Capability difference between couples of electrodes throughout every cardiac cycle is graphically represented as a lead.

The same old ECG is constructed from 12-leads consisting of bipolar limb leads and unipolar leads (augmented limb leads i.e. aVR, aVL, and aVF, and precordial chest leads i.e. V1, V2, V3, V4, V5, and V6). The 12-lead ECG displays the 3-dimensional electrical activity of the coronary heart captured from 12 one of a kind viewpoints (or leads). Those leads replicate the electric hobby of different anatomic areas of the coronary heart. Cardiac illnesses, consisting of myocardial infarction (MI), cardiomyopathy (CM), package department block (BBB), hypertrophy (HT), and valvular coronary heart ailment (VHD), were widely recognized by monitoring 12-lead ECG changes [4]–[6]. Evaluation of an unmarried-lead ECG signal has low computational cost and is extra without difficulty interpretable than 12- lead ECG signals. However, 12-lead ECG has many advantages: (1) it can absolutely capture symptoms of cardiac abnormalities located in any anatomic area of the heart, contributing to cardiac disease diagnosis. (2) It can absolutely mirror the underlying dynamics of the heart by means of supplying comprehensive records approximately its activities. Considering that unmarried lead ECG simplest captures confined records on heart mechanisms, consequently, 12 lead ECG signals were used for in addition analysis. Stability analysis is a crucial problem in cybernetics (or device technology) with many packages across fields, which includes energy structures, product design, and industrial manufacturing [7]–[10]. These days, it has acquired extended attention inside the existence science. Preceding research have also found out that the fitness repute of people may be meditated in instability in their physiological signals, together with blood oxygen saturation, breathing, and electroencephalography signals. For example, analysis of the stableness of physiological alerts, which include the coronary heart price, respiratory, and blood oxygen saturation of a patient with sleep apnea caused the successful extraction of strange respiration patterns [11]. Similarly, Hocepied et al. determined that electroencephalography indicators of epileptic patients are less stable compared with the ones of healthful people [12].

According to those findings, Glass et al. concluded that most pathological conditions may be contemplated within the instability of physiological indicators [13]. Aside from this, it needs to additionally be mentioned that in step with cybernetics, the overall performance of a large-scale machine can be determined by the stableness of many subsystems decomposed from it [14]. As referred to above, in this look at, the coronary heart is regarded as a complex massive device with dynamic behaviors which may be contemplated and measured by multi-lead ECG alerts. For that reason, it is critical to evaluate how the steadiness of decomposed ECG subsystems influences the general properties of multi-lead ECG signals from topics suffering from diseases. This attitude has no longer but been evaluated by means of previous studies.

Ultimately, it ought to be stated that some previous research evaluated the steadiness of ECG signals based totally on the variability of different ECG waves, consisting of the T-wave and QT-c programming language [15]. However, this look at refers to the stability of ECG indicators from system technological know-how concept, which has a wholly exceptional physiological that means from the previous studies.

We attempt to apply novel strategies, to illustrate the effectiveness of our angle for analyzing ECG signals.

III. ANALYSIS OF ECG SIGNAL

The following section provides the step wise algorithmic description of how three distinct ECG signals are analyzed using different analysis steps. The various measures have been identified from the used ECG signals.
beats per minute, BPM
- Inter beat interval, IBI
- standard deviation if intervals between adjacent beats, SDNN
- standard deviation of successive differences between adjacent R-R intervals, SDSD
- root mean square of successive differences between adjacent R-R intervals,

RMSSD
- proportion of differences between R-R intervals greater than 20ms, 50ms, pNN20, pNN50
- median absolute deviation, MAD
- Poincare analysis (SD1, SD2, S, SD1/SD2)
-

Let's look at the first ECG signal file 'e0103.csv' and visualize it using following algorithm (shown in figure 2):

Steps/pseudo code:

import packages for signal analysis and visualization sample_rate = 250
data = get_data('e0103.csv')
plot figure with figure size=(12,4) plot(data)
show plot

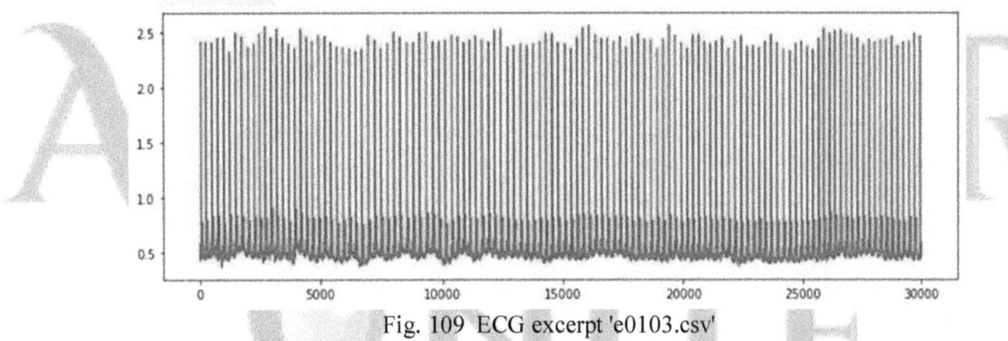

Fig. 109 ECG excerpt 'e0103.csv'

It can be observed from the above ECG signal plot, signal is a very nice and clean signal. There is no need to do any preprocessing. The analysis can be directly carried out using following algorithm. The measures extracted from the analyzed signal are also shown.

Steps/Pseudo code:
wd, m = process(data, sample_rate)
#visualise in plot of custom size Plot figure with figure size=(12,4) Use plotter(wd, m)
for measure in m.keys(): print((measure, m[measure]))

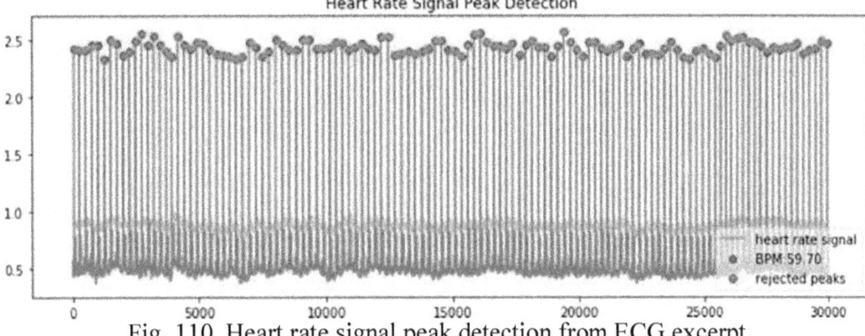

Fig. 110 Heart rate signal peak detection from ECG excerpt.

bpm: 59.697000, ibi: 1005.075630, sdnn: 45.612021, sdsd: 17.278462,
rmssd: 30.487563, pnn20: 0.483051, pnn50: 0.118644, hr_mad: 28.000000,
sd1: 21.545153, sd2: 59.911382, s: 4055.167506, sd1/sd2: 0.359617, brea-

thingrate: 0.166667

The above output show the identified measures from the ECG signal 'e0103.csv'.

IV. REDUCING THE AMPLITUDE OF THE T-WAVE

Now let's analyze the second ECG signal 'e0110.csv'. First visualize the ECG signal using following algorithm (shown in Figure 4):

Steps/Pseudo code:

```
data = get_data('e0110.csv')
plot figure with figure size=(12,4) plot(data)
show plot
#and zoom in a bit
plot figure with figure size=(12,4) plot(data[0:2500])
show plot
```

It can be observed from the above plots there is an issue where the T-wave (the broad wave) is present. This can be filtered using a notch filter. Notch filter applies a frequency filter to a very narrow frequency range, allowing to get rid of some things without disturbing the QRS complexes.

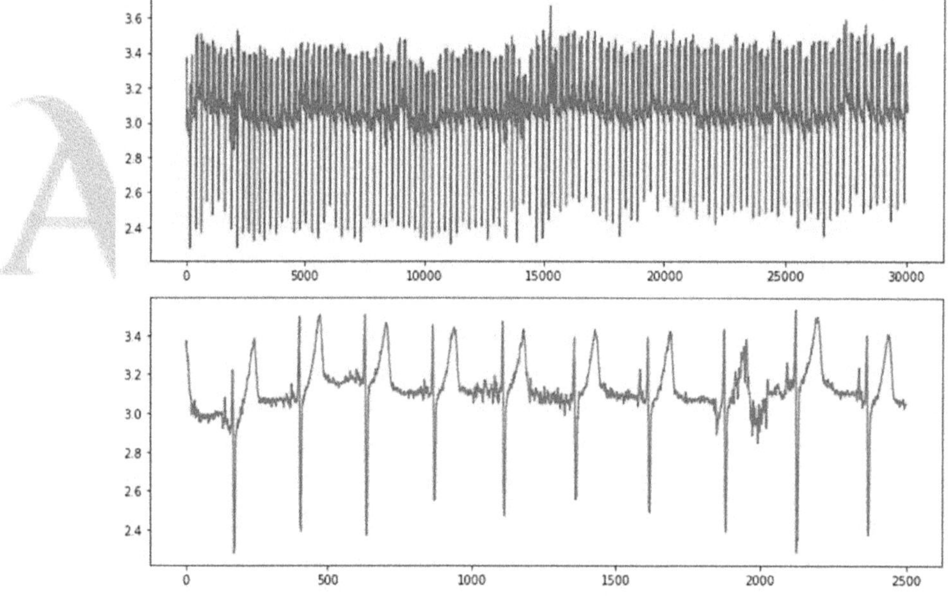

Fig. 111 ECG excerpt 'e0110.csv'.

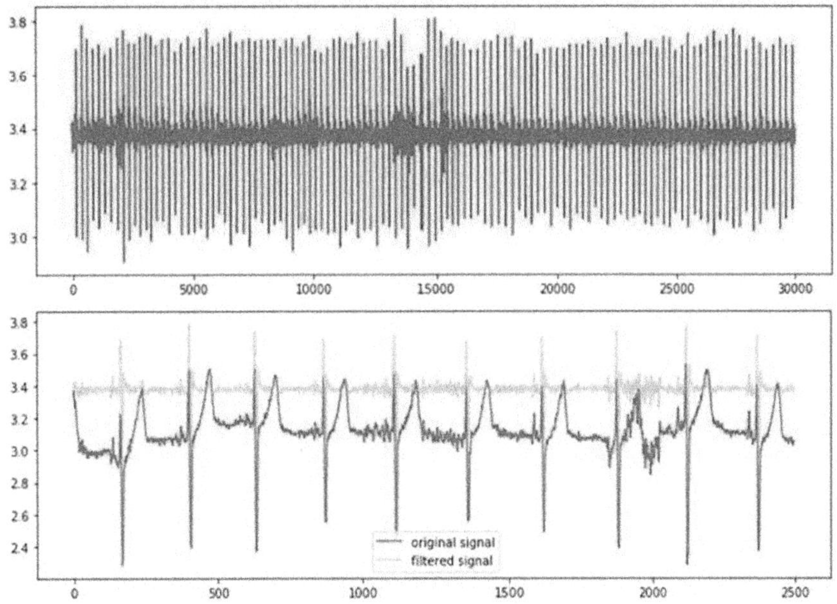

Fig. 112 Filtered ECG signal with reduced T-wave amplitude.

Steps/Pseudo code:

```
filtered = filter_signal(data, cutoff = 0.05, sample_rate = sam- ple_rate, filtertype='notch')

#visualize again
plot figure with figure size=(12,4) plot(filtered)
show plot
#and zoom in a bit
plot figure with figure size=(12,4) plot(data[0:2500], label = 'original signal')
plot(filtered[0:2500], alpha=0.5, label = 'filtered signal') plot legend()
show plot
```

It can be observed from the above plots that the amplitude of the T-wave has been reduced and now we can analyze the ECG signal 'e0110.csv' using following algorithm.

Steps/Pseudo code:

```
#run analysis
wd, m = process(scale_data(filtered), sample_rate) #visualise in plot of custom size
plot figure with figure size=(12,4) use plotter(wd, m)
#display computed measures for measure in m.keys():
print((measure, m[measure]))
```

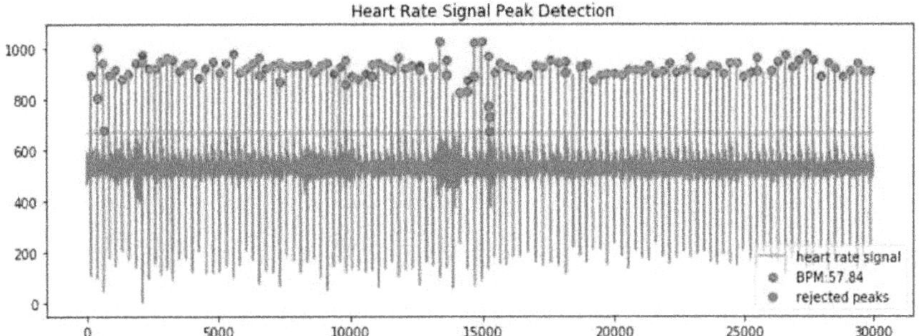

Fig. 113 Heart rate signal peak detection from filtered ECG signal comprising distrusted peaks.

bpm: 57.843015, ibi: 1037.290323, sdnn: 60.906871, sdsd: 20.513036,

rmssd: 33.059617, pnn20: 0.493827, pnn50: 0.135802, hr_mad: 36.000000
sd1: 23.285718, sd2: 84.305770, s: 6167.324586, sd1/sd2: 0.276206,
breathingrate: 0.075000

V. Eliminating Distrusted Peaks

From the above measures and plot it can be observed that the output has some dis- trusting some peaks. This is because optimizer likes broader peaks than some ECG recordings provide (especially lower sampling rates). This issue is caused when filter- ing the peak width decreases. To eliminate this issue we can unsample the signal us- ing following algorithm:

Steps/Pseudo code:

import scipy.signal.resample

#resample the data. Usually 2, 4, or 6 times is enough depending on original sampling rate

resampled_data = resample(filtered, len(filtered) * 2) #And run the analysis again

wd, m = process(scale_data(resampled_data), sample_rate * 2) #visualise in plot of custom size

plot figure with figure size=(12,4) use plotter(wd, m)

#display computed measures for measure in m.keys():

print((measure, m[measure]))

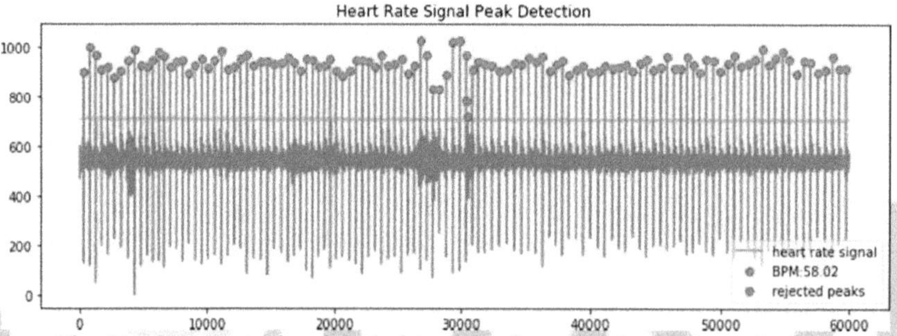

Fig. 114 Heart rate signal peak detection after removing distrusted peaks.

bpm: 58.018220, ibi: 1034.157895, sdnn: 59.536305, sdsd: 21.549303,
rmssd: 34.825073, pnn20: 0.544643, pnn50: 0.133929, hr_mad: 35.000000
sd1: 24.588644, sd2: 80.051446, s: 6183.774312, sd1/sd2: 0.307161,
breathingrate: 0.116667

It can be observed from the above output, Upsampling the signal has enabled to optimize and find the position for all peaks in the signal. The use of scale_data() in the processing function is recommended when the amplitude is low (2.4-3.8 in the original data).

VI. Conclusions

In this paper good to reasonable quality ECG signals are analyzed using Anaconda with Python 3.8 distribution. Three ECG excerpts from https://physionet.org/content/edb/1.0.0/ the European ST-T ECG Database. All the ECG signals are recorded at 250 Hz. The algorithms for analysis of ECG signals, reducing the amplitude of the T-wave, and eliminating distrusting peaks are presented in this paper. It can be observed from the presented results the T-wave amplitude reduction and distrusting peaks removal helps for the proper analysis of the ECG signals. In future the presented algorithms can be evaluated for analyzing the noisy ECG signals.

.

References

[1] Taddei A, Distante G, Emdin M, Pisani P, Moody GB, Zeelenberg C, Marchesi C. The Eu- ropean ST-T Database: standard for evaluating systems for the analysis of ST-T changes in ambulatory electrocardiography. European Heart Journal 13: 1164-1172 (1992).

[2] Goldberger, A., Amaral, L., Glass, L., Hausdorff, J., Ivanov, P. C., Mark, R., & Stanley, H. E. (2000). PhysioBank, PhysioToolkit, and PhysioNet: Components of a new research re- source for complex physiologic signals. Circulation [Online]. 101 (23), pp. e215–e220

[3] G. Guven et al., "Biometric identification using fingertip electrocardiogram signals," Sig- nal, Image Video Process., vol. 12, no.5, pp. 1–8, Jan. 2018.

[4] A. L. Goldberger, Ed., "Clinical electrocardiography: a Simplified Approach ," Seventh Ed., Philadelphia: Mosby, 2006, pp. 329–337.

[5] J. A. Drezner et al., "Abnormal electrocardiographic findings in athletes: recognising changes suggestive of cardiomyopathy," Br. J. Sports Med., vol. 47, no. 3, pp. 137–152, Feb. 2013.

[6] K. Thygesen et al., "Third universal definition of myocardial infarction," Circulation, vol. 126, no. 16, pp. 2020–2035, Jun. 2012.

[7] R. C. Dorf and R. C. Bishop, "Modern control systems," IEEE Trans. Syst., Man, Cy- bern.Syst., vol.11, no.8, pp.580, 2011.

[8]   P. Kundur et al., "Power system stability and control," New York, NY, USA: McGraw- Hill, 1994.
[9]   M. V. Cook, "Flight dynamics principles: a linear systems approach to aircraft stability and control," Butterworth-Heinemann, 2012.
[10]   F. Tahami et al., "A novel driver assist stability system for all-wheeldrive electric ve- hicles," IEEE Trans. Veh. Technol., vol. 52, no. 3, pp. 683–692, May. 2003.
[11]   L. A. Aguirre and Á. V. P. Souza, "Stability analysis of sleep apnea time series using iden- tified models: A case study," Comput. Biol. Med., vol. 34, no. 3, pp. 241–257, Apr. 2004.
[12]   G. Hocepied et al., "Stability analysis of epileptic EEG signals," in 8th IEEE Int. Conf. BIBE, 2008, pp. 1–5.
[13]   L. Glass and M. C. Mackey, "Pathological conditions resulting from instabilities in physio- logical control systems," Ann. N. Y. Acad. Sci., vol. 316, no. 1, pp. 214–235, Feb. 1979.
[14]   J. Lunze, "Stability analysis of large-scale systems composed of strongly coupled similar subsystems," Automatica, vol. 25, no. 4, pp. 561–570, Jul. 1989.
[15]   M. A. Hasan et al., "Increased beat-To-beat T-wave variability in myocardial infarction patients," Biomed. Eng., vol. 63, no. 2, pp. 123–130, Nov. 2018.